The Elements
of
Public Speaking

The Elements
of
Public Speaking

SIXTH EDITION

Joseph A. DeVito

HUNTER COLLEGE OF THE CITY UNIVERSITY OF NEW YORK

 LONGMAN

An imprint of Addison Wesley Longman, Inc.

New York • Reading, Massachusetts • Menlo Park, California • Harlow, England
Don Mills, Ontario • Sydney • Mexico City • Madrid • Amsterdam

Senior Acquisitions Editor: Deirdre Cavanaugh
Developmental Editor: Dawn Groundwater
Project Coordination and Text Design: Thompson Steele Production Services
Cover Designer: Kay Petronio
Cover Photograph: Kindra Clineff/The Picture Cube
Art Studio: Thompson Steele Production Services
Photo Researcher: Diane Kraut
Electronic Production Manager: Eric Jorgensen
Manufacturing Manager: Hilda Koparanian
Electronic Page Makeup: Thompson Steele Production Services
Printer and Binder: Quebecor Printing/Hawkins, Inc.
Cover Printer: The Lehigh Press, Inc.

For permission to use copyrighted material, grateful acknowledgment is made to the copyright holders on p. 473, which are hereby made part of this copyright page.

DeVito, Joseph A.
    The elements of public speaking / Joseph A. DeVito.
    —6th ed.
          p.   cm.
    Includes bibliographical references and index.
    ISBN 0-673-98008-1
    1. Public Speaking.   I. Title.
PN4121.D389   1996
808.5'1—dc20   95–47223
                                          CIP

ISBN 0-673-98008-1

12345678910—ARH—99989796

BRIEF CONTENTS

v

DETAILED CONTENTS

PART TWO

Elements of Subjects and Audiences   97

PART THREE

Elements of Organization   209

PART FOUR

Elements of Style and Delivery 265

PART FIVE

Elements of Public Speeches   321

SPEECHES & OUTLINES

SPEECHES

It is a pleasure to write an introduction to the sixth edition of this text and gratifying to know that so many instructors and students enjoyed and profited from earlier editions. This edition is similar in purpose to previous editions but dramatically different in several important ways. It is a major revision with many significant improvements.

The general goal of the text remains the same: to provide a **comprehensive treatment of public speaking skills.** *Elements of Public Speaking* continues to offer a serious, in-depth study of public speaking designed for the beginning college student. *Elements* is now, however, more easily accessible to the beginning public speaker and more adaptable to a variety of classroom structures.

Major Themes and Features

One major change in this edition is the integration of **cultural dimensions** throughout the text. Our students, the audiences they will address, and the speakers they will hear represent a broad mosaic of cultures. Similarly, the topics of public discourse are increasingly coming to focus on cultural and multicultural issues. Heightened mobility, changing immigration patterns, economic interdependency spanning continents, and advances in communication technology have made intercultural communication inevitable. This edition recognizes these changes and focuses on making public speaking more effective in this multicultural context. Because this integration of culture is new to this edition, the major headings that focus on culture (as well as gender differences—considered by many theorists to be an aspect of culture) are signaled by a marginal icon of ✂. In the next several years the integration of culture in college textbooks will be so commonplace that icons such as these will be superfluous. For now, however, they call

special attention to this previously most-neglected issue. Here are examples of these cultural dimensions that appear throughout the text:

- culture and public speaking: the relevance of culture; race, nationality, and culture; the aim of a cultural perspective (Unit 1)
- culture and speaker apprehension (Unit 3)
- listening and culture: language and speech; nonverbal differences; ethnocentrism; racist, sexist, and heterosexist listening (Unit 4)
- listening and gender (Unit 4)
- cultural differences in criticism (Unit 5)
- cultural differences in topics and thesis expression (Unit 6)
- cultural influences on meanings for icons and colors (Unit 9)
- culture in audience analysis, culture and age, secular and sacred cultures (Unit 10)
- gender in audience analysis (Unit 10)
- cultural considerations in organization: high- and low-context cultures, the influence of cultural context on organization (Unit 12)
- culture and meaning, culture and formality (Unit 15)
- culture and language; racist, sexist, and heterosexist language (Unit 16)
- cultural differences in persuasion (Unit 20)
- argument and evidence in cultural perspective (Unit 21)
- cultural influences on motivational appeals (Unit 22)
- culture and credibility perception (Unit 23)
- culture and the special occasion speech (Unit 24)
- the small group as a culture (Unit 25)

Critical thinking, a major feature of the previous edition, is further enhanced in this edition. Most of the principles of public speaking are also principles of critical thinking, for example, analyzing and adapting to audiences, evaluating and limiting speech topics and purposes, organizing the speech for ease of understanding, remembering, and persuasiveness. But the text also contains numerous specific sections on critical thinking, for example:

- critical listening (Unit 4)
- critically evaluating research (Unit 7)
- critically evaluating examples, narration, testimony, and statistics (Unit 8)
- critically evaluating audiovisual aids (Unit 9)
- critically evaluating arguments (Unit 21)
- critically evaluating motivational appeals (Unit 22)
- critically evaluating credibility appeals (Unit 23)
- thinking critically with the six hats technique (Unit 25)
- recognizing and critically analyzing groupthink (Unit 25)

In addition, many of the speeches are annotated with Critical Thinking questions to guide the student through the process of preparing and delivering a public speech. Questions focus on such critical thinking skills as discovery, evaluation, problem solving, and application.

The new design enables the Critical Thinking questions—formerly at the ends of the units—to be placed in the margins and thus to be increased in number and more clearly coordinated with the text material to which they refer.

The interactive format has been further enhanced:

- *Eleven self-tests,* interspersed throughout the text, not only promote active learning but also personalize the material for the reader.
- *Critical Thinking questions* in the margins ask the student to analyze, evaluate, and apply what she or he is reading.
- *Practically Speaking exercises* at the end of each unit provide opportunities to work actively with the ideas discussed in the text.

Introduced for the first time in this edition is **the short speech technique (SST).** The first exercise in each Practically Speaking section is a short speech exercise. Each of these provides the student with several choices for preparing and delivering a two-minute speech on some aspect of unit content.

Because of the short length format, an entire class or a good part of it could deliver their speeches with time left for discussion in one class period. This short speech exercise provides a kind of bridge connecting the content of the unit and the development of public speaking skills. The SST is designed with several purposes in mind:

- It gives students the opportunity to analyze or apply and to verbalize some important aspect of the unit's content and will therefore reinforce learning of the ideas. At the same time, these short speeches give students lots of opportunities to practice the skills of public speaking.
- These frequent and brief opportunities for speaking should help to reduce the fear of public speaking.
- These frequent speeches will also provide ample practice opportunities in organizing thoughts, in adapting to an audience, and in phrasing issues so that they are clearly understood.

These short speeches are not presented as a substitute for the longer, more sustained efforts that are already built into the course. The SST is useful—with appropriate feedback—for mastering skills, gaining confidence, and reducing apprehension. The longer speeches work best to emphasize research, organizational patterns, style and language, and in-depth audience analysis and adaptation. Suggestions for these longer or "regular" speeches appear throughout the text and in the *Instructor's Manual.*

Criticism in the classroom is emphasized in this text with an entire unit (Unit 5) devoted to this important concept and its related skills. In addition, numerous sections throughout the text, in the marginal Critical Thinking questions, and in the sample speeches ask for critical evaluations.

Focus On boxes (14 in all) are included in this edition. Set off from regular text, these boxes contain elaboration on some aspect of the regular text discussion. They include the following:

- Q&A Strategies (Unit 2)
- Conversations: How Apprehensive Are You? (Unit 3)
- Memory: Do You Really Remember What You Hear? (Unit 4)
- Plagiarism and How to Avoid It (Unit 7)
- Additional Organizational Patterns (Unit 12)

- Oral and Written Style: A Comparative Example (Unit 15)
- Mnemonic Devices (Unit 16)
- A Long-Term Delivery Improvement Program (Unit 18)
- Informative Speeches: Some Other Classifications (Unit 19)
- Compliance-Gaining Strategies (Unit 22)
- How We Form Credibility Impressions (Unit 23)
- More Special Occasion Speeches (Unit 24)
- The Group Agenda (Unit 25)
- The Six Critical Thinking Hats Technique (Unit 25)

Elements continues to provide an **overview of the public speaking process** early in the text so that students can begin to give their speeches early in the semester. The steps for preparing a speech, explained in Unit 2, have been increased to ten, to include delivery.

Improvements

This edition has been extensively revised, an aspect signaled visually by the change in the book's design and size.

Cultural dimensions, new to this edition, are an integral feature of just about every major concept.

Critical thinking skills are stressed more extensively than in the previous edition and appear throughout the text as part of the principles of public speaking and also in special sections.

Computer research has been updated and now includes introductions to such popular CD-ROM databases as ERIC, Medline, and America: History and Life and to the Internet.

Ethics has been expanded and moved to Unit 1. A discussion of plagiarism has also been added to the research unit (Unit 7).

Speaking in small groups has been added to this edition and appears as Unit 25. This unit emphasizes the role of speaking in groups and provides a useful transition between public speaking and small group communication.

New **speeches** have been added. A second poorly constructed speech has been added to further illustrate what not to do and to enable students to practice classroom criticism on an anonymous target. Four new student speeches have been added, and all appear with Critical Thinking questions to help the student master the skills of public speaking in an interactive

format. Besides the special occasion speeches, of which there are nine, eight complete informative and persuasive speeches are presented.

Also new are:

- Numerous speech excerpts added to clarify important principles
- New and revised preparation and delivery outlines added to Unit 12
- An annotated speech introduction and conclusion added to Unit 13

The Table of Contents for all speeches and outlines appears on page xix.

Learning Aid Notes, appearing in the first two units, identify the pedagogical features of the text and suggest ways in which they can be used most effectively.

The **TIPS from Professional Speakers** have been revised and expanded in number. They continue to emphasize the very practical aspects of public speaking. These TIPS are placed in the margins in this edition, where they can be more easily appreciated as comments and expansions on the text rather than as interruptions.

Tabular summaries at the end of each unit replace the internal summaries of the previous edition. These summaries are useful for review but also for seeing the relationships among the parts of the unit and the unit as a whole.

Coverage of speaker apprehension, a major problem faced by beginning speakers, has been expanded to provide a more systematic presentation of ways of dealing with it. Cognitive restructuring and performance visualization, systematic desensitization, and skill acquisition (including self-affirmation) are included as ways of dealing with speaker apprehension.

The **text organization** has been changed to more accurately reflect the way most people teach the course. Style and delivery now come before the types of speeches (informative, persuasive, special occasion, and in-group). Further, amplifying materials (Unit 8) and audiovisual aids (Unit 9) now follow the research unit (Unit 7). The use of **25 relatively brief units**—instead of the traditional long chapters—makes it easy to rearrange the units to suit more specific course purposes.

Eight new **exercises** have been added, and many others have been revised, updated, and streamlined.

A discussion of the **roots of public speaking** has been added and combined with the table identifying major contributors to the growth and development of the field (Unit 1).

Supplements

This sixth edition of *Elements of Public Speaking* comes with a wide variety of supplements to make this specific public speaking course both effective and enjoyable.

Instructor's Manual and Test Bank by Andrew John Bell, Grove City College

Instructor's Manual

- Text Overview
- Suggestions for Teaching the Course
- Sample Syllabi
- Student Speech Assignments and Exercises
- Unit Overviews and Learning Objectives
- Practically Speaking Exercises and Follow-Up
- Reading and Media Reference Listings

Test Bank

The Test Bank contains more than 1,000 questions, including multiple-choice, true-false, short-answer, and essay items. Referenced to text page number and targeted skill level (factual recall and applied and critical thinking), this collection of questions has been thoroughly revised and is designed to challenge students at all levels of learning.

TestMaster DOS and TestMaster Mac

The Test Bank is also available in TestMaster, a powerful computerized test-generation system that allows instructors to construct customized tests from existing and/or new items.

Overhead Transparency Package to Accompany *The Elements of Public Speaking*

This set of 75 four-color acetates is available free to qualified adopters.

The Speech Writer's Workshop (IBM/PC and Mac)

A virtual handbook for public speaking, this software provides students with practice in topic selection, outlining, citation format, and more.

Grades (IBM/PC)

Available to adopters, this software program simplifies class management and maintains grades for up to 200 students.

The Video Library

This collection includes a wide variety of films on such topics as preparation for public speaking, communication apprehension, and analyzing your audience. Please contact your sales representative for more information on titles and availability.

Acknowledgments

As always, it is a pleasure to express my great appreciation to the many people who influenced the development and production of this edition. My first debt is to the many instructors of public speaking who reviewed the manuscript at various stages of development. I want to again thank those who reviewed earlier manuscripts and editions of this text and to whose insights I continue to turn. Thank you: Suzanne Lindsey, Belmont University; Peter O'Rourke, Daytona Beach Community College; James Carlsen, Corpus Christi State University; Vincenne Waxwood, University of Pittsburgh; Gloria Kellum, University of Mississippi; Lisa Merrill, Hofstra University; Gaut Ragsdale, Northern Kentucky University; Conrad Awtrey, University of Wisconsin, Lacrosse; John E. Baird, Jr., Modern Management Methods; Michael Bartanen, Pacific Lutheran University; John D. Bee, University of Akron; Part G. Burgess, Queens College; James Chesebro, Indiana State University; Stephen Coletti, Ithaca College; Catherine R. Cowell, Angelo State University; Kathleen German, Miami University of Ohio; Joseph Giordano, University of Wisconsin, Eau Claire; Jeffrey Hahner, Pace University; Richard Jensen, University of New Mexico; Larry Judd, University of Houston; Bradford L. Kinney, Wilkes College; Cal M. Logue, University of Georgia; Joseph M. Mazza, Central Missouri State University; Kevin E. McCleary, Southern Illinois University at Edwardsville; Constance Morris, Wichita State University; Elizabeth Norwood, Loyola University of Chicago; Janice Peterson, University of California, Santa Barbara; Bennett Raforth, University of Illinois, Urbana; Ellen Ritter, University of Missouri; Susan M. Ross, Clarkson University; John R. Schedel,

Medaille College; Roselyn Schiff, Loop College; Curt Siemers, University of Nebraska, Omaha; Malcolm O. Sillars, University of Utah; Mary Ann Smith, University of Vermont; Ralph R. Smith, Southwest Missouri State University; Debra Stenger, Mississippi State University; David E. Walker, Jr., Middle Tennessee State University; William E. Wiethoff, Indiana University; and Russel R. Windes, Queens College.

To those who reviewed the fifth edition text and the manuscript for this sixth edition I am especially grateful. Their detailed and perceptive comments resulted in enormous improvements and refinements. Thank you: James Benjamin, University of Toledo; Douglas B. Hoehn, Community College of Philadelphia; David D. Hudson, Golden West College; Cindy Kistenberg, University of Houston, Downtown; Deborah Lamm, Lenoir Community College; Charles E. Lester, Palm Beach Atlantic College; Rick Roberts, University of San Francisco; Polly Rogers, Arapahoe Community College; Sheida Shirvani, Ohio State University, Zanesville; Debra Stevens, University of Montana

I also wish to thank Virginia Tiefel, Library Information Specialist, Ohio State University, for reviewing the unit on research and for offering a wealth of insights.

As always it is a pleasure to thank the many people at Addison Wesley Longman for all their help. I especially want to thank Cynthia Biron, who was editor of the fifth edition; Deirdre Cavanaugh, present communications editor; Dawn Groundwater, developmental editor; and Peter Glovin, marketing manager for communications. I also want to thank the people at Thompson Steele Production Services, especially Joanne Lowry, project editor; Ellen Coolidge, designer; and Bonnie Van Slyke, page layout artist.

—*Joseph A. DeVito*

PART ONE

Elements of Public Speaking

UNIT 1

The Nature of Public Speaking

Unit Contents

Unit Objectives

After completing this unit, you should be able to:

1 Identify the benefits to be derived from studying public speaking

2 Explain how public speaking differs from conversation

3 Diagram and explain the elements of public speaking

4 Explain the suggestions for speaking and listening ethically

5 Explain the role of culture in public speaking

6 Explain the relationship between critical thinking and public speaking

O f all the courses you will take in college, public speaking will surely be the most demanding, satisfying, frustrating, stimulating, ego-involving, and useful now and throughout your professional life. In this first unit we introduce the study of public speaking.

STUDYING PUBLIC SPEAKING

Begin your study by examining your own beliefs about public speaking; take the self-test "What Do You Believe About Public Speaking?"

Reasons for Studying Public Speaking

Here are just a few of the benefits you will derive from the time and effort you invest in studying public speaking.

> **Learning Aid Note**
>
> *Throughout this text are several self-tests that ask you to pause and reflect on your thoughts and behaviors. In working with these self-tests, focus on the statements in the test, on the issues they raise, and on the thoughts they help generate. The number you get "right" or "wrong" or the score you get (some tests yield scores for comparison purposes) is far less important.*

 Do you agree with Ralph Waldo Emerson's observation "All the great speakers were bad speakers at first"?

Self Test

What Do You Believe About Public Speaking?

For each of the following statements, respond with *T* if the statement is a generally accurate reflection of your thinking about public speaking or with *F* if the statement is a generally inaccurate reflection.

_____ 1. Public speaking is a useful art for formal occasions but has little place in my own professional or social life.

_____ 2. Good public speakers are born, not made.

_____ 3. The more speeches you give, the better you will become at it.

_____ 4. You'll never be a good public speaker if you're afraid to give a speech.

_____ 5. It is best to memorize your speech, especially if you are fearful.

_____ 6. Public speaking is a one-way process, going from speaker to audience and rarely from audience to speaker.

_____ 7. If you're a good writer, you'll be a good public speaker; a poor writer, a poor speaker.

_____ 8. Like a good novel, play, or essay, a good speech is applicable to all people at all times.

_____ 9. The First Amendment allows the public speaker total freedom of expression.

_____10. The skills of public speaking are similar throughout the world.

SCORING: All ten of these statements are false, and as you will see throughout this book, these assumptions can get in the way of learning the skills of public speaking. For example, fear may be unpleasant and uncomfortable but may also energize you and lead you to work at top efficiency. Similarly, and as we'll see throughout the numerous discussions of cultural differences, public speaking—like all forms of communication—will differ greatly from one culture to another.

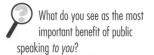

What personal and social abilities would you like to improve? How might these be cultivated through public speaking training?

Increase Personal and Social Abilities   Public speaking provides training in a variety of personal and social competencies. For example, in the pages that follow we cover skills for increasing self-awareness, enhancing self-confidence, and dealing with the fear of communicating. These certainly are skills that you will apply in public speaking. But they will also prove valuable in all of your social interactions. It's relevant to note that students from varied cultures (Anglo Americans, Hispanics, African Americans, and Asian Americans) studying in the United States see public speaking as a method for climbing up the socioeconomic ladder (Collier & Powell 1990).

Enhance Your Academic and Career Skills   As you learn public speaking, you'll also learn a wide variety of academic and career skills. These skills are central but not limited to public speaking. Among these are your abilities to:

- do research efficiently and effectively
- explain complex concepts clearly
- support an argument with all the available means of persuasion
- understand human motivation and be able to use your insights in persuasive encounters
- organize a variety of messages for clarity and persuasiveness
- present yourself to others with confidence and self-assurance
- analyze and evaluate the validity of persuasive appeals

Refine Your General Communication Abilities   Public speaking will also develop and refine your general communication abilities by helping you to improve competencies such as:

- developing a more effective communication style
- adjusting messages to specific listeners
- giving and responding appropriately to criticism
- developing logical and emotional appeals
- communicating your credibility
- improving listening skills
- organizing extended messages
- refining your delivery skills

What do you see as the most important benefit of public speaking *to you*?

Increase Your Public Speaking Abilities   Speakers aren't born; they're made. Through instruction, exposure to different speeches, feedback, and individual learning experiences, you can become an effective speaker. Regardless of your present level of competence, you can improve through proper training—hence this course and this book.

At the end of this course, you should be a more competent, confident, and effective public speaker. You should also be a more effective listener—more open yet more critical, more empathic yet more discriminating. And you should emerge a more competent and discerning critic of public communication.

What is the most important asset that you bring to the public speaking situation? How can you make your listeners aware of it?

As a leader (and in many ways you can look at this course as one in leadership training skills), you will need the skills of effective communication to help preserve a free and open society. These skills apply to you as a speaker

What specific means can you use to increase your public speaking abilities? What specific abilities might this course in public speaking help you improve?

who wants your message understood and accepted, as a listener who needs to evaluate and critically analyze ideas and arguments before making decisions, and as a critic who needs to evaluate and judge the thousands of public communications heard every day.

Historical Roots of Public Speaking

Public speaking is both a very old and a very new art. It is likely that public speaking principles were developed soon after our species began to talk. Much of contemporary public speaking, however, is based on the works of the ancient Greeks and Romans, who articulated an especially insightful system of rhetoric or public speaking. This tradition has been enriched by experiments, surveys, field studies, and historical studies that have been done since then.

Aristotle's *Rhetoric*, written some 2,300 years ago, was one of the earliest systematic studies of public speaking. It was in this work that the three kinds of proof—logos (or logical proof), pathos (emotional appeals), and ethos (appeals based on the character of the speaker)—were introduced. This three-part division is still followed today, and in fact Units 21, 22, and 23 discuss these specifically.

Roman rhetoricians added to the work of the Greeks. Quintilian, who taught in Rome during the first century, built an entire educational system—from childhood through adulthood—based on the development of the effective and responsible orator.

TIPS
From Professional Speakers

When we consider candidates for promotion in management, much of our impression comes from the time those candidates have spoken in office meetings.

Or from the memos or letters they've prepared.

When we consider candidates for a state vice presidency, we think about their primary role:
■ communicating with employees, customers, and regulators.

When we promote people to our holding company, U.S. West in Denver, we think about their primary role:
■ communicating with shareowners, stock analysts, and subsidiaries.

Without a doubt, communication skills continue to grow more important.

Richard D. McCormick, president, Northwestern Bell. "Business Loves English," *Vital Speeches of the Day* 51 (November 1, 1984):53.

Throughout these 2,300 years, the study of public speaking has grown and developed. Contemporary public speaking builds on this classical heritage and also incorporates insights from the humanities and the social and behavioral sciences. Likewise, perspectives from different cultures are being integrated into our present study of public speaking.

Table 1.1 shows some of the contributions to contemporary public speaking and illustrates the wide research and theory base from which its principles are drawn.

How might the other courses you are taking this semester give you insights into effective public speaking?

TABLE 1.1	The Growth and Development of Public Speaking
Academic Roots	**Contributions to Contemporary Public Speaking**
Classical rhetoric	Emphasis on substance; ethical responsibilities of the speaker; using a combination of logical, ethical, and emotional appeals; the strategies of organization
Literary and rhetorical criticism	Approaches to and standards for evaluation; insights into style and language
Philosophy	Emphasis on the logical validity of arguments; continuing contribution to ethics
Public address	Insights into how famous speakers dealt with varied purposes and audiences to achieve desired effects
Psychology	How language is encoded and decoded and made easier to understand and to remember; theories and findings on attitude change; emphasis on speech effects
General Semantics	Emphasis on using language to describe reality accurately; techniques for avoiding common thinking errors that faulty language usage creates
Communication theory	Insights into information transmission; the importance of viewing the whole of the communication act; the understanding of such concepts as feedback, noise, channel, and message
Interpersonal communication	Concepts from transactionalism; emphasis on mutual influence of speaker and audience
Sociology	Data on audiences' attitudes, values, opinions, and beliefs; how these influence people's exposure and responses to messages
Anthropology	Insights into the attitudes, beliefs, and values of different cultures and how these influence communications

...IVERSATION

depend on how
ublic speaking.
e your listeners
asons why they

is to compare it to conversation.
milarities and differences. We can
in purpose, audience, feedback,
and delivery.

a stranger, you
ler. For example,
ties, then explain
ganization is even
top you during a
predict what orga-
d remember your

you communicate with some
you might want to tell a friend
ne. In this case your purpose is
r boss to give you a raise. Here
you also communicate with a

he person you are
ce you're in. When
words and shorter
o impress someone,
ing you adjust your
the same way as in
cannot interrupt you
r to repeat that last

isteners will influence what
convince a friend to go to a
convince an instructor to
how your listeners so well
sages to them. But you do.
ay the events of the day to

r audience quite so well,
ady know (so you don't
't waste time persuading
In public speaking you
a conversation.

livery; you wouldn't
f course, you might if
was your promotion.
at first you will proba-
example, find yourself
not you should move
ur delivery will follow
nversation. Perhaps the
speaking as "enlarged"
sing with a large group.

al feedback from the
the other person will
gestures, and facial
s or make comments.
from one person to
e speaking and the
edback during the
ence speak back to
riod following the

rge audience with a rela-
n a face-to-face situation:
u ask your co-workers to

you would not
rould offer some
s the last day it's

playing." The number of arguments or reasons you offer will
resistant you think your friend might be. The same is true in
You don't simply say, "Vote for Johnson." Rather, you would gi
reasons why they should vote for Johnson and perhaps re
should not vote for Johnson's opponent.

Organization

In explaining how to bake a cake or in giving directions t
would organize your message so that it follows a logical or
you would start with the cake's ingredients and their quanti
how they are combined, and finally how they are cooked. Or
more important in public speaking because listeners can't
speech and ask you to fill in the missing parts. You have to
nizational pattern will best help listeners to understand ar
message.

Language

In conversation you vary your language on the basis of
speaking with, the topic you're talking about, and the pla
talking with children, for example, you might use easier
sentences than you would with friends. If you were trying
you might use a more sophisticated style. In public speak
language to your audience, the topic, and the situation in
conversation. In public speaking, however, your listeners
to ask, for example, what a particular word means o
sentence. So, your language must be instantly intelligible

Delivery

In conversation you normally don't even think of de
concern yourself with how to sit or stand or gesture. O
the conversation was with your boss and the topic
Because public speaking is a relatively new experience,
bly feel uncomfortable and self-conscious. You may, for
wondering what to do with your hands or whether or
about. With time and experience, you will find that y
naturally from what you are saying, just as it does in co
best advice to give you at this time is to view public
conversation. Deliver your speech as if you were conve
We review delivery in detail in Units 17 and 18.

▬ HOW PUBLIC SPEAKING WORKS

In public speaking a speaker addresses a relatively la
tively continuous discourse. Usually, it takes place i
You deliver an oral report in your economics class, y

TIPS
From Professional Speakers

You can become a speaker if you
have these assets:

1. A voice.
2. Ordinary knowledge of
language; that is, a working vocabulary and a reasonable acquaintance with grammar.
3. Something to say.
4. A desire to convey your thoughts
to others.

You have been using these assets for
years. You have been saying something to others, informally, dozens of
times daily. Under these circumstances, you call it "conversation."
Conversation is speech to the few.
Public speaking is, basically, conversation adapted to a larger group.

Maurice Forley, former executive
director, Toastmasters International,
Inc. *A Practical Guide to Public
Speaking* (North Hollywood, CA:
Wilshire Book Company, 1965), p. 2.

elect you as shop steward, you try to convince your neighbors to clean up the streets or other students to donate blood. These are all public speaking situations.

Unlike conversation, where the "audience" is one listener, public speaking involves a relatively large audience, from groups of perhaps 10 or 12 to audiences of hundreds of thousands. During conversation, the role of speaker shifts repeatedly from one person to another. In public speaking, on the other hand, the speaker gives a relatively continuous talk. This does not mean, however, that only the speaker communicates. Both speaker and audience communicate throughout the public speaking situation; the speaker communicates by delivering the speech and the audience by responding with feedback. Throughout the public speaking transaction, a mutual and simultaneous exchange of messages occurs between speaker and audience. Figure 1.1 shows the relationships among public speaking's major elements: speaker, listeners, noise, effects, context, messages, and channels.

How would you diagram the process of public speaking?

FIGURE 1.1
The public speaking transaction.

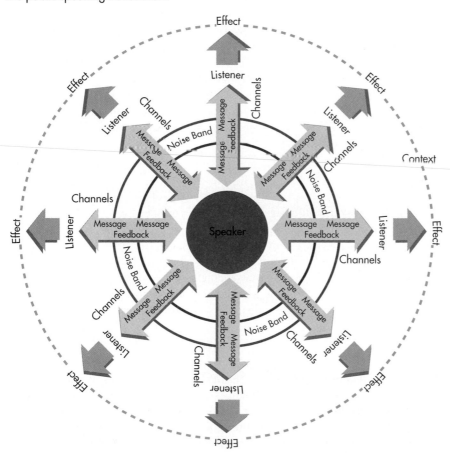

Speaker

As a speaker, you bring to the public speaking situation all that you are and all that you know. Further, you bring with you all that the audience thinks you are and thinks you know. Everything about you becomes significant and contributes to the total effect of your speech. Your knowledge, speech purpose, speaking ability, attitudes toward the audience, and other factors tell the audience who you are. As the public speaker, you are the center of the transaction; you and your speech are the reason for the gathering.

Listeners

What type of person would be the ideal listener for your classroom speeches?

Although we often speak of "the audience" as a collective body, it actually consists of separate and often very different individuals. Each of these listeners comes to a public speaking situation with different purposes, motives, expectations, attitudes, beliefs, and values. Therefore, each listener is going to respond differently to you and to the entire public speaking process.

Noise

Noise is interference. Noise is anything—audible or not—that interferes with your listeners receiving the messages you are sending. Noise may be physical (from traffic or others talking), psychological (from prejudices and stereotypes), or semantic (from language or dialect differences).

As a speaker, you may reduce the sources of some noise or lessen its effects, but you cannot eliminate all of it. Therefore, the speaker needs to learn to combat its effects by, for example, speaking louder, repeating important assertions, confronting biases and stereotypes, recognizing ethnocentric tendencies to see differences as inferior to one's own, or explaining idioms or technical terms.

Effects

As a public speaker, you design and deliver your speeches to influence listeners: Politicians give campaign speeches to secure your vote; advertisers give sales pitches to get you to buy their products; teachers give lectures to influence your thinking about history, psychology, or communication.

Because each listener is unique, each effect is also unique. While listening to the very same speech, one person may agree completely, another may disagree, and still another may misunderstand the entire message.

Context

Speaker and listeners operate in a physical, sociopsychological, temporal, and cultural context. The context influences you as the speaker, the audience, the speech, and the effects of the speech. The **physical context** is the actual place in which you give your speech (the room, hallway, park, or auditorium). A presentation in a small, intimate room needs to be very different from one in a sports arena.

What do you feel is the one major similarity and the one major difference between public speaking and two-person conversation?

The **sociopsychological context** includes, for example, the relationship between speaker and audience: Is it a supervisor speaking to workers or a worker speaking to supervisors? A principal addressing teachers or a parent addressing principals? It also includes the audience's attitudes toward and knowledge of the speaker and subject. You cannot, for example, treat a supportive audience and a hostile one similarly.

The **temporal context** includes, for example, the time of day and, more importantly, where your speech fits in with the sequence of events. For example, does your speech follow one that has taken an opposing position? Is your speech the sixth in a series exploring the same topic?

The **cultural context** refers to the beliefs, lifestyles, values, and ways of behaving that the speaker and the audience bring with them and that bear on the topic and purpose of the speech. Appealing to the "competitive spirit" and "financial gain" may prove effective with Wall Street executives but may insult Buddhists.

How would you describe the context for the speeches you will give in this course?

Messages and Channels

Messages are the signals sent by the speaker and received by the listener or from listener to speaker. These signals pass through one or more channels on their way from speaker to listener and from listener to speaker. The channel is the medium that carries the message signals from sender to receiver. Both the auditory and the visual channels are significant in public speaking. Through the auditory channel, you send your spoken messages—your words and your sentences. At the same time, you also send messages through a visual channel—through eye contact (or the lack of it), body movement, hand and facial gestures, and clothing.

Are there elements important to public speaking that are not covered here and that should be added to the model of the public speaking transaction?

Transactional Process

Public speaking, like all forms of communication, is a transactional process (Watzlawick, Beavin, & Jackson 1967; Watzlawick 1978). A "transactional process" is one in which (1) all elements are interdependent and (2) there is mutual influence between speaker and listener.

All elements of the public speaking process are interdependent. Each element in the public speaking process depends on and interacts with all other elements. For example, the way in which you organize a speech will depend on such factors as the speech topic, the specific audience, the purpose you hope to achieve, and a host of other variables—all of which are explained in the units to follow. Keep this interrelatedness in mind as you prepare your speeches.

Public speaking involves a mutual influence between speaker and audience. True, when you give a public speech you do most of the speaking and the listeners do most of the listening. The listeners, however, also send messages in the form of feedback, for example, applause, bored looks, nods of agreement or disagreement, and attentive glances. To be an effective public speaker, you must attend to these feedback messages and make appropriate adjustments. The audience also influences how you will prepare and present your speech. It influences (or should influence) your arguments, language, method of organization, and in fact every choice you make. You would not, for example, present the same speech on saving money to high school students as you would to senior citizens.

ETHICS AND PUBLIC SPEAKING

You have been put in charge of an advertising campaign to sell a new deodorant hand soap. You are considering printing ads with sexual terms and symbols embedded in the soap bubbles. Although the evidence of the effectiveness of this subliminal technique is—at best—weak, your immediate concern is with ethics. Would this be ethical?

You are pressed to deliver a speech in your public speaking class. You find a *Reader's Digest* article that could be used without anyone being aware that it was not your work. Should you use this article for your speech? Explain.

Both conversation and public speaking, and in fact all forms of communication, have an ethical dimension (Jaksa & Pritchard 1994; Johannesen 1990; Bok 1978), something our characters in the accompanying cartoon are beginning to notice. Yet for many communications, it is not easy to agree on what is and what is not unethical. Consider, for example:

- Is it ethical to tell voters what they want to hear just to get elected? To tell your grandmother she is getting well when you know she is terminally ill?
- Is it ethical to use emotional appeals to get someone to buy an inferior product? Would it be ethical if the product were a superior one?
- Is it ethical to persuade an audience to do something by scaring them? By threatening them? By making them feel guilty? Is it ethical to scare people into doing what is good for them, for example, to practice safe sex or to have a physical examination?

Speaker Ethics

Ethics concerns the rightness or wrongness of both the speaker's and the listener's behavior. What principles should speakers and listeners follow if their public speaking behavior is to be ethical?

The standards applied here grow out of the assumption that each person has a right to make his or her own choices. Each person has a right to the information and the knowledge necessary to make informed choices. Of

"Have you noticed ethics creeping into some of these deals lately?"

Drawing by H. Martin; © 1992 The New Yorker Magazine, Inc.

course, it is assumed that the individual is intellectually and emotionally capable of making reasoned and reasonable choices. It is further assumed that these choices will not restrict or prevent other persons from making their choices. Thus, we cannot always grant the freedom of choice to young persons or to mentally ill persons. We cannot grant the drunken driver the freedom to drive, since this restricts the freedom of others to drive in relative safety. Mothers and fathers, doctors and psychiatrists, and judges and law enforcement officers may have to prevent the exercise of some individual choices.

Five guidelines prove useful in evaluating the ethics of the public speaker. These guidelines are, at the same time, the ethical responsibilities of a public speaker. As you review these guidelines, think about your own ethical standards and behaviors.

Truth   Present the truth as you understand it. Your audience has a right to expect that you speak the truth as you know it. Obviously, you should not lie, but you should also avoid misrepresenting the truth because it might better fit your purpose. Avoid distorting information (no matter how small) because in undistorted form it might not be as useful.

Further, be truthful about the sources of your materials. Failure to properly credit sources can lead you to commit plagiarism, even though you have no intention of deceiving anyone. The issue of plagiarism is addressed in a box in Unit 7.

It is also unethical—and illegal—to defame another person. We defame (or commit defamation against) another person when we falsely attack his or her reputation, causing damage to it. We call such defamation libel when done in print or in pictures and slander when spoken. So, be careful of your facts, especially when talking about another person.

You are running for student body president and need to deliver speeches to the various clubs on campus. But you do not have the time or the abilities needed to construct these speeches. A few friends offer to write your speeches for a slight fee you could easily afford. Would this be ethical? Explain.

What ethical standards or principles do you feel should govern your own public speaking? Would you apply these same standards to contemporary political or religious speaking?

Knowledge and Preparation If you speak on a specific subject—as a teacher lecturing or as a political candidate debating—prepare yourself thoroughly. Be so informed, so knowledgeable, that the audience will be able to get the information they need to make reasoned and reasonable choices.

Audience Centered Have the audience's interests in mind. This is not to say that you should not speak out of personal interest; speakers should never exploit their audiences. If a speaker asks an audience to listen to a speech and to do certain things, it should be for their ultimate benefit. It would be unethical, for example, to persuade an audience to take up arms in a self-destructive war or to buy homes in a flood zone. It would be unethical to ask an audience to donate money to an embezzling organization.

It is also unethical (and illegal) to create what is legally termed a clear and present danger (Verderber 1991). This injunction, which derives from a Supreme Court decision (Oliver Wendell Holmes presiding in *Schenck v. U.S.* 1919), prohibits speech that is potentially dangerous to the welfare of the people and the country; Causing people to riot or to commit illegal acts may actually prove illegal if it can be determined that the speech posed a clear and present danger.

Understandable Closely related to preparedness is understandability (Jensen 1970). As a speaker, you have an obligation to make your speech understandable to your audience. In talking above the level of the audience, for example, you prevent the audience from clearly understanding what you are arguing or explaining. In talking in oversimplified terms, you can fool your audience into thinking they understand what they really do not. Each of these approaches is unethical because it prevents the audience from learning what they need to learn to make their choices.

Accountability Part of the ethical responsibility you have as a public speaker is to be accountable for everything you say. Although you may say virtually anything (with notable exceptions already mentioned), you have an obligation to take responsibility for what you say. Communication researcher Jon Hess (1993) suggests that because as a speaker you'll be held accountable for your comments, you should do the following:

- If you're not sure if certain information is correct, tell your audience. They have a right to know.
- Make clear when you are using facts and when you are using your own opinions. Both are important, but the audience should know which is which.
- Avoid misleading the audience in any way. Fooling the audience or encouraging them to believe what is not true is unethical.

Ethical Listening

Because public speaking is a two-way process, both speaker and listener share in the success or failure of the interaction. And both share in the moral implications of the public speaking exchange. Two major principles govern the ethics of listening.

Ethicist J. Vernon Jensen (1985) argues that ethical judgments should be made on a scale ranging from highly ethical to highly unethical. Do you agree? Or do you view any specific communication and behavior as being either of two values: ethical or unethical?

In what ways are the ethical responsibilities of the public speaker different from those of the interpersonal communicator? The newscaster or journalist?

Should elected officials (or teachers, doctors, or therapists) be held to a higher standard of ethics than, say, the post office worker or the owner of a small hardware store? Why?

Honest Hearing   Give the speaker an honest hearing. Avoid prejudging the speaker before hearing her or him. Try to put aside prejudices and preconceptions so you can evaluate the speaker's message fairly. At the same time, try to empathize with the speaker. You don't have to agree with the speaker, but do try to understand emotionally as well as intellectually what the speaker means. Then accept or reject the speaker's ideas on the basis of the information offered, and not on the basis of some bias or incomplete understanding.

Honest Responding   Just as the speaker should be honest with the listener, the listener should be honest with the speaker. This means giving open and honest feedback. In a learning environment such as your public speaking class, it means giving honest and constructive criticism to help the speaker improve. It also means reflecting honestly on the questions the speaker raises. Much as the listener has a right to expect an active speaker, the speaker has a right to expect an active listener. The speaker has a right to expect a listener who will actively deal with rather than just passively hear the message.

You might find it interesting to think about these few questions involving ethical listening and cultural differences. To what extent are your answers a statement of ethical principles?

- Do you listen differently (for example, less or more openly) to a speech by a culturally different person compared with the way you listen to one by a culturally similar person?
- Would you listen fairly to a speaker explaining religious beliefs and practices that are very different from your own?
- Do you see speakers from culturally different groups as equally believable (all other things being equal)?

How might the skills of public speaking prove useful in other communication situations, for example, interviewing for a job? Meeting a group of new people? Asking someone for a date?

CULTURE AND PUBLIC SPEAKING

A walk through any large city, many small towns, and just about any college campus will convince you that the United States is largely a collection of lots of different cultures, coexisting somewhat separately but also with each influencing the others. We need to see public speaking within this cultural context.

The Relevance of Culture

There are several reasons for the cultural emphasis you will find in this book (and probably in all your other textbooks). Most obvious, perhaps, are the vast demographic changes taking place throughout the United States. Whereas at one time the United States was largely a country populated by Europeans, now it is a country greatly influenced by the enormous number of new citizens from South America, Africa, and Asia. And the same is even more true on college and university campuses throughout the United States. With these changes come different communication customs and the need to understand and adapt to these new ways of looking at communication generally and public speaking specifically.

Learning Aid Note

Throughout this text, you'll see icons of four converging arrows, representing a coming together of differences. They call special attention to discussions of culture and gender and their role in public speaking. As noted in this discussion, public speaking in the United States is now, and will be more so in the future, an intercultural experience. It is therefore essential to understand the role of culture in order to achieve meaningful and effective public discourse.

Irish dramatist and philosopher George Bernard Shaw once observed that "It is difficult, if not impossible, for most people to think otherwise than in the fashion of their own period." What implications might this have for intercultural communication?

How would public speaking differ in a democracy and in a dictatorship? In a tribal and in an industrialized society? In a blue-collar and in a white-collar society?

We are also living in a time when people have become increasingly sensitive to cultural differences. From an originally assimilationist perspective (the view that people should leave their native culture behind and adapt to their new culture), we have moved to one that values cultural diversity (the belief that people should retain their native cultural ways). And, with some notable exceptions—hate speech, racism, sexism, classism, and homophobia come quickly to mind—we seem to be more concerned with saying the right thing and with ultimately developing a society where all cultures can coexist and in fact enrich each other.

In many cases the ability to interact effectively in public speaking situations (as well as interpersonally and in small groups) with members of other cultures translates into financial gain. The increased economic interdependence of the United States and widely different cultures makes it essential to gain the needed intercultural communication understanding and skills.

Race, Nationality, and Culture

Culture is the collection of beliefs, attitudes, values, and ways of behaving shared by a group of people and passed down from one generation to the next through communication rather than through genes. Thus, culture does not refer to color of skin or shape of eyes, since these are passed on through genes, not communication. Culture does refer to beliefs in a supreme being, to attitudes toward family, and to the values placed on friendship or money, since these are transmitted not by genes but by communication.

Culture is not synonymous with race or nationality, although members of a particular race are often enculturated into a similar set of beliefs, attitudes, and values. Similarly, members living in the same country are often taught similar beliefs, attitudes, and values. This similarity makes it possible for us to speak of "Hispanic culture" or "African American culture." But lest we be guilty of stereotyping, we need to recognize that within any large culture—especially a culture based on race or nationality—there will be enormous differences. The Kansas farmer may in some ways be closer to the Chinese farmer than to the Wall Street executive. Further, as an individual born into a particular race and nationality, you do not necessarily have to adopt the attitudes, beliefs, and values that may be dominant among the people of that race and nationality.

The Aim of a Cultural Perspective

A cultural emphasis will help us distinguish what is universally true from what is true in one culture and false in another (Matsumoto 1994). The principles for communicating information and for changing attitudes differ from one culture to another. If we're to understand public speaking, then we have to know how its principles vary on the basis of culture and therefore need to be qualified.

In what ways have your courses integrated cultural diversity?

And, of course, we need this cultural emphasis to help us communicate more effectively in a wide variety of contexts, contexts that are becoming increasing intercultural. Success in public speaking—as on your job and in your social life—will depend in great part on your understanding of and ability to communicate effectively with persons who are culturally different from yourself.

CRITICAL THINKING AND PUBLIC SPEAKING

Throughout this book, you will cover a wide variety of skills that educators now group under the topic of "critical thinking." The objective of critical thinking training is to foster more reasoned and more reasonable decision making. It is the process of analyzing and evaluating logically what you say and hear. Here are just a few skills that critical thinking theorists have identified (Ennis 1987; Nickerson 1987; McCarthy 1991; Adams & Hamm 1991; Bransford, Sherwood, & Sturdevant 1987):

- to evaluate and use evidence
- to organize thoughts clearly and logically
- to define concepts and problems specifically and unambiguously
- to discover valid and relevant information
- to distinguish between logical and illogical assumptions and inferences
- to evaluate the validity of an argument
- to judge critically and with good reasons

 Do you think you will change any of your attitudes or beliefs as a result of the speeches you hear in this class? What, if any, attitudes or beliefs would you never consider changing and why?

For the most part, the principles of public speaking are also the principles of critical thinking. It is impossible to be an effective speaker (or listener or critic) without also being an effective critical thinker. So, this is a particularly good opportunity to learn the skills of critical thinking as you learn public speaking. The two will work together; each will reinforce the other.

To best achieve this blend, numerous sections of this text cover critical thinking skills explicitly (for example, listening critically in Unit 4, criticizing the speech in Unit 5, discovering information in Unit 7, analyzing arguments in Unit 21, evaluating credibility in Unit 23, and ensuring accuracy in language in Unit 16). In addition, "Critically Speaking" questions appear in the margins.

In examining these critical thinking skills, look for ways you might transfer these skills to other areas of your personal and professional life (Sternberg 1987). Research shows that such transfers will be more efficient if you:

- think about the principles flexibly and recognize exceptions to the rule.
- seek analogies between the situation you are now in and previous experiences. What are the similarities? Differences?
- look for situations at home, at work, and at school where you might transfer the critical thinking skills. For example, might the skills of effective listening also prove valuable in listening to your friends, family, or romantic partner?

In what ways have your courses integrated critical thinking?

The five speeches in the Appendix are annotated with questions suggesting areas to explore in thinking critically about speeches.

UNIT IN BRIEF

Benefits of public speaking	■ Increases your personal and social abilities ■ Enhances related academic and professional skills in organization, research, style, and the like ■ Refines general communication competencies ■ Improves public speaking abilities—as speaker, as listener, and as critic
Public speaking compared with conversation	■ Similar to and yet different from conversation in purpose, audience, feedback, supporting materials, organization, language, delivery, and ethics
Elements of public speaking	■ Transactional process in which (a) a speaker, (b) addresses (c) a relatively large audience with (d) a relatively continuous discourse that is (e) usually in a face-to-face situation
Ethics in public speaking	■ Rightness or wrongness, morality or immorality, of public speaking ■ Speaker ethical guidelines: truth, knowledge and preparation, audience centered, understandable, and accountability ■ Listener ethical guidelines: give the speaker an honest hearing and honest responses
Culture in public speaking	■ Because of demographic changes and economic interdependence, cultural differences have become more significant ■ The aim of this perspective is to increase understanding of the role of culture in communication and to improve public speaking skills in a context that is becoming increasingly intercultural
Critical thinking	■ Effective public speaking depends on critical thinking from speaker, listener, and critic and incorporates a wide variety of critical thinking skills

PRACTICALLY SPEAKING

Short Speech Technique

Prepare and deliver a two-minute speech in which you:

1. explain the role of public speaking in a particular profession
2. tell the audience something about your attitudes and beliefs that may help them understand you as an audience member
3. identify what you like and what you dislike in listening to a public speaker
4. explain one important cultural artifact
5. explain one concept and how one culture defines it
6. compare two cultures in their views of a particular concept
7. explain how one belief common in your culture influences you
8. explain one difference or one similarity between any two cultural groups

1.1   Metaphors, Similes, and Public Speaking

Try your hand at creating metaphors or similes to help explain public speaking. Select an element from the Public Speaking Elements column and a field from the Metaphorical Fields column and explain the element with a specific metaphor drawn from the field; for example, pairing *speaker* and *transportation* might yield a metaphor such as "The effective speaker is like a locomotive; it takes time to get up the steam for effective movement."

Public Speaking Elements

speaker	context
speech	noise
channel	effect
audience	ethics
feedback	delivery

Metaphorical Fields

transportation	military
animals	music
environment	economic
nature	artistic
sports	communication

Learning Aid Note

At the end of every unit are practical experiences to stimulate you to think more actively about the concepts and skills covered in the unit and to practice your developing public speaking abilities.

*The first exercise in each unit is the SST, the **short speech technique**. This exercise provides a vehicle for integrating lots of short speeches into the course in addition to the traditional longer and more carefully crafted speeches. These short speeches all deal with the contents of the unit and so serve the dual function of covering the text material but also affording opportunities to practice your new skills. As the course progresses, these short speeches should incorporate increasingly sophisticated application of the public speaking principles. The next unit will provide specific guidelines to follow for these and all other speeches. For the short speeches in this first unit, rely on whatever principles of public speaking you think are appropriate.*

UNIT 2

Preparing a Public Speech: An Overview

Unit Objectives

After completing this unit, you should be able to:

1. Explain the three major types of speeches

2. Explain the ten steps for preparing a public speech

Y*ou're going to give a speech and you're anxious and unsure of what to say. What do you do? What do you speak about? How do you decide what to include in the speech? How should a speech be organized? At this point you probably have a lot more questions than answers, but that is the way it should be. The purpose of this unit is to start stimulating answers to your questions. In this way you'll be able to begin public speaking almost immediately. By following the ten steps outlined in this unit, you will be able to prepare and present effective first speeches.*

The ten steps for preparing a public speech will also provide you with a framework for structuring all of the remaining information in this text. Look at the rest of the text as an elaboration of these ten steps. As the course progresses and as you continue reading, we will return to these principles and further clarify them. This will help you gradually perfect and improve the public speaking skills outlined here. For each of the ten steps, we note where in the text you can find additional information.

Figure 2.1 presents these ten steps in a linear fashion. The process of constructing a public speech, however, often does not follow a logical and linear sequence. That is, you will probably not progress simply from Step 1, to 2, to 3, and so on. Instead, your progression might go more like this: Step 1, Step 2, back again to Step 1, Step 3, back again to Step 2, and so on throughout the preparation of your speech. For example, after selecting your subject and purpose (Step 1), you may

FIGURE 2.1
The steps in preparing and
delivering a public speech.

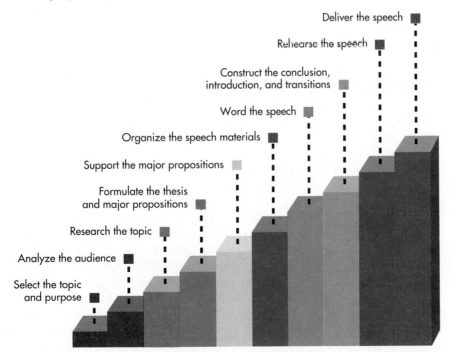

TIPS
From Professional Speakers

Most of us are mean to ourselves. We constantly tell ourselves that we are not good enough. We tell ourselves how dumb we are, how stupid we are, that we forgot to do this or forgot to do that. We do it so often that we begin to believe it! In fact, it's like what the prophets have said in the Bible, "What things you say and believe in your heart all come to pass."

The negative public relations we put out reaps negative public relations from others. You don't have to say "I'm so great" to everyone you meet, but you need to put across some self-confidence.

Lillian Glass, vocal image consultant and frequent lecturer. *How to Win: Six Steps to a Successful Vocal Image* (New York: Putnam/Perigee Books, 1987), pp. 161–163.

progress to Step 2 and analyze your audience. On the basis of this analysis, however, you may wish to go back and modify your subject, your purpose, or both. Similarly, after you research the topic (Step 3), you may want more information on your audience. You may therefore return to Step 2.

In some situations you will begin with your audience. For example, let's say you're invited to speak to a group of high school seniors. They probably will want you to address a specific topic, which is why they have asked you to speak. In this case you would begin your process by asking, What does this audience want? What do they need to know or do? For your classroom speeches you may also wish to focus first on your audience. In other cases you may wish to examine your own feelings about what is especially important. For example, you may feel strongly about the importance of recycling, amnesty, gay/lesbian rights, or abortion—issues about which you may feel it is important to instruct or convince others. Here you would begin with your own convictions and ask how you might adapt or relate this topic to your specific audience.

Going from one step to another and then back again should not throw you off track. This is the way most people prepare speeches and written communications. So, although we present the steps in the order a speaker normally follows, remember that you are in charge of the process. Use the order of these steps as guidelines but break the sequence as you need to. As long as you cover all ten steps thoroughly, you should accomplish your goal.

SELECT YOUR TOPIC AND PURPOSE

The first step in preparing a speech is to select the topic (or subject) and the purposes you hope to achieve. Let's look first at the topic.

The Topic

What topics would you like to hear other students speak on? What topics would you definitely not like to hear about? What accounts for your likes and dislikes?

Perhaps the question students in a public speaking class most often ask is, "What do I speak about?" For your classroom speeches—where the objective is to learn the skills of public speaking—there are hundreds of things to talk about. Suggestions are to be found everywhere and anywhere. In Unit 6 this topic is pursued in depth and many suggestions are offered; suggestions also appear in the Practically Speaking exercises at the end of this unit.

Worthwhile   The topics of a public speech should be worthwhile. Such topics should address issues that have significant implications for the audience. Topics should also be appropriate both to you as the speaker and to your audience. Select a topic you are interested in and feel is important to you and your audience. Try not to select a topic merely because it will fulfill the requirements of an assignment. Try to select a topic about which you know something and would like to learn more. You not only will acquire new knowledge but also will discover how to learn more about the topic—the relevant journals, the noted authorities, and so on. Unless you are a very accomplished speaker, your enthusiasm or lack of it will show during the speech. If you select a topic you are not interested in, you will have an extremely difficult time concealing this from the audience.

Like the penguin in the accompanying cartoon, each person sees the world from a unique point of view, so look at your topic from the audience's perspective. What are they interested in? What would they like to learn more about? On what topics would they find the time listening to your speech well spent? It is a lot easier to please an audience when you speak on a topic that interests them.

Also, recognize the important role that culture plays in the topics people consider appropriate or worthwhile. For example, it would be considered inappropriate for an American businessperson in Pakistan to speak of politics or in Nigeria of religion (Axtell 1993). In the same way there are often cultural taboos in public speaking, as we frequently witness when one from another culture or social group tries to appear to be a member of the audience's. Because you are all college students, probably studying in North America or Australia, you can assume—to some extent—that the topics you are interested in will also prove interesting to your classmates. But beyond this exceptionally homogeneous and accepting atmosphere—one you are unlikely to meet anytime after college—the culture will always play a role in the selection of the topic.

Limited in Scope   A suitable topic for a public speech is one that is limited in scope. Probably the major problem for beginning speakers is that they attempt to cover a huge topic in five minutes: the history of Egypt, why our tax structure should be changed, or the sociology of film. Such topics are too broad and attempt to cover too much. The inevitable result is that nothing specific is covered—everything is touched on but only superficially. No depth is achieved when the topic is too broad, and all the speaker succeeds in doing is telling the audience what it already knows. Invariably, your listeners will go away with the feeling that they have gained nothing as a result of listening to your speech.

Do men and women differ in what they consider an appropriate or an interesting topic in public speaking? In what ways has your culture influenced your thinking concerning what should be or should not be an appropriate topic for public speaking?

On the basis of your likes and dislikes, can you offer general principles to guide others in selecting topics?

Drawing by Leo Cullum; © 1992 The New Yorker Magazine, Inc.

The Purpose

The three major or general purposes of public speeches are to inform, to persuade, and to serve some ceremonial or special occasion function:

- The informative speech seeks to create understanding; the speaker clarifies, enlightens, corrects misunderstandings, demonstrates how something works
- The persuasive speech seeks to influence attitudes or behaviors; the speaker strengthens or changes the existing attitudes or gets the audience to take action
- The special occasion speech, containing elements of information and persuasion, serves varied purposes; for example, the speaker might introduce another speaker or a group of speakers, present a tribute, secure the goodwill of the listeners, or entertain the audience

Your speech will also have a specific purpose. For example, specific informative purposes might include informing your audience of the proposed education budget or the way a television pilot is audience tested. Specific persuasive purposes might include persuading your audience to support the proposed budget or to vote for Smith. Specific purposes for special occasion speeches might include introducing the newest Nobel Prize winner, who will speak on advances in nuclear physics, or defending a company policy of an all-male board of directors to the shareholders.

ANALYZE YOUR AUDIENCE

In public speaking your audience is central to your topic and purpose (see accompanying TIPS). In most cases, and especially in a public speaking class, you will be thinking of both your audience and your topic at the same time; it is difficult to focus on one without also focusing on the other. Your success in informing or persuading an audience rests largely on the extent to which you know them and to which you have adapted your speech. Ask yourself, "Who are they? What do they already know? What would they want to know more about? What special interests do they have? What opinions, attitudes, and beliefs do they have? Where do they stand on the issues I wish to address? What needs do they have?"

To illustrate this process of audience analysis (a topic discussed in depth in Units 8 and 9), consider age and gender as just two factors that need to be analyzed.

Age

If you are going to speak on social security and health care for the elderly or the importance of the job interview, it is obvious that the age of your listeners should influence how you develop your speech. But age is always an important if not so obvious factor. Ask yourself some questions about the age of your listeners. What is the general age of the audience? How wide is the range? Are

 How would you describe your public speaking class as an audience?

there different age-groups that you should address? Does the age of the audience impose any limitations on the topic? On the language you will use? On the examples and illustrations you will select?

Gender

Men and women view a variety of topics differently. They each have special knowledge and special interests as a result of their socialization. Ask yourself how the gender of the audience might influence your speech development. What is the predominant gender of your listeners? Do men and women view the topic differently? If so, how? Do men and women have different backgrounds, experiences, and knowledge concerning the topic? If so, how will this influence the way you develop the topic?

For example, if you plan to speak on caring for a newborn baby, you would approach an audience of men very differently from an audience of women. With an audience of women, you could probably assume a much greater knowledge of the subject and a greater degree of comfort in dealing with it. With an audience of men, you might have to cover such elementary topics as the type of powder to use, how to test the temperature of a bottle, and the way to prepare a formula.

RESEARCH YOUR TOPIC

If the speech is to be worthwhile and if you and the audience are to profit from it, you must research the topic. For your initial speeches, this will probably entail research in the library. First read some general source—an encyclopedia article or a general article in a journal or magazine. You might pursue some of the references in the article or seek out a book or two in the library. For some

Visit the library and select one research source (in print, video, audio, or electronic form) that you think would be useful to students preparing speeches for this class. What types of information does this reference source contain? Why do you think this would prove useful?

Why is research necessary for a public speech? Would it ever be legitimate to give a public speech totally devoid of research?

topics, you might want to consult individuals: professors, politicians, physicians, or other people with specialized information are useful sources.

Or you might begin with accessing a database, assembling a bibliography, and reading the most general source first and continuing with increasingly specific articles. See Unit 7 for in-depth coverage of research.

FORMULATE YOUR THESIS AND MAJOR PROPOSITIONS

What do you want your audience to get out of your speech? What single idea do you want them to retain? This single idea is the thesis of your speech. It is the essence of what you want your audience to get out of your speech. If your speech is an informative one, then your thesis is the main idea you want your audience to understand. Examples of such theses would be "Human blood consists of four major elements" and "The new computerized billing system is easy to understand."

If your speech is a persuasive one, then your thesis is the central idea you wish your audience to accept or act on. Examples of such theses would be "We should support Grace Moore for union representative" and "We should contribute to the college athletic fund."

Once you word the thesis statement, ask yourself—as would an audience—questions about the thesis in order to identify its major components. For an informative speech, the most helpful questions are, What? and How? So, for the thesis "Human blood consists of four major elements," the logical question seems to be, "What are they?" For the thesis "The new computerized billing system is easy to understand," the logical question seems to be, "Why is it easy?" or "How is it easy?" The answers to these questions identify the major propositions you should cover in your speech. The answer to the question, "What are the major elements of human blood?" would, in the form of a brief speech outline, look like this:

THESIS: "Human blood consists of four major elements." (What are they?)

    I. Plasma

   II. Red blood cells (erythrocytes)

  III. White blood cells (leukocytes)

  IV. Platelets (thrombocytes)

In a persuasive speech, the question an audience would ask would be more often of the Why? type. If your thesis is "We should support Grace Moore for union representative," then the inevitable question is, "Why should we support Grace Moore?" Your answers to this question will then enable you to identify the major parts of the speech, which might look like this:

THESIS: "We should support Grace Moore for union representative" (Why should we support Grace Moore?)

Select a recent television show or movie and identify its thesis. Are there subordinate theses?

Learning Aid Note

Throughout this text, we present a large number of examples of outlines and excerpts from speeches. These outlines and excerpts are designed to illustrate the principles discussed in the text and so should be examined carefully. Even if you feel you fully understand the principle, do not skip these sample outlines and speech excerpts. They will illustrate in concrete terms what the principle is designed to capture. Don't be concerned if you don't know the topic of the outline or excerpt; enough of a context is provided to illustrate the relevant principle of public speaking.

I. Grace Moore is an effective negotiator.

II. Grace Moore is honest.

III. Grace Moore is knowledgeable.

SUPPORT YOUR MAJOR PROPOSITIONS

Now that you have identified your thesis and your major propositions, turn your attention to how to support each of them. You must tell the audience what it needs to know about the elements in human blood. You need to convince the audience that Grace Moore is in fact honest, knowledgeable, and an effective negotiator.

In the informative speech, your support primarily amplifies—describes, illustrates, defines—the various concepts you discuss. You want the "causes of inflation" to come alive for the audience. You want the audience to see and feel the drug problem, the crime, or the economic hardships of the people you are talking about. Amplification accomplishes this. Specifically, you might use examples, illustrations, and the testimony of others to explain a concept or issue.

Presenting definitions helps the audience to understand specialized terms. Definitions breathe life into concepts that may otherwise be too abstract or vague. Statistics (summary figures that explain various trends) are essential for certain topics. Audiovisual aids—charts, maps, actual objects, slides, films, audiotapes, records, and so on—enliven normally vague concepts.

In a persuasive speech, your support is proof—material that offers evidence, argument, and motivational appeal and that establishes your credibility. Proof helps you convince the audience to agree with you. Let us say, for example, that you want to persuade the audience to believe that Grace Moore is an effective negotiator (your first major proposition, as noted above). To do this, you need to give your audience good reasons for believing in Moore's effectiveness as a negotiator. Your major proposition might be supported as illustrated here:

I. Grace Moore is an effective negotiator.
    A. Moore effectively negotiated the largest raise we ever received.
    B. Moore prevented management from reducing our number of sick days.
    C. Moore has been named Negotiator of the Year for the past three years by our own union local.

Support your propositions with reasoning from specific instances, from general principles, from analogy, and from causes and effects. These are logical supports. You can also support your position with motivational appeals. For example, you might appeal to the audience's desire for status, for financial gain, or for increased self-esteem.

You also add persuasive force through your own personal reputation or credibility. If the audience sees you as competent, of high moral character, and charismatic, they are likely to believe what you say.

What types of supporting materials would you find most useful in explaining to children the nature of advertising? In persuading class members to contribute blood?

In public speaking you have the opportunity to use visual aids. A pie chart to make your statistics clearer, a picture of the forest that is being destroyed, or a map showing military bases is an important form of support that will make your ideas more appealing, informative, and persuasive. An entire unit (Unit 9) is devoted to this important form of support.

ORGANIZE YOUR SPEECH MATERIALS

Organize your materials to help your audience understand and retain what you say. You might, for example, select a simple topical pattern. This involves dividing your topic into its logical subdivisions or subtopics. Each subtopic becomes a main point of your speech, and each is treated approximately equally. You would then organize the supporting materials under each of the appropriate points. The body of the speech, then, might look like this:

I. Main point I
   A. Supporting material for I
   B. Supporting material for I

II. Main point II
   A. Supporting material for II
   B. Supporting material for II
   C. Supporting material for II

III. Main point III
   A. Supporting material for III
   B. Supporting material for III

For a persuasive speech you may wish to consider other organizational patterns. For example, a problem-solution pattern might be effective for a number of topics. Let us say you want to persuade your listeners that medical schools should require communication courses. You might use a problem-solution pattern. Your speech in outline form might look like this:

I. Doctors cannot communicate effectively. (problem)
   A. They are inarticulate in expressing ideas. (problem 1)
   B. They are ineffective listeners. (problem 2)
   C. They do not see beyond the literal meaning. (problem 3)

II. Medical schools should require communication courses. (solution)
   A. Communication courses will train doctors to express themselves. (solution 1)
   B. Communication courses will train doctors in listening skills. (solution 2)
   C. Communication courses will train doctors to listen for meaning beyond the literal. (solution 3)

What thought pattern would you use to describe your college campus to a group of high school students who have never seen a college campus? To persuade your audience to eat a healthy diet?

WORD YOUR SPEECH

The audience will hear your speech only once. Make sure that your listeners readily understand everything you say by being instantly intelligible. Do not speak down to your audience, but do make your ideas, even complex ones, easy to understand at one hearing.

Use words that are simple rather than complex, concrete rather than abstract. Use personal and informal rather than impersonal and formal language. For example, use lots of pronouns (*I, me, you, our*) and contractions (*can't* rather than *cannot, I'll* rather than *I will*). Use simple and direct rather than complex and indirect sentences. Say, "Vote in the next election" instead of "It is important that everyone vote in the next election."

In wording the speech, be careful not to offend members of your audience. Remember that not all doctors are men. Not all secretaries are women. Not all persons are or want to be married. Not all persons love parents, dogs, and children. The hypothetical person does not have to be male.

Perhaps the most important advice to give is this: Do not write out your speech word for word. This will only make you sound like you're reading a text to your audience. You will thus lose the conversational quality that is so important in public speaking. Instead, outline your speech and speak with your audience, using this outline to remind yourself of your main ideas and the order in which you want to present them. Units 21 and 22 offer more extensive style suggestions.

What suggestions for using language more effectively would you offer your typical college instructor? Are these suggestions useful to students preparing public speeches?

Title the Speech

In some ways the title of a speech is a kind of frill. On the other hand, the title may be effective in gaining the interest of the audience and perhaps stimulating them to listen. In more formal public speech presentations, the title helps to gain audience attention and interest in announcements advertising the speech.

A title should be relatively short (so it's easy to remember), attract the attention and arouse the interest of the listeners, and have a close and clear relationship to the major purpose of the speech.

CONSTRUCT YOUR CONCLUSION, INTRODUCTION, AND TRANSITIONS

The last items to consider are the conclusion, introduction, and transitions, topics covered in depth in Unit 13.

Conclusion

In concluding your speech, do at least two things. First, summarize the speech. Identify the main points again and sum up what you have told the audience:

> *Let's all support Grace Moore. She's our most effective negotiator; she's honest; and she knows what negotiation and our union are all about.*

What problems do speakers often create when they conclude their speeches? How might these problems be avoided?

Second, wrap up your speech. Develop an appropriate closure, a crisp ending. Do not let the speech hang. End the speech clearly and distinctly.

I hope, then, that when you vote on Tuesday, you'll vote for Moore. She's our only choice.

Introduction

Because you must know in detail all you are going to say before you prepare the introduction, construct your introduction last. Your introduction should immediately gain the attention of the audience. Most often, your coming to the front of the room will attract their attention. However, as you start to speak you may lose them if you do not make a special effort to hold their attention. A provocative statistic, a little-known fact, an interesting story, or a statement explaining the topic's significance will help secure this initial attention.

How might a speaker gain attention in the introduction? How might these same techniques be used throughout the speech?

Second, establish a relationship among yourself, the topic, and the audience. Tell the audience why you are speaking on this topic. Tell them why you are concerned with the topic and why you are competent to address them. These are questions most audiences will automatically ask themselves. Tell them before they need to ask you. Here is one example of how this might be done.

You may be wondering why a 25-year-old woman with no background in medicine or education is talking to you about AIDS education. I'm addressing you today as a mother of a child with AIDS, and I want to talk with you about my child's experience in class and about every child's experience in class—your own children's as well as mine.

Third, orient the audience. Tell them what you are going to say in the order you are going to say it.

With which of the ten steps covered in this unit do you anticipate having the most difficulty? The least difficulty?

I'm going to explain the ways in which war movies have changed through the years. I'm going to discuss examples of movies depicting World War II, the Korean War, and Vietnam.

Transitions

After you have completed the introduction, review the entire speech to make sure that the parts flow into one another and that the movement from one part to another (say, from the introduction to the first major proposition) will be clear to the audience. Transitional words, phrases, and sentences will help you achieve this smoothness of movement. These linguistic devices are often called "connectives" because they connect pieces of the speech to each other.

Here are a few suggestions:

- Connect your introduction's orientation to your first major proposition: "*Let's now look at the first of these three elements,* the central processing unit, in detail. The CPU is the heart of the computer. It consists of . . ."
- Connect your major propositions to each other: "*But not only is* cigarette smoking dangerous to the smoker, *it also is* dangerous to the nonsmoker; Passive smoking is harmful to everyone. . . ."
- Connect your last major proposition to your conclusion: "*As we saw,* there were three sources of evidence against the butler. He had a motive; he had no alibi; he had the opportunity."

How does the advice on transitions given here compare with the advice given in your English composition course?

REHEARSE YOUR SPEECH

You've prepared your speech to be delivered to an audience, so your next step is to practice it. Rehearse your speech, from start to finish, out loud, at least four times before delivering it in class. During these rehearsals, time your speech so that you stay within the specified time limits.

Practice any terms that you may have difficulty with; consult a dictionary to clarify any doubts about pronunciation.

Include in your outline any notes you want to remember during the actual speech—notes to remind you to use your visual aid or to read a quotation.

DELIVER YOUR SPEECH

In your actual delivery, use your voice and bodily action to reinforce your message. Make it easier for your listeners to understand your speech. Obviously, any vocal or body movements that draw attention to themselves (and away from what you are saying) should be avoided. Here are a few guidelines that will prove helpful. Units 17 and 18 offer more suggestions.

When called on to speak, approach the front of the room with enthusiasm; even if, like most speakers, you feel nervous, show instead your desire to speak with your listeners.

F O C U S **O** N

Question and Answer Strategies

In many public speaking situations, a question-and-answer period will follow. So, be prepared to answer questions after your speech. Here are a few suggestions for making this Q&A session more effective.

- Consider if you need to repeat the question. If you suspect the audience did not hear it, then repeat it.
- Control any tendency to get defensive. Don't assume that the question is an attack. Assume, instead, that the question is an attempt to secure more information or perhaps to challenge a position you have taken.
- If appropriate, thank the person for asking the question or note that the question is a particularly good one.
- Don't bluff. If you are asked a question and if you don't know the answer, say so.
- As you develop your public speaking skills, you'll find many instances where you'll be able to connect the question with one or more of your major assertions or points of view: "I'm glad you asked about child care because that is exactly the difference between the two proposals we're here to vote on."

What one delivery suggestion would you offer the beginning speaker?

When at the front of the room, don't begin immediately; instead, pause, engage your audience eye to eye for a few brief moments, and then begin to talk directly to the audience. Talk in a volume that can be easily heard without straining.

Throughout your speech, maintain eye contact with your entire audience; avoid concentrating on only a few members or looking out of the window or at the floor.

UNIT IN BRIEF

Step 1: Select your topic and purpose	■ Is the topic worthwhile and limited in scope? ■ Is the purpose clearly defined?
Step 2: Analyze your audience	■ Is the speech appropriate? ■ Is the speech adapted to this specific audience?
Step 3: Research your topic	■ Is the speech adequately researched?
Step 4: Formulate your thesis and major propositions	■ Does the speech have one clearly identifiable thesis?

	■ Do all the major propositions support this thesis?
Step 5: Support your major propositions	■ Are the major propositions adequately supported so that they are clear and, if appropriate, persuasively presented?
Step 6: Organize your speech materials	■ Is the speech presented in a logical, clearly identifiable pattern that will aid comprehension?
Step 7: Word your speech	■ Is the speech instantly intelligible to listeners, who will hear the speech only once?
Step 8: Construct your conclusion, introduction, and transitions	■ Does the conclusion summarize and close the speech? ■ Does the introduction gain attention and orient the audience? ■ Are the parts of the speech adequately connected with transitions?
Step 9: Rehearse your speech	■ Have you rehearsed the speech to the point where you are comfortable giving it to an audience?
Step 10: Deliver your speech	■ Do your voice and bodily action reinforce your message? ■ Do you focus your eyes and body on the listeners?

PRACTICALLY SPEAKING

Short Speech Technique

Prepare and deliver a two-minute speech in which you:

1. describe a public speech you heard recently
2. explain a print advertisement in terms of the steps for preparing a public speech
3. explain any one of the steps of public speaking as it might apply to intercultural conversation
4. describe how you see your class as an audience for your next speech

2.1   Thinking Critically About Informative Speaking

Here are suggestions for informative speech topics built around the three types of informative speaking to be discussed in detail in Unit 19: definition, description, and demonstration. Select one topic from each of the three types of speeches, then:

1. formulate a specific thesis
2. formulate a specific purpose suitable for an informative speech of approximately five minutes
3. analyze this class as your potential audience and identify ways you can relate this topic to their interests and needs
4. generate at least two major propositions from your thesis
5. support these propositions with examples, illustrations, definitions, and so on
6. construct a conclusion that summarizes your main ideas and brings the speech to a definite close
7. construct an introduction that gains attention and orients your audience

Discuss these outlines in small groups or with the class as a whole. Try to secure feedback from other members on how you can improve these outlines.

Topics for Speeches of Definition

alcoholism	free speech
art and science	friendship
artificial intelligence	happiness
assault and battery	id, ego, superego
atheism	infallibility
baseball's rules	libel and slander
cartel	love and sex
censorship	Marxism
codependency	mysticism
cognitive therapy	neurosis and psychosis
counterfeiting	prejudice
creative thinking	primitivism
culture	propaganda
discrimination	rap, opera, chant, hip-hop
drug abuse	religion
ESP	sexual ethics
ethics	sexual harassment
etiquette	truth
fear and jealousy	violence
felony and misdemeanor	
feminism	

Topics for Speeches of Description

academic garb
bee colony
Buckingham Palace
college hierarchy
college newspaper office
computer
computer department of an ad
    agency
courtroom
exercise guidelines
Fort Knox
houseboat
how cholesterol works in the
    body
insurance policy
library
lie detector
monetary systems

national government
nuclear power plant
operation of the heart
photography darkroom
publishing company
rental lease
shopping center
skeletal structure of the
    body
stock exchange
structure of an airplane, boat,
    car
time management tech-
    niques
TV station (studio)
types of paintbrushes
weather bureau
weight control techniques

Topics for Speeches of Demonstration

how television is censored
how advertising influences
    the media
how graduate and professional
    schools select students
how a magazine or newspaper
    is put together
how to conduct an interview
how to form a campus organi-
    zation or club
how to complain
how advertisers choose where
    to place ads
how to lessen guilt
how the brain works
how radar works
how to organize your time
how nicotine affects the
    body
how steroids work
how sound is produced
how clothing communicates
    status
how to buy insurance

how to save for retirement
how to apply for a student
    loan
how to apply to graduate
    school
how satellite TV works
how to write a will
how to adopt a child
how a bill becomes law
how political candidates raise
    money
how to organize a protest
how power works in an organi-
    zation
how to publicize your ideas
how an experiment is con-
    ducted
how IQ is measured
how dreams reveal the sub-
    conscious
how to apply for life experience
    credits
how a jury is selected

2.2   Thinking Critically About Persuasive Speaking

Here are 20 topics for persuasive speeches. Select any one topic and then:

1. formulate a specific thesis
2. formulate a specific purpose suitable for a persuasive speech of approximately five minutes.
3. analyze this class as your potential audience; try to predict their relevant attitudes and beliefs; and identify ways you can relate this topic to their interests and needs
4. generate at least two major propositions from your thesis
5. support these propositions with examples, illustrations, definitions, facts, opinions, and so on
6. construct a conclusion that summarizes your main ideas and brings the speech to a definite close
7. construct an introduction that gains attention and orients your audience

Share your outline in small groups or with the class as a whole. Try to secure feedback from other members on how you can improve your outline.

1. Vote in the next election (college, city, state, national).
2. Capital punishment should be abolished (extended).
3. Support (Do not support) college athletics.
4. Gay men and lesbians should (not) be permitted to adopt children.
5. Military recruitment should (not) be allowed on college campuses.
6. Join the Peace Corps.
7. Sex education in elementary schools should be expanded (eliminated).
8. Volunteer to read for the blind.
9. Teachers, police, and firefighters should (not) be permitted to strike.
10. Personal firearms should be prohibited (permitted).
11. Alcohol should be prohibited (permitted) on college campuses.
12. Marijuana should (not) be legalized.
13. Marriage licenses should be denied to any couple who have not known each other for at least one year.
14. Nuclear plants should be abolished (expanded).
15. The government should (not) support the expansion of solar energy.
16. Required college courses should be eliminated.
17. Condoms should (not) be made available to high school students on request.
18. Cheating on an examination should (not) result in automatic dismissal from college.
19. This country should (not) establish a system of free legal services for all of its citizens.
20. Church property should (not) be taxed.

Learning Aid Note

Throughout this text, a number of speeches are presented. These speeches, together with their annotations and questions, are presented to illustrate the principles and skills of public speaking. With the exception of those in Unit 5, which were written to illustrate what poorly constructed speeches look like, the rest of the sample speeches are particularly good ones. Read these speeches as carefully as you would read the text; they are concrete illustrations of the principles discussed in the text. They will prove extremely useful as models of excellence.

2.3   Analyzing a Speech

The following speech is presented as a summary of the major parts of a public speech. The annotations will guide you through the speech and will illustrate the principles considered in this unit. The questions will give you an opportunity to apply your newly acquired public speaking skills. This speech is an excellent one. It was given by Jay Lane, a student at Southern Utah State College, and won the award for the best informative speech at the 1987 National Individual Events Tournament.

Dust—Jay Lane

Webster's says it's fine, dry, and pulverized. We rarely think about it. Strange, really. For there's twice as much in this room as there is anywhere outside. And those who study it tell us that 43 million tons will fall on the United States alone. What it is, in a word, is dust. And I know what you're thinking, but wait. For there is an inspiration in the examination of such a microscopic phenomenon. The November 1986 issue of *Discover* magazine relates the account of author Penny Ward Mosier and the coming of age of Dust. In that article she writes, "I only noticed the dust because my mind was desperately seeking a diversion. That happens during tax time. And so it was one day that I found myself pushing around little clumps of dust, and then it happened, from behind the corner of my desk there appeared a giant dust ball, piloted by my big toe. I picked it up. Intrigued, 'What is this dust ball?' I wondered." The experience of the author is one that is shared by us all at one time or another. How many times have you sat and watched the lazy, floating particles falling slowly in the sunlight. The dust is more than the mystical substance that makes up daydreams. It is also the thesis of a speech. One that deals with a subject which "touches us" literally every day of our lives.

And so, with your kind permission, I present dust. What it is, where it comes from, and how on earth it can affect us. Now, I have to admit that until fairly recently, I had never given dust more than a speck of thought. But as my understanding has increased, so has my appreciation. You see, what we often think of as, well, as dust, blossoms under a microscope, becoming what some might even consider to be exotic. But, I should slow myself down before my story loses its structure. According to the Library of Congress, there are 322 books that have been published on the subject of dust. Let's see what information they can provide.

In his book entitled *The Secret House* author David Bodine provides a great deal of information. It seems that the principal element that makes up what we refer to as dust is soil. That's a fancy word for dirt. Followed closely by of, all things, salt. That's right. These tiny crystals dance out of our oceans at a rate of 300 million tons every year. In addition, you will find fabric fibers, fungi, pollens, and a variety of things that, quite

The attention-getting device used here is to arouse curiosity. We wonder what the speech will be on, and so we listen to get the answer to our question. The speaker also maintains our attention throughout the speech with humor and with little-known facts. In what other ways might the speaker have captured the audience's attention?

The topic is itself interesting because dust is something we all experience but few of us really know anything about it.

The purpose of the speech is clearly stated. We know the speech is an informative one by the way the topics are identified in the opening sections of the speech. Might there be situations where the speaker would not want the audience to know the purpose so early in the speech?

Lane orients the audience in two ways. First, he presents a general idea of his speech topic when he says, "It [dust] is also the thesis of a speech." Second, he orients us in more detail by identifying the three major points he will cover: "And so, with your kind permission, I present dust: [1] What it is, [2] where it comes from, and [3] how on earth it can affects us." The audience is thus set up to hear these three aspects of dust. This very clear orientation is favored in much of the United States but may be less favored by cultures that encourage a more indirect style. How might the speaker have introduced the topic less directly?

Throughout the speech he repeats the thesis, that dust is a significant topic: "The dust is more than the mystical substance that makes up daydreams," "a subject which 'touches us' literally every day of our lives," and "an entire world of fascination." Did you become convinced of the importance of dust?

Throughout the introduction, the author directly involves the audience. For example, he says, "We rarely think about it," "in this room," and "I know what you're thinking, but wait." Also, he earlier related the experience of Penny Mosier to the audience members: "The experience . . . is shared by us all." How might you involve an audience in a topic such as abortion, drug legislation, or immigration policies?

The speaker neatly establishes his credibility by his references to his thorough research. How else might a speaker establish his or her credibility? (Unit 23 discusses this in depth.)

In this section the speaker covers his first point, namely, the nature of dust ("what it is").

Throughout the speech, the speaker reminds the audience that he appreciates their feelings about dust but that they should continue listening because he will tell them something new and useful. Does this make you want to continue reading? What else might the speaker have done to encourage the audience to stay with him?

A neat transition connects the first topic, what dust is, to the second topic, where dust comes from. Do the transitions in this speech help you follow where the speaker is going? What kinds of transitions do we use in conversation? What kinds of transitions do talk-show hosts use?

Note how the speaker uses a conversational style that engages and involves the listener. Generally, the conversation style is recommended, but can you think of situations where a more formal, more elevated style of public speaking would prove more effective?

Note how the use of specific numbers communicates about the speaker's research efforts and concern for accuracy. In what other ways does the speaker show that he did his research? Is this a style that would be evaluated favorably in all cultures?

Lane again introduces his next point with a transition: "With so much dust in the air [covered just previously], it seems like it should have some kind of impact on your life, shouldn't it [the third part of the speech: how it can affect us]?" This he covers in two parts: the negative aspects of dust and the more positive side. The transition could have been clearer, and

frankly, you don't want to hear about. But don't worry, I am merely saving the best part for last. Now I realize that at times dust can be a hard sell. Still, I press boldly forward. For dust is becoming a serious business. For this reason, the Maryland Medical Laboratories donated several of their shelves, taking them away from growing cultures of new biotechnologies and bacteria in order to grow samples of Mrs. Mosier's dust balls. They immediately blossomed into a collage, warranting closer examination. Of the experience she wrote, "Everyone came by to stare at my dust, oohed and aahed over the slides that we had made. Under a microscope my stained dust was a work of art. I now understood that not only could dust be anything, it could be everything."

She also notes that in addition to being everything, it also comes from everything. For example, forest fires. In a good year, for dust, seven percent of the world's total comes from forest fires. In addition, much of it comes from our oceans, as mentioned earlier. And, of course, we can't forget man-made pollutants, industrial dust. But, the single largest contributors to the world supply of dust are volcanoes. In fact, the infamous eruption of Krakatoa in 1883 was the dust event of recorded history. But, you know, that happened a long time ago. So the dust that you see must come from someplace else. But where?

How about Africa? Seriously, *Nature* magazine in November of 1986 notes that the winds that blow across the African deserts carry with them so much dust that in times it falls as a light pink rain on Miami. But is it possible that the dust carries all the way across the country, that the dust here in San Diego is from Africa, that the dust in your home has an international flavor? Yes. Says dust buster John Ferguson, who last year helped sell some 750 thousand gallons of Endust! He knows. It is not only possible that the dust in your homes comes from all over the world, it does. What's more, much of it comes from outer space. Extra-terrestrial dust. Coming principally from comets and disintegrating meteorites, at a rate of 10,000 tons every year. Well, with so many things coming from so many places, it's not surprising that everything you own is covered by that fine, thin layer, and you don't know half the story yet. Again, according to *Discover* magazine, the average six-room city or urban dwelling takes in 40 pounds of dust every year, 40 pounds. And a single cubic inch of air space can contain 1,600,000 tiny particles. (Cough) Sorry, it got just a little difficult to breathe.

With so much dust in the air, it seems like it should have some kind of impact on your life, shouldn't it? Good point. Let's see. Now you've already heard about dust and how it affects us through hay fever. Of course, that's pollen, a significant source of dust. And I know you've seen a cobweb at one time or another. But there was something else, something

Lane's language is appropriate to the audience. He creates images (Penny Mosier with her dust ball, looking at a sunset, wrapping one's body in Saran Wrap), involves the audience through questions ("But where?" "Do you remember the ones under your bed?"), uses language that is easily understood and is personal (there are numerous personal pronouns and direct references to the speaker and the audience, and he uses concrete rather than abstract language). How would you evaluate the speaker's use of language? What do you like best about his style? What do you like least?

Talk about a direct link to your past, AT&T has nothing on these guys in terms of long-distance communication.

But, seriously, Dr. Bryant notes that there is some information that we get from dust we simply cannot get anywhere else. There are also some implications and impacts of dust that are a little bit closer to home. It seems that dust has an interesting effect on light waves. It breaks up the blues and the purples at the short end of the spectrum, but leaves the reds and oranges untouched. The result, beautiful red, orange, yellow in the sunset you saw last night. Oh, yes, there was one more thing. According to the *American Academic Encyclopedia* of 1983, dust serves as an interesting tricha, and essential foundation. It seems that as the dust floats around in the atmosphere and allows water molecules to bond, the result, condensation and precipitation. In case you're wondering if dust has any social significance, try getting a drink of water without it. Dust, what a simple term. But it is anything and everything. It is a glass of water, a sunset, a very ugly bug. But whatever dust may be, the dust ball discovered by Mrs. Mosier was more than just a word, rather an entire world of fascination.

SOURCE: From "Dust" by Jay Lane in *1987 Championship Debates and Speeches* by the American Forensic Association. Reprinted by permission of the American Forensic Association.

significant, that I wanted to share. Now, I don't want to be the cause of anyone's nightmares, and I don't want to keep you awake tonight, but this is the point where I re-create all of your childhood fears. You know, as kids it's fairly easy for us to handle dirt. We roll around with the fungi and the fabric fibers and never really give it a second thought, but it's the monsters, do you remember, the ones under your bed? Well, I'm here today to tell you that those childhood foes are very real in a sense. For this was discovered by the Maryland Medical Laboratories in the research they did for Mrs. Mosier. Dr. and Scientist Charles McCloud discovered under the microscope something he said that he had never seen before. He said it had mouth parts on its legs, and described it as an angry rhinoceros with crustation appendages. In short he said, it's the ugliest thing you have ever seen. So go ahead. Even that tough group of scientists uttered their share of icks and uggs when they saw this little guy. He is a member of a family of house mites.

The scientific name is am-uh-huh, I wrote it down. *Dermitoffaginous sparnine*, I think. Personally, I just write dust. There are 15 species of these little guys that live in various parts around the world. They live in your pillows, in your mattresses, in your sheets, and in your dust balls. They eat the 50 million or so skin scales that your body sheds every day. Don't worry, they can't eat anything if it's still attached. Although they will chew on your toenail dirt if you give them half a chance.

But now I don't want you to leave with the idea that this isn't really a significant problem. According to Ian Fielding in his book entitled *Dust* there are about two million of these dust mites in every twin-sized bed. Kind of makes you want to wrap your body in Saran Wrap, doesn't it? Well, that was the response of Mrs. Mosier, but don't worry, even after finding all this out, she, her husband, and their two million tiny pets have learned to share the bed just fine. Of course, that was before she found out her air conditioner had gangrene. Yet another element, that simple term that we call dust.

But I don't want to leave you with a negative impression. Like everything that has to do with dust is bad. For there are many benefits from dust as well. Consider as you would a *Forbes* magazine article of August 12, 1985, entitled "A Handful of Dust." The article relates a revolution in scientific research. It seems that Dr. Von Bryant, a pollentologist, that's a term for someone who studies dust, and Texas A&M University are conducting a group of experiments that they call "chomap." The purpose of the project is to re-create environmental conditions over the past ten thousand years by using dust. According to Dr. Von Bryant, they have already discovered some pollen samples as old as 2.5 billion year

it might have summarized both his previous and previewed his third point. How would phrase this?

The significance of the topic and the s most clearly established in the coverage point, how dust affects us. Some additio earlier in the speech to establish the si the topic might have helped. How mi have done this?

The speaker might have answere question, "Why should we listen?" than curiosity (which he did use ef reasons would you give your liste giving this speech?

Usually, a speaker is any inadequacies or lo speaker's mentioning term work for him or technique work in yo

The source *Forbes, Dust Encyclopedi* being intru speaker is He might author c of *Dust* about

D

UNIT 3

From Apprehension to Confidence

Unit Objectives

After completing this unit, you should be able to:

1. Define *speaker apprehension*

2. Identify the suggestions for dealing with speaker apprehension

3. Identify three suggestions listeners might follow to help the speaker deal with apprehension

4. Identify at least four suggestions for increasing self-confidence as a public speaker

*I*f you are like most students, your first concern is not with organization or audience analysis but with stage fright or what we call speaker apprehension. Apprehension is experienced not only by the beginning public speaker but also by even the most experienced speakers. Most public speakers don't eliminate apprehension; they learn to control it.

"*Communication apprehension*," note researchers James McCroskey and Lawrence Wheeless (1976), "*is probably the most common handicap that is suffered by people in contemporary American society.*" According to a nationwide survey conducted by Bruskin Associates, speaking in public ranks as the number one fear of adult men and women. It ranks above fear of heights and even fear of snakes. According to college students surveyed by McCroskey and Wheeless, between 10 and 20 percent suffer "severe, debilitating communication apprehension." Another 20 percent suffer "from communication apprehension to a degree substantial enough to interfere to some extent with their normal functioning."

You may wish to pause here and take the self-test "How Apprehensive Are You in Public Speaking?" on the next page.

 In what situations do you experience the greatest degree of communication anxiety? What do these situations have in common?

WHAT IS SPEAKER APPREHENSION?

Speaker apprehension affects the way you feel and the way you act. Many people develop negative feelings about their ability to communicate orally. They predict that their communication efforts will fail. They feel that whatever gain they would make as a result of engaging in communication is not worth the fear they would experience. As a result, apprehensive speakers avoid communication situations and, when forced to participate, participate as little as possible.

General and Specific Apprehension

Some people have a general speaker apprehension that manifests itself in all communication situations. These people suffer from trait apprehension—a fear of communication generally, regardless of the specific situation. Their fear appears in conversations, small-group settings, and public speaking situations.

Other people experience speaker apprehension in only certain communication situations. These people suffer from state apprehension—a fear specific to a given communication situation. For example, a speaker may fear public speaking but have no difficulty in talking with two or three other people. Or a speaker may fear job interviews but have no fear of public speaking. State apprehension is extremely common. Most people experience it for some situations. As already mentioned, public speaking is the state that provokes the most apprehension.

Degrees of Apprehension

Speaker apprehension exists on a continuum. Some people are so apprehensive that they are unable to function in any communication situation. They suffer greatly in a society oriented around communication, since success often

TIPS
From Professional Speakers

When the subject of nerves comes up, there is both good news and bad news. The bad news is that, more than likely, you will be nervous. You aren't alone. Almost all speakers, including professionals, experience uneasiness before speeches. So do athletes, rock stars, actors, and other performers just before their game or performance. The good news is that, not only is this normal, but it's good!!! More news—Nervous energy IS energy. You can use it to your advantage.

Thomas J. Murphy, teacher and author, & **Kenneth Snyder,** professional speaker and trainer. *What! I Have to Give a Speech?* (Bloomington, IN: Grayson Bernard Publications, 1995), p. 160.

Self Test

How Apprehensive Are You in Public Speaking?

This questionnaire is composed of six statements concerning your feelings about public speaking. Indicate in the space provided the degree to which each statement applies to you by marking whether you

1 = strongly agree
2 = agree
3 = are undecided
4 = disagree
5 = strongly disagree

There are no right or wrong answers. Many of the statements are similar to other statements; do not be concerned about this. Work quickly; record your first impression.

_____ 1. I have no fear of giving a speech.
_____ 2. Certain parts of my body feel very tense and rigid while giving a speech.
_____ 3. I feel relaxed while giving a speech.
_____ 4. My thoughts become confused and jumbled when I am giving a speech.
_____ 5. I face the prospect of giving a speech with confidence.
_____ 6. While giving a speech, I get so nervous that I forget facts I really know.

SCORING: Compute your score as follows:

1. Begin with the number 18; this is just used as a base so that you will not wind up with negative numbers.
2. To 18, add your scores for items 1, 3, and 5.
3. Subtract your scores for items 2, 4, and 6 from your Step 2 total.

Your score should range from 6 to 30; the higher the score, the greater the apprehension. Any score above 18 indicates some degree of apprehension. Most people score above 18 on this test, so if you scored relatively high you are among the vast majority of people. You might also want to take the test for apprehension in conversations, presented on page 45. An apprehension test for group discussions and meetings appears in Unit 25, Speaking in Small Groups. You may want to take this test now and compare your scores. If you are like most people, your apprehension score will be higher for public speaking than for group discussions or meetings or for conversations.

SOURCE: From James C. McCroskey, *An Introduction to Rhetorical Communication*, 6th ed. (Englewood Cliffs, N.J.: Prentice Hall, 1993).

How accurately do you feel the self-test "How Apprehensive Are You in Public Speaking?" identified your apprehension in public speaking?

How closely do your scores on the "How Apprehensive" self-test and on the shyness test (see Practically Speaking exercise 3.1) match? Do the scores and their degree of similarity seem reasonable?

depends on the ability to communicate effectively. Other people are so mildly apprehensive that they appear to experience no fear at all. They actively seek out a wide variety of communication experiences. Most of us fall between these two extremes.

For some people, apprehension is debilitating and hinders personal effectiveness in professional and social relationships. For others, apprehension is motivating and may actually help in achieving one's goals. By the end of this course, you should be in this second category.

Positive and Normal Apprehension

Apprehension in public speaking is normal. Everyone experiences some degree of fear in the relatively formal public speaking situation. In public speaking you are the sole focus of attention and are usually being evaluated for your performance. Therefore, experiencing fear or anxiety is not strange or unique.

Although you may at first view apprehension as harmful, it is not necessarily so—as the TIPS from Dorothy Leeds make clear. In fact, apprehension can work for you. Fear can energize you. It may motivate you to work a little harder to produce a speech that will be better than it might have been. Further, the audience cannot see the apprehension you might be experiencing. Even though you may think the audience can hear your heart beat faster and faster, they cannot. They cannot see your knees tremble. They cannot sense your dry throat—at least, not most of the time.

Culture and Speaker Apprehension

Intercultural communication can create uncertainty, fear, and anxiety, all of which are intimately related to speaker apprehension (Stephan & Stephan 1985).

When you are in an intercultural situation—say, when your audience is composed largely of people of cultures very different from your own—you are more uncertain about the situation and about the audience's possible responses. Not surprisingly, most people react negatively to high uncertainty and develop a decreased attraction for these other people (Gudykunst & Nishida 1984; Gudykunst, Yang, & Nishida 1985). When you are sure of the situation and can predict what will happen, you are more likely to feel comfortable and at ease. But when the situation is uncertain and you cannot predict what will happen, you become more apprehensive (Gudykunst & Kim 1992 a,b).

Intercultural situations can also engender fear. You might, for example, have a greater fear of saying something that will prove offensive or of revealing your own prejudices. The fear easily translates into apprehension.

Intercultural situations can also create anxiety, a feeling very similar to apprehension. Anxiety may be felt for a number of reasons (Stephan & Stephan 1985). For example, your prior relationships with members of a culturally different group can influence your apprehension. If your prior relationships were few or unpleasant, then you are likely to experience greater apprehension when dealing with these members than if those prior experiences were numerous and positive.

Your thoughts and feelings about the group will also influence your apprehension. For example, if you hold stereotypes and prejudices or feel you are very different from these others, then you are likely to experience more apprehension than if you saw these people as similar to you.

The situation you are in can also influence your anxiety and apprehension. If, for example, you feel that members of another group are competing with or evaluating you, then you are likely to experience more apprehension than if the situation were more cooperative and equal.

Why do intercultural communication situations seem to create more uncertainty, fear, and anxiety than communication between members of the same culture?

Self
Test

Conversations: How Apprehensive Are You?

 What factors of conversation increase apprehension?

This following six statements concern your feelings about communication with other people. Think about the degree to which each statement applies to you, that is, whether you (1) strongly agree, (2) agree, (3) are undecided, (4) disagree, or (5) strongly disagree with each statement. There are no right or wrong answers. Some of the statements are similar to other statements; do not be concerned about this. Work quickly; record your first impression.

_____ 1. While participating in a conversation with a new acquaintance, I feel very nervous.
_____ 2. I have no fear of speaking up in conversations.
_____ 3. Ordinarily I am very tense and nervous in conversations.
_____ 4. Ordinarily I am very calm and relaxed in conversations.
_____ 5. While conversing with a new acquaintance, I feel very relaxed.
_____ 6. I'm afraid to speak up in conversations.

SCORING: Compute your score as follows:

1. Begin with the number 18 .
2. To 18, add your scores for items 2, 4, and 5.
3. Subtract your scores for items 1, 3, and 6 from your total for Step 2.
3. The result (which should be somewhere between 6 and 30) is your apprehension score for interpersonal conversations.

The higher the score, the greater your apprehension. A score above 18 indicates some degree of apprehension.

SOURCE: From James C. McCroskey, *An Introduction to Rhetorical Communication*, 6th ed. (Englewood Cliffs, N.J.: Prentice Hall, 1993).

Factors Influencing Communication Apprehension

Understanding the factors that influence communication apprehension will help you control them and therefore control your own fear of speaking (Beatty 1988).

Perceived Novelty   Situations that are new and different contribute to anxiety. As the novelty of the situation is reduced (as you gain experience in public speaking), your anxiety is also reduced.

Subordinate Status   When you feel that others are better speakers than you or that they know more about the topic than you do, anxiety increases. Thinking more positively about yourself and being thorough in your preparation are helpful techniques for reducing this particular cause of anxiety.

TIPS
From Professional Speakers

Whether you face real or imaginary fear, physical danger, or emotional stress, the reaction is the same. And speakers benefit: The adrenaline becomes energy; their minds seem more alert; new thoughts, facts, and ideas arise. In fact, some of my best ad libs come to me in front of my toughest audiences; it's yet another gift from the adrenaline.

Nervousness can give your speech the edge—and the passion—all good speeches need. It has always been so; two thousand years ago Cicero said all public speaking of real merit was characterized by nervousness.

Dorothy Leeds, president, Organizational Technologies, Inc., a management and sales consulting firm. *Powerspeak: The Complete Guide to Persuasive Public Speaking and Presenting* (New York: Prentice Hall, 1988), pp. 9–10.

bursts into wild applause. Throughout this visualization, avoid all negative thoughts.

As you visualize yourself as an effective public speaker, take special note of how you walk, look at your listeners, handle your notes, and respond to questions and especially how you feel about the whole experience.

The second part of performance visualization is designed to help you model your performance on that of a particularly effective speaker. Here you would view a particularly competent public speaker on video and make a mental movie of it. As you review the actual and mental movie, you begin to shift yourself into the role of speaker. In effect, you become this effective speaker.

Systematic Desensitization

Systematic desensitization is a technique for dealing with a variety of fears, including those involved in public speaking (Wolpe 1957; Goss, Thompson, & Olds 1978; Richmond & McCroskey 1992). The general idea is to create a hierarchy of behaviors leading up to the desired but feared behavior (say, speaking before an audience). One specific hierarchy might look like this:

> Giving a speech in class
> Introducing another speaker to the class
> Speaking in a group in front of the class
> Answering a question in class
> Asking a question in class

How would you create a desensitization hierarchy for "fear of nonpoisonous snakes," "fear of asking for a date," or "fear of expressing a difference of opinion to a superior"?

You would begin at the bottom of this hierarchy and rehearse this behavior mentally over a period of days until you can clearly visualize asking a question in class without any uncomfortable anxiety. Once you can accomplish this, you can move to the second level. Here you would visualize the somewhat more threatening answering of a question. Once you can do this, you can move to the third level, and so on, until you get to the desired behavior.

In creating your hierarchy, try to use small steps. This will enable you to get from one step to the next more easily. Each success will make the next step easier.

You might then go on to engage in the actual behaviors after you have comfortably visualized them: Ask a question, answer a question, and so on.

Skill Acquisition

The third general approach to dealing with speaker apprehension is to acquire specific skills and techniques for greater control over apprehension and for increased speaking effectiveness. Here are some useful techniques.

Prepare and Practice Thoroughly   Much of the fear you experience is a fear of failure. Adequate and even extra preparation will lessen the possibility of failure and the accompanying apprehension. Jack Valenti (1982), president of the Motion Picture Association of America and speechwriter for Lyndon Johnson, put it this way: "The most effective antidote to stage fright and other calamities of speechmaking is total, slavish, monkish preparation."

Because apprehension is greatest during the beginning of the speech, try memorizing the first few sentences of your speech to eliminate any possibility of saying them incorrectly or forgetting them.

If the speech contains complicated facts or figures, be sure to write these out and plan to read them. Again, this procedure will help lessen your fear of making a mistake.

Gain Experience   Learning to speak in public is similar to learning to drive a car or ski down a mountain. With experience, the initial fears and anxieties give way to feelings of control, comfort, and pleasure. Experience will prove to you that a public speech can be effective despite your fears and anxieties. It will show you that the feelings of accomplishment in public speaking are rewarding and will outweigh any initial anxiety.

Move About and Breathe Deeply   Physical activity—gross bodily movements as well as the small movements of the hands, face, and head—eases or lessens apprehension. Using a visual aid, for example, will temporarily divert attention from you and will allow you to get rid of your excess energy.

Deep breathing relaxes the body. By breathing deeply a few times before getting up to speak, you will sense your body relax. This will help you overcome your initial fear of getting out of your seat and walking to the front of the room. If during your speech you find yourself becoming a bit more nervous than you'd hoped, just breathe deeply during a pause.

Avoid Chemicals as Tension Relievers   Unless they are prescribed by a physician, avoid any chemical means for reducing apprehension. Tranquilizers, marijuana, alcohol, or artificial stimulants, for example, are likely to create problems rather than reduce them. They are likely to impair other functions. For example, chemicals are likely to impair your ability to remember the parts of your speech, to accurately read audience feedback, and to regulate the timing of your speech.

What other suggestions might you offer for helping speakers to manage their apprehension in public speaking?

LISTENER GUIDELINES

Listeners can do a great deal to assist speakers with their apprehension. Here are just a few suggestions.

Positively Reinforce the Speaker

A nod, a pleasant smile, an attentive appearance throughout the speech will help put the speaker at ease. Resist the temptation to pick up a newspaper or talk with a friend. Try to make the speaking experience as easy as possible for the speaker.

Ask Questions in a Supportive Manner

If there is a question period after the speech, ask information-seeking questions rather than fire critical challenges. Instead of saying "Your criticism of heavy metal music is absurd," say "Why do you find the lyrics of heavy metal harmful?" or "What is there about rap music that you find offensive?" Ask questions in a tone and manner that do not make the speaker defensive.

Do Not Focus on Errors

If the speaker fumbles in some way, do not focus on it. Do not put your head down, cover your eyes, or otherwise nonverbally communicate your intense awareness of the fumble. Instead, continue listening to the content of the speech. Nonverbally, try to communicate to the speaker that you are concerned with what is being said.

DEVELOPING CONFIDENCE

Confidence separates the effective from the ineffective public speaker. Confidence also seems to separate the speaker who experiences enjoyment from the speaker who feels only pain and anxiety. Fortunately, confidence is a quality everyone can develop and improve. A few suggestions for developing your self-confidence as a public speaker should help.

Prepare Thoroughly

Preparation is probably the major factor in instilling confidence in a speaker, as it is in reducing apprehension. Preparation includes everything you do from the time you begin thinking about your speech to the time you deliver it. The more you know about your topic, the more confident you will feel and the more confidence you will project. Thorough rehearsal will lessen any fears of forgetting.

What kinds of listening behaviors help to lessen your anxiety when you are speaking?

Preparing thoroughly is probably your best offensive strategy for reducing anxiety and developing confidence in public speaking situations. What other advice would you give to a speaker on the path from apprehension to confidence?

Familiarize Yourself with the Public Speaking Situation

Familiarize yourself with the arrangement of the room in which you will speak, the type of audience you will address, and so on. Familiarity with any situation increases your ability to control it. The public speaking situation is no exception. Perhaps a day or two before you are to speak, stand in front of the room and look it over. Try to imagine the entire speaking situation as it will be when you deliver your speech. Then, when you do go to the front of the room to give your first speech, you will face the familiar instead of the unexpected.

Develop the Desire to Communicate

Avoid rehearsing fear responses (*I'm going to forget my speech. No one will like my speech. I'm going to look foolish*). Replace any thoughts of fear with thoughts of control. Avoid self-critical statements; replace these with thoughts of confidence—substitute positive "scripts." Tell yourself that the experience can be an enjoyable one—it really can be! With time, you will find that you are operating with a more positive and confident view of the entire public speaking experience.

Rehearse

Rehearsing your speech and its presentation—and thus sensing your control over it—is essential for increasing self-confidence. Rehearse your speech often. Rehearse out loud. If possible, rehearse your speech in front of a few supportive listeners. Rehearsals that approximate the actual speaking situation will especially help reduce the novelty of the situation and help build your confidence as a public speaker.

Rehearse your speech as a confident, fully-in-control public speaker. Rehearse with a positive attitude and perspective. When you then present the actual speech, you will find you can present it as you rehearsed it, with confidence.

Each public speaking experience—like each rehearsal—should add to your self-confidence. After five or six speeches, you should be looking forward to future speaking engagements.

Engage in Self-Affirmation

Because the way you talk to and about yourself will influence what you think of yourself, it is often helpful to engage in self-affirmation. Try telling yourself that you are competent and that you will be successful. Read through the list of self-affirming phrases presented here and try to feel what they are trying to convey.

- I'm a generally competent person and speaker.
- I have some good personality characteristics that will come across effectively in public speaking.
- Neither I nor my speech has to be loved by everyone.
- I am worthwhile listening to because I'm me.
- My past failures and inadequacies do not have to influence everything I do.
- I am creative, and that will come across in my speaking.

Shortly before you get up to make your remarks is the time to visualize yourself delivering a confident, well-received speech. It works—if you've done your homework well and have earned the right to psych yourself up.

Think of times you've succeeded at your endeavors in any field rather than the times you've failed. Think in terms of how good it'll be to succeed rather than how bad it'll be to fail. Think about your purpose in delivering the speech.

Concentrate on what you want to do. Concentrate on the emotions you want to spread outward, not on the emotions you want to keep inside. Concentrate on what you're saying, not how you're saying it or how you look.

Ed McMahon, television emcee and frequent public speaker. *The Art of Public Speaking* (New York: Ballantine, 1986), pp. 101–102.

 What other suggestions might you offer for developing self-confidence?

What well-known celebrity do you feel displays confidence most effectively? What is there about this person's behaviors that led you to this judgment?

Are the methods for increasing self-confidence the same for men and women? For members of different cultures?

- I think critically and will be able to analyze and present complex ideas to others.
- I'm a self-starter.
- I can be effective in most things I do, including public speaking.
- I'm flexible and can adjust to different situations and different audience responses.

Develop a Communicator Self-Image

A "communicator self-image" implies a view of yourself as a capable, proficient, and confident communicator. See yourself as an advocate who is effective in getting her or his message across to others. Think of yourself as a confident speaker. In addition to thinking of yourself as confident, act like a confident speaker. For example, maintain eye contact with your listeners; stand tall as would a leader. Acting confidently will go a long way toward actually increasing your confidence. This process occurs in three steps:

You act as if you are confident.

↓

You come to think of yourself as confident.

↓

You become confident.

Build your positive qualities by acting as if you already have them. This "acting as if" will help you make these positive qualities a more integral part of your thinking and behaviors.

UNIT IN BRIEF

Speaker apprehension	■ Speaker apprehension is a fear of speaking and may involve trait apprehension (fear of communication generally) or state apprehension (fear of a specific communication situation) ■ In addition to culture, the following influence apprehension: novelty, subordinate status, conspicuousness, dissimilarity, and prior history

Dealing with speaker apprehension	■ As a speaker:
	    Try **cognitive restructuring**: substituting rational beliefs for irrational beliefs
	    Try **systematic desensitization**: mastering a behavior by first mastering its less threatening parts
	    Try **skills acquisition**: acquiring the specific techniques for managing apprehension

■ As a listener:
 Positively reinforce the speaker
 Ask questions supportively
 Avoid focusing on errors

Developing confidence ■ Prepare thoroughly
  ■ Familiarize yourself with the public speaking
   situation
  ■ Develop the desire to communicate
  ■ Rehearse often and with a positive attitude
  ■ Engage in self-affirmation
  ■ Develop an image of yourself as a successful
   speaker

PRACTICALLY SPEAKING

Short Speech Technique

Prepare and deliver a two-minute speech in which you:

1. explain how apprehension relates to your professional life
2. explain how apprehension might have an impact on a student's dating and general social life
3. explain how uncertainty, fear, and anxiety operate in communication generally and in intercultural communication specifically
4. describe the confidence as displayed by a fictional character in literature, film, or television

3.1   Shyness

Earlier you assessed your own communication apprehension in a variety of communication contexts. Often but not always, communication apprehension and shyness are related. Here is a shyness scale that will enable you to measure your own degree of shyness. Respond to these statements as noted in the directions, and then consider the questions presented after the test.

> The following 14 statements refer to talking with other people. If the statement describes you very well, circle *YES*. If it somewhat describes you, circle *yes*. If you are unsure whether or not it describes you or if you do not understand the statement, circle the *?* If the statement is a poor description of you, circle *no*. If the statement is a very poor description of you, circle *NO*. There are no right or wrong answers. Work quickly; record your first impression.

1. I am a shy person.	YES	yes	?	no	NO
2. Other people think I talk a lot.	YES	yes	?	no	NO
3. I am a very talkative person.	YES	yes	?	no	NO

*P*reparing and presenting a public speech is the task you are most concerned with and most anxious about. But that is really only half the process of public speaking. The other half is critical listening. Before reading about this area of human communication, examine your own listening habits by taking the self-test "How Good a Listener Are You?"

 ## THE LISTENING PROCESS

How would you describe the listening process? Does the five-step model presented here adequately describe listening as you understand it? How might you improve on this model?

The process of listening can be described as a series of five steps: receiving, understanding, remembering, evaluating, and responding. This process is represented in Figure 4.1.

Receiving

Unlike listening, hearing begins and ends with this first stage of receiving. Hearing is something that just happens when you get within earshot of some auditory stimuli. Listening is quite different; it begins (but does not end) with receiving the messages the speaker sends. The messages are both verbal and nonverbal; they consist of words as well as gestures, facial expressions, variations in volume and rate, and lots more, as we will see throughout this text.

At this stage you recognize not only what is said (verbally and nonverbally) but also what is omitted. The politician's summary of accomplishments

FIGURE 4.1
A five-step model of the listening process. This five-step model draws on a variety of previous models developed by listening researchers (for example, Barker 1990; Steil, Barker, & Watson 1983; Brownell 1987; Alessandra 1986).

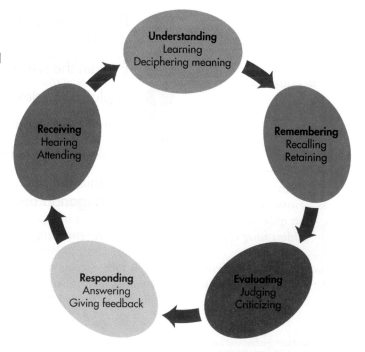

How would you describe yourself as a listener in a public speaking situation? What is your greatest strength? Your greatest weakness?

Self Test

How Good a Listener Are You?

Respond to each question using the following scale:

1 = always
2 = frequently
3 = sometimes
4 = seldom
5 = never

___ 1. I consider listening and hearing to be essentially the same, so I listen by simply keeping my ears open.
___ 2. I allow my mind to wander away from what the speaker is talking about.
___ 3. I simplify messages I hear by omitting details.
___ 4. I focus on a particular detail of what the speaker is saying instead of the general meanings the speaker wishes to communicate.
___ 5. I allow my attitudes toward the topic or speaker to influence my evaluation of the message.
___ 6. I assume that what I expect to hear is what is actually said.
___ 7. I stop listening when the speaker attacks my personal beliefs.
___ 8. I listen to what others say, but I don't feel what they are feeling.
___ 9. I judge and evaluate what the speaker is saying before I fully understand the meanings intended.
___10. I rehearse my questions and responses while the speaker is speaking.

SCORING: Add up the scores for all ten statements. Your score should be somewhere between 10 and 50. Since all statements describe ineffective listening tendencies, high scores reflect effective listening and low scores reflect ineffective listening. If you scored significantly higher than 30, then you probably have better-than-average listening skills. Scores significantly below 30 represent lower-than-average listening skills. Regardless of the score, however, most people can significantly improve their listening skills. Each of the questions in this listening test refers to an obstacle or effectiveness principle discussed in this unit.

in education and his or her omission of failures in improved health care programs are both received at this stage.

Receiving messages is a highly selective process. You do not listen to all the available auditory stimuli. Rather, you selectively tune in to certain messages and tune out others. Generally, you listen carefully to messages that you feel will prove of value to you or are particularly interesting. At the same time, you give less attention to messages that have less value or interest. Thus, you may, for example, listen carefully when your instructor tells you what will

What types of audience responses are helpful to you as a speaker? What types are detrimental?

appear on the examination but listen less carefully to an extended story or routine announcements. When receiving:

- focus your attention on the speaker's verbal and nonverbal messages, on what is said and on what is not said
- avoid focusing your attention on distractions in the environment
- focus your attention on what the speaker is saying rather than on any questions you may wish to ask later

Understanding

Understanding is the stage at which you learn what the speaker means. This understanding includes both the thoughts that are expressed and the emotional tone that accompanies these thoughts, for example, the urgency or the joy or sorrow expressed in the message. To enhance understanding:

Are you a better listener in interpersonal situations than in public speaking ones? If so, why do you behave differently in the two types of situations?

- relate the new information the speaker is giving to what you already know (In what way will this new proposal change our present health care?)
- see the speaker's messages from the speaker's point of view; avoid judging the message until you fully understand it as the speaker intended it
- rephrase (paraphrase) the speaker's ideas into your own words as you continue to listen

Remembering

Messages that you receive and understand need to be retained for at least some period of time. In public speaking situations, you can augment your memory by taking notes or by taping the messages.

What you remember is actually not what was said but what you think (or remember) was said. Memory for speech is not reproductive; you don't simply reproduce in your memory what the speaker said. Rather, memory is reconstructive; you actually reconstruct the messages you hear into a system that seems to make sense to you. This is well illustrated in the accompanying box, "Do You Really Remember What You Hear?"

In remembering:

- identify the thesis or central idea and the major propositions
- summarize the message in a more easily retained form, being careful not to ignore crucial details or qualifications
- repeat names and key concepts to yourself
- identify the organizational pattern and use it (visualize it) to organize what the speaker is saying

Evaluating

Evaluating consists of judging the messages' and the speaker's credibility (Unit 19), truthfulness, or usefulness in some way. At this stage your own biases and prejudices become especially influential. These will influence what you single out for evaluation and what you will just let pass. They will influence what you judge good and what you judge bad. In some situations, the evaluation is more

FOCUS **O**N

Do You Really Remember What You Hear?

To illustrate the reconstructive nature of memory, try to memorize the following list of 12 words (Glucksberg & Danks 1975). Don't worry about the order of the words; only the number remembered counts. Take about 20 seconds to memorize as many words as possible. Don't read any further until you have tried to memorize the list of words.

Word List

bed	dream	comfort
rest	wake	sound
awake	night	slumber
tired	eat	snore

Now close the book and write down as many of the words from this list as you can remember.

How did you do? If you are like my students, you not only remembered a good number of the words on the list but also "remembered" at least one word that was not on the list: *sleep*. You did not simply reproduce the list; you reconstructed it. In this case you gave the list a meaning and part of that meaning included the word *sleep*. This happens with all types of messages; the messages are reconstructed into a meaningful whole, and in the process a distorted version of what was said is often "remembered."

"If you can hear me, give me a sign."

Drawing by Cotham; © 1993 The New Yorker Magazine, Inc.

in the nature of critical analysis, a topic we explore in detail in Unit 5. When evaluating:

- resist evaluation until you fully understand the speaker's point of view
- distinguish facts from inferences (see Unit 5), opinions, and personal interpretations that you are making as well as those made by the speaker
- identify any biases, self-interests, or prejudices that may lead the speaker to slant unfairly what he or she is presenting
- identify any biases that may lead you to remember what supports your attitudes and beliefs and to forget what contradicts them

Responding

Responding occurs in two phases: (1) nonverbal (and occasionally verbal) responses you make while the speaker is talking and (2) responses you make after the speaker has stopped talking. Responses made while the speaker is talking should support the speaker and show that you are listening. These include what nonverbal researchers call backchanneling cues (Burgoon, Buller, & Woodall 1989), such as nodding your head, smiling, leaning forward, and similar signals that let the speaker know you are attending to the message.

Responses made after the speaker has stopped talking are generally more elaborate and might include questions of clarification ("I wasn't sure what you meant by reclassification"), expressions of agreement ("You're absolutely right on this, and I'll support your proposal when it comes up for a vote"), and expressions of disagreement ("I disagree that Japanese products are superior to those produced in the United States"). When responding:

It might be argued that responding is not a part of listening in the same way that receiving or understanding are. What do you think? Would you include responding in your model of listening?

- support the speaker throughout the talk by using a variety of backchanneling cues; using only one backchanneling cue—for example, nodding constantly—will make it appear that you are not listening but are on automatic pilot
- support the speaker in your final responses by saying something positive
- own your own responses; state your thoughts and feelings as your own; use I-messages (for example, say "I think the new proposal will entail greater expense than you outlined" rather than "Everyone will object to the plan for costing too much")

Throughout the listening process, try to be supportive of the speaker; make the speaker see that you are listening and that you are actively thinking about what he or she is saying. Try to avoid listening behavior that can distract and make the speaker feel uncomfortable (see Table 4.1).

Can you think of other types of distracting listeners?

LISTENING AND CULTURE

Listening is difficult in part because of the inevitable differences in the communication systems between speaker and listener. Because each person has had a unique set of experiences, each person's communication and meaning system is going to be different from each other person's. When speaker and listener come from different cultures, the differences and their effects are naturally much greater. Here are just a few areas where misunderstandings can occur.

TABLE 4.1	Distracting Listening	
Listener Type	**Listening Behavior**	**Speaker (Mis)Interpretations**
The static listener	gives no feedback, remains relatively motionless, reveals no expression.	Why isn't he reacting? Am I not producing sound?
The monotonous feedback giver	seems responsive but the responses never vary; regardless of what the speaker says, the response is the same.	Am I making sense? Why is she still smiling? I'm being dead serious.
The reader/writer	reads or writes, always looking at the newspaper, never at the speaker.	Am I that boring? Is last week's student paper more interesting than I am?
The eye avoider	looks all around the room but never at the speaker.	Why isn't he looking at me? Do I have spinach on my teeth?
The overly expressive listener	reacts to just about everything with extreme responses.	Why is she so expressive? I didn't say anything that provocative. She'll have a heart attack when I get to my conclusion.

Language and Speech

Even when speaker and listener speak the same language, they speak it with different meanings and different accents. No two speakers speak exactly the same language. Every speaker speaks an idiolect: a unique variation of the language (King & DiMichael 1992). Speakers of the same language will, at the very least, have different meanings for the same terms because they have had different experiences.

Speakers and listeners who have different native languages and who may have learned English as a second language will have even greater differences in meaning. Translations are never precise and never fully capture the meaning in the other language. If your meaning for *house* was learned in a culture in which everyone lived in his or her own house with lots of land around it, then communicating with someone whose meaning was learned in a neighborhood of high-rise tenements is going to be difficult. Although you will each hear the same word, the meanings you'll each develop will be drastically different. In adjusting your listening—especially when in an intercultural setting—understand that the speaker's meanings may be very different from yours even though you each know the same language.

Still another aspect of speech is accents. In many classrooms throughout the country, there will be a wide range of accents. Those whose native language is a tonal one, such as Chinese (where differences in pitch signal important differences in meaning), may speak English with variations in pitch that may seem unnatural to others. Those whose native language is Japanese may have trouble distinguishing *l* from *r*, since Japanese does not make this distinction.

The directness or indirectness with which a speaker presents his or her ideas varies greatly from one culture to another. Some cultures—Western Europe and the United States, for example—favor a direct style in communication; they advise us to "say what you mean and mean what you say." Many Asian cultures, on the other hand, favor an indirect style; they emphasize politeness and the maintenance of a positive public image rather than absolute truth. Listen carefully to persons with different styles of directness. Consider the possibility that the meanings the speaker wishes to communicate with, say, indirectness may be very different from the meanings you would communicate with indirectness.

The case of feedback provides a good example of the difference between direct and indirect styles. Members of some cultures give very direct and very honest feedback. Speakers from these cultures—the United States is a good example—expect the feedback to be an honest reflection of what their listeners are feeling. In other cultures—Japan and Korea are good examples—it's more important to be positive than to be truthful, and so members of such cultures may respond with positive feedback even though they don't feel it. Listen to feedback, as you would all messages, with a full recognition that different cultures view feedback very differently.

Nonverbal Behavioral Differences

Speakers from different cultures have different display rules, cultural rules that govern which nonverbal behaviors are appropriate and which are inappropriate in a public setting. As you listen to another person, you also "listen" to her or his nonverbal messages. If these are drastically different from what you

Feedback is elaborated on in the next unit. Consider now, however, how you feel about giving and receiving feedback on your public speaking efforts. What kinds of feedback do you want? What kinds of feedback do you specifically *not* want?

expect on the basis of the verbal message, they may be seen as a kind of noise or interference or as contradictory messages. Also, different cultures may give very different meanings to the same nonverbal gesture, a point well illustrated in the accompanying photo of four hand signals.

Ethnocentrism

One problem that hinders effective listening is the tendency to see others and their behaviors through your own cultural filters. *Ethnocentrism* is the tendency to evaluate the values, beliefs, and behaviors of your own culture as being more positive, logical, and natural than those of other cultures. The nonethnocentric, on the other hand, would see both himself or herself and others as different but equal, with neither being inferior or superior.

Ethnocentrism exists on a continuum. People are not either ethnocentric or not ethnocentric; rather, most are somewhere between these polar opposites. And, of course, your degree of ethnocentrism varies depending on the

How does ethnocentrism influence your listening behavior? Does it influence the television shows you watch? The movies you see? The music you listen to?

What do these nonverbal gestures mean to you? Do they all mean the same thing? Actually, they are all slightly different, and mean different things depending on their cultural context. (a) is American for "OK." (b) is from the Mediterranean, and means "zero." (c) is from Japan, and means "money." (d) is from Tunisia, and means "I will kill you."

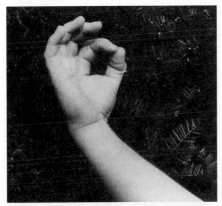

(a)

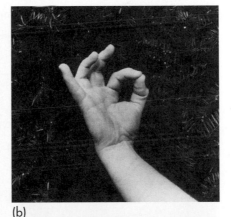

(b)

(c)

(d)

group on which you focus. For example, if you are Greek American you may have a low degree of ethnocentrism when dealing with Italian Americans (because of the similarities in the cultures of Greeks and Italians) but a high degree when dealing with Japanese Americans (because of the greater differences between the Greek and the Japanese cultures). Most important for our purposes is that your degree of ethnocentrism—and we are all ethnocentric, at least to some degree—will influence your listening effectiveness.

Table 4.2, drawing on the findings of a number of researchers (Lukens 1978; Gudykunst & Kim 1984; Gudykunst 1991), summarizes some of the interconnections between ethnocentrism and communication. In this table five degrees of ethnocentrism are identified; in reality, of course, there are as many degrees as there are people. The "communication distances" are general terms that highlight the attitude dominating that level of ethnocentrism. Under "Listening" are some of the major ways people might listen given their particular degree of ethnocentrism.

Recognizing the tendency toward ethnocentrism is the first step in combating any excesses. In addition, try following the suggestions for effective listening offered in this unit, especially when you are in an intercultural public speaking situation. Also, expose yourself to culturally different experiences. At the same time, resist the temptation to evaluate these through your own

Where would you place yourself on the ethnocentrism continuum?

TABLE 4.2	The Ethnocentrism Continuum

Degree of Ethnocentrism	Communication Distance	Listening
Low	Equality	Treats others as equals; finds it natural to listen fairly to culturally different speakers and openly to different cultural ways
	Sensitivity	Makes an effort to decrease the distance between self and culturally different others and to lessen any conscious ethnocentrism
	Indifference	Lacks concern for others; prefers to listen to culturally similar speakers and to not seriously consider other cultural customs or perspectives
	Avoidance	Actively avoids and limits listening to culturally different speakers or to culturally different perspectives
High	Disparagement	Engages in hostile behavior; belittles others; views different cultures and ways of behaving as inferior to one's own

cultural filters. For many, this will not be easy. But, in light of the tremendous advantages to be gained through increased intercultural experiences, the effort seems well worth it.

Racist, Sexist, and Heterosexist Listening

Just as racist, sexist, and heterosexist attitudes will influence your language (as illustrated in the popular press and in Unit 16 of this text), so too, can they influence your listening.

When we evaluate a speaker on the basis of the speaker's race, sex, or affectional orientation, we may be in danger of racist, sexist, or heterosexist listening. Understanding the speaker from the speaker's point of view and empathizing with the speaker are useful techniques for effective listening. However, when we listen through positive or negative filters or stereotypes based on sex, race, or affectional orientation, we are in danger of failing to listen to what the speaker is really saying. We come to listen less to the speaker and more to our own assumptions and preconceptions. For example, it is sexist listening when you discount or put a positive slant on what a male or female speaker says because of the speaker's gender when gender is logically irrelevant. This is also true when we listen in this way based on a person's race or affectional orientation.

Is racism, sexism, or heterosexism a part of your listening behavior? If so, how does it influence your listening?

As a general rule, do you think that people are more easily informed by persons who are culturally similar to them or by those who are culturally different from them? Are they more easily persuaded by those who are culturally similar? What implications do your responses have for the process of education?

✖ ▬ LISTENING AND GENDER

According to Deborah Tannen (1990) in her best-selling *You Just Don't Understand: Women and Men in Conversation,* women seek to build rapport and establish a closer relationship and so use listening to achieve these ends. Men, on the other hand, will play up their expertise, emphasize it, and use it in dominating the interaction. Women play down their expertise and are more interested in communicating supportiveness. Tannen argues that the goal of a man in conversation is to be accorded respect and so he seeks to show his knowledge and expertise. A woman, on the other hand, seeks to be liked and so she expresses agreement.

Men and women also show that they are listening in different ways. In conversation, a woman is more apt to give lots of listening cues, such as interjecting *yeah*, *uh-uh*, nodding in agreement, and smiling. A man is more likely to listen quietly, without giving lots of listening cues as feedback. Tannen argues, however, that men do listen less to women than women listen to men. The reason, says Tannen, is that listening places the person in an inferior position whereas speaking places the person in a superior one.

We can try to apply these gender differences to listening in public speaking. Men may seem to assume a more argumentative posture while listening, as if getting ready to argue. They may also appear to ask questions that are more argumentative or are designed to puncture holes in your position as a way to play up their expertise. Women are more likely to ask supportive questions and perhaps offer criticism that is more positive than men. Women also use more cues in listening in a public speaking context. They let the speaker see that they are listening. Men, on the other hand, use less listening cues in conversation and probably also in public speaking. Men and women act this

How useful is Tannen's distinction between men and women as listeners? Can you think of exceptions to this general principle?

way to both men and women; their customary ways of communicating do not seem to change depending on whether the listener is male or female.

There is no evidence to show that these differences represent any negative motives on the part of men to prove themselves superior or of women to ingratiate themselves. Rather, these differences in listening are largely the result of the way in which men and women have been socialized.

OBSTACLES TO EFFECTIVE LISTENING

The first step in improving listening abilities is to recognize and combat the various obstacles to effective listening (Nichols & Stevens 1957; Nichols 1961; Murphy 1987; Roach & Wyatt 1988).

Preoccupation with Other Issues

Probably the most serious and most damaging obstacle to effective listening is the tendency to become preoccupied with yourself. Sometimes the preoccupation with yourself centers on assuming the role of speaker. You begin to rehearse your responses, to think of what you will say to answer the speaker or perhaps a question you want to ask the public speaker. While focusing on yourself, you inevitably miss what the speaker is saying. Similarly, you may become preoccupied with external issues. You think about what you did last Saturday or your plans for the evening. Of course, the more you entertain thoughts of external matters, the less effectively you listen.

The obvious noise obstacle to effective listening in this photo is the physical noise from the operation of the machinery. What other noise obstacles might exist in this situation? What noise obstacles might arise in the room in which you will give your speeches?

Assimilation

Another obstacle to listening is assimilation: the tendency to reconstruct messages so they reflect your own attitudes, prejudices, needs, and values. It is the tendency to hear relatively neutral messages ("Management plans to institute drastic changes in scheduling") as supporting your own attitudes and beliefs ("Management is going to screw up our schedules again").

Friend-or-Foe Factor

You may also distort messages because of the friend-or-foe factor: the tendency to listen for positive qualities about friends and negative qualities about enemies. For example, if you dislike Fred, then it will take added effort to listen objectively to Fred's speeches or to criticism that might reflect positively on Fred.

Hearing What You Expect to Hear

Another obstacle is the failure to hear what the speaker is saying and instead hear what you expect. You know that your history instructor frequently intersperses lectures with long personal stories, and so when she says, "I can remember . . . ," you automatically hear a personal story and perhaps tune out.

Prejudging the Speech or Speaker

Whether in a lecture auditorium or in a small group, avoid the tendency to prejudge some speeches as uninteresting or irrelevant. All speeches are, at least potentially, interesting and useful. If you prejudge them and tune them out, you will never be proven wrong; at the same time, however, you close yourself off from potentially useful information. Most important, perhaps, is that you are not giving the other person a fair hearing. Avoid jumping to conclusions before you've heard the speaker; the conclusions you reach may in reality be quite different from the conclusions the speaker draws.

Rehearsing Your Responses

Often a speaker may say something with which you disagree. Then, during the remainder of the speech, you rehearse your response or question, you then imagine the speaker's reply to your response, and then your response to the speaker's response. The dialogue goes back and forth in your mind. Meanwhile, you miss whatever else the speaker said. You may even miss the very part that would answer your question. If appropriate, jot down the point or question and go back to listening.

Filtering Out Unpleasant Messages

Resist the temptation to filter out difficult or unpleasant messages: You don't want to hear that something you believe is untrue or that people you care for are unpleasant, and yet these are the very messages you need to listen to with great care. These are the messages that will lead you to examine and reexamine

What obstacles to effective listening do you think occur most often? How might these obstacles be related to listening in an interpersonal situation?

Can you supply specific advertising examples that illustrate any of the ten distortions discussed under Critical Listening? Which of these distortions do you see most often?

 What other distortions do you identify in the various persuasive messages you hear?

your implicit and unconscious assumptions. If you filter out this kind of information, you risk failing to correct misinformation. You risk losing new and important insights.

PRINCIPLES OF EFFECTIVE LISTENING

Effective listening is extremely important because you spend so much time listening. In fact, if you measured importance by the time you spend on an activity, listening would be your most important communication activity. Most of your communication time is spent in listening. You will improve your listening if you listen actively, for total meaning, with empathy, and with an open mind.

Listen Actively

The first step in listening improvement is to recognize that it is not a passive activity. You cannot listen without effort. Listening is a difficult process. In many ways it is more demanding than speaking. In speaking you control the situation; you can talk about what you like in the way you like. In listening, however, you have to follow the pace, the content, and the language of the speaker.

The best preparation for active listening is to act like an active listener. Recall, for example, how your body almost automatically reacts to important news. Almost immediately, you sit up straighter, cock your head toward the speaker, and remain relatively still and quiet. You do this almost reflexively because this is how you listen most effectively. This is not to say that you should be tense and uncomfortable, only that your body should reflect your active mind. In listening actively:

- Because your mind can process information faster than the average rate of speech, there is often a time lag. Use this time to summarize the speaker's thoughts, formulate questions, draw connections between what the speaker says and what you already know.
- Work at listening. Listening is hard work, so be prepared to participate actively. Avoid what James Floyd (1985) calls "the entertainment syndrome," the expectation to be amused and entertained by a speaker. Remove distractions or other interferences (newspapers, magazines, stereos) so that your listening task will have less competition.
- Assume there is value in what the speaker is saying. Resist assuming that what you have to say is more valuable than the speaker's remarks.
- Take notes if appropriate. In some instances, you will want to take notes while the speaker is speaking. Taking notes may be helpful if you want to ask a question about a specific item of information or want to include a specific statement in your critical evaluation (see Unit 5). Try not to distract the speaker. Have your pen and paper on your desk rather than shuffle through your book bag, which could disturb the speaker. Write only what you need to. Resist the temptation to turn the exercise into a writing one rather than a listening one.

TIPS

From Professional Speakers

Select a position in the room that provides for a better listening environment. Stay away from entrances or exits; do not select a place too far away from the speaker. Do not sit next to a group that may be talking during the speech. When people enter a room, they tend to sit at the back. Change that habit. Take a front row seat, and see how your listening skills improve.

Marjorie Brody & Shawn Kent, communication consultants and trainers. *Power Presentations: How to Connect with Your Audience and Sell Your Ideas* (New York: Wiley, 1993), p. 31.

Listen for Total Meaning

The meaning of a message is not only in the words used; it is also in the speaker's nonverbal behavior. Sweating hands and shaking knees communicate as surely as do words.

The meanings communicated in a speech will also depend on what the speaker does not say. For example, the speaker who, in a speech on contemporary social problems, omits references to the homeless or to drugs communicates meaning by these very omissions. Exactly what inferences listeners will draw from such omissions will depend on a variety of factors. Some possible inferences might be that the speaker is poorly prepared, the speaker's research was inadequate, the speaker forgot part of the speech, the speaker is trying to fool the audience, the speaker is trying to cover up certain issues and thinks we won't notice, or the speaker thinks we are uninformed, stupid, or both.

As a listener, therefore, be particularly sensitive to the meanings significant omissions may communicate. As a speaker, recognize that most inferences audiences draw from omissions are negative. Most such inferences will reflect negatively on your credibility and on the total impact of the speech. Be careful, therefore, to mention significant issues the audience expects to be discussed. In listening for total meaning:

- Focus on both verbal and nonverbal messages. Recognize both consistent and inconsistent "packages" of messages and take these cues as guides for drawing inferences about the meaning the speaker is trying to communicate. Ask questions when in doubt.
- See the forest, then the trees. Connect the specifics to the speaker's general theme rather than merely remembering isolated facts and figures.
- Balance your attention between the surface and the underlying meanings. Do not disregard the literal (surface) meaning of the speech in your attempt to uncover the more hidden (deeper) meanings.

Listen with Empathy

Try to feel what the speaker feels—empathize with the speaker. To empathize with others is to feel what they feel, to see the world they see, to walk in their shoes. Only when you achieve this will you be able to understand fully another's meaning (Eisenberg & Strayer 1987). Listen to feelings as well as to thoughts and ideas; listen to what the speaker is feeling and thinking.

- See the speaker's point of view. Before you can understand what the speaker is saying, you have to see the message from the speaker's point of view. Try putting yourself in the role of the speaker and feel the topic from the speaker's perspective.
- Understand the speaker's thoughts and feelings. Do not consider your listening task complete until you have understood what the speaker is feeling as well as thinking.
- Avoid "offensive listening." Offensive listening is the tendency to listen to bits and pieces of information that will enable you to attack the speaker or find fault with something the speaker has said.

TIPS
From Professional Speakers

Be a responsive listener. Be responsive in your demeanor, posture, and facial expression. Let your whole being show you are interested in other people and their ideas.

As you listen, look at the other person and show some signs of hearing and understanding. Nod your head occasionally—gently, not vigorously. Nod slightly with a yes for agreement or a no when it's something sad or unhappy. Show through your posture, whether seated or standing, that you are concentrating on listening totally. . . .

To understand this important principle of being responsive, it helps to ask, "How do we turn people off?" The answers come quickly: by not looking at them, not asking questions, not showing any positive response, by looking at our watch or out the window, shuffling papers, interrupting, and giving other negative types of feedback.

Robert L. Montgomery, professional speaker, trainer, author, and president of his own consulting firm. *Listening Made Easy* (New York: American Management Associations, 1981), pp. 75–76.

Listen with an Open Mind

Listening with an open mind is difficult. It is not easy to listen to arguments attacking your cherished beliefs. It is not easy to listen to statements condemning what you fervently believe. Listening often stops when such remarks are made. Yet it is in these situations that it is particularly important to continue listening openly and fairly. To listen with an open mind, try these suggestions:

What principle of effective listening do you think is the most important? Why? What other principles would you suggest to make the listening process more effective?

- Avoid prejudging. Delay both positive and negative evaluation until you have fully understood the intention and content of the message being communicated.
- Avoid filtering out difficult, unpleasant, or undesirable messages. Avoid distorting messages through oversimplification or leveling, the tendency to eliminate details and to simplify complex messages to make them easier to remember.
- Recognize your own biases. They may interfere with accurate listening and cause you to distort message reception through assimilation, the tendency to interpret what you hear (or think you hear) in terms of your own biases, prejudices, and expectations. Biases may also lead to "sharpening"—when an item of information takes on increased importance because it seems to confirm your stereotypes or prejudices.

CRITICAL LISTENING

Throughout this discussion of listening, we have emphasized listening for understanding. There is also, however, critical listening. Critical listening depends on the skills already noted but also demands focused attention to the truth and accuracy of the information and to the honesty and motivation of the speaker. Thus, in addition to keeping an open mind and delaying judgments, for example, it is necessary to focus on other issues as well: Is what the speaker says the truth as far as you understand it? For example, is this car really that great? Are there any disadvantages to this particular car? Has the speaker presented the information in enough detail? Have crucial parts been left out? For example, has the speaker identified all the costs?

In addition, pay special attention to the following distortions speakers may introduce. The first seven distortions were first identified in *The Fine Art of Propaganda*, prepared for the Institute for Propaganda Analysis (Lee & Lee 1972, 1995). The last three are taken from a more contemporary study of propaganda (Pratkanis & Aronson 1991). The propagandist (one who distorts the truth, an unethical persuader) uses these techniques to gain our compliance without logic or evidence. These devices are as important today as they were in the 1930s, when some of them were first identified. They appear in public messages of all sorts, most notably in speeches and in the appeals of advertisers. They also appear in our own thinking as we try to evaluate the messages we hear and as we try to make important decisions. Learn to identify these devices so that you will not be fooled by them.

Name-Calling

In name-calling, the speaker gives an idea, a group of people, or a political philosophy a bad name ("atheist," "neo-Nazi"). In this way, the persuader tries to make you condemn the idea without analyzing the argument and evidence.

The purpose here is to give listeners a negative impression of the person or the person's proposal and to turn their attention away from analyzing the issues to responding only to the negative label.

Glittering Generality

A glittering generality is the opposite of name-calling. Here the speaker tries to make you accept some idea by associating it with things you value highly ("democracy," "free speech," "academic freedom"). By using "virtue words," the speaker tries to get you to ignore the evidence and to simply approve of the idea.

What "bad names" do you hear persuaders use? What "good names" do you hear?

Transfer

In using the device of transfer, the speaker associates her or his idea with something you respect (to gain your approval) or with something you detest (to gain your rejection). For example, a proposal for condom distribution in schools may be characterized as a means for "saving our children from AIDS" (to encourage acceptance) or as a means for "promoting sexual promiscuity" (to encourage disapproval). Sports car manufacturers try to get you to buy their cars by associating them with high status and sex appeal, and exercise clubs and diet plans, by associating themselves with health, self-confidence, and interpersonal appeal.

Testimonial

The testimonial device involves using the image associated with some person to gain your approval (if you respect the person) or your rejection (if you do not respect the person). This is the technique of advertisers who use people dressed up to look like doctors or plumbers or chefs to sell their products. And, it seems, the technique works.

Sometimes this technique takes the form of using only vague and general "authorities." For example, we frequently hear such appeals as "experts agree," "scientists say," "good cooks know," and "dentists advise." Exactly who these experts are or how many of them have agreed is seldom made clear. The advertisers hope, however, that we will simply remember that "experts agree" (with the commercial).

Sometimes the testimonials are from people who have no recognizable authority in the field in which they are speaking. Does Bill Cosby have a specialized knowledge of Jell-O or of photography? Does Angela Lansbury have specialized knowledge of painkillers? Does Susan Lucci have specialized knowledge of cars and trucks?

Plain Folks

Using the "plain folks" device, the speaker identifies himself or herself and the proposition with the audience. The speaker and the proposition are good—so the "reasoning" goes—because they are one of the people. They are just "plain folks" like the rest of you. Consider, for example, the following excerpt for a hypothetical proposal. Notice that it provides absolutely no evidence. Instead, it seeks to associate the proposal with "plain folks."

> *This bill will benefit the small farmers and small businesses—the backbone of this country. Let's give average people a break, people who struggle to make a living for their families, people like you and like me. Let's respond to their needs and give people like us a break.*

Card-Stacking

The speaker using card-stacking selects only the evidence and arguments that support the case. The speaker might even falsify evidence and distort the facts to better fit the case. Despite these lies, the speaker presents the supporting materials as "fair" and "impartial." For example, when advertisers say, "Ninety percent of the dentists surveyed endorse Whiter-White Toothpaste as an effective cleansing agent," what are they really saying? Are they saying that Whiter-White is better than any other toothpaste on the market? Or are they saying that 90 percent of the dentists endorse Whiter-White compared to not brushing your teeth at all?

Bandwagon

Using the bandwagon method, the speaker persuades the audience to accept or reject an idea or proposal because "everybody is doing it." The persuader might also try to show that the "right" people are doing it. The propagandist persuades by convincing you to jump on this large and popular bandwagon. This technique is often used in political elections where results of polls are used to get undecided voters to jump on the bandwagon with the candidate leading in the polls. After all, the implication goes, we don't want to vote for a loser.

Granfallon

Granfallon is a term taken from a novel by Kurt Vonnegut and refers to the tendency of people to see themselves as constituting a cohesive and like-minded group because they are given a label. The name might be religious: "As Christians [Jews, Muslims, Hindus], we know that . . ." Or it might be cultural: "As Native Americans [African Americans, Hispanics, Arabs], we should . . ." Or the label might be occupational: "As teachers [blue-collar workers, artists, journalists, athletes] we should agree that . . ."

The problem with this line of reasoning is that it tends to divide the world into "we" and "they" and therefore inevitably simplifies the situation and ignores the vast individual differences in any group covered by such broad labels.

Agenda-Setting

In agenda-setting, a speaker might argue that XYZ is the issue and that all others are unimportant and insignificant. This appeal is heard frequently: "Balancing the budget is the key to the city's survival" or "There is only one issue confronting elementary education in our largest cities, and that is violence." In almost all situations, however, there are many issues and many sides to each issue. Often the person proclaiming "X is the issue" really means "I'll be able to persuade you if you focus solely on X and ignore the other issues."

Attack

Attack involves accusing another person (usually an opponent) of some serious wrongdoing so that the issue under discussion never gets examined. "Arguments" such as "How can we support a candidate who has been unfaithful [smoked pot, avoided the military]?" are heard often in political discussions.

This technique effectively describes the negative campaign ads that have become so popular. Does this strategy work with you?

A person's personal reputation and past behavior are often relevant. When, however, personal attack is used to draw attention away from other issues, then it becomes fallacious and should be identified as such by the critical listener.

"Once we know these devices well enough to spot examples of their use," say Lee and Lee (1972), "we have taken a great and long step towards freeing our minds from control by propagandists. It is not the only step necessary, but it is certainly the most important."

UNIT IN BRIEF

The five-step listening process	■ **Receiving** or hearing what is said (verbally and nonverbally) as well as what is omitted ■ **Understanding** the thoughts and emotions the speaker conveys ■ **Remembering** the messages and retaining them for some time ■ **Evaluating** or judging the messages in some way ■ **Responding** or reacting to the messages
Suggestions for avoiding obstacles to listening	■ Don't become preoccupied with yourself or external issues ■ Beware of assimilation ■ Watch for the friend-or-foe factor ■ Be aware of the tendency to hear what you expect to hear and not to hear what you do not expect to hear ■ Avoid prejudging the speech or speaker ■ Avoid rehearsing your own responses ■ Avoid filtering out unpleasant messages

Four principles of effective listening	■ **Listen actively:** use listening time, work hard, assume value, and, if appropriate, take notes ■ **Listen for total meaning:** focus on both verbal and nonverbal messages, connect specifics to the general thesis, attend to both surface and deep meanings ■ **Listen with empathy:** see the speaker's point of view, understand the speaker's feelings and thoughts, avoid offensive listening ■ **Listen with an open mind:** avoid prejudging and filtering out difficult messages, recognize your own biases
Ten fallacies to detect as a listener and to avoid as a speaker	■ **Name-calling:** giving an idea a negative name to encourage condemnation ■ **Glittering generality:** associating a proposal with things valued highly ■ **Transfer:** associating ideas with what we respect (to gain approval) or with what we detest (to gain rejection) ■ **Testimonial:** using an authority to gain audience approval ■ **Plain folks:** identifying oneself with the audience ■ **Card-stacking:** selecting only what supports one's case and ignoring what is not supportive ■ **Bandwagon:** Claiming that one's proposal is good because everyone believes it is ■ **Granfallon:** giving a group a name and implying that everyone is now similar ■ **Agenda-setting:** focusing attention on one issue to the exclusion of other perspectives ■ **Attack:** attacking the speaker personally rather than addressing the issues

PRACTICALLY SPEAKING

Short Speech Technique

Prepare and deliver a two-minute speech in which you:

1. explain how a current television or print advertisement relies on or makes use of one of the distortions discussed under Critical Listening
2. explain the role of listening in effective interpersonal relationships
3. describe a communication breakdown (problem) occasioned by ineffective listening
4. describe what a speaker can do to make listening easier

4.1   Your Own Listening Barriers

Most people put on blinders when they come upon particular topics or particular spokespersons. Sometimes these blinders prevent information from getting through fairly and objectively. For example, you may avoid listening to certain people or reading certain newspapers because they frequently contradict your beliefs. Sometimes these blinders color the information you take in, influencing you to form a positive view of some information (because it may support one of your deeply held beliefs) and a negative view of other information (because it may contradict such beliefs).

Read over the following situations and identify any barriers that may get in the way of your listening to these people and these messages fairly and objectively. Some situations may seem likely and others extremely unlikely. For this exercise, however, assume that all speakers are speaking on the topic indicated and that you are in the audience. Ask yourself the following questions about each of the 20 situations presented below.

Questions

- What are your initial expectations?
- How credible do you find the speaker—even before he or she begins to speak?
- Will you begin listening with a positive, a negative, or a neutral attitude? How will these attitudes influence your listening?
- What will you be saying to yourself as you begin listening to the speaker? Will this influence what you receive, understand, and remember of the speech? Will this influence how you evaluate and respond to the speech?
- What do you think your final assessment of the speech will be? On a ten-point scale (10 = extremely sure; 1 = extremely unsure), how sure are you that this will be your assessment?
- Can you identify at least one barrier that you (or someone else) might set up for each of these speech situations?

Situations

1. Elizabeth Taylor speaking on the need to contribute to AIDS research
2. Gloria Steinem criticizing (or praising) the contemporary women's movement
3. Former Vice-President Dan Quayle (or President Bill Clinton) speaking on the role of the military in defending American democracy
4. A noted and successful business leader addressing the futility of a college education in today's economy
5. Senator Edward Kennedy speaking on the importance of moderation
6. Spike Lee speaking on race relations
7. Ross Perot or Bill Gates discussing financial mistakes the government must avoid
8. A Mexican business leader urging American businesses to consider relocating to Mexico
9. Oprah Winfrey or Geraldo Rivera speaking on the mistakes of modern psychology
10. A representative from General Motors, Toyota, or Mercedes-Benz urging greater restrictions on foreign imports

11. A Catholic priest speaking on why you should remain a virgin until marriage
12. A homeless person petitioning to be allowed to sleep in the local public library
13. A representative of the leading tobacco companies voicing opposition to (or support for) the legalization of marijuana
14. An Iranian couple talking about the need to return to fundamentalist values
15. A person with AIDS speaking in favor of lower drug prices
16. A successful Japanese business leader talking about the mistakes of contemporary American businesses
17. A lesbian mother speaking against lesbians being granted custody of their children
18. A person without sight or hearing speaking in favor of including persons with disabilities in the definition of multiculturalism used on campus
19. A man (or woman) speaking on the failings of the opposite sex and how to tolerate them without going crazy
20. An 85-year-old multimillionaire speaking on why social security must be given to everyone regardless of income or need

UNIT 5

Speech Criticism in the Classroom

Unit Objectives

After completing this unit, you should be able to:

1. Define *criticism* and explain its values

2. Explain the difficulties involved in public speaking criticism

3. Explain the influence of culture on criticism

4. Explain effectiveness, universality, and conformity to the principles of the art as standards of criticism

5. Identify the principles of giving and receiving criticism

6. Identify the guidelines for speech criticism

*I*n learning the art of public speaking, much insight will come from the criticism of others as well as from your criticism of others. This unit considers some of the values and difficulties of criticism, the influence of culture on criticism, the standards for evaluating a speech, and some of the ways to make criticism easier and more effective.

THE VALUES OF CRITICISM

Critics and criticism are essential parts of any art. The term *criticism* comes from the Latin *criticus*, which means "able to discern," "to judge." There is nothing inherently negative about criticism; it is a process of judging and evaluating a work of art, a movie, or a public speech.

The major purpose of criticism in the classroom is to improve your public speaking skills. Through constructive criticism, you will learn the principles of public speaking more effectively. You will be shown what you do well and what you could improve.

As a listener-critic, you will also learn the principles of public speaking through assessing the speeches of others. Just as you learn when you teach, so too do you learn when you criticize.

Criticism also helps identify standards for evaluating the wide variety of speeches you'll hear throughout your life. This critical frame of mind and the guidelines for critical evaluation will prove useful in assessing all communications: the salesperson's pitch to buy a new car, the advertiser's plea to buy Tylenol rather than Excedrin, and the network's editorial.

When you give criticism—as you do in a public speaking class—you are telling the speaker that you have listened carefully and that you care enough about the speech and the speaker to offer suggestions for improvement.

What do you see as the major value of criticism in your particular public speaking class?

THE DIFFICULTIES OF CRITICISM

Criticism is difficult for the critic as well as for the person criticized (Weisinger 1990; Heldmann 1988). As a critic, you may feel embarrassed or uncomfortable to offer criticism. After all, you might think, "Who am I to criticize another person's speech? My own speech won't be any better." Or you may be reluctant to offend anyone and fear that your criticism will make the speaker feel uncomfortable. Or you may view criticism as a confrontation that will do more harm than good.

Still another obstacle is that in offering criticism, you put yourself on the line; you state a position that others may disagree with and that you may be called upon to defend. Considering these difficulties, you may conclude that the process is not worth the effort and decide to leave the criticism to others.

But reconsider. By offering criticism, you are helping the speaker; you are giving the speaker another perspective for viewing her or his speech, and this perspective will prove valuable for future speeches. When you offer criticism,

Assume you just heard a truly terrible speech and are called upon to comment on it. What difficulties would you experience in expressing your honest feelings? What would be your first two sentences?

you do not claim to be a better speaker. Again, you are simply offering another perspective. It is true that by stating your criticism, you put yourself in a position with which others may disagree. But that is what will make this class and the learning of the principles exciting and challenging.

Criticism is also difficult to receive. After you have worked on a speech for a week or two and dealt with the normal anxiety that comes with giving a speech, the last thing you want is to stand in front of the class and hear others say what you did wrong. Public speaking is ego-involving, and to personalize criticism is normal. If you learn how to give and how to receive criticism, however, it will become an effective teaching and learning tool. And it will help you sharpen your skills and improve every aspect of the public speaking process. It will also serve as an important support mechanism for the developing public speaker, as a way of patting the speaker on the back for all the positive effort.

Do you think you'll experience any difficulties in giving and receiving criticism? If so, might it be wise to discuss these at this point in the semester?

CULTURAL DIFFERENCES

When it comes to criticism, there are vast cultural differences in what is considered proper. In some cultures, public criticism—even if it is designed to help teach important skills—is considered inappropriate. Some cultures place a heavy emphasis on saving face, on allowing the other person to always remain in a positive light. The alternative is loss of face. In some ways it is similar to embarrassment in the United States. Loss of face (in Asian cultures, for example) is, however, much more intense and long-lasting than embarrassment (James 1995). In the United States, embarrassment can often be humorous (especially if you're not the one being embarrassed); loss of face is never humorous to anyone.

In cultures where saving face is important, members may prefer not to say anything negative in public and may even be reluctant to say anything positive, for fear that the omissions may be construed as negatives. The Japanese, for instance, are reluctant to say *no* in a business meeting, for fear of offending the

What cultural perspective on criticism do you bring to this class? How will this affect your behavior in this class?

other person. But their *yes,* properly interpreted in light of the context and the general discussion, may mean *no.* In cultures in which saving face is especially important, such communication rules as the following would prevail:

- Don't express negative evaluation in public; instead, compliment the person.
- Don't prove someone wrong, especially in public; express agreement even if you know the person is wrong.
- Don't correct someone's errors; don't even acknowledge them.
- Don't ask difficult questions, lest the person not know the answer and lose face or be embarrassed; generally, avoid asking questions.

In some cultures, being kind to the person is more important than telling the truth, and so members may say things that are complimentary but untrue in a logical sense.

Those who come from cultures that are highly individual and competitive (the United States, Germany, and Sweden are examples) may find public criticism a normal part of the learning process. Those who come from cultures that are more collective and emphasize the group rather than the individual (Japan, Mexico, and Korea are examples) are likely to find giving and receiving public criticism uncomfortable. Thus, people from individualistic cultures may readily criticize others and are likely to expect the same "courtesy" from other listeners. "After all," one of these persons might reason, "if I'm going to criticize your skills to help you improve, I expect you to help me in the same way."

Persons from collectivist cultures, on the other hand, may feel it is more important to be polite and courteous than to help someone learn a skill. Cultural rules to maintain peaceful relations among the Japanese (Midooka 1990) and politeness among many Asian cultures (Fraser 1990) may conflict with the classroom cultural norm to express honest criticism.

The difficulties are compounded when you interpret unexpected behavior through your own cultural filters. For example, if a speaker who expects comments and criticism gets none, he or she may interpret the silence to mean that the audience didn't care or wasn't listening. But they may have been listening very intently. They may simply be operating with a different cultural rule, a rule that says it is impolite to criticize or evaluate another person's work, especially in public.

These cultural differences may cause difficulty if they are not discussed openly. Some people may become comfortable with public criticism once it is explained that the cultural norms of most public speaking classrooms include public criticism (cf. Verderber 1991), just as norms may incorporate informative and persuasive speaking assignments or written outlines. Other people may feel more comfortable offering written criticism as a substitute for oral and public criticism. Or perhaps private consultations can be arranged.

STANDARDS OF CRITICISM

What standards do you use when you criticize a speech? How do you measure the excellence of a speech? On what basis do you say that one speech is weak, another is good, and still another is great? Three major standards quickly suggest themselves: effectiveness, universality, and conformity to the principles of the art.

Effectiveness

The effectiveness standard judges the speech in terms of whether or not it achieves its purpose. If the purpose is to sell soap, then the speech is effective if it sells soap and is ineffective if it fails to sell soap. Increased sophistication in measuring communication effects makes this standard tempting to apply.

There are, however, problems with this approach. In many instances—in the classroom, for example—the effects of a speech cannot always be measured. Sometimes the effect of a speech is long-term and you may not be present to see it take hold. Also, some effects are simply not measurable; you cannot always measure changes in attitude and belief, for instance.

Sometimes audiences may be so opposed to a speaker's position that even the greatest speech will have no observable effect. It may take an entire campaign to get such an audience to change their position even slightly. At other times audiences may agree with the speaker and even the weakest speech will secure their compliance. In situations like these, the effectiveness standard will lead to inaccurate and inappropriate judgments.

Lincoln's "Gettysburg Address" was negatively critiqued when it was delivered in 1863. Today it is regarded as one of the greatest speeches of all time. What problems do situations like this present for evaluating speeches with the effectiveness standard?

Universality

The universality standard (Murphy 1957) asks to what extent the speech addresses values and issues that have significance for all people in all times. This standard is often the one used in evaluating literature. By this standard, Martin Luther King, Jr.'s "I Have a Dream" (see Appendix for the complete text) would be judged positively because it argues for beliefs, values, and actions that most of the civilized world view positively.

A similar standard is the **historical justification** standard. This standard asks to what extent the speech's thesis and purpose were justified by subsequent historical events. By this standard, William Jennings Bryan's famous "Cross of Gold" speech (delivered in 1896)—although it won Bryan the Democratic nomination for president—would be judged negatively because it argued for a rejected monetary standard and against a monetary standard (gold) that the entire world had accepted.

Another similar standard is **ethical merit**. This standard asks to what extent the speech argues for what is true, moral, humane, or good. By this standard, the speeches of Adolf Hitler would be judged negatively because they supported ideas most people find repugnant. Other situations would not be so easy to judge with the ethical merit standard. For example, consider how different cultures would respond to such seemingly simple theses as the following:

By this standard of universality, how would you evaluate the typical religious sermon? The typical advertisement?

- Try eating beef.
- Try eating pork.
- Try eating dog meat.
- Get divorced when things don't work out.
- Never get divorced.
- Support gay or lesbian marriage proposals.
- Defeat gay or lesbian marriage proposals.

Obviously, different cultures will respond with very different attitudes; some will judge some speeches ethical and others unethical. Members of another culture may do exactly the opposite.

Conformity to the Principles of the Art

Do you agree with the conformity-to-the-principles-of-the-art standard for evaluating a public speech? Can you identify disadvantages with this standard?

A more useful standard (and one I use in my own public speaking classes) is to evaluate the speech on the basis of its conformity to the principles of the art. With this standard, a speech is positively evaluated when it follows the principles of public speaking established by the critics, theorists, and practitioners of public speaking (and as described in this text) and negatively evaluated as it deviates from these principles.

This standard is, of course, not totally separate from the effectiveness standard, since the principles of public speaking are largely principles of effectiveness. When you follow the principles of the art, your speech will in all likelihood be effective.

The great advantage of this standard (especially in a learning situation such as this) is that it will help you master the principles of public speaking. When your speech is measured by its adherence to these principles, you will be learning the principles by applying them to your unique situation.

What standards other than effectiveness, universality, and conformity might you apply to evaluating a public speech? What are the advantages and disadvantages of those additional standards?

The principles of public speaking are presented throughout this book, and it is by these principles, supplemented by whatever principles your instructor adds, that your public speech efforts will be evaluated. In your early speeches, follow the principles as closely as you can, even if their application seems mechanical and unimaginative. After you have mastered their application, then begin to play with the principles, altering them to suit your own personality, the uniqueness of the situation, and your specific goals.

EXPRESSING CRITICISM

Before reading the specific suggestions for expressing criticism, take the test on the next page, which asks you to identify what's wrong with selected critical comments.

Here are a few suggestions for making critical evaluations a more effective part of the total learning process and for avoiding some of the potentially negative aspects of criticism.

Say Something Positive

Egos are fragile and public speaking is extremely personal. Speakers are all like Noel Coward when he said, "I love criticism just as long as it's unqualified praise." Recall that part of your function as a critic is to strengthen the already positive aspects of someone's public speaking performance. Positive criticism is particularly important in itself, but it is almost essential as a preface to negative comments. There are always positive characteristics, and it is more productive to concentrate on these first. Thus, instead of saying (as in the self-

What's Wrong with These Comments?

Examine each of the following critical comments. For the purposes of this exercise, assume that each comment represents the critic's complete criticism. What's wrong with each?

1. I loved the speech. It was great. Really great.
2. The introduction didn't gain my attention.
3. You weren't interested in your own topic. How do you expect us to be interested?
4. Nobody was able to understand you.
5. The speech was weak.
6. The speech didn't do anything for me.
7. Your position was unfair to those of us on athletic scholarships; we earned those scholarships.
8. I found four things wrong with your speech. First, . . .
9. You needed better research.
10. I liked the speech; we need more police on campus.

The following discussion will identify how to express your criticism effectively and will illustrate why each of these ten comments gives ineffective feedback.

How do you feel about serving as a critic for your classmates? How do you feel about others criticizing your speeches?

test) "The speech didn't do anything for me," tell the speaker what you liked first, then bring up some weakness and suggest how it might be corrected.

When you are criticizing a person's second or third speech, it is especially helpful if you can point out specific improvements ("You really held my attention in this speech," "I felt you were much more in control of the public speaking today than in your first speech").

Remember too the irreversibility of communication. Once you say something, you cannot take it back. Remember this when offering criticism, especially criticism that may be too negative. If in doubt, err on the side of gentleness, a lesson the parents in the cartoon on the next page seem not to have learned.

How is criticism in a public speaking class similar to or different from interpersonal criticism? For example, criticism of your friendship behavior? Your behavior as a lover? Your parenting behavior?

Be Specific

Criticism is most effective when it is specific. Statements such as "I thought your delivery was bad," "I thought your examples were good," or, as in the self-test, "I loved the speech. . . . Really great" and "The speech was weak" are poorly expressed criticisms. These statements do not specify what the speaker might do to improve delivery or to capitalize on the examples used. In commenting on delivery, refer to such specifics as eye contact, vocal volume, or whatever else is of consequence. In commenting on the examples, tell the speaker why they were good. Were they realistic? Were they especially interesting? Were they presented dramatically?

Even though we are using the conformity-to-the-art standard, cultural differences in how to evaluate a speech or speaker will not be erased. Each of us will approach the speaker and speech in part through our own cultural filters. When you can identify particular cultural influences, discuss these. These different perspectives will add new dimensions to public speaking criticism.

The Subject and Purpose   The speech subject should be worthwhile, relevant, and interesting to the audience. The speech purpose should be clear and sufficiently narrow so that it can be achieved in the allotted time. Here are some questions to guide your criticism:

1. Is the subject a worthwhile one?
2. Is the subject relevant and interesting to the audience and to the speaker?
3. Is the information presented beneficial to the audience in some way?
4. What is the general purpose of the speech (to inform, to persuade, to secure goodwill, and so on)? Is this clear to the audience?
5. Is the specific topic narrow enough to be covered in some depth in the time allotted?

The Audience, Occasion, and Context   A public speech is designed for a specific audience and occasion and takes into account the characteristics of the audience.

6. Has the speaker taken into consideration the age; sex; cultural factors; occupation, income, and status; and religion and religiousness of the audience? How are these factors dealt with in the speech?
7. Is the speech topic appropriate to the specific occasion and the general context?

Research   A public speech needs to be based on accurate and reliable information. The topic needs to be thoroughly researched, and the speaker needs to demonstrate a command of the subject matter.

8. Is the speech adequately researched? Do the sources appear reliable and up-to-date?
9. Does the speaker have a thorough understanding of the subject?
10. Is the speaker's competence communicated in some way to the audience?

The Thesis and Major Propositions   The public speech should have one clear thesis to which the major propositions in the speech are clearly related.

11. Is the thesis of the speech clear and limited to one central idea?
12. Are the main propositions of the speech clearly related to the thesis? Does the speech contain an appropriate number of major propositions (not too many, not too few)?

Supporting Materials   The speech's propositions need to be supported by a variety of appropriate supporting materials that explain or prove their validity.

13. Is each major proposition adequately supported? Are the supporting materials varied and appropriate to the speech and the propositions?

14. Do the supporting materials amplify what they purport to amplify? Do they prove what they purport to prove?

Organization   The speech materials need to be organized into a meaningful whole to facilitate audience understanding.

15. Is the body of the speech organized in a pattern that is appropriate to the speech topic? To the audience?
16. Is the pattern of organization clear to the audience? Does it help the audience follow the speech?

Style and Language   The language and style of the speech should help the audience understand the speaker's message. These elements should be consistent in tone with the speech topic and purpose.

17. Does the language help the audience to understand clearly and immediately what the speaker is saying? For example, are simple rather than complex, concrete rather than abstract, words used? Is personal and informal language used? Are simple and active sentences used?
18. Is the language offensive to any person or group of persons?

The Conclusion, Introduction, and Transitions   The conclusion should summarize the major points raised in the speech and provide clear and crisp closure. The introduction should gain attention and orient the audience. Transitions should connect the various parts of the speech so that they flow into one another and should provide guideposts for the audience to help them follow the speaker's train of thought.

19. Does the conclusion effectively summarize the main points identified in the speech and effectively wrap up the speech, providing recognizable closure?
20. Does the introduction gain the attention of the audience and provide a clear orientation to the subject matter of the speech?
21. Are there adequate transitions? Do the transitions help the audience to better understand the development of the speech?

Delivery   Effective delivery should help maintain audience attention and help the speaker to emphasize the ideas in the speech.

22. Does the speaker maintain eye contact with the audience?
23. Are there any distractions (of mannerism, dress, or vocal characteristics) that will divert attention from the speech?
24. Can the speaker be easily heard? Are the volume and rate of speech appropriate?

THE SPEECH CRITIQUE

It is often helpful to have a form for recording your evaluation of a particular speech. The accompanying critique form is organized around the steps identified for preparing a speech and highlights just some of the important characteristics to look for. As you progress through this course, you will focus on a larger number of characteristics and on their greater refinement.

Critically evaluate the Public Speaking Critique Form presented. How would you revise it so that it becomes a more useful tool in your learning the art of public speaking?

Public Speaking Critique Form

Evaluation key: 1 = excellent; 2 = good; 3 = fair; 4 = needs improvement;
5 = needs lots of improvement. Circle or underscore items the speaker needs to "Work on"; write in additional items requiring attention.

Speaker _____ Date _____

Speech _____

_____ **Subject and Purpose**
Work on: selecting more worthwhile subject; making subject relevant and interesting to audience; clarifying purpose; narrowing purpose

_____ **Audience, Occasion, Context**
Work on: relating topic and supporting materials to specific audience, occasion, and context

_____ **Research**
Work on: doing more extensive research; using more reliable sources; stressing your command of the subject

_____ **Thesis and Major Propositions**
Work on: clarifying thesis; limiting thesis to one central idea; relating propositions to thesis

_____ **Supporting Materials**
Work on: using more support; using more varied and appropriate support; relating support more directly to the propositions

_____ **Organization**
Work on: using a clear thought pattern; making pattern clear to audience

_____ **Style and Language**
Work on: clarity, vividness, appropriateness, personal style, forcefulness/power

_____ **Conclusion, Introduction, Transitions**
Work on: conclusion's summary, closure; introduction's attention, orientation; using more transitions

_____ **Delivery**
Work on: eye contact, eliminating distracting mannerisms, gestures, volume, rate

_____ **General evaluation**

_____

_____

_____

_____

_____

UNIT IN BRIEF

The nature of criticism	■ Helps to identify strengths and weaknesses and thereby helps you improve as a public speaker ■ Helps to identify standards for evaluating all sorts of public speeches ■ Shows that the audience is listening and is concerned about the speaker's progress ■ Cultures differ in their views of criticism and in the rules they consider appropriate
Standards of criticism	■ **Effectiveness:** How effectively did the speaker accomplish the purpose? ■ **Universality:** Does the speech have application to all people in all times? 　Historical justification: Is the speech's thesis justified by history? 　Ethical merit: Does the speech defend what is moral or good? ■ **Conformity to the principles of the art:** How effectively did the speaker apply the principles of public speaking?
Suggestions for offering criticism	■ Say something positive ■ Be specific ■ Be objective ■ Limit criticism ■ Be constructive ■ Focus on behavior ■ Own your own criticism
Suggestions for receiving criticism	■ Accept the critic's viewpoint and support the critic's efforts ■ Listen openly ■ Respond without defensiveness ■ Separate speech from self-criticism ■ Seek clarification as appropriate

PRACTICALLY SPEAKING

Short Speech Technique

Prepare and deliver a two-minute speech in which you:

1. explain what you think would be the ideal critical evaluation for a speaker to receive from a critic
2. explain why criticism is so difficult to give or to receive (select one)

3. explain what you think is the most appropriate standard to use for criticizing the classroom speech, the religious sermon, the college lecture, the political campaign speech, or the advertiser's pitch (select one or compare two)
4. offer a critical evaluation of any one of the speeches contained in this text or of a speech from some other source

5.1   Analyzing and Criticizing a Poorly Constructed Informative Speech

The sample speeches presented elsewhere in this book are all good ones, designed to illustrate the effective application of the principles of public speaking. Here, however, is an especially poor speech, constructed to illustrate clearly and briefly some of the major faults with informative speeches. This exercise can be returned to several times throughout the course. As the course progresses, the responses will become more complete, more insightful, and more effective.

After you have reviewed the speech and the comments to the side, phrase your criticism in the form of a relatively formal critique of one to two minutes. Assume that this is a student's first speech and you are the public speaking instructor. What do you say?

The title seems adequate, though not terribly exciting. Try to give it a more appealing title.

This nervous reaction is understandable but is probably best not shared with the listeners. After all, you don't want them to be uncomfortable for you.

Going through your notes makes the audience feel that you didn't prepare adequately and may just be wasting their time.

This is the speaker's orientation. Is this sufficient? What else might the speaker have done here?

Here the speaker shows such uncertainty that we question his or her competence.

And we begin to wonder, "Why is the speaker talking about this to us?"

Reading the *Star* may be entertaining, but it doesn't constitute evidence. What does this reference do to the credibility you ascribe to the speaker?

Everything in the speech must have a definite purpose. Asides such as not liking to go to the dentist are probably best omitted.

Here was an opportunity for the speaker to connect the topic with important current political events but fails to say anything that is not obvious.

Three Jobs

Well, I mean, hello. Er . . . I'm new at public speaking, so I'm a little nervous. I've always been shy. So, don't watch my knees shake.

Um, let me see my notes here. [Mumbles to self while shuffling notes:] One, two, three, four, five—oh, they're all here. OK, here goes.

Three Jobs. That's my title, and I'm going to talk about three jobs.

The Health Care Field. This is the fastest-growing job in the country, one of the fastest, I guess I mean. I know that you're not interested in this topic and that you're all studying accounting. But there are a lot of new jobs in the health care field. The *Star* had an article on health care and said that health care will be needed more in the future than it is now. And now, you know, like, they need a lot of health care people. In the hospital where I work—on the West Side, uptown— they never have enough health aides and they always tell me to become a health aide, like, you know, to enter the health care field. To become a nurse. Or maybe a dental technician. But I hate going to the dentist. Maybe I will.

I don't know what's going to happen with the President's health plan, but whatever happens, it won't change the need for health aides. I mean, people will still get sick; so, it really doesn't matter what happens with health care.

The Robotics Field. This includes things like artificial intelligence. I don't really know what that is, but it's, like, growing real fast. They use this in making automobiles and planes and I think in computers. Japan is a leading country in this field. A lot of people in India go into this field, but I'm not sure why.

The Computer Graphics Field. This field has a lot to do with designing and making lots of different products, like CAD and CAM. This field also includes computer-aided imagery—CAI. And in movies, I think. Like *Star Wars* and *Terminator 2*. I saw *Terminator 2* four times. I didn't see *Star Wars*, but I'm gonna rent the video. I don't know if you have to know a lot about computers or if you can just, like, be a designer and someone else will tell the computer what to do.

I got my information from a book that Carol Kleiman wrote, *The 100 Best Jobs for the 1990s and Beyond*. It was summarized in last Sunday's *News*.

My Conclusion. These are three of the fastest-growing fields in the United States and in the world, I think—not in Third World countries, I don't think. China and India and Africa. More like Europe and Germany. And the United States—the United States is the big one.

I hope you enjoyed my speech. Thank you.

I wasn't as nervous as I thought I'd be. Are there any questions?

Introducing these topics like this is clear but not very interesting. How might each of the three main topics have been introduced more effectively? Notice, too, how vague the speaker is—"includes things like," "and I think in computers," and "I'm not sure why."

Here too there is little that is specific. CAD and CAM are not defined and CAI is explained as "computer-aided imagery," but unless we already knew what these were, we would still not know even after hearing the speaker.

Again, the speaker inserts personal notes (for example, seeing *Terminator 2* four times) that have no meaningful connection to the topic.

The speaker uses only one source and, to make matters worse, doesn't even go to the original source but relies on a summary in the local newspaper.

Using the word *conclusion* to signal that you are concluding is not a bad idea, but work it into the text instead of using it as a heading in a book chapter.

Again, the speaker makes us question his or her competence and preparation by the lack of certainty. And, again, personal comments are best left out.

5.2   Analyzing and Criticizing a Poorly Constructed Persuasive Speech

Like the informative speech in Practically Speaking 5.1, this speech was written to illustrate some really broad as well as some rather subtle errors that a beginning speaker might make in constructing a persuasive speech. First, read the entire speech without reading any of the questions in the column at the side. Then, after you have read the entire speech, reread each paragraph and respond to the critical thinking questions. What other questions might prove productive to ask?

XXX Has Got to Go

You probably didn't read the papers this weekend, but there's an XXX movie, I mean video, store that moved in on Broad and Fifth Streets. My parents, who are retired teachers, are protesting it and so am I. My parents are organizing a protest for the next weekend.

There must be hundreds of XXX video stores in the country, and they all need to be closed down. I have a lot of reasons.

What do you think of the title of the speech?

Visualizing yourself as a listener, how would the opening comment make you feel? Does the speaker gain your attention? What thesis do you think the speaker will support? Does mentioning "my parents" help or hurt the speaker's credibility?

What is the speaker's thesis? What impression are you beginning to get of the speaker?

PART TWO

Elements of Subjects and Audiences

UNIT 6

Topic, Purpose, and Thesis

Unit Contents

Your Topic
Your Purpose
Your Thesis

Unit in Brief
Practically Speaking

Unit Objectives

After completing this unit, you should be able to:

1 Identify the characteristics of an effective speech topic

2 Explain how to find topics through surveys, news items, brainstorming, and the Dictionary of Topics

3 Explain how to limit a topic with *topoi* and tree and fishbone diagrams

4 Identify the three general speech purposes and distinguish these from specific speech purposes

5 Define *thesis* and explain its major uses

*I*n this unit we explain how to find a suitable topic and limit it to manageable proportions, how to establish your purpose, and how to develop your thesis.

YOUR TOPIC

Before explaining how to find and limit topics, we need to distinguish between topics that are suitable and topics that are not.

Suitability

A suitable speech topic should be (1) worthwhile and deal with matters of substance and (2) appropriate to the speaker, audience, and occasion.

The topics should be **worthwhile**. Such topics should address issues that have significant implications for the audience. Topics that are worthwhile have consequences (social, educational, political, and so on) that are significant for your listeners. The topic must be important enough to merit the time and attention of a group of intelligent and educated persons.

A suitable topic is **appropriate** to you as the speaker, to the audience you will address, and to the occasion. When you select a topic you are interested in, you will enjoy thinking and reading about it and this will come through in your speech. Look also at your topic in terms of its appropriateness to the audience. What are they interested in? What would they like to learn more about? On what topics would they find the time listening to your speech well spent? It is a lot easier to please an audience when the topic interests them.

What three topics would you like to hear other students speak on? (You may find it helpful to share these topics with others so that a pool of interesting topics can be established.) What three topics would you like to see other students avoid? (Again, you may find it helpful to share these.)

Cultural Considerations

Cultural differences will greatly influence appropriateness. In many Arab, Asian, and African cultures, discussing sex in an audience of both men and women would be considered obscene and offensive. In other cultures— Scandinavia is a good example—sex is expected to be discussed openly and without embarrassment or discomfort.

Each culture has its own taboo topics, subjects that should be avoided, especially by visitors from other cultures. Table 6.1 presents several examples that Roger Axtell in *Do's and Taboos Around the World* (1993) recommends be avoided by visitors from the United States. These examples are intended not to be exhaustive but rather to serve as a reminder that each culture defines what is and what is not an appropriate topic for discussion.

As with criticism, your college or your communication classroom is very likely to have its own cultural norm in terms of what is and what is not appropriate. Consider, for example, if the following speeches would be considered "appropriate" by members of your public speaking class or by the general college community:

How appropriate would the following topics be for speeches in your class? To inform my audience of how we can reverse the current economic situation; to inform my audience of why they should take a health education course; to inform my audience of how to use the Windows software program; to persuade my audience to change their eating habits; to persuade my audience that street gangs should be government-regulated; to persuade my audience to buy products with minimal packaging.

- A speech that seeks to convert listeners to a specific religious cult
- A speech supporting neo-Nazi values
- A speech supporting racial segregation

- A speech supporting the legitimacy of killing those who defend or perform abortion
- A speech advocating violence against a specific group of people because of their race, affectional orientation, nationality, or religious beliefs
- A speech that teaches listeners how to cheat on their income tax

Do you agree with Gilbert Keith Chesterton's observation that "There is no such thing as an uninteresting subject; there are only uninteresting people"? Can you identify one topic that would be inappropriate for every conceivable audience? Can you identify one television talk show that dealt with an uninteresting topic?

The topic should also be appropriate for the occasion. For example, time limitations will exclude certain topics because they are too complex. You could not explain problems with our educational system or solutions to the drug problem in a five-minute speech. While the "occasion" creates few difficulties in the classroom, it imposes a number of serious restrictions outside the classroom. For example, some occasions call for humorous subjects that would be out of place in other contexts. Then too, speeches of personal experience may be appropriate in one context but inappropriate in another.

TABLE 6.1	Taboos Around the World
Culture	**Taboos**
Belgium	Politics, language differences between French and Flemish, religion
Bolivia	Politics, religion
Caribbean	Race, local politics, religion
Colombia	Politics, criticism of bullfighting
Egypt	Middle Eastern politics
Iraq	Religion, Middle Eastern politics
Japan	World War II
Libya	Politics, religion
Mexico	Mexican-American war, illegal aliens
Nigeria	Religion
Norway	Salaries, social status
Pakistan	Politics
Philippines	Politics, religion, corruption, foreign aid
South Korea	Internal politics, criticism of the government, socialism or communism
Spain	Family, religion, jobs, negative comments on bullfighting

Many students who are returning to college some years after graduating from high school will remember libraries that looked like the one in this photo—with card catalogs instead of computer screens. How might the new computer technologies available at your college library help you in finding topics? Are there specific Web sites that you might recommend for someone seeking a topic?

Finding Topics

Perhaps the question students in a public speaking class most often ask is, "What will I talk about?" A student may think, "I'm not knowledgeable about international affairs [or the Middle East or environmental issues]." Or "I'm not up on an issue like mass transit [or national health insurance or gay rights]." This situation is not uncommon; many if not most college students feel the same way. This need not lead to despair; all is not lost.

The answer to "What do I speak about?" will change as your life situations change. For your classroom speeches—where the objective is to learn the skills of public speaking—there are hundreds of things to talk about. Searching for speech topics is a relatively easy process. Here are four ways to generate topics: surveys, news items, brainstorming, and the Idea Generator.

Surveys   Look at some of the national and regional polls concerning what people think is important—the significant issues, the urgent problems. For example, a survey conducted by the Roper organization for H&R Block in 1978, as reported in *The American Public and the Income Tax System*, found that Americans felt the following to be among the most significant issues: lowering the crime rate, making the tax system fair, improving the educational system, improving the nation's defense capabilities, setting up a program to provide national health insurance for everyone, lowering unemployment, improving and protecting the environment, lowering social security taxes, and improving public transportation. The concerns look very much like those of today.

From Professional Speakers

Pick a topic that you know something about. This doesn't mean you have to know more than everyone in the audience about the topic, but you should at least be familiar with your topic. No professional speaker would get up in front of an audience and speak on a topic that was totally unfamiliar. You shouldn't, either. For a beginning speaker there will be enough nervousness just facing an audience. You don't want to compound that nervousness by trying to remember information you don't really know.

Thomas J. Murphy, teacher and author, & **Kenneth Snyder,** professional speaker and trainer. *What! I Have to Give a Speech?* (Bloomington, IN: Grayson Bernard Publications, 1995), p. 25.

A more recent survey of 10,000 executives and meeting planners identified the ten topics that they consider the most important and that will continue to be important for the net few years: dealing with change, customer service, global marketplace opportunities, future strategies, total quality, new technologies, productivity and performance in business, diversity, legal issues, and health and fitness (Weinstein 1995).

Or you can conduct a survey yourself. Roam through the nonfiction section of your bookstore and you'll quickly develop a list of the topics book buyers consider important. A glance at your newspaper's best-seller list will give you an even quicker overview. Here, for example, are the topics of the best-sellers as reported by the *New York Times* (May 28, 1995): near-death experiences; spirituality, inspirational, and moral stories; changing society; love, family, and relationships; effective argument; religion; success; animal behavior; advances in medicine; siblings; male-female communication; government regulations; and health and diet. Business best-sellers, in addition to those noted above, include increasing personal wealth, tips for investing, organizing your life, the use of modeling in business, competitive business strategies, computers and how they will change our lives, the information superhighway, managing change in the corporation, principles of success, business innovation, and career advice (*New York Times* June 4, 1995, Business, p. 8).

Naturally, all audiences are different. Yet such surveys are useful starting points for giving you some insight into what others think is important and hence what should be of interest to them.

News Items   Another useful starting point is a good newspaper or magazine. Here you will find the important international and domestic issues, the financial issues, and the social issues all conveniently packaged in one place. The editorial page and the letters to the editor are also useful in learning what people are concerned about.

Newsmagazines like *Time* and *Newsweek*, as well as financial magazines such as *Forbes*, *Money*, and *Fortune*, will provide a wealth of suggestions. Similarly, news shows like *20/20, 60 Minutes*, and *Meet the Press* and even the ubiquitous talk shows often identify the very issues with which people are concerned and on which conflicting points of view exist.

Brainstorming   Another useful method is to brainstorm, a technique discussed in detail in Unit 25 (Osborn 1957). Using brainstorming to help yourself generate topics is simple. You begin with your "problem," which in this case is, "What will I talk about?" You then record any idea that occurs to you. Allow your mind to free-associate. Don't censor yourself; instead, allow your ideas to flow as freely as possible. Record all your thoughts—regardless of how silly or inappropriate they may seem. Write them down or record them on tape. Try to generate as many ideas as possible. The more ideas you think of, the greater the chances a suitable topic will be in the pile. After you have generated a sizable list—it should take you no longer than five minutes—read over the list or replay the tape. Do any of the topics on your list suggest other topics? If so, write these down as well. Can you combine or extend your ideas? Which ideas seem workable?

Read through your local newspaper. What topics for public speaking does just one issue suggest? Try the same for *Time, Newsweek,* or *U.S. News & World Report.* What topics do these magazines suggest?

How would you define "hate speech"? Should hate speech be protected by the First Amendment? Should hate speech be permitted in the college classroom? In the high school classroom?

The Idea Generator: Dictionary of Topics   The Idea Generator is actually a method both for discovering topics and for limiting them. This system consists of using a dictionary of general topics and a series of questions that you can ask of any subject. The first part of the idea generator, "Ideas: The Dictionary of Topics," will prove helpful in finding a suitable topic. It consists of a dictionarylike listing of subjects within which each topic is broken down into several subtopics. These subtopics should begin to suggest potential subjects for your informative and persuasive speeches (Table 6.2). The second part of the Idea Generator, "*Topoi:* The System of Topics," will prove useful in helping you limit your topic—the subject to which we now turn.

TABLE 6.2   Ideas: The Dictionary of Topics*

Presented here are ideas for speech topics. This list is not intended to provide specific topics for any of your speeches; it should, however, alleviate any anxiety over "having nothing to talk about." The list should stimulate you to think of subjects dealing with topics you're interested in but may not have thought of as appropriate to a public speech. Each topic is broken down into several subtopics that you might see as potential ideas for your informative and persuasive speeches.

Abortion arguments for and against; techniques of; religious dimension; legal views; differing views of

Academic freedom nature of; censorship; teachers' role in curriculum development; and government; and research; restrictions on

Acupuncture nature of; development of; current practices in; effectiveness of; dangers of

Adoption agencies for; procedures; difficulties in; illegal; concealment of biological parents; search for birth parents

Advertising techniques; expenditures; ethical; unethical; subliminal; leading agencies; history of; slogans

Age ageism; aging processes; aid to the aged; discrimination against the aged; treatment of the aged; different cultural views of aging; and sex differences

Aggression aggressive behavior in animals; in humans; as innate; as learned; and territoriality

Agriculture science of; history of; in ancient societies; technology of; theories of

Air pollution; travel; embolism; law; navigation; power; raids

Alcoholism nature of; Alcoholics Anonymous; Al Anon; abstinence; among the young; treatment of

Amnesty in draft evasion; in criminal law; and pardons; in Civil War; in Vietnam War; conditions of

Animals experimentation; intelligence of; aggression in; ethology; and communication

Arts theater; dance; film; painting; support for; apathy; social aspects of; economic aspects of; styles in the arts

Athletics professional; Little League; college; support for;

corruption in; benefits of; little-known sports; records; Olympics

Automobiles development of; economics of; advances in; new developments; mass production

Awards Academy; sports; Tony; Cleo; Emmy; scholarship; athletic

Bicycling as exercise; as transportation; touring; Olympic; development and types of cycles; social aspects; ecological aspects

Birth defects; control; rites; racial differences; natural

Blind number of blind persons; training of the blind; Braille; communication and the blind; prejudice against; adjustment of; famous blind persons

Books binding; burning; collecting; rare; making; publishing; writing

Boxing professional; amateur; great fights; styles of; famous fighters; economics of

Continued

*This dictionary of topics is available in computerized form on *The Speech Writer's Guide* (see "Supplements" in Preface).

TABLE 6.2   Continued

Brain trust; washing; damage; genius; intelligence; aphasia

Business cycles; associations; laws; in performing arts; finance

Cable television; underground; development of; economics of

Calorie nature of; and exercise; and diets; and weight gain

Capitalism nature of; economics of; development of; depression and inflation; philosophy; alternatives to

Cards playing; tarot; fortune-telling; development of games; rules for games

Censorship arguments for and against; and violence; and sex; television; literacy

Chauvinism and patriotism; and sexism; and learning; changing conceptions of

Cities problems of; population patterns; and tourism; crime; government of

Citizenship different conceptions of; acquiring loss of; naturalization; tests; in different countries

College functions of; economics of; differences among; historical development of; and job training; and education

Communication public; media; intrapersonal; interpersonal; satellite

Computer memory; music; programming; and communication; chess; personal; and education

Copyright laws; infringements; rules; practices

Credit nature of; public; agricultural; card use; unions; bureau

Crime prevention; types of; and law; and punishment

Cults types of; programming; deprogramming; influences of; power of

Culture cultural relativism; lag; drift; diffusion; change; shock

Death legal aspects of; and religion; and suicide; and life; reincarnation

Debt management; retirement; limit; and credit cards

Defense national; mechanisms; self; techniques; karate

Depression nature of; and suicide; among college students; dealing with

Diet water; Scarsdale; dangers of; alternatives to; fasting; Cambridge

Disasters natural; wartime; prevention of; famous; economics of

Discrimination sensory; and prejudice; racial; religious

Diseases major diseases of college students; prevention; detection; treatment; recovery

Divorce rate; throughout world; causes of; advantages of; disadvantages of; proceedings

Drugs addiction; treatment; allergies; poisoning; problems; effects; legalizing

Earthquakes nature of; famous; Alaskan; San Francisco; volcanos; seismic readings

Ecology nature of; approaches of; applications of

Economics principles of; macro; micro; schools of; of education; in education

Education system of; social; religious; medical; legal;

economics of; segregation; desegregation

Emigration migration; changing population patterns; uses of; problems with

Employment theory; and unemployment; service; insurance

Energy conservation; nature of; types of; crisis; sources; nuclear; solar; fusion

Entertainment industry; benefits; abuses; tax; functions of; and communication

Environment biological; influences; versus innate factors in learning; pollution of

Ethnicity meaning of; and prejudice; theories of; and culture

Ethology nature of; animal behavior patterns; pioneers; theories of

Evolution philosophical; theological; of human race; theories of; and revolution

Exercise importance of; methods of; dangers of; gymnastics

Farming techniques; government subsidies; equipment; effect of droughts

Federal Communications Commission (FCC) structure of; powers; functions; and television programming; rulings of; licenses

Feminism meaning of; implications of; changing concepts of

Folk literature; medicine; music; poetry; society; tales; wisdom

Food health; preservatives; additives; red dye; and allergies; preparation; stamps

Football rules; college; professional; abuses in; training in

TABLE 6.2   Continued

Freedom of speech laws protecting; and Constitution; significance of; abuses of; and censorship; and economics

Freedom of the press and the Constitution; revealing sources; importance of; investigative reporting

Gambling types of; legal aspects of; casino; houses; and chance; legalization of

Game(s) history of; theory; shows; children's psychological; destructive

Gay and lesbian rights; lifestyle; laws against; prejudice against; and religion; statistics; relationships

Gender roles; identification; differences

Government federal; state; city; powers of

Guilt causes of; symptoms; dealing with; effects of; and suicide; and religion

Health services; human; education; laws; audiology

Heroes nature of; and adolescence; fictional; social role of; real-life heroes

Hospital(s) structure; function; and preventive medicine; and concern for community; and cost

Housing urban; cost; inflation; discrimination in; subsidized; underground

Humor theories of; nature of; situational; verbal; cultural differences in

Hypnotism nature of; and memory; and age regression; potentials of; uses of; dangers of; medical uses of

Immigration migration; patterns; laws governing

Imports and exports; laws regulating; and tariffs; and protection of workers

Income personal; national; and employment theory; tax; statement

Industrialization social aspects; economics of; political aspects of; development of; psychological aspects

Infant mortality causes of; prevention of; racial differences; preventive medicine

Intelligence quotient; tests; theories of; cultural differences

Internet accessing information; e-mail; and researching; and finding jobs

Journalism as profession; investigative; photojournalism; education

Kidnapping nature of; famous; laws governing; penalties; Act; Lindberg

Labor types of; division of; hours; in pregnancy; economics of; and management; unions

Languages artificial; sign; natural; learning of; loss of; pathologies of

Laws international; criminal; of nature

Libraries functions; support; science; design; largest; collections; types of

Life definition of; extraterrestrial; cycle; insurance; support; systems

Literacy rate; world distribution; definition; problems in rising rate of

Love nature of; theories of; romantic; family; and hate; and interpersonal relationships; of self; and materialism

Magic nature of; and religion; significance of; types of; and science; history of; and magicians; and sleight of hand

Marriage and divorce; vows; traditions; open; contracts; bans; changing views of; laws against

Media forms of; contributions of; abuses; regulations; popularity of; influences of; and violence; and censorship

Medicine preventive; forensic; and health insurance; history of; holistic; and poisoning; alchemy; industrial

Men education of; problems of; and women; and chauvinism; changing roles of; and sexism; and prejudice; and homosexuality; in groups; as fathers

Military organizations; preparedness; confrontations and conflicts; governments; law

Morality nature of; cultural variations in views; teaching of; and crime

Music festivals; forms; instruments; compositions; styles; drama

Myth(s) nature of; origin of; symbolism of; and ritual; contemporary significance of

Narcissism nature of; and Narcissus; Freudian view of; and autoeroticism; and love of others

National Organization for Women (NOW) structure of; functions of; influences of; contributions of; beliefs of

Newspapers functions of; advertising; reporters; famous; structure of; economics of

Continued

TABLE 6.2   Continued

Noise pollution; white; and communication; redundancy and; combating; causes of; types of

Nuclear plants; explosion; family; war; reaction; weapons; arguments for and against nuclear plants

Nutrition nature of; functions of food; essential requirements; animal; human; and starvation; and diet

Obscenity nature of; laws prohibiting; and pornography; effects of; influences on

Occupational diseases; psychology; satisfaction; therapy

Peace Corps; treaty; pipe; economics of

Personality development of; measurement of; theories of; disorders; tests

Photography nature of; types of; art of; color; development of; infrared; technology; holography

Police functions of; structure of; crime prevention; and education; community relations; civilian review; abuses by

Pollution air; atmospheric research; chemical radiation; water; and food; sources; effects; laws governing

Population(s) beliefs; theories; Malthusianism; Marxism; and education; and elderly; and family size; world; innate factors; racial typing; evolution; mutation

Pornography and censorship; types of; influences of; restrictions on

Prison reform; systems; security; routine; effect on crime; personality; behavior; and sex; and conditioning

Psychic phenomena ESP; psychokinesis; reliability of; and frauds; theories of

Psychoanalysis development of; leaders; impact of; training in; theories of

Public relations in colleges; and propaganda; public opinion; advertising

Public schools support of; changing curriculum; and parochial schools; problems with; PTAs

Publishing economics of; history of; copyright; and media exposure; trade and textbook; magazine and newspaper

Racing auto; dog; horse; corruption in; jockeys; fame

Racism nature of; self-hatred; genetic theory; human rights; education; religious; UN position; in United States

Radio development of; advertising; air traffic control; police; surveillance; radioactivity

Religion different religions; leaders in; influence of; beliefs of; and agnosticism; and atheism; and God; social dimensions of; and art; and architecture

Salaries minimum wage; professional; white- and blue-collar; racial variation; and unions; and inflation

Sales advertising; methods; forecasting; and excise taxes; effects on consumers

Satellite communication; launchings; research

Sciences history of; procedures in; empirical data; methods of; fiction

Security personal; social; national

Segregation genetic; racial; leaders in fight against; legal aspects; and legal decisions; effects of; education

Self-concept meaning of; and communication; and depression; and conditioning

Self-defense in criminal law; international laws; and war; martial arts

Self-disclosure benefits of; cautions in; influences of; influences on; effects of; types of; conditions conducive to

Sex education; roles; therapy; surrogate; change; and love; and the concepts of deviation; variations; and learning

Social security; facilitation; class; control; differentiation; Darwinism; equilibrium; groups; movement; realism

Solar system; wind; radiation; energy; heating

Space exploration; flight; probes; age

Sports nature of; psychology of; fans; in college; professional; records; Little League; figures; salaries; international competition; Olympics; invention of; stadiums

Strikes famous; violence; unions; essential-service occupations; teacher; causes and effects

Subconscious Freud; development of concept; defense mechanisms

Subversive activities definition of; political; legislation penalties for

Suicide causes; among college students; laws regulating; methods; aiding the suicide of

TABLE 6.2   Continued

another; philosophical implications; religious dimension

Superstition beliefs; mythology; influences on history

Supreme Court judicial review; decisions; makeup of; chief justices; jurisdiction

Taxation alcohol; cigarette; history of; purposes of; historical methods of; types of; without representation; evasion; tariffs

Teaching methods; teachers; machines; programmed learning; behavioral objectives; and conditioning

Technology benefits of; and undeveloped areas; as threat to workers; and economics; history of

Telepathy nature of; evidence for; tests of; and fraud

Television development of; history of; working of satellite; commercials; propaganda; and leisure time; programming; economics of; effects of; and violence; and radio; and film; producing; Nielsen ratings

Test-tube babies developments in; opposition to; methods; dangers; variations

Theater Greek; Roman; commedia dell'arte; American; British; Eastern; Italian; French; performers; styles of; and television; and film; Broadway; and critics

Theology forms; development of; different religions; education

Therapy physical; psychological; language; techniques of; schools of

Time management; travel; records

Tobacco production of; smoking; effects of; causes of; meth-

ods of stopping; nicotine; dangers of; economics of

Translation computer; missionary impetus; problems in; history of; kinds of

Transplants nature of; rejection of; donor selection; legal aspects of; ethical aspects of; future of; advances in

Transportation history; urban; water; air; land

Trust nature of; and love; and self-disclosure; types of; and communication

UFOs evidence for; types of; reported sightings; theories of; agencies in charge of

Unemployment urban; seasonal; and violence; insurance; disguised

Unions development of; problems with; advantages of; arguments for and against; unionism

United Nations (UN) development of; functions of; agencies; and League of Nations; structure; veto powers; Security Council; Declaration of Rights

Urban living; problems; benefits; stress; crime; transportation; development; decay

Vaccine nature of; types; vaccination; immunization

Values and attitudes; and communications; social; economic; changing; religious; axiology; and sex differences

Vietnam country; people; War; language; rehabilitation

Virtue natural; religious; nature of; changing conceptions of; learning and

Vitamins deficiency; excess; types of

Voice qualities; voiceprints; and personality; training; and persuasion; paralanguage

Wages minimum; and inflation; and fringe benefits; average; differences among cultures

War conduct of; financing; destruction by; causes of; debts; games; casualties; effects of

Weapons hand and missile; firearms; artillery; rockets; automatic; nuclear; biological; psychological

Weather forecasting; hurricanes; control of; rain; snow; heat; cold; and population patterns; and health; and psychology; diving

Weightlifting techniques in; as exercise; as sport; leading weightlifters; competition; dangers in; benefits of; societal attitudes toward; and sexual attraction

Witchcraft meaning of; white and black; and magic; structure of; functions of; theories of; in primitive societies; contemporary

Women and sexism; biology; learning and programming; in different societies; accomplishments of; prejudices against; ERA; social roles

Words history; coinage; foreign contributions; semantics; and meaning

Youth problems of; crime; education; hostels; music; communication problems; generation gap

Zodiac nature of; different conceptions of; constellations; myths surrounding; and horoscopes

Limiting Topics

To be suitable for a public speech—or any other type of communication—a topic must be limited in scope; it must be narrowed down to fit the time constraints. Probably the major problem for beginning speakers is that they attempt to cover a huge topic in too short a time. The inevitable result is that nothing specific is covered—everything is touched on but only superficially. No depth is achieved with a broad topic, so all you can succeed in doing is telling the audience what it already knows. Here are three popular methods for narrowing and limiting your topic.

The Idea Generator—*Topoi*: The System of Topics   The second half of the Idea Generator is "*Topoi*: The System of Topics," a technique that comes to us from the classical rhetorics of ancient Greece and Rome. Using this method of *topoi*, you would ask yourself a series of questions about your general subject. The process will enable you to see divisions or aspects of your general topic on which you might want to focus. In Table 6.3 the columns on the left contain seven general questions (Who? What? Why? When? Where? How? and So?) and a series of subquestions. The right-hand column illustrates how some of the questions on the left might suggest specific aspects of the general subject of "dictionary." By asking these general and specific questions about a subject, you will see how you can divide and analyze a topic into its significant parts.

Let's take another idea: You want to give a speech on "homelessness." Applying the system of *topoi*, you would ask such questions as:

- Who are the homeless?
- Who is the typical homeless person?
- Who is responsible for the increase in homelessness?
- What does it mean to be homeless?
- What does homelessness do to the people themselves?
- What does homelessness do to the society in general?
- What does homelessness mean to you and me?
- Why are there so many homeless people?
- Why did this happen?
- When did homelessness become so prevalent?
- Where is homelessness most prevalent?
- Where is there an absence of homelessness?
- How does someone become homeless?
- How can we help the homeless?
- How can we prevent others from becoming homeless?
- Why is homelessness such an important social problem?
- Why must we be concerned with homelessness?

Such questions should be helpful to you in using general topics to generate more specific ideas for your speeches. Try this system on any one of the topics listed in the Dictionary of Topics in Table 6.2. You'll be amazed at how many topics you will generate. Your problem will quickly change from "What can I speak on?" to "Which one of these should I speak on?"

What other questions might you want to add to the system of *topoi?* Why might these additional questions prove useful?

TABLE 6.3   *Topoi:* **The System of Topics**

General Questions	Subject-Specific Questions
Who? Who is he or she? Who is responsible? Who did it? To whom was it done? Who is in favor of (against) this?	Who are the people responsible for making dictionaries? What is the role of the linguist? The lexicographer? The grammarian? Who was Noah Webster? Who was Samuel Johnson?
What? What is it? What are its parts? What is it like? What is it different from? What does it do? What are its functions? What are some examples? What should we do?	What is a dictionary? What does a dictionary contain? What are other dictionarylike works? What is a thesaurus? What are some different types of dictionaries? What is a dictionary used for? What is the difference between an abridged and an unabridged dictionary?
Why? Why use it? Why do it? Why did it happen? Why did it not happen?	Why were dictionaries developed? Why were specialized dictionaries developed?
When? When did it happen? When will it occur? When should it be done? When did it begin? When did (will) it end?	When were dictionaries developed? When should students learn about dictionaries? When will dictionaries be computerized for everyday use?
Where? Where did it come from? Where is it going? Where is it now?	What is the history of the dictionary? What were early dictionaries like? What is the state of the art? What will the dictionary of the future look like?
How? How does it work? How is it used? How do you do it? How do you operate it? How is it organized?	How do you use a dictionary? What do you look for in a dictionary? What questions are better answered by other reference books?
So? What does it mean? What is important about it? Why should I be concerned with this? Who cares?	Why should I be concerned with dictionaries? What is the value of a dictionary? What kind of dictionary should I use?

Tree Diagrams   Tree diagrams help you to repeatedly divide your topic into its significant parts. Starting with the general topic, you divide it into its parts. Then you take one of these parts and divide it into its parts. You continue with this process until the topic seems manageable, one that you can reasonably cover in some depth in the allotted time.

Take the topic of television programs as the first general topic area. You might divide this topic into such subtopics as comedy, children's programs, educational programs, news, movies, soap operas, quiz shows, and sports. You might then take one of these subtopics, say, comedy, and divide it into sub-subtopics. Perhaps you might consider it on a time basis and divide television comedy into its significant time periods: pre-1960, 1961–1979, 1980 to the present. Or you might focus on situation comedies. Here you might examine a topic such as women in television comedy, race relations in situation comedy, or family relationships in television comedies. The resultant topic is at least beginning to look manageable. Television programs, without some limitation, would take a lifetime to cover adequately.

The construction of tree diagrams (actually, they resemble upside-down trees) might clarify the process of narrowing a topic. Let us say, for example, that you want to give a speech on mass communication. You might develop a tree diagram with branches for the division that interests you most, as shown in Figure 6.1. Thus, you can divide mass communication into film, television, radio, and advertising. If television interests you most, then develop branches from television. Comedy, news, soaps, sports, and quiz shows would be appro-

How would you draw a tree diagram for limiting topics beginning with such general subjects as immigration, education, sports, transportation, or politics?

FIGURE 6.1
A tree diagram for limiting speech topics.

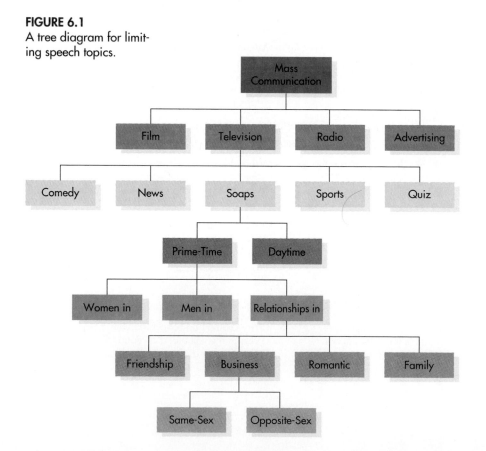

priate. Now, let us say that it is soaps that most interest you. In this case you would create branches from soaps, perhaps prime-time and daytime. Keep dividing the topic until you get something that is significant, appropriate to you and your audience, and manageable in the allotted time.

Fishbone Diagrams   Another useful diagram is the fishbone. The fishbone is widely used as a problem-solving tool in business organizations but can easily be adapted to analyzing and limiting a topic. Often called the Ishikawa diagram after its developer, Kaoru Ishikawa (Higgins 1994; Lumsden & Lumsden 1993), the diagram resembles the bones of a fish. The major topic appears at the head of the fish. The bones emanating from the spine are the major subtopics. The smaller bones coming out of these larger bones are the subdivisions of the subtopics. Let's say, for example, that you wanted to give a speech on the family. Your fishbone diagram might come to look like that in Figure 6.2.

How would you draw a fishbone diagram for limiting such topics as psychology, religion, crime, or economics?

FIGURE 6.2
A fishbone diagram for limiting speech topics.

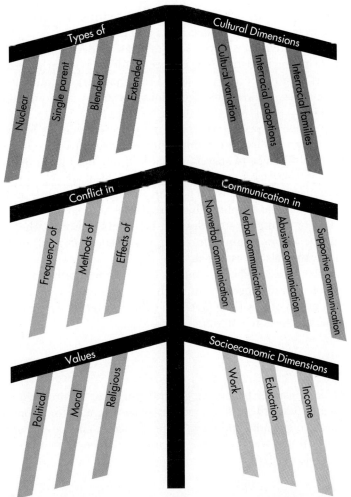

Once the major topic is dissected in this way, you can easily see a variety of specific and more limited topics on which you might speak. Let's say you wanted to give your speech on family values. Your major propositions are already identified: political, moral, and religious. Or you might want to limit your topic still further and focus exclusively on moral values. If so, you would then need to dissect the bones of "moral values" so that you could identify your major propositions. You might, for example, focus on types of moral values, their decay or improvement, or their characteristics in different cultures.

Can you think of a persuasive speech that would not also contain some elements of information?

YOUR PURPOSE

The purpose of your speech is your goal; it is what you hope to achieve during your speech. It identifies the effect you want your speech to have on your audience. In constructing your speech, identify first your general purpose and second your specific purpose.

General Purposes

The three major purposes of public speeches are to inform, to persuade, and to serve some ceremonial or special occasion function.

In the informative speech, you seek to create understanding: to clarify, to enlighten, to correct misunderstandings, to demonstrate how something works. In this type of speech, you would rely most heavily on materials that amplify—examples, illustrations, definitions, testimony, audiovisual aids, and the like.

In the persuasive speech, you try to influence attitudes or behaviors; you seek to strengthen or change existing attitudes or to get the audience to take some action. In this type of speech, you would rely heavily on materials that offer proof—on evidence, argument, and psychological appeals, for example.

Any persuasive speech is in part an informative speech and as such contains materials that amplify, illustrate, define, and so on. In its focus on strengthening or changing attitudes and behaviors, however, the persuasive speech must go beyond simply providing information. Logical, motivational, and credibility appeals are essential.

The special occasion speech contains elements of information and persuasion. For this type of speech you might, for example, introduce another speaker or a group of speakers, present a tribute or try to secure the goodwill of the listeners, or seek to entertain your listeners.

Specific Purposes

After you have established your general purpose, identify your specific purpose, which identifies more precisely what you aim to accomplish. For example, in an informative speech your specific speech purpose would identify that information you want to convey to your audience. Here are a few examples on the topic of AIDS:

GENERAL PURPOSE: to inform
SPECIFIC PURPOSES:

> to inform my audience of the recent progress in AIDS research
>
> to inform my audience of our college's plans for AIDS Awareness Day
>
> to inform my audience of the currently used tests for HIV infection

In a persuasive speech, your specific purpose identifies what you want your audience to believe, to think, or perhaps to do. Here are a few examples, again on the topic of AIDS:

GENERAL PURPOSE: to persuade
SPECIFIC PURPOSES:

> to persuade my audience to contribute to AIDS research
>
> to persuade my audience that they should be tested for HIV infection
>
> to persuade my audience to become better informed about how AIDS can be transmitted

In formulating your specific purpose, keep the following guidelines in mind.

Use an Infinitive Phrase Begin the statement of your specific purpose with the word *to* and elaborate on your general purpose, for example, *to inform my audience of the schedule of events for AIDS Awareness Day* or *to persuade my audience to contribute a book for the library fund-raiser* or *to introduce the main speaker of the day*.

Limit Your Specific Purpose Limit your specific purpose in two ways. First, avoid the common pitfall of trying to accomplish too much in too short a time. For example, "to persuade my audience that AIDS is prevalent in our community and that they should contribute money for AIDS services" contains two specific purposes. Select either "to persuade my audience that AIDS is prevalent in our community" or "to persuade my audience that they should contribute money for AIDS services." Beware of specific purposes that contain the word *and*; it's often a sign that you have more than one purpose.

Second, limit your specific purpose to what can reasonably be developed in the allotted time. Specific purposes that are too broad are useless. Note how broad and overly general the following purposes are:

> to inform my audience about clothing design
>
> to persuade my audience to improve their health

Note how much more reasonable the following restatements are for a relatively short speech:

> to inform my audience of the importance of color in clothing design
>
> to persuade my audience to exercise at least three times a week

Why is it so important to clearly limit your specific purpose for your classroom speeches?

Use Specific Terms   Phrase your specific purpose with precise terms. The more precise your specific purpose, the more effectively it will guide you in the remaining steps of preparing your speech. Compare, for example, the following statements of specific purpose:

I. to persuade my audience to do something about AIDS

II. to persuade my audience to contribute food to homebound persons with AIDS

Statement I merely identifies the general topic area; it does not state what you hope to accomplish in your speech. Note how much more specific Statement II is.

YOUR THESIS

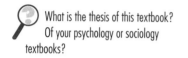

What is the thesis of this textbook? Of your psychology or sociology textbooks?

Your thesis is your main assertion: what you want the audience to absorb from your speech. The thesis of Lincoln's Second Inaugural Address was that Northerners and Southerners should work together for the entire nation's welfare; the thesis of the Rocky movies was that the underdog can win; the thesis of Martin Luther King, Jr.'s "I Have a Dream" speech was that true equality must be granted to African Americans and, in fact, to all people (see Appendix for the complete speech).

Do your term papers for other courses have theses? If so, what were the theses of your last three papers? If not, would they have profited from being built around specific theses?

Let's say, for example, that you are planning to deliver a speech against using animals for experimentation. Your thesis statement might be something like this: "Animal experimentation should be banned." This is what you want your audience to believe as a result of your speech. In an informative speech, the thesis statement focuses on what you want your audience to learn. For example, a suitable thesis for a speech on jealousy might be "There are two main theories of jealousy." Be sure to limit the thesis statement to one central idea. Statements such as "Animal experimentation should be banned and companies engaging in it should be prosecuted" contain not one but two basic ideas.

Notice that in persuasive speeches, the thesis statement puts forth a point of view, an opinion. The thesis is an arguable, debatable proposition. In informative speeches, the thesis is relatively neutral and objective.

Using Thesis Statements

The thesis statement serves three useful purposes. First, it helps you generate your main ideas or assertions. Second, it suggests suitable organizational patterns and strategies. Third, it focuses the audience's attention on your central idea. Let's look at each of these functions in more detail.

Generating Main Ideas   Each thesis contains an essential question within it; this question allows you to explore and subdivide the thesis. Your objective is to find this question and pose it to your thesis. For example, let's say your thesis is "The Hart bill provides needed services for senior citizens." Stated in this form, the obvious question suggested is "What services are they?" The answer to this question suggests the main parts of your speech, for example, health, food, shelter, and recreational services. These four areas then become the four main points of your speech. An outline of the main ideas would look like this:

I. The Hart bill provides needed health services.

II. The Hart bill provides needed food services.

III. The Hart bill provides needed shelter services.

IV. The Hart bill provides needed recreational services.

The remainder of the speech would then be filled in with supporting materials. Under *I*, you might identify the several needed health services and explain how the Hart bill provides for these services. This first main division of your speech might, in outline form, look something like this:

I. The Hart bill provides needed health services.
A. Neighborhood clinics will be established.
B. Medical hotlines for seniors will be established.

What is the thesis of a recent television show? What is the thesis of the last novel you read? What is the thesis of the last movie you saw?

What questions might you ask of such thesis statements as these? (1) Vote for the Student Rights Party, (2) all students need computer skills, (3) organize your time more effectively, (4) insist on prenuptial agreements, and (5) tuition should not be raised.

In the completed speech, this first major proposition and its two subordinate statements might be spoken like this:

The Hart bill provides senior citizens with the health services they so badly need. Let me give you some examples of these badly needed health services. One of the most important services will be the establishment of neighborhood health clinics. These clinics will help senior citizens get needed health advice and services right in their own neighborhoods.

A second important health service will be the establishment of health hotlines. These phone numbers will be for the exclusive use of senior citizens. These hotlines . . .

Suggesting Organizational Patterns   The thesis provides a useful guideline in selecting your organizational pattern. For example, let's suppose your thesis is "We can improve our own college educations." Your answer to the inherent question "What can we do?" will suggest a possible organizational pattern. If, for example, you identify the remedies in the order in which they should be taken, then a time-order pattern would be appropriate. If you itemize a number of possible solutions, all of which are of about equal importance, then a topical pattern would be appropriate. These and other patterns are explained in detail in Unit 12: The Body of the Speech.

Focusing Audience Attention   The thesis sentence also focuses the audience's attention on your central idea. In some speeches you may wish to state your thesis early in your speech, for example, in the introduction or perhaps early in the body of the speech. There are instances, however, when you may not want to state your thesis. Or you may want to state it late in your speech. For example, if your audience is hostile to your thesis, it may be wise to give your evidence and arguments first and gradually move the audience into a more positive frame of mind before stating your thesis.

In other cases you may want the audience to infer your thesis without actually spelling it out. However, do realize that most audiences, and especially uneducated ones, are not persuaded by speeches in which the speaker does not explicitly state the thesis. Listeners often fail to grasp what the thesis is and so do not change their attitudes or behaviors.

Make your decision as to when (or if) to state your thesis on the basis of what will be more effective in helping you achieve your specific purpose with your specific audience. Here are a few guidelines to help you make the right decision.

Do you agree with the suggestions offered here for focusing or not focusing audience attention on your thesis? How would you revise these suggestions? What other suggestions might you offer?

1. In an informative speech, state your thesis early, clearly, and directly.
2. In a persuasive speech where your audience is neutral or positive, state your thesis explicitly and early in your speech.
3. In a persuasive speech where your audience is hostile to your position, delay stating your thesis until you have moved them closer to your position.

Wording the Thesis

State your thesis as a simple declarative sentence. This will help you focus your thinking, your collection of materials, and your organizational pattern. You may, however, phrase your thesis in a number of different ways when you present it to your audience. At one extreme, you may state it to your audience as you phrased it for yourself, for example:

Animal experimentation must be banned.

I want to tell you in this brief speech why animal experimentation must be stopped.

Or you may decide to state your thesis as a question, for example:

Why should we ban animal experimentation?

Are there valid reasons for banning animal experimentation?

In persuasive speeches in which you face a hostile or mildly opposed audience, you may wish to state your thesis in vague and ambiguous terms. Here is an example:

I want to talk about animal experimentation. Is there a problem with our current policy? Let's look at what our policy is and see if it should be changed.

 In what different ways might you phrase these thesis statements in an actual speech? What advantages or disadvantages can you identify for each phrasing? (1) Buy American-made cars, (2) thinking can make you happy, (3) condoms should be distributed in the schools, (4) dramatic tax cuts will improve the economy, and (5) take the HIV/AIDS test.

In these cases you focus the audience's attention on your central idea but delay presenting your specific point of view until a more favorable time.

Recognize that there are cultural differences in the way a thesis should be stated. In some Asian cultures, for example, making a point too directly or asking directly for audience compliance may be considered rude or insulting.

A Note on Thesis and Purpose

The thesis and the purpose are similar in that they both guide you in selecting and organizing your materials. In some ways, however, they are different.

Thesis and purpose differ in their form of expression. The thesis is phrased as a complete declarative sentence. The purpose is phrased as an infinitive phrase (to inform . . . , to persuade . . .).

The thesis is message-focused; the purpose is audience-focused. The thesis identifies the central idea of your speech; it summarizes—epitomizes—the speech content. The purpose identifies the change you hope to achieve in your audience, for example, to gain information, to change attitudes, to act in a certain way.

Further, the purpose limits what you hope to achieve given the practical limitations of time and your audience's expectations and attitudes. The thesis,

TIPS

From Professional Speakers

One of my "secrets" for doing creative work of any sort is simply to do what I call "getting out of my own way." I discovered, quite early in life, that there is some strange creative center in my brain that, once stimulated, will give up a considerable volume of whatever I ask it to produce: jokes, stories, philosophical observations, or ideas for essays, newspaper or magazine features, television comedy sketches, plays, songs, and so on. Part of the process involves shutting "me" up, calming myself down, relaxing, and just listening to the ideas as an internal computer cranks them out. . . .

By simply agreeing to give a speech, or by self-generating a plan to do so, you will have stimulated your own mysterious idea center. What you must do next is listen to its responses. At this stage don't—whatever you do—serve as a censorious judge, telling yourself, "Oh, that's no good" or "That will never work." Stopping self-criticism at once is part of the process of getting out of your own way.

Steve Allen, writer and performer. *How to Make a Speech* (New York: McGraw-Hill, 1986), pp. 24–25.

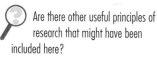
Are there other useful principles of research that might have been included here?

Here are some general principles to keep in mind as you are taking your research notes.

1. *Key your notes to the topics in your preliminary speech outline.* For example, let us say that your speech is to be on surrogate motherhood. Your preliminary outline looks like this:

Surrogate Motherhood

   I. Legal aspects

  II. Moral aspects

 III. Psychological aspects

You might then classify your notes under these three major topics. Simply head the page with *Legal*, *Moral*, or *Psychological*. Taking notes with your preliminary outline will help focus your research and will remind you of those topics for which you need more information.

Because this is a preliminary outline, you will need a large category for miscellaneous information. Here you would file all the interesting information that you are not sure you will use and yet don't want to lose.

2. *Make sure your notes are complete (and legible).* If you have to err, then err on the side of having notes that are too detailed. You can always cut the quotation or select one example out of the three at a later time. As you take notes, be sure to identify the source so that you can find that reference again should you need it. You might also want to include the catalog number or otherwise indicate where you can again find the book or periodical.

3. *Use only one side of the paper and leave plenty of white space on all sides of your notes.* Never write on the back of your notes. One-sided pages are easier to rearrange and to cut in half if, for example, you decide to divide up a topic. One-sided pages will also save you lots of time in locating your materials. By leaving white space on the sides, you'll be able to write in your comments or indicate headings that might be appropriate. The white space gives you a chance to interact with your notes by writing in your comments, questions, and ideas.

Use Research Time Effectively

Manage the time you have effectively and efficiently. If you are going to give two speeches on the same topic, do the research for both at the same time. Don't wait until you have finished the first speech to begin researching the second. You might, for example, divide the loose-leaf notebook into two sections and insert the material with appropriate cross-references.

Learn the Available Sources of Information

Research is a chore for many people because they are unfamiliar with the available sources of information. When you know how to research, it will be easy, pleasant, and rewarding. Learn what is available, where, and in what form. For example, spend a few hours in the library learning where some of the most useful source materials are located.

- Where are the encyclopedias? The almanacs? The indexes to the various journals?
- How are newspapers and journals maintained in your library?
- What material is on microfilm?
- How does your library operate interlibrary loans? How long do such loans take? Can you borrow both journals and books? Are there any restrictions?
- What other libraries are available in your area? Are there municipal libraries that might complement your college library? Do other colleges allow students from your college to use their facilities? Are they better equipped in certain areas?
- What computer search facilities are available at your library? Most libraries have facilities for accessing various on-line databases (information stored electronically that can be accessed or retrieved by computer). How can you access the Internet?

 Can you identify three research works that are especially important in your college major? If you cannot, how might you go about finding out what these are?

SOURCES FOR RESEARCH

More than 30 million different books have been published since the invention of the printing press. Currently, approximately 400,000 titles are published each year. Millions of articles are published every year in thousands of different journals and magazines. There are now more than 100,000 journals and magazines in the area of science alone.

Computerized databases are now common on campuses throughout the country. Old ones are being expanded and new ones are being created. The Internet has made vast amounts of information available with just a few keystrokes on a computer. The information currently available on just about any topic is so vast that it is understandably daunting for many people. The research process will be easier and less forbidding once you know some of the more significant sources of information.

Experts

The faculty is one of the best, if rarely used, sources of information for almost any speech topic. Regardless of what your topic is, a faculty member of some department knows a great deal about the topic. At the very least, he or she will be able to direct you to appropriate sources. Experts in the community can serve similar functions. Local politicians, religious leaders, doctors, lawyers, museum directors, and the like are often suitable sources of information.

Another obvious expert is the librarian. Librarians know the contents and mechanics of libraries; they are experts in the very issues that may be giving you trouble. Librarians will be able to help you in finding biographical material, indexes of current articles, materials in specialized collections at other libraries, and so on. Your librarian will also help you access the appropriate computerized databases that will help you retrieve the information you need.

inexpensive versions published annually are among the most up-to-date sources of information on many topics. The most popular are *The World Almanac and Book of Facts* (also available on CD-ROM), the *Information Please Almanac*, and *The Universal Almanac*. The *Canadian Almanac and Directory* is the best source for Canadian data.

Government Publications

If you are working on a speech on government, history, population, law, farming, or any of a wide variety of other topics, you may find useful sources in government publications. The U.S. government is in fact the country's largest publisher. It prints more pages per year than any other publisher. Here is just a small sampling of the publications available in most libraries or directly from the Government Printing Office in Washington, D.C.

The annual *Statistical Abstract of the United States* contains the most complete statistical data on population, vital statistics, health, education, law, geography and environment, elections, finances and employment, defense, insurance, labor, income, prices, banking, and a host of other topics. Other valuable statistical sources include *Vital Statistics of the United States* (especially useful for demographic statistics) and *Morbidity and Mortality Weekly Report* (useful for health-related issues). For international statistics see *United Nations Statistical Yearbook*, *World Statistics in Brief*, and *UNESCO Statistical Yearbook*.

The *Official Congressional Directory* (1809 to date) and the *Biographical Directory of the American Congress* provide biographical information on government personnel, maps of congressional districts, and various other helpful information to those concerned with the workings of Congress.

The *Congressional Record* (1873 to date) is issued daily when Congress is in session. The Record contains all that was said in both houses of Congress. It also contains materials that members of Congress wish inserted.

Government publications originate in the various divisions of its 13 departments, each of which is a prolific publisher. The Departments of Agriculture, Commerce, Defense, Education, Energy, Health and Human Services, Housing and Urban Development, Interior, Justice, Labor, State, Treasury, and Transportation each issue reports, pamphlets, books, and assorted other documents dealing with its various concerns. Because of the wealth of published material, you will have to first consult one of the guides to government publications. A few of the more useful ones that should be in your college library include *Government Reference Books* (1968 to date), *A Bibliography of United States Government Bibliographies*, and *U.S. Government Books: Recent Releases* (published quarterly).

To what specific source of information would you first go in researching "abortion"? "Sexual harassment"? "Civil disobedience"?

▬ RESEARCHING ON-LINE

As already noted, many of the indexes and abstracts formerly available only in print are now available on-line (enabling you to access an "outside" database) and on CD-ROM (with which you access a database contained on high-density compact discs that have read-only memory). A "database" is simply informa-

Examine the available computerized databases in your library. What one database will prove most valuable to you as you continue your college education?

tion contained in one place. A dictionary, an encyclopedia, and an index to magazines are all examples of databases. A computerized database is similar except that it is accessed through a computer. These systems enable you to access many of the sources discussed previously as well as many information sources available only on-line.

There are numerous advantages to researching your speeches by computer:

- You don't have to copy each reference you find; instead, you can print out your search or download it to your own computer disk.
- You can do combined searches. If you are researching the topic of drugs and violence, for example, you do not have to review all the references to drugs to see if any also deal with violence (as you would with print indexes). You can request a computer search for all and only the references dealing with "drugs and violence."
- Computer searches are more accurate and more complete than any that could be done manually.
- Computer researching is more convenient; in many cases you can search the literature from your home at any time you wish.
- Computer researching is extremely efficient; you can search many more sources in far less time than you could manually.
- Many computerized information sources, such as World Wide Web, discussed below, are hypertext-based and thus allow you to select highlighted terms in a document to go to related documents. Hypermedia-based systems allow you to go not only to additional text but to video or audio material as well.

What other advantages can you identify? What are the disadvantages of researching by computer?

Here are a few examples of databases your college library is likely to have on CD-ROM. All of these databases contain information on the nature and scope of the database and user-friendly directions for searching, displaying, printing, and saving the retrieved information to disk. Many contain examples you can work through to get to know the system and an explanation of the technical terminology used in the database.

America: History and Life   The America: History and Life on Disc database contains citations and abstracts of the major scholarly literature in history. In scope and contents, this on-line source is identical to the print version, *America: History and Life*. This database contains abstracts (approximately 75 to 100 words in length) from more than 2,100 journals in 40 different languages. Approximately 900 of these journals are printed in the United States and Canada. Foreign journals are surveyed for all articles dealing with American history and life. One of the useful features of this database (and various others) is that articles and the commentaries written in response to them are combined so that you can access all the relevant articles at the same time. This database also contains reviews from about 140 mainly U.S. and Canadian journals as well as reviews of works on microfilm, film, and video.

Psychlit and Sociofile   The Psychlit and Sociofile databases are similar in format and so can be considered together. Psychlit is a database of citations from approximately 1,300 journals in psychology and related fields in 27 languages published in some 50 different countries. Sociofile is the sociological counterpart and contains citations from about 1,600 journals in sociology and related fields in 30 different languages published in approximately 55 countries.

Both databases also contain citations for books, book chapters, and dissertations of psychological and sociological relevance. Abstracts of around 250 words are provided for each article or book.

Medline   The Medline database is the computerized version of *Index Medicus*, the *Index to Dental Literature*, and the *International Nursing Index*; it is the National Library of Medicine's bibliographic database, the definitive source in the United States for biomedical literature. This database is enormous and contains citations from over 3,700 journals "selected for inclusion because of their importance to health professions." The index is international in scope; 75 percent of the citations are published in English. Medline covers such categories as anatomy, diseases, chemicals, drugs, equipment, psychiatry, biological sciences, information science and communications, and health care. Articles since 1975 contain abstracts of about 250 words.

You can also limit your search to, for example, an abridged index that covers 118 journals in English, dental information, or nursing information. An example from Medline appears in Figure 7.1.

ERIC   Should you be preparing a speech on some topic related to education—bilingualism, school violence, leadership training, teacher preparation, test

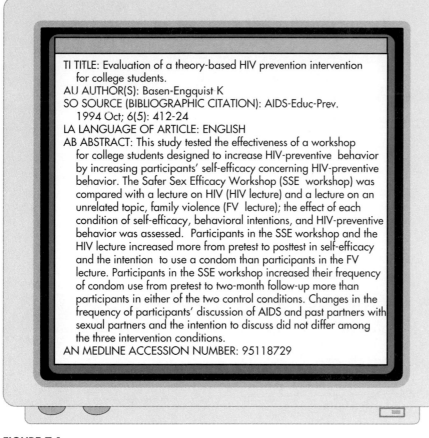

FIGURE 7.1
A sample citation from Medline.

anxiety, communication apprehension, and multiculturalism are a few examples—the Educational Resources Information Center (ERIC) database will prove useful. ERIC is a network of 16 contributing clearinghouses, each of which specializes in a separate subject area. Together they survey more than 750 journals and provide complete citations and abstracts of 200 to 300 words. Further, more than 850 ERIC Digest records containing the full text of the original work are also available. In addition to journal articles, ERIC also includes dissertations, convention papers, books, computer programs, nonprint media, and speeches. A sample citation from ERIC appears in Figure 7.2.

Can you think of speech topics that might effectively use material from all the computerized databases identified here?

The New York Times   The *New York Times* CD-ROM database contains the full editorial content of the *New York Times*, one of the world's most comprehensive newspapers. All aspects of news, sports, editorials, columns, obituaries, New York and regional news, and the *New York Times Book Review* and *Magazine* are included. You can search this database by subject terms, personal names, or company names. Many features also contain brief, 25-word

AN ACCESSION NUMBER: EJ451223
AU PERSONAL AUTHOR: Rancer,-Andrew-S; And-Others
TI TITLE: Beliefs about Arguing as Predictors of Trait
    Argumentativeness:
Implications for Training in Argument and Conflict Management.
PY PUBLICATION YEAR: 1992
JN JOURNAL CITATION: Communication-Education; v41 n4
    p375-87 Oct 1992
AV AVAILABILITY: UMI
AB ABSTRACT: Finds that five composite beliefs about arguing
    (enjoyment, self-concept, pragmatic outcomes, dysfunctional
    outcomes, and ego-involvement) explain significant variance in
    underlying motivation to argue and to discriminate between
    individuals who vary in the predisposition. Discusses implications
    for pedagogy and curriculum design in argumentation and
    conflict management courses. (SR)

FIGURE 7.2
A sample citation from ERIC.

abstracts. A sample entry from the *New York Times* database is included in Figure 7.3.

What one computer database would you find especially useful for your next speech? How would you go about accessing this database?

Other frequently available databases include the Linguistics and Language Behavior Abstracts database, which contains references to studies on language; the Social Science database, which covers the social and behavioral sciences; and the Legal Resource Index, which covers periodicals devoted to law. The LEXIS/NEXIS System allows you to retrieve the complete text of articles from hundreds of newspapers, magazines, journals, and even newsletters, in addition to a wide variety of legal and statutory records.

There is probably an appropriate database for just about any topic you might think of. Once you have selected your topic, you might wish to consult a directory of the available databases to locate the database that would be most appropriate for you. Your library will have directories of the available databases for which access can be secured. In these directories you would discover the particular database containing the subject area you wish to research. Your librarians will be familiar with the various databases; avail yourself of their expertise.

Personal CD-ROMS The CD-ROM databases discussed above are available through libraries, as well as through a variety of private vendors, such as CompuServe, Pipeline, America Online, Delphi, and Prodigy. But there are other CD-ROMs that are much more limited and that you can purchase for your own computer. Comprehensive encyclopedias, as mentioned above, are readily available on CD-ROM as are dictionaries, thesauruses, books of quotations, atlases, almanacs, the *Guinness Book of Records*, and a wide variety of other reference volumes.

Recently, articles appearing in professional academic journals have been made available on CD-ROMs that are regularly being upgraded and expanded and which your college may have. For example, articles appearing in many communication journals are now available on *CommSearch 95* along with a variety of convenient ways to access the material.

These CD-ROMs have the same advantages of speed of access and printing as those you might use in your college library. In addition, many of these contain photos, audio clips, and animations that clarify complex processes. The hypertext-hypermedia feature makes these as enjoyable to use as they are efficient.

The Internet

If you want to access copies of Supreme Court decisions, works of literature, congressional speeches, census statistics, quotations, weather reports, scientific articles, or newspaper reports, or even job listings (see Jandt & Nemnich

Personal CD-ROMs are technically not "on line." Where would you have discussed these sources in this unit?

FIGURE 7.3
A sample citation from the *New York Times* Index.

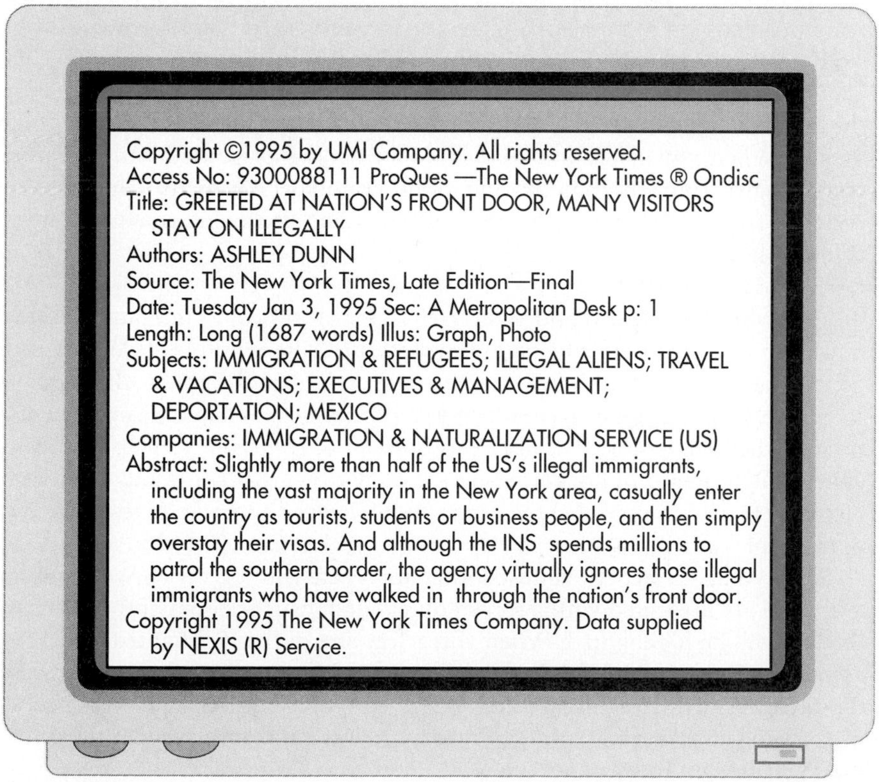

Copyright ©1995 by UMI Company. All rights reserved.
Access No: 9300088111 ProQues —The New York Times ® Ondisc
Title: GREETED AT NATION'S FRONT DOOR, MANY VISITORS
    STAY ON ILLEGALLY
Authors: ASHLEY DUNN
Source: The New York Times, Late Edition—Final
Date: Tuesday Jan 3, 1995 Sec: A Metropolitan Desk p: 1
Length: Long (1687 words) Illus: Graph, Photo
Subjects: IMMIGRATION & REFUGEES; ILLEGAL ALIENS; TRAVEL
    & VACATIONS; EXECUTIVES & MANAGEMENT;
    DEPORTATION; MEXICO
Companies: IMMIGRATION & NATURALIZATION SERVICE (US)
Abstract: Slightly more than half of the US's illegal immigrants,
    including the vast majority in the New York area, casually enter
    the country as tourists, students or business people, and then simply
    overstay their visas. And although the INS spends millions to
    patrol the southern border, the agency virtually ignores those illegal
    immigrants who have walked in through the nation's front door.
Copyright 1995 The New York Times Company. Data supplied
    by NEXIS (R) Service.

1995), or if you simply want to network with others who share your interests, the Internet may be your answer. Your college probably provides you with access to the Internet and e-mail capability.

Because the Internet is so vast and is changing so rapidly (as are the tools or "browsers" that help you find the information you want) this brief section can only give you a glimpse of the potential uses of the Internet for the public speaker. Complement this discussion with a more detailed publication on the Internet—now a major section in the computer area of your bookstore (for example, Campbell 1995, Maloni, Greenman, Miller, & Hearn 1995, Glossbrenner 1995).

Usenet Newsgroups   Currently, there are thousands of "newsgroups" devoted to specific interests (for example, science, social issues, news, talk, recreation, and computers). These are useful for reading news items and letters and papers on a specific topic. You can also save the news items you are particularly interested in to your own file. In addition, you can ask questions and get the opinions of scientists, say, for your next speech on "recent advances in cryonics."

Reading through the FAQ file (frequently asked questions) will help you get the maximum benefit from your Usenet connections. Starting this type of search early will allow you time to receive useful responses. It always seems to take longer than you expect, so build this inevitable time-delay into your research schedule.

Gopherspace   A huge part of the Internet is gopherspace, a kind of file system of information that you can access with a user-friendly (though visually drab) system of menus that become increasingly more specific as you narrow your search. When you log on to Gopher, you are presented with a general menu such as the one in Figure 7.4, which is the Gopher menu for the City University of New York. Note that in addition to a few documents (noted by the word "document" in the left-hand column) the menu consists of other menus. When you select one of these, you will be presented with a screen consisting of some documents and some more specific menu choices. You continue selecting menus or documents depending on the information you are trying to find.

World Wide Web   The World Wide Web is, for most people and purposes, the most valuable and interesting part of the Internet. The World Wide Web is, like gopherspace, a collection of documents but, unlike gopherspace, these documents may include not only words but graphic, video, and audio components. Because the Web is so vast, you need a browser of some sort to help you navigate through the sea of documents to the one or two that you want. Currently, Netscape is the browser of choice and most colleges and universities make use of this tool.

The Web is a hypertext-based system. When you log on to World Wide Web, you are presented with a screen of text and visuals. Some of the terms in the text will be highlighted. When you select one of the highlighted terms (or some visual), you will be shifted to a document dealing with that concept. By repeatedly selecting highlighted terms, you will move around the Web, probably pausing at numerous points of interest as you make your way to the information you want for your speech.

What information might you find on the Internet that would be of value to your next speech?

Like cultures and small work groups and teams, newsgroups have their own system of etiquette—"netiquette"—that users are expected to follow. What are some of these rules?

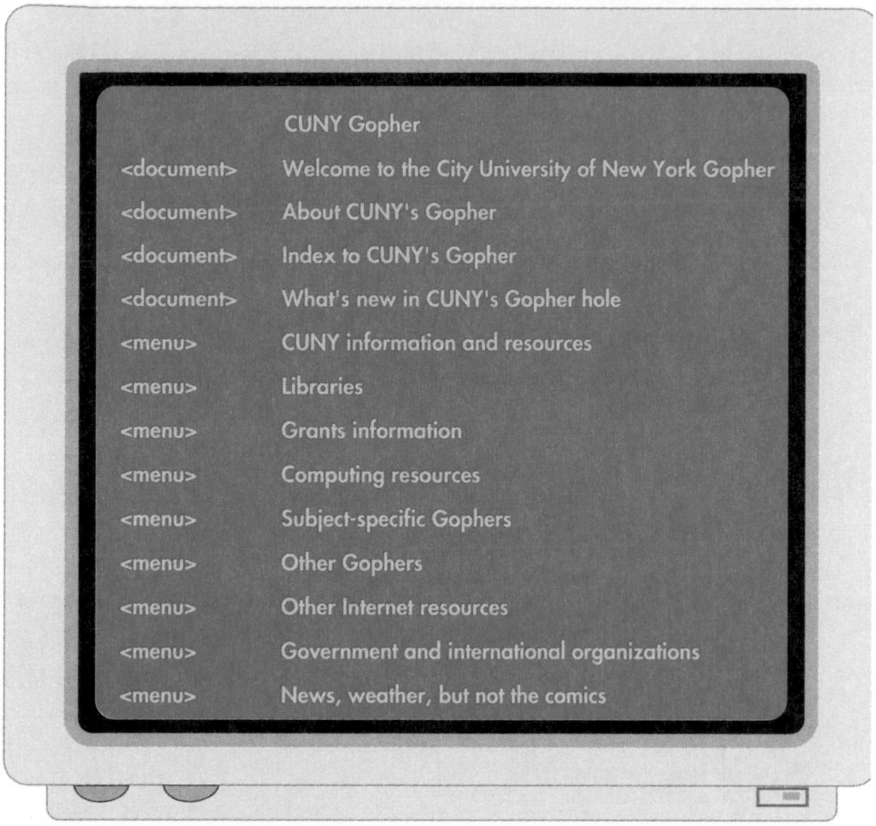

FIGURE 7.4
A sample Gopher menu.

Many colleges and academic organizations generally, business and government organizations, and interest groups of all kinds are establishing Web sites. You've probably noticed that Internet addresses are increasingly appearing in print and television advertisements. These addresses invite you to visit their Web site and read their varied materials. A sample Web site home page appears in Figure 7.5.

Table 7.1 provides a variety of Internet addresses to get you started using this vast resource for your speeches.

One of the great advantages of Netscape and other browsers, especially for the researching public speaker, is its abundance of searching instruments—tools for finding exactly the right information quickly and easily. If you don't know the address of the source you want to reach or don't know what source contains the information you want, these tools will prove invaluable. Yahoo, EINet Galaxy, Lycos, and WebCrawler are just a few of the many tools that will help you locate just the right documents out of literally millions of other documents by simply typing your topic.

E-mail E-mail (electronic mail) is similar to regular mail in many ways and yet it is more convenient, faster, and in many cases less expensive. E-mail, however, is especially helpful in securing information. For example, you can

Another part and one of the older parts of the Internet are FTP sites, which contain shareware and freeware software, graphics, and text files that can be assessed and downloaded. Try accessing an FTP site. Try, for example, *Oak.oakland.edu, rtfm.mit.edu,* or *ftp.csd.uwm.edu* (suggestions from Grossbrenner 1995). What is one useful thing about the Internet that might be of value to the researching public speaker?

FIGURE 7.5
A sample World Wide Web page. By typing the Internet address, you would be able to retrieve this page on your computer screen. You would then be able to move through this site by selecting any of the highlighted words.

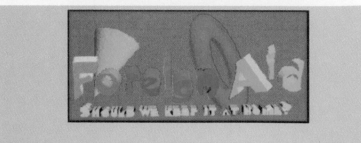

Foreign Aid: Should We Keep It At Home?

We are a group of first year English composition students instructed by Tonya Browning at The University of Texas at Austin. Our project concerns the United States and its involvement in providing foreign assistance to underprivileged nations. This presentation examines both sides of the debate regarding foreign aid to other countries.

The Drawbacks of U.S. Foreign Assistance

The United States sends billions of dollars in supplies, labor, and actual funds to other countries each year. Even though we are experiencing record unemployment, increased racial tension, skyrocketing infant mortality rates, woeful underfunding of education, crumbling infrastructure and a record budget deficit that will probably mortgage our grandchildren's grandchildren, we are still sending the taxpayer's hard earned money to countries thousands of miles away. The question remains: if the government has billions of dollars to spend on these other countries, then why are Americans suffering at home? These funds need to stay in our own country to help fight these domestic problems. Not only should we keep this money at home, but United States officials need to consider reallocation of current funds.

The Advantages of U.S. Foreign Assistance

There are a number of reasons why foreign assistance programs are a sound investment for the future of the United States. First and foremost, they help the US economically while insuring global stability. In addition, trading partners are gained, strategic allies are secured, and democracies are fostered around the world. Humanitarian acts also play a substantial role in the intervenment of the US because the welfare of the underdeveloped is advanced. Hence, the advantages to solid foreign aid programs benefit not only the US, but the impoverished countries as well. Most importantly, it is through foreign aid and the compassion of the American people, that peace and prosperity are allowed to advance around the globe.

TABLE 7.1   Some Internet Sites for the Researching Public Speaker

This table lists a range of Internet sites that you can visit to secure (in many cases) authoritative and up-to-the-minute information for a variety of speech topics. The list here is designed to suggest a few generally useful sites (quotations, dictionaries, and speeches, for example) but also to give you an idea of the tremendous range of more specific topics you can access on the Internet.

Research Applications	Internet Address
Quotations (from *Bartlett's*) for just about any topic or purpose	www.cc.columbia.edu/acis/bartleby/bartlett/
Identifies the newest and best sites on the web	gnn.com/gnn/wn/whats-new.html
News	
Associated Press	www.trib.com/NEWS/Apwire.html
Telecommunications news	wtn.com/wtn/wtn.html
News and information from CNN	www.nmis.org/NewsInteractive/CNN/Newsroom/contents.html
Lists the sites especially useful to journalists and public speakers	gopher://gopher.tamu.edu:70/11/.dir/journalism.dir
A wide variety of dictionaries, including English-to-German [French, Japanese, and Russian], technical, and popular dictionaries	gopher://gopher.uiuc.edu
A wide variety of reference books including almanacs, the *King James Bible,* and the 1990 census	http://jg.cso.uiuc.edu/pg/lists/subjects2.html
Historical documents and speeches	gopher://dewey.lib.ncsu.edu:70/11/library/stacks/historical-documents-US
Congressional Record, Federal Register, and lots more	htpp://www.law.csuohio.edu
Extensive law library	www.law.indiana.edu/law/lawindex.html
Information on health and sickness	www.cdc.gov
	www-hsl.mcmaster.ca/tomflem/top.html
	www.mayo.edu/
Supreme Court cases, decisions, and more	www.law.cornell.edu/supct/supct.table.html
Wide variety of education issues	www.ed.gov
Information on a broad range of ecological issues	www.ecology.com/
A vast human rights database	www.law.uc.edu/Diana/
Connections to sources of information on international trade	http://www.helsinki.fi:80/~lsaarine/internat.html
A wide variety of business information	http://www.helsinki.fi:80/~lsaarine/ssbusg.html
Best place to start for issues geographical	http://hpb1.hwc.ca:10002/www_VL_Geography.html
Starting place for accessing a number of presidential libraries	http:www.yahoo.com/Reference/Libraries/Presidential-Libraries
Clearinghouse for public policy information appearing on the Internet	http://info.heinz/cmu.edu
The great documents on freedom, including Aristotle's *Politics* and the U.S. Bill of Rights	http://nw.com/jamesd

Continued

TABLE 7.1	Continued	
Research Applications		**Internet Address**
The FBI's site for information on law enforcement, counterintelligence, and more		http://naic.nasa.gov/fbi/
Provides links to UN information on the Internet		http://www.undcp.org/unlinks.html
Reference sources for researching a wide variety of religions		gopher://chico.rice.edu:70/11/Subject/RelPhil
Links to resources on economics		gopher://una.hh.lib.umich.edu/11/ebb

write to people doing research in an area you're interested in, government officials, business organizations, and students in other universities quickly and easily through e-mail. You are also more likely to get a quick response when you use e-mail. E-mail addresses, like Web addresses, are becoming more easily available and are often included in books, articles, directories of professional organizations and, of course, in e-mail phone books.

You can also join mailing lists and receive messages from other members. By subscribing to a mailing list that focuses on your public speaking topic, you'll likely receive lots of interesting and relevant material (and probably much that is uninteresting and irrelevant). You can always unsubscribe when you want to move on to other topics or your interests change.

THE RESEARCH INTERVIEW

Earlier we noted that among the best sources of information are the experts. Here are some suggestions to make your dealing with the experts more productive and efficient.

Select the Person You Wish to Interview

Let us say you wish to speak on family therapy. You look through your college catalog and find that a course in family communication is offered by Professor Bernard Brommel. You think it might be worthwhile to interview him. You are now on your first step; you've selected one of the people you hope to interview. But don't stop there. Before you pursue the interview, try to learn something about this instructor. Has the instructor written a book or articles in the field? If so, use your research skills to track these down.

Secure an Appointment

Phone the instructor or send a letter requesting an interview. In your call or letter, identify the purpose of your request and state that you would like a brief

---

TIPS
From Professional Speakers

It's amazing how many people pose question after question in their conversations, as if they were rhetorical, and never pause for an answer. When you ask a question and then rush ahead with an answer yourself or move on to the next topic, the other person notices the pattern and decides you don't intend to take any answer seriously. Nervousness also plays a big part in someone's talking right through where the pauses should go. Be aware of that habit; ask, pause, wait.

Dianna Booher, business communications consultant and author and president of Booher Consultants. *Communicate with Confidence: How to Say It Right the First Time* (New York: McGraw-Hill, 1994), p. 169.

interview. For example, you might say, "I'm preparing a speech on family therapy and would appreciate it if I could interview you to learn more about the subject. The interview would take about 15 minutes." (This time limitation helps, since Brommel now knows it will not take very long and is more likely to agree to being interviewed.) Generally, it is best to be available at the interviewee's convenience, so indicate flexibility on your part—for example, "I can interview you any day after 12:00 P.M."

For what topics would you consider the following sources credible? Sally Jesse Raphael, a textbook in American history, the National Organization for Women, and the astrology column in your local newspaper.

Prepare Your Questions

Prepare in advance the questions you wish to ask. This will ensure that you use the time available to your best advantage. Of course, as the interview progresses other questions will come to mind and should be asked. But having a prepared list of questions will help you feel more relaxed and will help you most easily obtain the information you need.

Throughout the interview, be especially alert to nonverbal cues that tell you the interviewee wishes to say more (so avoid interrupting) or that he or she has finished and you should go on to another question. Try to avoid cutting short the interviewee's discussion but at the same time try to avoid awkward and prolonged silences.

Who might you realistically interview (given your present location, resources, time limitations, and so forth) on the following topics: marital problems faced by young couples, gay and lesbian rights, bias crimes, modern art, religion, and politics?

Arrive on Time

Attitudes toward time, promptness, and lateness vary greatly from culture to culture. It is important to know that these attitudes are extremely important; to one who values promptness, lateness in others is rarely tolerated or excused. Arriving on time will thus enable you both to make the right impression and to use the time set aside to your advantage. It will also demonstrate your seriousness of purpose.

Establish Rapport with the Interviewee

Open the interview with an expression of thanks for making the time available to you and again state your purpose. Many people receive lots of requests and it helps if you remind the person of your purpose. You might say something like this: "I really appreciate your making time for this interview. As I mentioned, I'm preparing a speech on family therapy, and your expertise and experience in this area will help a great deal."

Ask for Permission to Tape the Interview

Generally, it is a good idea to tape the interview. Taping will enable you to focus your total attention on the interview and will eliminate your worry about taking notes and having to ask the interviewee to slow down or repeat. It will also provide you with a much more accurate record of the interview than handwritten notes will. But ask permission first. Some people prefer not to have informal interviews taped. Even if the interview is being conducted by phone, ask permission if you intend to tape the conversation.

TIPS
From Professional Speakers

Requesting a fact limits a person's thinking. He or she generally answers with the fact and grows silent again. If you want to have the person expand so that you can gather a wide range of information and impressions, suggest a topic rather than ask a question: "Tell me what you think about the way the President is handling the economy." "What do you know about nuclear energy—have you given it any thought for heating your home?" "How about employee morale around here?"

Dianna Booher, business communications consultant and author and president of Booher Consultants. *Communicate with Confidence: How to Say It Right the First Time* (New York: McGraw-Hill, 1994), pp. 168–169.

Ask Open-Ended and Neutral Questions

Use questions that provide the interviewee with room to discuss the issues you want to raise. Thus, instead of asking, "Do you have formal training in the area of family therapy?" (a question that requires a simple yes or no and is unlikely to yield a very informative response), you might ask, "Can you tell me something of your background in this field?" (a question that is open-ended and allows the interviewee to tell you about his or her background).

Ask questions phrased in a neutral manner. Try not to lead the interviewee to give you answers you want. Asking, "What do you think of the administration's recent policy?" gives the interviewee free range and does not bias the answer, as would, for example, "What problems do you think the administration's recent policy is likely to create?"

Close the Interview with a Note of Appreciation

Thank the person for making the time available for the interview and for being informative, cooperative, helpful, or whatever. In short, let the person know that you do in fact appreciate the effort made to help you with your speech. On the more practical side, this will also make it a great deal easier if you want to return for a second interview.

Follow Up on the Interview

Follow up on the interview with a brief note of thanks. Or you might send the person you interviewed a copy of your speech, again with a note of thanks for the help.

CRITICALLY EVALUATING RESEARCH

Collecting research materials is only part of the process; the other part is critically evaluating them. Although evaluating specific amplifying materials and arguments is discussed in later units (see Units 14 and 17, for example), some general questions to ask of all researched information are suggested here.

1. *Is the information recent?* Generally, the more recent the material, the more useful it will be. With some topics—for example, unemployment statistics, developments in AIDS research, and tuition costs—the recency of the information is crucial to its usefulness. Check your figures in a recent almanac or newspaper.

2. *Is the information fair and unbiased?* Bias is not easy to determine, but try to examine any sources of potential bias. Obvious examples come quickly to mind: cigarette manufacturers' statements on the health risks from smoking; newspaper and network editorials on the fairness of news reporting; and the National Rifle Association's arguments against gun control. But other examples are not so easy to see as potentially biased. Try checking the credibility of your

In critically evaluating research, what other issues should you consider (in addition to recency, bias, relevance, and sufficiency)?

sources in a biographical dictionary or in relevant newspaper articles. Look at your sources to see if they represent all sides of an issue. If, for example, all your information comes from liberal publications or from conservative publications, then your arguments are likely to be biased. Try securing information from a wide range of positions.

3. *Is the information directly relevant to your topic and purpose?* An interesting quotation or a startling statistic is useful only if it relates directly to the point you wish to make. Avoid including information solely because of its interest value; make sure that all your information relates directly to issues you wish to discuss.

4. *Is the information sufficient?* Ask yourself if the collected information is sufficient to illustrate your point, to prove that one proposal is better than another, or to show why your system will work better than the existing system. The opinion of one dietitian is insufficient to support the usefulness of a particular diet; the statistics from five private colleges on tuition increases are insufficient to illustrate national trends in rising tuition costs.

Always ask these questions with your specific audience in mind. Remember that you are collecting, evaluating, and communicating this information because you want to achieve some effect on your audience.

Can you find examples from recent advertising that violate the principles for evaluating research discussed here?

INTEGRATING RESEARCH INTO YOUR SPEECH

Now that you have amassed this wealth of research material, how do you integrate it into your speech? Here are a few suggestions.

Mention the sources in your speech by citing at least the author and, if helpful, the publication and date. Here is how C. Kenneth Orski (1986) did it:

> *In assessing what the future may hold for transportation, I will lean heavily on a technique pioneered by John Naisbitt, author of* Megatrends. *Naisbitt believes that the most reliable way to anticipate the future is to try to understand the present. To this end he methodologically scans 6000 daily local newspapers from around the country.*

Provide smooth transitions between your words and the words of the author you're citing. In this excerpt Marilyn Loden (1986) does this most effectively:

> *In his book,* Leadership, *James MacGregor Burns advocates new leadership styles which encourage employees to take more risk, to be more self-reliant and manage more creatively. He calls this new management approach "transformational leadership."*

Avoid such useless expressions as "I have a quote here" or "I want to quote an example." Let the audience know that you are quoting by pausing before

F OCUS **O** N

Plagiarism and How to Avoid It

Plagiarism is committed when you use material from another source without properly crediting it. There are a number of forms this can take:

Using the exact words of another person. If you are going to use another person's exact words, then cite them exactly as written or spoken and credit the source.

For example, in a speech on nonverbal communication in different cultures, you might say something like this:

> According to Roger Axtell, in his *Gestures: The Do's and Taboos of Body Language Around the World*, touching varies from one culture to another. Axtell says, for example, "In the Middle East, two Arab male friends may even be seen walking down the street hand-in-hand and all it signifies is friendship."

In your outline give the full bibliographic reference, just as you would in a history paper. Be sure you use quotation marks for any citation in which you use the person's exact words, just as you would in a written essay.

And make it clear to your listeners that you are using the person's exact words, as was done in the example above. You can do this by changing your inflection, stepping forward, or reading the specific words from your notes. In this way the audience knows the exact words belong to someone else.

Using the ideas of another person. Even if you are not quoting directly, you still have to acknowledge your source if you are using the ideas, arguments, insights, or examples taken from another source.

If you are using the ideas of another, simply acknowledge this in your speech and in any written materials, such as an outline. Much as readers of an essay have the right to know where your arguments or data came from, so do listeners. Therefore, weave into your speech the sources of your materials. Do this with subtlety and without disturbing the natural flow and rhythm of your speech. Here are a few examples:

- A recent article in *Time* magazine noted that . . .
- Professor Fox, in her lecture last week on Western Civilization, argued that . . .
- This week Nielsen reported that the number of homes with color televisions . . .

Follow the same rules for crediting sources as you would in writing term papers. And just as you would be guilty of plagiarism if you didn't cite the sources in your history paper, so too would you be guilty of plagiarism if you didn't credit your sources in your speech.

Using the organizational structure of another. Even if you are "only" following the organizational structure of another source, you need to acknowledge your indebtedness to this other source. In such cases you can say something like this:

- Here I'm following the arguments given by Professor Marishu in her lecture on culture and racism.
- This pattern for explaining how a car is designed comes from the work of Edward Frid in his new book, *Designing a Car*.

the quote, taking a step forward, or referring to your notes to read the extended quotation. Marilyn Loden (1986) again does this effectively:

> *Mary Kay Ash believes in feminine leadership. Recently she said: "A woman can no more duplicate the male style of leadership than an American businessman can exactly reproduce the Japanese style."*

If you feel it is crucial that the audience know you are quoting and you want to state that this is a quotation, you might do it this way:

> *Recently, Mary Kay Ash put this in perspective, and I quote: "A woman can no more duplicate the male style of leadership . . ."*

Be sure to credit the sources of information derived from personal interviews or from the Internet with as much fidelity as you do with journal articles or books. Include these sources in your speech, as illustrated above, and in the list of references following the speech.

By integrating and acknowledging your sources of information in the speech, you will give fair credit to those whose ideas and statements you are using and at the same time you will help establish your own reputation as a responsible researcher.

UNIT IN BRIEF

General principles of research	■ Examine what you know
	■ Work from the general to the specific
	■ Take accurate notes
	■ Use research time effectively
	■ Learn the available sources of information

Sources for research	■ Experts
	■ Catalogs
	■ Encyclopedias
	■ Biographical materials
	■ Newspaper, magazine, and journal indexes and abstracts
	■ Almanacs
	■ Government publications

Researching on-line	■ America: History and Life
	■ Psychlit and Sociofile
	■ Medline
	■ ERIC

	■ The New York Times
	■ Personal CD-ROMS
	■ The Internet
	■ Usenet newsgroups
	■ Gopherspace
	■ World Wide Web
	■ E-mail
Research interview	■ Select the person
	■ Secure an appointment
	■ Prepare questions
	■ Arrive on time
	■ Establish rapport
	■ Ask permission to tape
	■ Ask open-ended and neutral questions
	■ Close with appreciation
	■ Follow up the interview
Critically evaluating research	■ Is the information recent?
	■ Is the information fair and unbiased?
	■ Is the information directly relevant to your topic?
	■ Is the information sufficient?
Integrating research into your speech	■ Mention your sources
	■ Credit your sources for exact words as well as for ideas (to avoid even the suspicion of plagiarism)
	■ Provide smooth transitions between your words and the words of others

PRACTICALLY SPEAKING

Short Speech Technique

Prepare and deliver a one- to two-minute speech in which you:

1. explain the value for research of one reference book
2. explain one computer program that will prove helpful in research
3. explain an advertisement that is reportedly based on research and evaluate the research
4. explain how you used either one of the computerized databases discussed in this unit or some other database

7.1   Accessing Information

In order to gain some familiarity with the various ways of locating information, select one of the following questions and then report back to the class on both the answer and the reference sources you used to find it. In discussing how you found the answer, mention unproductive as well as productive sources you consulted. If you feel especially ambitious, try finding answers to these questions in two, three, or four different sources.

1. What does the Japanese flag look like?
2. What is the population of Nebraska?
3. What is the age of the president of the United States?
4. What are the ingredients of a Harvey Wallbanger?
5. What was the first capital of the United States?
6. Who is the current president of the Speech Communication Association, the American Psychological Association, or the International Communication Association?
7. What is the world's largest library? How many volumes does it contain?
8. Who won the Academy Award in 1952 for best director?
9. What is the literacy rate for China?
10. What are the main languages of Cambodia?
11. What is the prime interest rate for today?
12. What is the faculty-student ratio for Harvard?
13. What is the largest amount of money grossed by a film?
14. What were the profits or losses for IBM last year?
15. Who is the author of the quotation "Though it be honest, it is never good to bring bad news"?
16. What was the birthplace and real name of John Wayne?
17. What is the full name of the journals usually abbreviated *QJS, JC, CM,* and *CE*?
18. What is the use and origin of the word *meathead*?
19. What did John Travolta do before starring in films?
20. How many votes did Stephen Douglas receive from Illinois in the Lincoln-Douglas presidential election of 1860?
21. What is the text of John Kennedy's "Inaugural Address"?
22. What is the political configuration of Europe today?
23. What is the graduate program in communication at the University of Illinois like?
24. How much is the tuition at Brown University?
25. How much does it cost for a full-page, four-color advertisement in *Reader's Digest*?
26. Who were the major figures in the Hudson River school of painting?
27. What are the rules for playing chess?
28. Where are the texts of contemporary speeches on U.S. energy problems?
29. What were the major contributions of psychologist B. F. Skinner?
30. What is the political history of one of your state's senators?
31. What are the major principles and beliefs of Islam?
32. What is the history of the Boy Scouts in Canada?
33. Who said "My only love sprung from my only hate"?

34. What is the title of the Ph.D. dissertation of someone teaching at your school?
35. Where can the psychological studies on "learned helplessness" be found?

7.2   Researching On-Line

This exercise is designed to illustrate the wide variety of information you can easily secure from computer searches and to provide the opportunity for exploring your on-line sources. Look up and bring to class a copy of an abstract for one of the following:

- An article on public speaking that appears in the ERIC database for the last five years
- An article on a psychological study of fear—from the Psychlit database
- An article on persuasion from the Sociofile database
- An article appearing in the *Quarterly Journal of Speech*, *Communication Monographs*, or *Communication Education* that is of some interest to you
- An article from a business journal dealing with communication skills
- An article from the *New York Times* on college education
- An article on diabetes from Medline
- An article on divorce from any database
- An article on immigration patterns during the last 20 years from America: History and Life
- A review of a novel published in the last two years

UNIT 8

Amplifying Materials

Unit Objectives

After completing this unit, you should be able to:

 Explain the nature of examples, narration, testimony, and statistics as forms of amplification

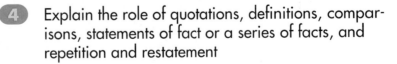 Explain the suggestions for critically evaluating examples, narration, testimony, and statistics

Explain the suggestions for using examples, narration, testimony, and statistics

Explain the role of quotations, definitions, comparisons, statements of fact or a series of facts, and repetition and restatement

*O*nce you have identified your specific purpose and your main assertions and know where and how to search for information, devote your attention to supporting or amplifying your assertions. Here we look at how to use examples, narration, testimony, and statistics, as well as such materials as quotations, definitions, comparisons, statements of fact, and repetition and restatement.

EXAMPLES

Examples are specific instances that are explained in varying degrees of detail. A relatively brief specific instance is referred to as an example. A longer, more detailed example is referred to as an illustration, while one told in storylike form is referred to as a narration, which is covered in the next section.

Examples are useful when you wish to make an abstract concept or idea concrete. For instance, it is difficult for the audience to see exactly what you mean by such abstract concepts as "persecution," "denial of freedom," "love," and "friendship" unless you provide specific examples. Your examples also encourage listeners to see *your* mental pictures of these concepts rather than seeing their own.

In a speech on lead poisoning, Brenda Dempsey (Boaz and Brey 1988), a student from Eastern Michigan University, uses a specific example to stress the importance of her topic:

> When Denise Waddle and her family moved to a nice, middle-class section of Jersey City, New Jersey, they had dreams of healthy living, block parties, even a big backyard so their kids could make mud pies. In less than one year in their new home, their two-year-old son had been poisoned, and their newborn showed high levels of poisoning in his bloodstream. Unknowingly, the Waddles had been poisoned by their own backyard, for high levels of lead contaminated their water, and their lives.

Here Carol W. Kinsley (1994, p. 41) uses an example to explain what community service learning is:

> One of Michelle Herbert's recent projects at Liberty School involved her fifth-grade writing class in visits to a retirement home. They acted as pen-pals, writing letters, drawing pictures, and relating their own experiences to the residents. They also corresponded with the residents via computer e-mail. As part of their experience, they recorded their impressions and reflections in a journal after every session.

What kind of example might you use to explain the feeling of love? Loneliness? Joy? Sadness? Poverty? Excellence of mind? Physical strength?

Critically Evaluating Examples

Ask yourself (as speaker, listener, and critic) the following questions about examples.

1. *Is the example typical or representative?* Generally, use an example that is representative of the class of objects about which you are speaking. Training

schools that advertise on television frequently show a particularly successful graduate. The advertiser assumes, of course, that the audience will see this example as representative. Perhaps this person is representative; more often than not, however, representativeness is not achieved or perhaps even desired by the advertiser.

At times you may want to draw an example that is purposefully far-fetched. Perhaps you wish to poke fun at a particular proposal or show the inadequacies of an alternative point of view. The important point is that both you and the audience see the example in the same way.

2. *Is the example relevant?* Use examples that relate directly to the proposition you wish to explain. Leave out irrelevant examples, however interesting or entertaining. Be certain too that the audience sees the relevance. Notice how Marvin Alisky (1985) uses his example to make his point:

> *In his play* Pygmalion, *George Bernard Shaw observes, "If you treat a girl like a flower girl, that's all she will ever be. If you treat her like a princess she may become one."*
>
> *If we treat those around us like extensions of our modern technology, that is all they will be. If we treat them like important assets with individual and changing needs, then they will become assets to our organizations and communities.*

Specific examples are often the part of the speech an audience remembers longest and most clearly. Can you develop a specific example for one of the following propositions? (1) Television sitcoms present an absurd view (a realistic view, an idealized view) of life; (2) unwed teenagers who have children are (not) doing the children and the country a service; (3) court TV should be eliminated (expanded); (4) computer literacy should (not) be a requirement for high school graduation.

Using Examples

In using examples, keep in mind that their function is to make your ideas vivid and easily understood. They are useful for explaining a concept; they are not ends in themselves. Make them only as long as necessary to ensure that your purpose is achieved.

Use enough examples to make your point. Make sure that the examples are sufficient to re-create your meaning in the minds of your listeners, but be careful not to use too many. If you use too many examples, the audience may become bored and lose the very point you wish to make.

Make the relationship between your assertion and your example explicit. Remember that this relationship is clear to you because you have constructed the speech. The audience is going to hear your speech only once. Show the audience exactly how your example relates to the assertion or concept you are explaining. Consider the following excerpt, in which Stella Guerra (1986) uses a series of examples to illustrate the progress made by women in government and the military. Notice how much more effective these examples are than if she had simply said, "Women have made great progress in government and in the military."

> In short, we are continuing to help America forge an environment that says "opportunities are abundant." In this environment of prosperity we've seen many firsts:
> - The first female brigadier general
> - The first female astronaut
> - The first female sky marshal
> - The first female ambassador to the United Nations
> - The first female justice of the Supreme Court
> - The first female director of Civil Service
> - The first female U.S. Customs rep in a foreign country
> - The first female to graduate at the very top of the class in a service academy—Navy '84; Air Force '86
>
> The list goes on and on—and this same progress can be seen in all sectors of our society.

Make clear the distinction between real and hypothetical examples. Do not try to make your audience believe that a hypothetical example is a real one. If they recognize it, they will resent your attempt to fool them. Use statements such as the following to let the audience know when you are using a hypothetical example:

> We could imagine a situation such as . . .
>
> I think an ideal friend would be someone who . . .
>
> A hypothetical example of this type of friendship would be like this.

If the example is real, let the audience know this as well. Help the audience to see what you want them to see with such statements as "A situation like this occurred recently; it involved . . . ," "I have a friend who . . . ," or simply "An actual example of this was reported . . . "

How effectively do your instructors use examples? What suggestions for improvement might you offer?

▬ NARRATION

Narratives are stories and are often useful as supporting materials in a speech. Narratives give the audience what it wants: a good story. Narration helps you maintain attention, since listeners seem automatically to perk up when a story is told. If the narrative is a personal one, then it is likely to increase your credibility and show you as a real person. Listeners like to know about speakers, and the personal narrative meets this desire. Notice how you remember the little stories noted personalities tell in television interviews.

The main value of narration is that it allows you to bring an abstract concept down to specifics. For example, the mythical story of Damon and Pythias, who were each willing to die for the other, illustrates friendship and love in a way a definition could never do.

Narratives can be of different types, and each serves a somewhat different purpose. Following Celia Jaffe (1995) we identify three types: explanatory, exemplary, and persuasive.

Explanatory narratives explain the way things are. The biblical book of Genesis, for example, explains the development of the world. In the following excerpt Jamie Lee Wagner (Schnoor, 1994, p. 7), a student from Arizona State University, uses an explanatory narrative to introduce her topic, sleep deprivation:

On September 9, 1993, a Greyhound bus bound for my hometown of Phoenix, Arizona, swerved off the road and flipped over. The accident injured 42 of the passengers, including David Mata, who was forced to have both of his hands amputated. The driver, the man responsible for the passengers' safety, had fallen asleep behind the wheel. And he was just one of the 100 million Americans who suffer from sleep deprivation, ranging in severity from occasional jet lag to chronic insomnia.

Exemplary narratives provide examples of excellence, examples to follow or admire. The stories of the lives of saints and martyrs are exemplary narratives, as are the Horatio Alger success stories. Similarly, many motivational speakers such as Susan Powter and Tony Little often include exemplary narratives in their speeches and will tell the story of how they were when they were out of shape. Here, for example, is just a part of a narrative used by Kathleen B. Cooper (1994, p. 85), chief economist for Exxon Corporation:

My story began like many others: I married early—after only one year of college. And I headed off to work to "put hubby through" doing clerical work, as was also so common then. What happened to get me back on the road to finish college? One extraordinarily boring job experience. It made me realize that I would probably work for most or all of my life, and I did not want to go through life without enjoying my work.

Persuasive narratives try to strengthen or change beliefs and attitudes. When Sally Struthers tells us of the plight of starving children, she's using a persuasive narrative. The parables in religious writings are persuasive in their urging listeners to lead life in a particular way. Here Richard A. Gephardt

TIPS

From Professional Speakers

It is easy to forget an idea, but stories, especially if they make your audiences laugh or cry, are very difficult to forget. Stories make the audience feel that these points and concepts you are teaching are universal because they are true experiences. The listeners feel, "Well, if it happened to 'them' and 'they' are not only OK but doing very well, I guess I can cope too." An illustration is easy for the audience to follow and can fit into various time limits.

Lilly Walters, director of Walters International Speakers Bureau, a professional lecture agency. *Secrets of Successful Speakers: How You Can Motivate, Captivate, and Persuade* (New York: McGraw-Hill, 1993), pp. 79–80.

Did you acquire any of your cultural beliefs through narratives? If so, what types of narratives were they? Who told them? At what times were they told?

(1995, p. 199), Missouri congressman, uses a persuasive narrative to emphasize the importance of economic recovery:

> *A few weeks ago, I met a man in Jefferson Country, Missouri, who had lost his job, and couldn't find a way of earn a living. His economic crisis shattered his marriage, as well as his self-confidence. He had loaded all of his worldly possessions into his car, and was headed down the road to nowhere.*
>
> *He looked at me with tears in his eyes, and said: "They took away more than my paycheck. They took away my pride. And that was all I had left to give."*
>
> *Your job is more than what you do—it's who you are. It's your identity.*

Often, the same narrative can serve a variety of functions. For example, consider the story from Greek mythology of Narcissus, the beautiful boy who so admired himself that he ignored the advances of the nymph Echo and wanted only to stare at and admire his own reflection in a lake. As a result of his total self-absorption, he fell into the lake and was "reborn" as the narcissus flower. The story is explanatory because it explains the myth of how the narcissus flower developed; it is exemplary because it portrays the evil that befalls a narcissistic personality; and it is persuasive because of its obvious injunction: Don't be so self-absorbed.

Narratives can be first-person or third-person accounts. In first-person narratives the speaker tells a story that happened to her or him. Kathleen Cooper's narrative, given earlier, is a good example. In third-person narrative the speaker tells a story about someone else—a parent deciding to give up a child to adoption, a person experiencing his or her first day in the military, a family undergoing conflict. Wagner's and Gephardt's accounts, given earlier, are good examples of third-person narratives.

Critically Evaluating Narratives

Like examples, narratives need to be assessed critically.

1. *Is the narrative relevant?* If the narrative is not relevant to the speech purpose, then it should not be used. Regardless of how humorous, heart-wrenching, or instructive the story is, use it only if it supports your purpose.

2. *Is the narrative presented fairly?* Although narratives are commonly thought of as true, narratives can be hypothetical or they can be composites of a variety of stories. Novelists, for example, often combine the lives of numerous people into one character. Regardless of the type of narrative you use, it should be clear to your audience when your story is real, when it is hypothetical, and when it is a composite drawn for purposes of illustration.

Using Narratives

Keep your narratives relatively short and few in number. In most cases, one or possibly two narratives are sufficient in a short, five- to seven-minute speech. Especially if the narrative is a personal one, be sure you don't get carried away

Can you create a narrative about some personal incident and connect it to a potential speech purpose?

and elaborate more than necessary. There are, of course, exceptions—such as in Kathleen Cooper's speech, where a large portion of the speech is devoted to personal narrative.

Maintain a reasonable chronological order. Events happen in time and are best recounted in a time sequence. Avoid shifting back and forth through time. Start at the beginning and end at the end.

Make explicit the connection between your story and the point you are making. Be sure the audience will see the connection between the story and the purpose of your speech. If they don't, you will lose not only the effectiveness of the story but also their attention as they try to figure out why you told it.

Consider using a climax order, in which you build to a high point. If possible, create suspense. If you do, your audience is likely to pay you greater attention than normal.

Use dialogue only if you can carry it off. Be especially careful of speaking in the dialogue of a person who is very different form you—say, someone of the opposite sex or of another race. You can easily revert to stereotypes or what can easily be perceived as stereotyping. The man who recites the dialogue of a frail woman and who raises his pitch too high or uses too many facial expressions may easily create a humorous effect. Generally, dialogues are easier to incorporate into your speech if the person is like you. And, with perhaps only the rarest of exceptions, avoid using foreign accents.

TESTIMONY

Testimony refers to the opinions of experts or to the accounts of witnesses. Testimony helps to amplify your speech by adding a note of authority to your arguments. Testimony may therefore be used in either of two ways. First, you might be concerned with the opinions, beliefs, predictions, or values of some authority or expert. You might, for example, want to state an economist's predictions concerning inflation and depression, or you might want to support your analysis by citing an art critic's evaluation of a painting or art movement.

As you might think, testimony is also of value when you wish to persuade an audience. Thus, you might want to use the testimony of a noted economist to support your predictions about inflation, or you might wish to cite an education professor's opinion about the problems confronting education in an effort to persuade your listeners that certain changes must be made in our schools.

In the following excerpt, for instance, former U.S. Congresswoman Shirley Chisholm (1978) addresses the Independent Black Women's Caucus of New York City and uses the testimony of noted psychologist Rollo May to bolster her argument that African American women must assume political power rather than wait for it to be given:

> As Rollo May has put it: "Power cannot, strictly speaking, be given to *another, for then the recipient still owes it to the giver. It must in some sense be assumed, taken, asserted, for unless it can be held against opposition, it*

What specific person or type of person would prove an effective spokesperson for:

a. The best way to bake a cake?
b. How to lead a happy life?
c. What the government has to do to solve economic problems?
d. Why religion is (not) important in everyday life?

For what propositions would you be an effective spokesperson? Why?

If you could interview anyone who ever lived, whom would you choose? What questions would you ask?

is not power and will never be experienced as real on the part of the recipient." And those of us in the room know all too well that whatever is given to us is almost always a trap.

Second, you might want to use the testimony of an eyewitness to some event or situation. You might, for example, cite the testimony of someone who saw an accident, the person who spent two years in a maximum-security prison, or the person who had a particular operation.

Critically Evaluating Testimony

Test the adequacy of your testimony by asking yourself the following questions.

1. *Is the testimony presented fairly?* In using the testimony of others, present it fairly. Include, for example, any qualifications made by the expert. When presenting the ideas of an authority, present them as that authority would want.

2. *Is the person an authority on this subject?* Authorities, especially today, reign over very small territories. Doctors, professors, and lawyers—to name just a few—are experts on very small areas of knowledge. A doctor may be an expert on the thyroid gland but may know little about skin, muscles, or blood. A professor of history might know a great deal about the Renaissance but little

about American history. When an authority is used, be certain the person is in fact an authority on your specific subject.

3. *Is the person unbiased?* This question should be asked of both expert and witness accounts. Try to discover if there are any biases in the sources being cited. The real estate salesperson who tells you to "Buy! Buy! Buy!" and the diamond seller who tells you "Diamonds are your best investment" obviously have something to gain and are biased. Be suspicious of the conclusions of any biased source. This does not mean that normally biased sources cannot provide unbiased testimony. Surely they can. This does mean that once a bias has been detected, you should be on the lookout for how it might figure into the testimony.

Using Testimony

When you cite testimony, stress first the competence of the person, whether that person is an expert or a witness. To cite the predictions of a world-famous economist of whom your audience has never heard will mean little unless you first explain the person's competence. You might say, for example:

> *This prediction comes from the world's leading economist, who has success-fully predicted all major financial trends over the past 20 years.*

Now the audience will be prepared to lend credence to what this person says.
Similarly, establish the competence of a witness. Consider the following two excerpts:

> *My friend told me that in prison drugs are so easy to get that all you have to do is pay the guard and you'll get whatever you want.*

> *My friend, who was a guard in three different prisons over the past 15 years, told me that in prisons drugs are so easy to get that all you have to do is pay the guard and you'll get whatever you want.*

Notice that in the second statement, you establish the credibility of your source. Your audience is much more likely to believe this second testimony.
Second, stress the unbiased nature of the testimony. If the audience perceives the testimony to be biased—whether or not it really is—it will have little effect. You want to check out the biases of a witness so that you can present accurate information. But you also want to make the audience see that the testimony is in fact unbiased.
Third, stress the recency of the statement to the audience. Notice that in the first excerpt that follows, we have no way of knowing when the statement was made and therefore no way of knowing how true this statement would be today. In the second excerpt, however, the recency of the statement is stressed. As demonstrated by the following example, recency is often a crucial factor in determining whether or not we will believe a statement:

> *General Bailey has noted that the United States has more than twice the military power of any other world power.*

What would be a person's ideal qualifications in order for you to accept his or her testimony on such issues as these: a report on an accident, the importance of a proper diet, how to lose your fear of public speaking, and how to integrate multiculturalism into a college curriculum.

If you were presenting testimony, how would you seek to establish the person's qualifications so that your class would accept what he or she says as true and reliable on such issues as these: The military budget should be cut drastically; buy mutual funds; current AIDS education programs are not working; you can rise in the corporation.

General Bailey, who was interviewed last week in the Washington Post, *noted that the United States has more than twice the military power of any other world power.*

STATISTICS

Statistics are summary numbers. Statistics help your audience to see at a glance the important characteristics of an otherwise complex set of numbers. For a teacher to read off 50 grades on the last examination would not help you to see where your score fell in relation to the others in your class. In such cases statistical information is much more helpful.

Measures of Central Tendency

Measures of central tendency tell you the general pattern of a group of numbers. The mean is the arithmetic average of a set of numbers; for example, the mean grade on the midterm was 89, the mean expenditure on personal grooming items is $40 per year, the mean income for scientists is $64,000.

The median is the middle score; 50 percent of the cases fall above the median and 50 percent fall below it. For example, if the median score on the midterm was 78, it means that half the class scored higher than 78 and half scored lower.

The mode is the most frequently occurring score. It is the single score that most people received. If the mode of the midterm was 85, it means that more students received 85 than any other single score.

Measures of Correlation

Measures of correlation tell you how closely two or more things are related. You might say, for example, that there is a high correlation between smoking and lung cancer or between poverty and crime. Recognize that high correlations do not mean causation. The fact that two things vary together (that is, are highly correlated) does not mean that one causes the other. They may each be caused by some third factor.

Measures of Difference

Measures of difference tell you the extent to which scores differ from the average or from each other. For example, the range tells us how far the lowest score is from the highest score. The range is computed by subtracting the lowest from the highest score. If the lowest score on the midterm was 76 and the highest was 99, the range was 23 points. Generally, a high range indicates great diversity, whereas a low range indicates great similarity.

How effectively do advertisements use statistics? What principles for using statistics do you think advertisers generally follow? Why do advertisers use statistics as they do?

Percentiles

Percentiles are useful for specifying the percentage of scores that fall below a particular score. For example, if you scored 700 on the College Entrance Examination Board test, you were approximately in the ninety-seventh percentile. This means that 97 percent of those taking the test scored lower than 700. Generally, the twenty-fifth, fiftieth, and seventy-fifth percentiles (also called, respectively, the first, second, and third quartiles) are distinguished. The second quartile, or fiftieth percentile, is also the median, since exactly half the scores are above and half are below.

Here Lee Brown (1995, p. 176) uses statistics to make clear the growth of heroin use:

> *Data on heroin-related emergency room visits show that the problems associated with long-term heroin use are on the rise. Data from the Drug Abuse Warning Network (DAWN), which reports on drug-related activity in our hospitals, shows a sharp increase in heroin emergency room incidents. The annual number of heroin-related emergency room visits rose from 38,100 in 1988 to 48,000 in 1992—a 26 percent rise.*

Critically Evaluating Statistics

In critically evaluating statistics, ask the following questions.

1. *Are the statistics based on a large enough sample?* The size of the sample is always important. This is one reason why few advertisers ever report the size of their sample. Advertisers may tell you, for example:

> *Buy Blotto milk for the health of your baby. Four out of five nutritionists surveyed chose Blotto milk.*

In this case and in similar claims, however, you are not told how large the entire sample was. If the researchers merely tested groups of five until they found one group where four would endorse Blotto, you would not put much confidence in those statistics. (Note too that the statement does not say what the nutritionists chose Blotto milk over. We assume it was other brands of milk, but nowhere is this made explicit.) The sample must be large enough to expect that if another group were selected, the results would be the same as those reported in the statistics. Enough nutritionists should have been surveyed so that if you went out and selected 100 at random, 80 would endorse Blotto.

2. *Is the sample a fair representation of the entire population?* If you wish to make inferences about an entire class of people, sample the group fairly and include representatives of all subgroups. Thus, it would be unfair to make inferences about the attitudes of college professors if you surveyed only those who taught communication.

3. *Is the statistic based on recent sampling?* Recency is particularly important, since things change so rapidly. To report mean income, church attendance, or smoking statistics without ensuring recency is meaningless. Here, for example, Martha Lamkin (1986), in a speech delivered October 24, 1986, uses the September 1986 issue of *American Demographics* for her statistics. Note too

What kinds of statistics would help you support the following propositions:
a. Robotics engineering pays well
b. Golden Gate Bridge is long
c. Adventure films are the most financially successful
d. College graduates are significantly happier than nongraduates
e. Whiterwhite fights tooth decay better than any other toothpaste
f. Excessive television viewing distorts the viewer's perceptions of reality

that she cites not only the current status of women in these professions but also what these figures mean in terms of growth:

> *Despite the persistence of occupational segregation, women's representation in several areas is growing rapidly. The September issue of* American Demographics *reports that, since 1970:*
>> *. . . [W]omen now make up over 20 percent of all lawyers—an increase of 400 percent; . . . we now comprise 18 percent of all doctors—up 80 percent; and . . . women now constitute 28 percent of all computer scientists—a 100 percent increase.*

4. *Are the statistics collected and analyzed by an unbiased source?* Remember our advertisers! They are intent on selling a product; they make their living that way. When they say "four out of five," ask who collected the data and who analyzed them.

Using Statistics

How might you use statistics to illustrate the following propositions:
a. School violence is increasing
b. Inflation is going down
c. The cost of war is astronomical
d. The use of drugs is increasing among the college-educated population

Keep in mind that the audience will ask essentially the same questions that a good researcher would ask in analyzing statistics. Answer these questions for your audience. For example, answer their questions about whether the source is biased. Stress the unbiased nature of the source who collected and analyzed the statistics, the representativeness of the sample, and the recency of the statistical collections and computations.

Further, make the statistics clear to an audience that will hear the figures only once. Round off figures so they are easy to comprehend and retain. Don't say that the median income of workers in this city is $12,347. This may be accurate, but it will be difficult to remember. Instead, say that it is "around $12,300" or even "a bit more than $12,000."

Make numbers meaningful to the audience. To say, for example, that the Sears Tower in Chicago is 1,559 feet tall does not visualize its height. So, consider saying something like:

> *The Sears Tower is 1,559 feet tall. Just how tall is 1,559 feet? Well, it's as tall as the length of more than four football fields. That's how tall. It's as tall as 260 6-foot people standing on each other's heads.*

Make explicit the connection between the statistics and what they show. To say, for example, that college professors make an average of $42,000 per year needs to be related specifically to the proposition that teachers' salaries should be raised or lowered, depending on your point of view.

Here Geneva Johnson (1991) uses statistics to dramatize the rapid population growth of the elderly:

> *Today's population is growing at a steady rate of 1 percent per year and now includes 6 million elderly. By 2030, we will have 17 million and by 2050, 26 million. Implication, today, is that 1 in 40 people are 80 or older. By 2050, 1 in 12 will be 80 or older.*

▬ SOME ADDITIONAL FORMS OF AMPLIFICATION

There are a variety of other forms of amplification that can be used. Here is just a brief mention of some of these.

Quotations

Quotations are useful for adding spice and wit as well as authority to your speeches. Quotations can, however, become cumbersome. Too often they are not related directly to the point you are trying to make and their relevance gets lost. If the quotation is in technical language that listeners will not understand, it then becomes necessary to interject definitions as you go along.

Therefore, unless the quotation is short, comprehensible to the audience, and related directly to the point you are trying to make, use your own words; paraphrase in your own words the essence of the idea. And credit the person you are quoting.

Here, for example, James H. Carr (1995, p. 219) uses a quotation from Martin Luther King, Jr.:

> *This is as true today as it was just over 30 years ago when Dr. Martin Luther King, Jr. stood on the steps of the Lincoln Memorial at the great civil rights march of 1963 and stated, "We have . . . come to this spot to remind America of the fierce urgency of now . . . now is the time to open the doors of opportunity to all."*
>
> *Now is the time for us to think rationally and act compassionately. Now is the time for us to consider the future of our great nation if we continue to place a priority on punishing people after their lives have been destroyed, rather than providing meaningful educational training and employment opportunities.*

Here Clifton R. Wharton, Jr. (1995, p. 207), uses his own words and also credits the source:

> *A Michigan senator, Arthur Vandenberg, once said that politics stop at the water's edge—meaning that the nation unites once action is taken. Unfortunately, we have forgotten that bit of wisdom.*

Definitions

Definitions are helpful when you introduce complex terms or wish to provide a particular perspective on a subject. In fact, an entire speech can be devoted to definition. The types of definitions and guidelines for using them are discussed in Unit 19.

Comparison and Contrast

Another form of amplification is comparison and contrast. You might want to compare or contrast one thing with another—living conditions in Germany and Japan, extroverted and introverted personalities, or computers and type-

Select a quotation from one of the many books of quotations available in your library or on-line. How might you use it in your next speech?

writers. This form of amplification is discussed in Unit 20 under "Reasoning from Analogy."

Simple Statement of Fact or a Series of Facts

It is often useful to cite facts or a series of facts to explain a statement or position. In a speech on the growing problem of drug trafficking, Lee Brown (1995, p. 177) uses a series of facts:

> *There are other critical developments:*
> - *Worldwide opium production has quadrupled in the last decade.*
> - *Poppy growing areas are expanding in Afghanistan and the new republics of the former Soviet Union.*
> - *Heroin addict populations, particularly in Asia, are increasing.*
> - *South American heroin from Colombia is now being shipped by the cocaine cartels to the United States.*

Repetition and Restatement

Still another way to amplify your thoughts is to use repetition or restatement. Repetition involves repeating your idea in the same words at strategic places throughout your speech. Restatement involves repeating your idea in different words.

Repetition and restatement are especially helpful in public speeches because of the inevitable lapses in audience attention. When you repeat or restate your ideas, you provide listeners with one more opportunity to grasp what you are saying.

Restatement is especially important when addressing a culturally mixed audience who may not have learned your language as their first language. Consequently, they may not easily understand certain idioms and figures of speech. Restating these ideas in different words increases the chances of audience comprehension.

UNIT IN BRIEF

Examples: specific instances explained in varying degrees of detail	■ Examples should be representative and relevant ■ Examples are most effective when: (1) they are used to explain a concept rather than as ends in themselves; (2) the relationship between the concept and the example is made explicit; and (3) the distinction between real and hypothetical is made clear

Narration: a story that illustrates some assertion and can be explanatory, exemplary, persuasive, and presented in first- or third-person	■ Narratives should be relevant to the subject and purpose of the speech and should be fairly presented ■ Narratives are most effective when they are (1) relatively short, (2) presented in chronological order, (3) connected clearly to the speech purpose, (4) presented in a climax order, and (5) presented in dialogue only when most effective (otherwise, use your own words)
Testimony: the opinions of experts or the accounts of witnesses, often used to lend authority or otherwise amplify assertions	■ Testimony should be presented fairly, should be authoritative on the specific subject, and should be unbiased ■ Testimony is most effective when (1) the competence of the authority is stressed, (2) the unbiased nature of the testimony is stressed, and (3) the recency of the observation or opinion is stressed
Statistics: an organized summary of figures that clarify trends or other important characteristics of an otherwise complex set of numbers	■ Statistics should be based on an adequate sample size, based on a representative sample, based on recent sampling, and collected and analyzed by unbiased sources ■ Statistics are most effective when (1) their unbiased nature is stressed, (2) they are understandable to an audience, (3) they are meaningful to the audience, and (4) the connection between the statistics and what they support is clear
Some additional forms of amplification	■ Quotations: useful in adding wit and authority ■ Definitions: especially helpful when the audience is new to a topic ■ Comparisons and Contrasts: helpful when you want to point out similarities or differences between things or concepts ■ Simple Statement of Fact or a Series of Facts: useful in fortifying your position ■ Repetition and Restatement: helpful because of the inevitable lapses in audience attention and for emphasis

PRACTICALLY SPEAKING

Short Speech Technique

Prepare and deliver a two-minute speech in which you:

1. develop two examples (real or hypothetical) to illustrate one of these propositions: Rewards come to those who work hard; having faith will solve all problems; being optimistic leads to happiness; use time, don't waste it; practice makes perfect; depression is a physiological, not a psychological, problem (or depression is a psychological, not a physiological, problem); good neighbors are nosy neighbors
2. tell a personal story to illustrate a specific point, being sure to follow the suggestions offered in this unit
3. retell a fairy tale or folktale to illustrate a moral or general principle
4. explain the kinds of testimonials that would convince you to buy a particular brand of toothpaste, cereal, car, dog food, or hearing aid
5. explain a print ad that relies on statistics and show how the advertiser uses statistics to make a point
6. explain the meaning of a quotation you find interesting
7. compare or contrast two people, cultures, or religions on any one specific feature

8.1   Amplifying Statements

Here are some rather bland, uninteresting statements. Select one of them and amplify it, using at least three different methods of amplification. Identify each method used. Since the purpose of this exercise is to provide greater insight into forms and methods of amplification, you may, for this exercise, manufacture, fabricate, or otherwise invent facts, figures, illustrations, examples, and the like. In fact, it may prove even more beneficial if you go to extremes in constructing these forms of support.

1. Abortion is wrong (is moral).
2. The Sears Tower in Chicago is the world's tallest building.
3. Dr. Kirk was a great instructor.
4. My grandparents left me a fortune in their will.
5. The college I just visited seems ideal.
6. The writer of this article is a real authority.
7. I knew I was marrying into money as soon as I walked into the house.
8. Considering what they did, punishment to the fullest extent of the law would be mild.
9. The fortune-teller told us good news.
10. The athlete lived an interesting life.

UNIT 9

Audiovisual Aids

Unit Contents

Unit Objectives

After completing this unit, you should be able to:

1. Explain the functions of audiovisual aids

2. Identify at least ten types of audiovisual aids

3. Explain the tests to use in critically evaluating the effectiveness of an audiovisual aid

4. Explain the guidelines for using audiovisual aids

*W*hen you are planning to give a speech, consider using some kind of audiovisual (AV) aid—a visual or auditory means of clarifying or amplifying your speech. At the start, ask yourself if you should you use an AV aid. How would the aid make your speech more effective? What type of aid should you use? Charts? Slides? Models? There are many types to choose from. How should you go about creating the AV aid? What principles should you follow to make sure that your aid helps achieve your public speaking purpose? How should you use the aid during your speech?

THE FUNCTIONS OF AUDIOVISUAL AIDS

AV aids are not an added frill. They are integral parts of your speech and serve essential functions. Let's look at some of the more important functions.

Audiovisuals Gain Attention and Maintain Interest

We are a generation that grew up on audiovisual entertainment. We are used to it and we enjoy it. It's not surprising, then, that we, as members of the audience, appreciate it when a speaker makes use of such aids. We perk up when the speaker says, "I want you to look at this chart showing the employment picture for the next five years" or "Listen to the way Springsteen uses vocal variety."

Audiovisual aids also help maintain attention and interest because they break up the speech and provide some variety in what we see and hear. Audiences will respond more favorably when you provide them with this variety, with this differently packaged message.

Audiovisuals Add Clarity

What other functions do audiovisual aids serve?

Let's say you want to illustrate the growth of the cable television industry in the United States over the last 30 years. You could say, for example, "In 1952 there were 14,000 subscribers, in 1955 there were 150,000 subscribers, in 1960 there were 650,000 subscribers, in 1965 there were 1,275,000 subscribers, . . . " This gets pretty boring and you still haven't covered the 1970s and the 1980s. Note how much easier this same information is communicated in the bar graph in Figure 9.1. At a glance we can see the rapid growth from practically nothing to more than 55,800,000 subscribers.

Audiovisuals Reinforce Your Message

What persuasive functions do audiovisual aids serve?

Audiovisuals help to add a reinforcement that is so necessary in making sure the audience understands and remembers what you have said. With a visual aid, you present the same information in two different ways—verbally as audience members hear you explain the aid and visually as they see the chart, map, or model. The same is true with audio aids. The audience hears you speak of vocal variety, but they also hear examples of it from the recording. This one-two punch helps the audience to understand more clearly and to remember more accurately what you have said.

TYPES OF AUDIOVISUAL AIDS

You are convinced of the value of using some kind of audiovisual aid, but what kind should you use? Let's look at some of the more popular aids used by speakers.

FIGURE 9.1
Growth of the cable TV industry in the United States as of January each year.

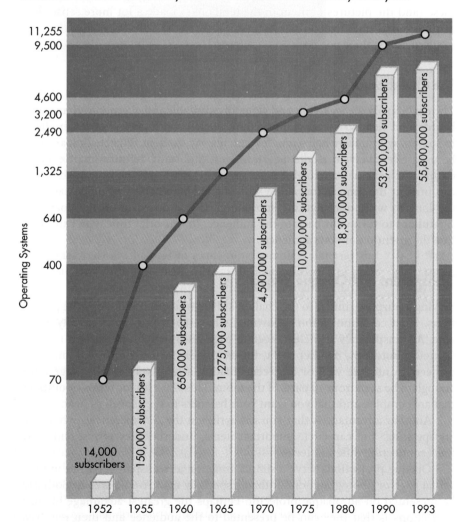

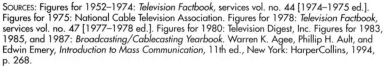

Sources: Figures for 1952–1974: *Television Factbook*, services vol. no. 44 [1974–1975 ed.]. Figures for 1975: National Cable Television Association. Figures for 1978: *Television Factbook*, services vol. no. 47 [1977–1978 ed.]. Figures for 1980: Television Digest, Inc. Figures for 1983, 1985, and 1987: *Broadcasting/Cablecasting Yearbook*. Warren K. Agee, Phillip H. Ault, and Edwin Emery, *Introduction to Mass Communication*, 11th ed., New York: HarperCollins, 1994, p. 268.

is
lig
po
tra
pe
yo

H

Ha
als
sp
wa

ye
wo
to
wł

Cł

Cł
ch
sp
wo
idé
wi
wi
thi
idé

equipped with transparency paper. If you don't have access to a transparency projector, you might consider blowing up your graphic until you get it to a size that can be seen by your entire audience.

Maps

How would you evaluate your local television weather forecaster's use of visual aids?

Maps are useful for showing geographic elements as well as changes throughout history: population density, immigration patterns, economic conditions, the location of various resources, and hundreds of other issues you may wish to develop in your speeches.

People

Oddly enough, people can function effectively as "audiovisual aids." For example, if you want to demonstrate the muscles of the body, you might use a bodybuilder. If you want to demonstrate different voice patterns, skin complexions, or hairstyles, you might use people as your aids. Aside from the obvious assistance they provide in demonstrating their physical qualities, people help to secure and maintain the attention and interest of the audience.

Slides

Slides are useful for showing various scenes or graphics that you cannot describe in words. The great advantages of slides are their visual appeal (and hence their attention-getting value) and their ease of preparation and use.

Maps are an often neglected form of visual aid. How might you incorporate maps into speeches dealing with, for example, the Middle East conflicts, the growth of the Sun Belt, the growth of the European Common Market, and political changes in Africa over the last 50 years?

Again, most departments of communication have slide projectors, so you should have no trouble getting the equipment. When planning to use slides, be sure to allow yourself sufficient time to shoot, develop, and organize them.

Films, Filmstrips, and Videotapes

I use a variety of films to illustrate some of the breakdowns that occur in interpersonal communication, the techniques for and the progress made in teaching animals to communicate, and various other topics. Filmstrips are also useful because they enable you to regulate timing more closely. If there are a number of questions during a lecture, you can easily stop a filmstrip to address them; stopping a film is a bit more cumbersome. Although it is a great deal to undertake, you might consider making your own videotape to illustrate your talk. But remember, a bad film is a bad audiovisual aid and detracts from rather than adds to the effectiveness of your speech.

 What types of audiovisual aids might be helpful in a speech on how to make great coffee or children's television commercials?

Pictures and Illustrations

Assuming that you do not have films or slides, the next best visual aid is a picture. There are, however, many hazards involved in using this type of aid, so I recommend its use only with reservations. If the picture is large enough for all members of the audience to see clearly (say, poster-size), if it clearly illustrates what you want to illustrate, and if it is mounted on cardboard, then use it; otherwise, do not.

Do not pass pictures around the room. This only draws attention away from what you are saying. Listeners will look for the pictures to circulate to them, will wonder what the pictures contain, and will miss a great deal of your speech in the interim.

Illustrations may at times be more useful than pictures. For example, Figure 9.4 presents an illustration of the human ear to show the structures of the ears, their shape, and how they are related to each other.

Recall the last college lecture you heard. Did the instructor use any audiovisual aids? What particular aids might have helped improve the class?

FIGURE 9.4
Human ear.

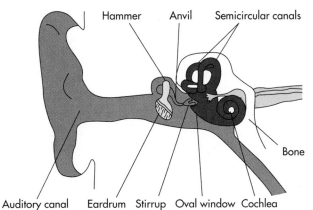

Hammer   Anvil   Semicircular canals

Bone

Auditory canal   Eardrum   Stirrup   Oval window   Cochlea

How would you illustrate with three or four audiovisual aids one of the topics listed in the Dictionary of Topics in Unit 6?

Tapes and CDs

To deliver a speech about music and not provide the audience with samples would seem strange. Very likely the audience's attention would be drawn away from your speech to wonder why you had not provided the actual music. Tapes and CDs, of course, can be useful for many other types of speeches as well. A speech on advertising would be greatly helped, for example, by having actual samples of advertisements as played on radio or television. A tape of such examples would go a long way toward helping to clarify your point. It would also provide for variety by breaking up the oral presentation most effectively.

CRITICALLY EVALUATING AUDIOVISUAL AIDS

In using audiovisual aids, ask yourself the following questions.

Is the Aid Clear?

Clarity of an AV aid is the most important test of all. If the aid is not clearly visible, it will not serve its purpose. Therefore, make the aid large enough so that everyone can see it. Poster-board paper is readily available and relatively inexpensive. The 24-by–36-inch size seems large enough for most purposes. It contains enough space for most charts or graphs, and it can be seen from any point in most classrooms. Black or red print on a white background is probably the clearest combination you can use (though also see Table 9.1). Also, make the aid simple so that its meaning is clear. Too many words or pictures will obscure your meaning.

Is the Aid Relevant?

It may be attractive, well-designed, easy to read, and possess all the features one could hope for in an audiovisual aid, but if it is not relevant to the topic, leave it at home.

Is the Aid Appealing?

Audiovisual aids work best when they are appealing. Sloppy, poorly designed, and worn-out aids will detract from the purpose they are intended to serve. Visual aids should be attractive enough to engage the attention of the audience but not so attractive as to be distracting. The almost nude body draped across a car may be effective in selling underwear but would probably detract if your object is to explain the profit-and-loss statement of the Chrysler Corporation.

Is the Aid Culturally Sensitive?

Just as what you say will be interpreted within a cultural framework, so too will the symbols and colors you use in your aid be so interpreted. For example, the symbols you use that you may assume are universal may not be

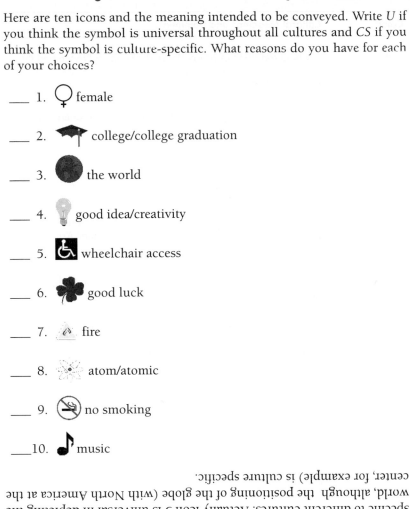

Self Test

Can You Distinguish Universal from Culture-Specific Icons?

Here are ten icons and the meaning intended to be conveyed. Write *U* if you think the symbol is universal throughout all cultures and *CS* if you think the symbol is culture-specific. What reasons do you have for each of your choices?

____ 1. female

____ 2. college/college graduation

____ 3. the world

____ 4. good idea/creativity

____ 5. wheelchair access

____ 6. good luck

____ 7. fire

____ 8. atom/atomic

____ 9. no smoking

____ 10. music

Icons 1, 5, 7, 8, 9, 10 would be considered universal; the others are specific to different cultures. Actually icon 3 is universal in depicting the world, although the positioning of the globe (with North America at the center, for example) is culture specific.

known by persons new to a culture (see accompanying self-test). And, of course, when speaking to international audiences, you need to use universal symbols or explain those that are not universal. Also, be careful that your icons do not reveal an ethnocentric bias. For example, using the American dollar sign to symbolize "wealth" may be quite logical in your public speaking class but interpreted as ethnocentric if used with an audience of international visitors.

Also, the meanings that different colors communicate will vary greatly from one culture to another. Table 9.1, constructed from the research reported by Nancy Hoft (1995), illustrates some of these different meanings. Before you look at the table, consider the meanings your own culture(s) gives to such colors as red, green, black, white, blue, yellow, and purple.

*P*ublic speaking audiences vary greatly. Thousands of people at Yankee Stadium listening to a politician or religious leader, 30 students in a classroom listening to a lecture, and 5 people listening to a street orator are all audiences. The characteristic that seems best to define an audience is common purpose. A public speaking audience is a group of individuals gathered together to hear a speech.

You deliver a speech to inform or persuade your audience. Or perhaps you give a speech to introduce a speaker, to present or accept an award, to secure the goodwill of your audience, or to pay tribute to someone. A teacher lectures on Gestalt psychology to increase understanding; a minister talks against adultery to influence behaviors and attitudes; a football coach gives a pep talk to motivate the team to improve—all of these persons are trying to produce change. If speakers are to be successful, then they must know their audience. If you are to be successful, you must know your audience. This knowledge will help you in a variety of ways; here are just a few:

- *in selecting your topic*
- *in phrasing your purpose*
- *in establishing a relationship between yourself and your audience*
- *in choosing examples and illustrations*
- *in stating your thesis, whether directly or indirectly*
- *in the arguments you use and the motives to which you appeal*

APPROACHING AUDIENCE ANALYSIS AND ADAPTATION

Your first step in audience analysis is to construct an audience profile in which you analyze the sociological or demographic characteristics of your audience. These characteristics help you estimate the attitudes and beliefs of your audience. If you want to effect changes in these attitudes and beliefs, you have to know what they are.

Attitudes and Beliefs

Attitude refers to your tendency to act for or against a person, object, or position. If you have a positive attitude toward the death penalty, you are likely to argue or act in favor of instituting the death penalty (for example, to vote for a candidate who supports the death penalty). If you have a negative attitude toward the death penalty, then you are likely to argue or act against it. Attitudes influence how favorably or unfavorably listeners will respond to speakers who support or denounce the death penalty.

Belief refers to the confidence or conviction you have in the existence or truth of some proposition. For example, you may believe that there is an afterlife, that education is the best way to rise from poverty, that democracy is the best form of government, or that all people are born equal. If your listeners

As you read this unit, think about possible evidence that might support or contradict any of the assumptions made throughout the unit. What types of evidence (philosophical generalizations, personal experience, survey data) would be especially significant in supporting or contradicting such assumptions?

What is the single most important characteristic about your specific public speaking audience to keep in mind? How will this one characteristic influence your speech preparation and presentation?

believe that the death penalty is a deterrent to crime, for example, then they will be more likely to favor arguments for (and speakers who support) the death penalty than listeners who do not believe in the connection between the death penalty and deterrence would.

As you can readily see from this last example, the attitudes and beliefs your listeners have will influence how receptive they will be to your topic, your point of view, and your evidence and arguments. It is therefore essential that you learn about your listeners' attitudes and beliefs before you prepare your speech.

Seeking Audience Information

In learning about your audience, you will need to analyze their demographic or sociological characteristics and then their psychographic or psychological makeup. In this unit we examine the sociological characteristics and in the next, the psychological.

You can seek out audience information using a variety of methods: observation, data collection, interviewing, and inference (Sprague & Stuart 1996).

Observe   Think about your audience. What can you infer about, say, their economic status from observing their clothing and jewelry? Might their clothing reveal any conservative or liberal leanings? Might clothing provide clues to attitudes on economics or politics? What do they do in their free time?

Where do they live? What do they talk about? Are different cultures represented? Does this give you any clue as to what their interests or concerns might be?

Collect Data Systematically   A useful means for securing information about your audience is to use a questionnaire. Let's say you took a course in desktop publishing and were thinking about giving an informative speech on the nature of desktop publishing. One thing you would need to determine is how much your audience already knows. This will help you judge the level at which to approach the topic, information you can assume is known, terms you'll need to define, and so on. You might also want to know if the audience has ever seen documents produced by desktop publishing. If they haven't, examples would provide interesting visual aids. To help you answer these and other relevant questions, you might compose a questionnaire such as that appearing in Figure 10.1.

Audience questionnaires are even more useful as background for your persuasive speeches. Let's say you plan to give a speech in favor of allowing single people to adopt children. To develop an effective speech, you need to know your audience's attitudes toward single-parent adoption. Are they in favor? Opposed? Do they have reservations? If so, what are they? To help you

FIGURE 10.1
Audience questionnaire for an informative speech.

Audience Questionnaire

I'm planning to give an informative speech on desktop publishing, a procedure in which printed pages similar to those appearing in magazines and newspapers are produced with a personal computer. I'd appreciate your responding to these four questions.

1. How much do you know about desktop publishing?
   ❑ a great deal
   ❑ something but not very much
   ❑ very little
   ❑ virtually nothing

2. Have you ever seen a publication produced by desktop software?
   ❑ yes
   ❑ no
   ❑ not sure

3. How interested are you in learning more about desktop publishing?
   ❑ very interested
   ❑ neither interested nor uninterested
   ❑ uninterested

4. Is there anything special about desktop publishing that you would like to learn?

   _____

   _____

   _____

In addition to giving you information on audience attitudes and beliefs, what other advantages might audience questionnaires have?

Audience Questionnaire

I'm preparing a speech on adoption and would like to know how you feel about a few key issues. Please respond to each of these three questions as completely as possible. Anything else you'd care to say about adoption would be greatly appreciated and would help me in preparing my speech.

1. How do you feel about single people adopting children?
   - ☐ strongly in favor of it
   - ☐ in favor of it
   - ☐ neutral
   - ☐ opposed to it
   - ☐ strongly opposed to it

2. Is your attitude the same for interracial adoption? For gays and lesbians adopting? Please explain.

   _____

   _____

3. What are the main reasons for your current attitudes?

   _____

   _____

FIGURE 10.2
Audience questionnaire for a persuasive speech.

What kind of questionnaire might prove useful in securing information about your audience for your next speech? Develop a questionnaire that seeks to assess how much your audience know about your topic, how interested they are in your topic, and what their attitudes and beliefs about the topic and your purpose are.

answer such questions, you might use a questionnaire such as that presented in Figure 10.2.

Interview Members of Your Audience   In a classroom situation, interviewing audience members is accomplished easily. But if you are to speak to an audience you will not meet prior to your speech, you might interview those who know the audience members better than you do. For example, you might talk with the person who invited you to speak.

If you do survey your audience—with a questionnaire or by interview—be sure to mention this in your speech. It will alert your listeners to your thoroughness and your concern for them. It will also satisfy their curiosity, since most people will be interested in how others responded. You might say something like this:

> *I want to thank you all for completing my questionnaire on single-parent adoption. Half of you were neutral; 40 percent were in favor, and 10 percent were opposed. The major reason in favor of single-parent adoption was that it would provide homes for an enormous number of children who would otherwise not be adopted. The major reason against such adoption was the belief that a child needs two parents to grow up emotionally healthy. Let's look more carefully at each of these reasons.*

Use "Intelligent Inference and Empathy"   Use your knowledge of human behavior and human motivation and try to adopt the perspective of the audience. For example, let's say you are addressing the entire teaching staff of your college on the need to eliminate (or expand) affirmative action. What might you infer about your audience? Are they likely to be in favor of affirmative

In your speech to the young executives, you might begin with something like this:

> I want to talk with you about investing for your future. In 20 years—years that will pass very quickly—many of you will be retiring. You will quickly learn that your company pension plan will prove woefully inadequate. Social security will be equally inadequate. With only these sources of income, you will have to lower your standard of living drastically. But that need not happen. In fact, with extremely small investments made now and throughout your high-income-earning years, you will actually be able to live at a much higher standard than you ever thought possible.

Note that in both of these examples, the speaker has made age-based inferences about the audiences' attitudes toward investments. The speaker has demonstrated a knowledge of the audience and their immediate concerns. As a listener hearing even these brief excerpts, you would feel that the speaker was addressing you directly and specifically. As a result, you would probably give this speaker more attention than you'd give to one who spoke in generalities and without any clear idea of who was listening.

Here are some questions about age that you might find helpful in analyzing and adapting to your audience. In examining these questions, do recognize that culture will greatly influence attitudes toward age. Among Native Americans and the Chinese, for example, there is great respect for the aged, whereas in the United States youth is valued and the aged are, perhaps, tolerated. Programs for the aged, scholarships for students, and parents' and children's responsibilities are likely to be met very differently by members of these different cultures.

In a famous observation on growing up, Mark Twain once said, "When I was a boy of fourteen, my father was so ignorant I could hardly stand to have the old man around. But when I got to be twenty-one, I was astonished at how much the old man had learned in seven years." What guidelines for audience analysis does Twain's remark suggest?

"You'd better ask your grandparents about that, son—my generation is very uncomfortable talking about abstinence."

Drawing by Mankoff; © 1994 The New Yorker Magazine, Inc.

1. *Do the age-groups differ in the goals, interests, and day-to-day concerns that may be related to your topic and purpose?* Graduating from college, achieving corporate success, raising a family, and saving for retirement are concerns that differ greatly from one age-group to another. Learn your audience's goals. Know what they think about and worry about. Connect your propositions and supporting materials to these goals and concerns. Show the audience how they can more effectively achieve their goals and you will win a favorable hearing.

2. *Do the groups differ in their ability to absorb and process information?* Will they differ in their responses to visual cues? With a young audience, it may be best to keep up a steady, even swift pace. If possible use visuals. Make sure their attention doesn't wander. With older persons, you may wish to maintain a more moderate pace.

3. *Do the groups differ in their respect for tradition and the past?* Is one age-group (usually, the young) more likely to view innovation and change positively? Might appeals to tradition be more appropriate for an older audience? Might appeals to discovery, exploration, newness, and change find a more receptive hearing among the young?

4. *Do the groups differ in the degree to which they are motivated by their peer group?* Young people have strong needs to be evaluated positively by their peer group; group identification is very important to the young. Use this motive in your speeches. Show a young audience that what you are advocating has the approval of like-minded young people. Show them why agreement with you will result in peer approval.

In what other ways do the young and the old differ? In what other ways do men and women differ?

Gender

Gender is one of the most difficult audience variables to analyze. The rapid social changes taking place today make it difficult to pin down the effects of gender. At one time, researchers focused primarily on biological sex differences. Now, however, many researchers are focusing on psychological sex roles. When we focus on a psychological sex role, we consider a person feminine if that person has internalized those traits (attitudes and behaviors) society considers feminine and rejected those traits society considers masculine. We consider a person masculine if that person has internalized those traits society considers masculine and rejected those traits society considers feminine. Thus, a biological woman may display masculine sex-role traits and behaviors and a biological man may display feminine sex-role traits and behaviors.

Because of society's training, biological males generally internalize masculine traits and biological females generally internalize feminine traits. So, while there is probably great overlap between biological sex and psychological sex roles, they are not equivalent. In fact, at times they may be quite different. Although we use the shorthand "men" and "women," remember that psychological sex roles may be more significant than biological sex in accounting for these differences.

Mary A. DeVries (1994, p. 194), in her *Internationally Yours*—a book addressed to American businesspeople working in other countries and with people from other cultures—advises, "Even in countries where women are more readily accepted in business dealings, it behooves them to avoid appearing aggressive and never to flaunt their feelings of equal status." What do you think of this advice?

Do you think you are at an advantage speaking to a same-sex, opposite-sex, or mixed-sex audience? As a listener, are you more responsive to a same-sex speaker, an opposite-sex speaker, or doesn't it matter? How can you be sure that your answers to the second question validly represent your normal listening behavior?

Attitudes toward men and women and even the traits that are considered masculine and feminine will vary from one culture to another. In the United States, Australia, and Western Europe, women and men are considered equal in most areas. In much of the rest of the world—Asia and the Arab world, for example—men make the business decisions and the important family decisions. In Islamic cultures, women are seen in "traditional" roles of mother and housewife, not as business partner, for example. And men and women do not compete with each other whether at school or at work. With even these few examples, it is easy to see the difficulties a female speaker would have addressing men from these cultures on topics heard every day in the United States— abortion, no-fault divorce, lesbians in the military, and sexual equality, for example.

Is this true generally of the men and women you know? What topics are women more interested in than men are? What topics are men more interested in than women are?

Let's say that you are a marriage counselor and are delivering a speech on how to communicate more effectively. Your speech should be very different if delivered to a group of women versus to a group of men. Women, it has been argued, will probably be more receptive to the topic and more willing to talk about their relationships than men will (Tannen 1990). In your speech to an audience of women, you might say:

Many of you are probably in relationships with those who have difficulty expressing themselves, especially when it comes to romance. Oh, they're good men, of course, but they don't know how to talk romance. They don't know the language of romance. You do; women have been taught this language and feel comfortable with it. And so, you have to assume the role of teacher and teach your partner this new and different language. But you must do it with subtlety; that is what I want to talk about.

To an audience of men, however, you might introduce your topic very differently. You might, for example, say something like this:

Most of you are probably in relationships with women who do all or most of the talking about the relationship. They are the ones who talk romance. Somehow you're not comfortable talking like this; you have difficulty using the language of romance. You're men of action. But maybe there are ways of talking this language that will make it less painful. In fact, I'm going to show you how to talk the language of romance so that you'll love each and every syllable.

Note that in these two examples, the speaker begins with and builds on the feelings the audience is assumed to have. The audience is made to see that the speaker knows who they are and intends not to contradict or criticize these feelings but rather to take these feelings into consideration in the speech.

Here are some questions to guide your analysis of this very difficult audience characteristic.

1. *Do men and women differ in the values that they consider important and that are related to your topic and purpose?* Traditionally, men have been found to place greater importance on theoretical, economic, and political values. Traditionally, women have been found to place greater importance on aesthetic, social, and religious values. In framing appeals and selecting examples, use the values your audience members consider most important.

2. *Will your topic be seen as more interesting by men? By women?* Will men and women have different attitudes toward the topic? Men and women do not, for example, respond in the same way to such topics as abortion, rape, and equal pay for equal work. Select your topics and supporting materials in light of the sex of your audience members. When your audience is mixed, make a special effort to relate "women's" topics to men and "men's" topics to women.

3. *Will men or women feel uncomfortable with your topic or purpose?* For example, women are generally more relationally oriented than men are. Women express their feelings more readily than men do. Many men operate with the "cowboy syndrome," the tendency to remain strong and silent regardless of what is happening. Relational topics—for example, friendship, love, and family—are more popular with women than with men. (All you have to do to convince yourself of this is to pick up a random selection of magazines addressed to women and magazines addressed to men. Look at the advertisements, the articles, and even the cartoons.) When speaking on these topics to women, you will probably find a receptive audience. When speaking on such topics to men, draw explicit connections between these topics and men's values, needs, and interests.

Educational and Intellectual Levels

An educated person may not be very intelligent, and, conversely, an intelligent person may not be well educated. In most cases, however, the two go together. Further, they seem to influence the reception of a speech in similar ways and

TIPS
From Professional Speakers

Another time, I prepared a speech for a client I hadn't worked with in over seven years. The speech was to be given at the end of a conference of 500 senior managers from around the world. I was not able to get a clear idea of how to focus my speech from discussions with the people who invited me, and other sources were not readily available. I planned my speech based on what I knew about the group seven years ago, but decided to travel to the conference site the evening before in order to gather "intelligence" from participants. I discovered that the group had changed dramatically, and realized that the focus of my speech was inappropriate. I altered my design and began by talking about the changes I'd observed. The audience knew immediately that I was speaking to them and this rapport created the context for success.

Whether you are leading a seminar, addressing a group of 500 or talking to your local PTA, it is critically important to know your audience and to think of them.

Michael J. Gleb, speaker and author. *Present Yourself* (Rolling Hills Estates, CA: Jalmar Press, 1988), p. 90.

Have your college experiences pushed you to be more critical of evidence and argument? If so, in what ways?

so are considered together. The shorthand *educated* is used here to refer to both qualities.

Let's say you are an advertising executive and are giving a speech on how spokespersons for television commercials are chosen. If your audience is highly educated and knowledgeable, you might say something like this:

> *The credibility of the spokesperson depends on three essential dimensions. First, it depends on the person's perceived competence. Second, it depends on the person's moral character. Third, it depends on the person's charisma. Rhetorical scholarship and experimental research have found support for these three factors.*

If your audience is less educated and less knowledgeable, you might communicate essentially the same information this way:

> *What makes us believe one person and disbelieve another person? Research tells us that there are three main characteristics. First, we believe someone we think has knowledge or competence. Second, we believe someone who is moral, who is essentially a good person. Third, we believe someone who is dynamic and outgoing.*

The first example assumes that the audience knows such technical terms as *credibility, competence, charisma,* and *rhetorical.* The second example does not take this knowledge for granted but instead uses everyday language to explain the same concepts. When technical vocabulary is used, the terms are explained (as in ". . . we think has knowledge or competence").

In looking at the education and intelligence of your audience, consider asking questions such as the following.

1. *Is the educational level related to the audience's level of social or political activism?* Generally, the more educated are more responsive to the needs of others. They more actively engage in causes of a social and political nature. Appeals to humanitarianism and broad social motives should work well with an educated audience. However, when speaking to less educated groups, concentrate on the value your speech has to their immediate needs and to the satisfaction of their immediate goals.

2. *Will the interests and concerns of the audience differ on the basis of their educational level?* Generally, the educated are more concerned with issues outside their immediate field of operation. They are concerned with international affairs, economic issues, and the broader philosophical and sociological issues confronting the nation and the world. The educated recognize that these issues affect them in many ways. Often the uneducated do not see the connection. Therefore, when speaking to a less educated audience, draw the connections explicitly and relate such topics to their more immediate concerns.

Note too that groups from different educational levels will be familiar with different sources of information. Thus, for example, only a relatively educated audience would be familiar with such periodicals as *Architectural Digest, Byte,* and *Barron's.* The educated and the less educated will probably also read

Do you find the generalizations made here reasonable? Would you qualify any of them? What other generalizations would you make about audiences and educational levels?

different newspapers and watch different television shows. Recognize these differences and use the relevant sources appropriately.

3. *Will the educational levels influence how critical the audience will be of your evidence and argument?* The more educated will probably be less swayed by appeals to emotion and to authority. They will be more skeptical of generalizations (as you may and should be of my generalizations in this unit). They will question the validity of statistics and frequently demand better substantiation of your propositions. The educated are more likely to apply the tests of evidence discussed in later units (see Units 14 and 17). Therefore, pay special attention to the logic of your evidence and arguments in addressing an educated audience.

4. *Will the educational level relate to what the audience knows about your topic?* As a speaker, you will be able to assume more background knowledge when addressing an educated than an uneducated audience. Fill in the necessary background and detail for the less educated.

> How might you incorporate into your next speech the following principle suggested by Dr. Samuel Johnson: "No man forgets his original trade: the rights of nations, and of kinds, sink into questions of grammar, if grammarians discuss them."

Occupation, Income, and Status

Occupation, income, and status, although not the same, are most often positively related. Therefore, they can be dealt with together. Consider asking such questions as these.

1. *How will job security and occupational pride be related to your topic and purpose?* Appeal to these when appropriate, and attack them only with extreme caution. If you can show your audience how your topic will enhance their job, give them greater job security or mobility, or make them more effective and efficient workers, you will have a most attentive and receptive audience.

2. *Will people from different status levels view long-range planning and goals differently?* Higher-status people are generally more future-oriented. They train and plan for the future. Their goals are clear, and their efforts are directly addressed to achieving these goals. Even their reading matter relates directly to these goals. For example, high-status individuals read *Forbes*, *Fortune*, and the *Wall Street Journal* to help them achieve their financial goals. When speaking to a lower-status audience, relate future-oriented issues to their more immediate and demanding situations.

3. *Will the different status groups have different time limitations?* Higher-status, more financially secure people may be more likely to devote their time to social and political issues. Lower-status people may be more concerned with meeting their immediate needs. Time is extremely valuable to the poor. The speaker who asks anything that would take their time is demanding a great deal—perhaps more than many can afford. Relate any request for them to see "the larger picture" to the fulfillment of their present needs.

Religion

Today there is great diversity within each religion. Almost invariably, there are conservative, liberal, and middle-of-the-road groups within each. As the differences within each religion widen, the differences between and among religions seem to narrow. Different religions are coming closer together on various social and political, as well as moral, issues. And, most people would argue, that direction is increasingly conservative (Roof & McKinney 1988), though religions in other parts of the world (for example, Europe) are becoming more liberal.

Secular and Sacred Cultures   Some cultures may be viewed as secular cultures, where religion does not dominate the attitudes and views of the people or greatly influence political or educational decisions (Dodd 1995). Liberal Protestant cultures such as the peoples of the Scandinavian countries would be clearly secular. Other cultures are sacred; in these cultures religion and religious beliefs and values dominate everything a person does and influence politics, education, and just about every other topic or issue imaginable. Islamic cultures are examples of traditional sacred cultures. Technically, the United States is a secular culture (the Constitution, for example, expressly separates church and state), but in some areas of the country religion does exert a powerful influence on schools (from prayers to condom distribution to sex education) and politics (from selection of political leaders to concern for social welfare to gay rights legislation).

Generalizations here, as with gender, are changing rapidly. So, use these questions as guides to exploring this extremely complex topic of religion and religious attitudes.

How might the religions of your class members influence the ways they might view two or three of today's news items?

1. *Will the religious see your topic or purpose from the point of view of religion?* Religion permeates all topics and all issues. On a most obvious level, we know that such issues as birth control, abortion, and divorce are closely connected to religion. Similarly, premarital sex, marriage, child rearing, money, cohabitation, responsibilities toward parents, and thousands of other issues are clearly influenced by religion. Religion is also important, however, in areas where its connection is not so obvious. For example, religion influences one's ideas concerning such topics as obedience to authority, responsibility to government, and the usefulness of qualities like honesty, guilt, and happiness.

2. *Does your topic or purpose attack the religious beliefs of any segment of your audience?* Even those who claim total alienation from the religion in which they were raised may still have strong emotional (though perhaps unconscious) ties to that religion. These ties may continue to influence their attitudes and beliefs.

When dealing with any religious beliefs (and particularly when disagreeing with them), recognize that you are going to meet stiff opposition. Proceed slowly and inductively. Present your evidence and argument before expressing your disagreement.

For your next speech, what would be your ideal audience (in terms of age; gender; cultural factors; educational and intellectual levels; occupation, income, and status; and religion)? What would be the most difficult audience imaginable?

3. *Do the religious beliefs of your audience differ in any significant ways from the official teachings of their religion?* Do not assume that a religious leader's opinion or pronouncement is accepted by the rank-and-file members.

Generally, opinion polls show that official statements by religious leaders take a more conservative position than members do.

4. *Can you make reliable inferences about people's behavior based on their religiousness?* One of the common beliefs about religious people is that they are more honest, more charitable, and more likely to reach out to those in need than the nonreligious are. A review of research, however, finds even this seemingly logical connection not true (Kohn 1989). For example, in a study of cheating among college students, religious beliefs bore little relationship to honesty; in fact, atheists were less likely to cheat than those who identified themselves as religious. Other studies have found that religious people were not any more likely to help those in need, for example, to give time to work with retarded children or to comfort someone lying in the street. So, be careful of making assumptions about people's behavior on the basis of their religiousness. You are much more likely to be accurate in judging attitudes than behaviors.

Other Factors

No list of audience characteristics can possibly be complete, and the list presented here is no exception. You will need another category—"other factors"—to identify any additional characteristics that might be significant to your particular audience. Such factors might include the following.

Expectations.   How will your audience's expectations about you influence their reception of your speech? Whether you intend to fulfill these expectations or explode them, you need to take them into consideration.

Relationship Status.   Will the relationship status of your audience members influence the way in which they view your topic or your purpose?

Special Interests.   Do the special interests of your audience members relate to your topic or purpose? What special interests do the audience members have? What occupies their leisure time?

Organizational Memberships.   How might the organizational memberships of your audience influence your topic or purpose? Might you use these organizational memberships in your examples and illustrations?

Political Affiliation.   Will your audience's political affiliations influence how they view your topic or purpose? Are they politically liberal? Conservative? What does this mean to the development of your speech?

TIPS
From Professional Speakers

Once you have gathered that [demographic] information and thought it through, the answers to these further questions will give you the detailed information you need to make your presentation more relevant to your audience's needs and interests:
■ What can you say that will be of most use or interest to participants?
■ What can you say about how well they perform the task you are there to discuss?
■ What other positive points can your talk include?
■ How can you let the audience know you are sincere and realistic?
■ How else can you help them see the benefits of your message?

Stephen C. Rafe, president of Rapport Communications and professional speech coach and adviser. *How to Be Prepared to Think on Your Feet* (New York: HarperBusiness, 1990), p. 58.

If you were writing this textbook, what other audience characteristics would you include? What would you advise the student of public speaking to do on the basis of these characteristics?

What audience analysis information might be relevant to the following speakers, who are, let us assume, scheduled to speak to your public speaking class: Dan Quayle on the legacy of the Reagan-Bush administration, Betty Friedan on the women's movement, and Al Gore on the environment?

▬ ANALYZING CONTEXT CHARACTERISTICS

In addition to analyzing specific listeners, devote attention to the specific context in which you will speak. Consider the size of the audience, the physical environment, the occasion, the time of your speech, and where your speech fits into the sequence of events.

Size of Audience

Generally, the larger the audience, the more formal the speech presentation should be. With a small audience, you may be more casual and informal. In a large audience, you will have a wider variety of religions, a greater range of occupations and income levels, and so on. All the variables noted earlier will be more intensified in a large audience. Therefore, you will need supporting materials that will appeal to all members.

Physical Environment

The physical environment—indoors or outdoors, room or auditorium, sitting or standing audience—will obviously influence your speech presentation. Take a few minutes to erase or lessen the problem of entering the public speaking environment totally cold. Spend some time in front of the room. See the room from the perspective of the speaker (and from the perspective of the listener), before you are ready to speak.

Another factor in speech effectiveness is audience density. Generally, audiences are easier to persuade if they are sitting close together than if they are spread widely apart. With listeners close together, it is easier to maintain eye contact and to concentrate your focus.

Occasion

What audience analysis information might be relevant to these speakers, who are, let us assume, to speak with the entire student body of your college: Ricki Lake on making it in the media, Colin Powell on gays and lesbians in the military, and Kevin Costner on preserving the heritage of Native Americans?

The occasion greatly influences the nature and the reception of the speech. Whether the speech is a class exercise (as most of your early speeches will be) or some invited address (as most of your professional-life speeches will be) will influence much of the speech. When the speech is given as a class assignment, for example, you will probably be operating under a number of restrictions—time limitations, the type of purpose you can employ, the types of supporting materials you can use, and various other matters. When your speech is invited because of who you are, you have greater freedom to talk about what interests you, which, by virtue of the invitation, will also interest the audience.

The occasion will in part dictate the kind of speech required. A speech at a wedding will differ drastically from a speech at a funeral, which will differ drastically from one at a political rally. In constructing the speech, focus on each element in relation to the occasion. Ask yourself in what way the particular public speaking variable (language, organization, or supporting materials, for example) might be made more responsive to this particular occasion.

Time of the Speech

If your speech is to be given in an early morning class, say, around 8:00 A.M., then take into consideration that some of your listeners will still be half-asleep. Tell them you appreciate their attendance; compliment their attention. If necessary, wake them up with your voice, gestures, attention-gaining materials, visual aids, and the like. If your speech is in the evening when most of your listeners are eager to get home, recognize this as well.

Sequence of Events

Also consider where your speech fits into the general events of the time. A useful procedure is to scan a recent newsmagazine as well as the morning newspaper to see if any items relate to what you will say in your speech. If one does, you might make reference to the story as a way of gaining attention, adding support to your argument, or stressing the importance of the topic.

Think too about where your speech fits in with the other speeches that will be heard that day or during that class. If you are to speak after one or more other speakers, try especially hard to build in some reference to a previous speech. This will help to stress your similarity with the audience members and will also help you demonstrate important connections between what you are saying and what others have said.

> What other context characteristics should a speaker in your class take into consideration in preparing her or his next speech?

UNIT IN BRIEF

Factors to consider in analyzing an audience	■ cultural factors ■ age ■ gender (biological sex and psychological sex role) ■ educational and intellectual levels ■ occupation, income, and status ■ religion and religiousness ■ other factors: expectations, relationship status, special interests, organizational memberships, and political affiliations
Factors to consider in analyzing the context	■ size of the audience ■ physical environment ■ occasion ■ time ■ sequence of events

PRACTICALLY SPEAKING

Short Speech Technique

Prepare and deliver a two-minute speech in which you:

1. explain how men and women see the world differently or similarly
2. explain the importance of culture in public speaking
3. explain a particularly strong belief that you hold
4. explain some of the things you don't understand about the influence of culture, age, gender, or any other sociological factor on audience analysis
5. explain the differences between attitudes and beliefs (with lots of examples)

10.1   Analyzing an Unknown Audience

This experience should familiarize you with some of the essential steps in analyzing an audience on the basis of relatively little evidence and in predicting their attitudes.

Break up into small groups of five or six members. Each group should focus on a different magazine; your task is to analyze the audience (that is, the readers or subscribers) of that particular magazine in terms of the characteristics discussed in this unit. The only information you will have about the audience is that they are avid and typical readers of the given magazine. Pay particular attention to the types of articles published in the magazine, the advertisements, the photographs or illustrations, the editorial statements, the price of the magazine, and so on. Magazines that differ widely from each other are most appropriate for this experience.

After the audience has been analyzed, try to identify at least three favorable and three unfavorable attitudes they probably hold on contemporary issues. On what basis do you make these predictions? If you had to address this audience advocating a position with which they disagreed, what adaptations would you make? What strategies would you use in preparing and presenting this persuasive speech?

Share with the rest of the class the results of your efforts, taking special care to point out not only your conclusions but also the evidence and reasoning you used in arriving at the conclusions.

UNIT 11

The Audience: Psychological Analysis and Adaptation

Unit Objectives

After completing this unit, you should be able to:

1   Identify the five dimensions of an audience

2   Explain how the public speaker might adapt to audiences that differ on the five dimensions

3   Explain at least three guidelines for dealing with a mixed audience

4   Explain the suggestions for analyzing and adapting to the audience during the speech

*I*n the preceding unit we looked at the demographic characteristics of an audience and how you can discover some of their attitudes and beliefs that may be relevant to your speech. In this unit we continue the discussion of audience analysis. Here, however, the focus is on psychological characteristics, such as how willing the audience members are to listen to you and how favorable they are to your topic.

You may view audiences along such scales as those in Figure 11.1. By indicating on each scale where you think a particular audience is, you can construct an audience profile. Since each audience is unique, each audience will have a unique profile.

What do you think Blaise Pascal meant when he said, "The more intelligent a man is, the more originality he discovers in men. Ordinary people see no difference between men"?

HOW WILLING IS YOUR AUDIENCE?

Audiences gather with varying degrees of willingness to hear a speaker. Some are eager to hear the speaker and might even pay a substantial admission price. The "lecture circuit," for example, is a most lucrative aspect of public life. While some audiences are willing to pay to hear a speaker, others do not seem to care one way or the other. Still other audiences need to be persuaded to listen (or at least to sit in the audience). A group of people who gather to hear Shirley MacLaine talk about supernatural experiences are probably there willingly; they want to be there, and they want to hear what MacLaine has to say. On the other hand, some groups gather because they have to. The union contract may require members to attend meetings, for example, and administrators may put pressure on instructors to attend college and department meetings. These people may not wish to be there, but they do not want to risk losing their vote or their jobs.

Your immediate concern, of course, is with the willingness of your fellow students to listen to your speeches. How willing are they? Do they come to class because they have to, or do they come because they are interested in what you'll say? If they are a willing group, then you have few problems. If they are an unwilling group, all is not lost—you just have to work a little harder in adapting your speech.

What other psychological factors might have been included in this unit?

FIGURE 11.1
The dimensions of an audience.

The Audience

Willing	__ :	__ :	__ :	__ :	__ :	__ :	__ Unwilling
Favorable	__ :	__ :	__ :	__ :	__ :	__ :	__ Unfavorable
Passive	__ :	__ :	__ :	__ :	__ :	__ :	__ Active
Knowledgeable	__ :	__ :	__ :	__ :	__ :	__ :	__ Not Knowledgeable
Homogeneous	__ :	__ :	__ :	__ :	__ :	__ :	__ Heterogeneous

Adapting to the Unwilling Audience

The unwilling audience demands special and delicate handling. Here are a few suggestions to help change your listeners from unwilling to willing.

Secure their interest and attention as early in your speech as possible. Reinforce this throughout the speech by using little-known facts, quotations, startling statistics, examples, narratives, audiovisual aids, and the like. These devices will help you secure and maintain the attention of an initially unwilling audience. Here, for example, Judith Maxwell (1987), chair of the Economic Council of Canada, uses humor to gain the interest and attention of her audience. She then quickly connects this humor to the topic of her talk:

> *Yogi Berra said something once that's relevant to a discussion of economic forecasting. "If you don't know where you're going, you could wind up somewhere else." Whether we are business economists or economists in the public sector, what society expects from us is advice on how to "know where we are going." Our mission is to help captains of industry or captains of the ship of state plot an orderly path forward. In that sense, we are navigators.*

Reward the audience for their attendance and attention. Do this in advance of your main arguments. Let the audience know you are aware they are making a sacrifice in coming to hear you speak. Tell them you appreciate it. One student, giving a speech close to midterm time, said simply:

> *I know how easy it is to cut classes during midterm time to finish the unread chapters and do everything else you have to do. So I especially appreciate your being here this morning. What I have to say, however, will interest you and will be of direct benefit to all of you.*

Once the speaker acknowledges this, it is difficult for an audience to continue to feel unwilling.

Relate your topic and supporting materials directly to your audience's needs and wants. Show the audience how they can save time, make more money, solve their problems, or become more popular. If you fail to do this, then your audience has good reason for not listening.

How willing to listen to speeches is your class generally? On what evidence do you base your answer? What one means might you use to increase their willingness to listen?

Lord Chesterfield once observed, "Never hold any one by the button or the hand in order to be heard out; for if people are unwilling to hear you, you had better hold your tongue than them." How might you "hold" people with the principles of public speaking?

▰ HOW FAVORABLE IS YOUR AUDIENCE?

Audiences will vary in the degree to which they are favorable or unfavorable toward your thesis or point of view. And, of course, within the same audience you may have some who agree with you, others who disagree, and perhaps still others undecided. If you intend to change an audience's attitudes, beliefs, or behaviors, you must understand their present position.

Audiences also differ in their attitudes toward you and toward your topic. At times the audience may have no real feeling, positive or negative. At other times they will have very clear feelings that must be confronted. Thus, when

ANALYSIS AND ADAPTATION DURING THE SPEECH

Can you identify any adaptations speakers made during the speeches so far this semester? If so, were they effective? Were there additional opportunities for such adaptations that were not made?

In your classroom speeches, you will face a known audience, an audience you have already analyzed and for which you have made appropriate adaptations. At other times, however, you may face an audience that you have not been able to analyze beforehand or one that differs greatly from the audience you thought you would address. In these cases you will have to analyze and adapt to them as you speak. Here are some suggestions for making this process easy and effective.

Ask "What If" Questions

As you prepare your speech, have your audience clearly in mind. For example, let us say you have been told that you are to explain the opportunities available to the nontraditional student at your college. You have been told that your audience will consist mainly of working women in their thirties and forties who are just beginning college. As you prepare your speech with this audience in mind, ask yourself "what if" questions, for example:

- What if the audience has a large number of men?
- What if the audience consists of women much older than 30 and 40?
- What if the audience members also come with their spouses or their children?

Keeping such questions in mind will force you to consider alternatives as you prepare your speech. And you will find them readily available if you face this new or different audience.

Speak Extemporaneously

How important is adapting to your audience during your speech? How important is this on-the-spot adaptation in teaching?

As explained in more detail in Unit 17, when you speak extemporaneously, you prepare a delivery outline that includes your main assertions and your supporting materials in the order in which they will be presented. But, avoid memorizing your speech or otherwise committing yourself to any exact wording. In this way you will maintain the flexibility to delete examples that may be inappropriate or to add examples that may be more relevant to this new audience. If you memorize your speech, you will find it impossible to make these essential last-minute adjustments.

Do Extra

The more preparation you put into your speech, the better prepared you will be to make on-the-spot adjustments and adaptations. For example, if you anticipate a knowledgeable audience you may decide not to include background material or definitions in your speech. But you should have these ready just in case you discover that your listeners are not as knowledgeable as you thought. The more alternatives you consider as you prepare your speech, the more alternatives you will have available as you deliver it.

Focus on Listeners as Message Senders

As you are speaking, look at your listeners. Remember that just as you are sending messages to your audience, so too are they sending messages to you. Just as they are responding to what you are communicating, so too do you need to respond to what they are communicating. Pay attention to these messages, and on the basis of what they tell you, make the necessary adjustments.

Do remember that members of different cultures will operate with different display rules, cultural rules that state what types of expressions are appropriate to reveal and what expressions are inappropriate to reveal and should be kept hidden. Some display rules call for open and free expression of feelings and responses; listeners with these rules will be relatively easy to read. Other display rules call for little expression, and listeners with these rules will be extremely difficult to read.

If your listeners are talking among themselves or reading their newspapers, then it should be clear that they are not paying attention and that you have to do something to win them back. But not all audience behaviors are so obvious. Wanda Vassallo, in the accompanying TIPS, offers a wide variety of cues that you may wish to look for. These are more subtle behaviors, and their meanings are harder to decode. You may wish to use Vassallo's suggestions for reading these cues as starting points, but remember that any bit of nonverbal behavior may mean many different things.

A wide range of adjustments could be made to each type of audience response. For example, if your audience shows signs of boredom, you might increase your volume, move closer to them, or tell them that what you are going to say will be of value to them. If your audience shows signs of disagreement or hostility, you might stress some similarity you have with them. If your audience looks puzzled or confused, you might pause a moment and rephrase your ideas, provide necessary definitions, or insert an internal summary. If your audience seems impatient, you might say, for example, "My last argument . . ." instead of your originally planned "My third argument . . . "

Address Audience Responses Directly

Another way of dealing with audience responses is to confront them directly and say to those who disagree, for example:

> *I know you disagree with this position, but all I ask is that you hear me out and see if this new way of doing things will not simplify your accounting procedures.*

Or, to those who seem puzzled, you might say:

> *I know this plan may seem confusing, but bear with me; it will become clear in a moment.*

TIPS
From Professional Speakers

These are some generally accepted messages listeners give a speaker by what they do.

Folding arms across chest—closed mind or hostile response

Moving chair forward, leaning forward toward speaker—open-mindedness, interest in message

Crossing legs—competitive attitude, opposition

Stroking chin—undecided, contemplating

Open hands—willingness to listen

Hands behind head—taking it all in

Fidgeting, looking around—bored

Swinging foot in circle, tapping foot—bored, impatient

Wrinkled brow—puzzled, contemplating

Wringing hands—nervous, anxious

Twiddling thumbs—bored

Shrugging shoulders—indifference

Gritting teeth—anger

Rolling eyes—disgust

Dropping mouth open—disbelief

Covering mouth with hand—surprise, shock

Biting lip—concentration, thinking

Looking off in distance—indifference, daydreaming

Touching nose with index finger quickly—doubt

Glancing sideways, drawing back—suspicion

Steepling hands—confidence

Wanda Vassallo, speaker, writer, and minister. From *Speaking with Confidence: A Guide for Public Speakers.* Copyright © 1990 by Wanda Vassallo. Reprinted by permission of Betterway Publications, Inc.

Americans speaking in Japan, to take one well-researched example, need to be careful lest they make their point too obvious or too direct and insult the audience. Speakers in Japan (and in other high-context cultures) are expected to lead their listeners to the conclusion through example, illustration, and various other indirect means (Lustig & Koestler 1996).

High-context cultures place a great deal more emphasis on saving face than low-context cultures do. As already noted in our discussion of criticism (Unit 5), members of high-context cultures may be less willing and less comfortable than members of low-context cultures to give and receive public criticism.

In the United States (and in other low-context cultures) speakers are encouraged to be explicit and direct, to tell the audience, for example, exactly what the speaker wants them to do (see the earlier discussion, in Unit 6, on focusing audience attention on the thesis).

In the United States each major proposition of a speech or written composition should be developed by itself. Only when this is fully developed and finalized would the speaker or writer move on to the next point. Hindu culture, however, is less rigid and allows for many ideas being considered in the same paragraph of an essay or in the same part of a speech (Lustig & Koestler 1996).

In what one way might your previous speech have been different were you addressing a homogeneous audience representing a high-context culture? A homogeneous audience representing a low-context culture? A heterogeneous audience?

MAJOR PROPOSITIONS

The major propositions are your main assertions—your major points of information or your major arguments, for example. Here we explain how to select and word these propositions and how to use them effectively in a speech.

Selecting and Wording Propositions

In discussing the thesis (Unit 6), you saw how you can develop your main points or propositions by asking strategic questions. To see how this works in detail, imagine that you are giving a speech to a group of high school students on the values of a college education. Your thesis is "A college education is valuable." You then ask, "Why is it valuable?" From this question you generate your major propositions. Your first step might be to brainstorm this question and generate as many answers as possible without evaluating them. You may come up with answers such as the following:

What main ideas might you generate from these theses: (a) College athletics should be expanded, (b) students need to be educated about AIDS, (c) college courses in foreign languages should be discontinued.

1. It helps you get a good job.
2. It increases your earning potential.
3. It gives you greater job mobility.
4. It helps you secure more creative work.
5. It helps you appreciate the arts more fully.
6. It helps you understand an extremely complex world.
7. It helps you understand different cultures.
8. It allows you to avoid taking a regular job for a few years.
9. It helps you meet lots of people and make new friends.
10. It helps you increase your personal effectiveness.

There are, of course, other possibilities, but for purposes of illustration these ten possible main points will suffice. But not all ten are equally valuable or relevant to your audience, so you should look over the list to see how to make it shorter and more meaningful. Try these suggestions:

1. *Eliminate those points that seem least important to your thesis.* On this basis you might want to eliminate No. 8, since this seems least consistent with your intended emphasis on the positive values of college.

2. *Combine those points that have a common focus.* Notice, for example, that the first four points all center on the values of college in terms of jobs. You might therefore consider grouping these four items into one proposition:

> *A college education helps you get a good job.*

This point might be one of the major propositions that could be developed by defining what you mean by a "good job." This main point or proposition and its elaboration might look like this:

> I. A college education helps you get a good job.
>   A. College graduates earn higher salaries.
>   B. College graduates enter more creative jobs.
>   C. College graduates have greater job mobility.

What motivated you to go to college? How might you use that motivation as a major proposition?

Note that A, B, and C are all aspects or subdivisions of a "good job."

3. *Select points that are most relevant to or that interest your audience.* On this basis you might eliminate No. 5 and No. 7 on the assumption that the audience will not see learning about the arts or different cultures as exciting or valuable at the present time. You might also decide that high school students would be more interested in increasing personal effectiveness, so you might select No. 10 for inclusion as a second major proposition:

> *A college education increases your personal effectiveness.*

Earlier you developed the subordinate points in your first proposition (the A, B, and C of I) by defining more clearly what you meant by a "good job." Follow the same process here by defining what you mean by "personal effectiveness." It might look something like this:

> I. A college education helps increase your personal effectiveness.
>   A. A college education helps you improve your ability to communicate.
>   B. A college education helps you acquire the skills for learning how to think.
>   C. A college education helps you acquire coping skills.

Follow the same procedure you used to generate the subordinate points (A, B, and C) to develop the subheadings under A, B, and C. For example, point A might be divided into two major subheads:

A. A college education helps improve your ability to communicate.
1. College improves your writing skills.
2. College improves your speech skills.

Develop points B and C in essentially the same way by defining more clearly (in B) what you mean by "learning how to think" and (in C) what you mean by "coping skills. "

4. *Use two, three, or four main points.* For your class speeches, which will generally range from 5 to 15 minutes, use two, three, or four main propositions. Too many main points will result in a speech that is confusing, contains too much information and too little amplification, and proves difficult to remember.

5. *Word each of your major propositions in the same (parallel) style.* Phrase points labeled with roman numerals in a similar (parallel) style. Likewise, phrase points labeled with capital letters and subordinate to the same roman numeral (for example, A, B, and C under point I or A, B, and C under point II) in a similar style. Parallel style is used in the example on college education.

This parallel styling helps the audience follow and remember your speech. Notice in the following that the first outline is more difficult to understand than the second, which is phrased in parallel style.

NOT THIS:

Mass Media Functions

  I. The media entertain.

 II. The media function to inform their audiences.

III. Creating ties of union is a major media function.

IV. The conferral of status is a function of all media.

THIS:

Mass Media Functions

  I. The media entertain.

 II. The media inform.

III. The media create ties of union.

IV. The media confer status.

How is parallel styling used in this textbook? In your other textbooks? Does this help to make the material easier to understand or remember?

6. *Develop your main points so they are separate and discrete.* Do not allow your main points to overlap each other. Each section labeled with a roman numeral should be a separate entity.

NOT THIS:

  I. Color and style are important in clothing selection.

THIS:

   I. Color is important in clothing selection.

  II. Style is important in clothing selection.

7. *Use the principle of balance.* Devote about equal time to each of your main points. A useful rule of thumb is to give about equal time to each item having the same symbol in your outline. Give each roman numeral about equal time, each item denoted by a capital letter about the same amount of time, and so on. Break this rule only when you have an especially good reason.

Coordination and Subordination

Central to a well-organized speech is the logical coordination and subordination of your assertions and supporting materials. Focus on the following partial outline dealing with two areas of study, some specific courses, and some areas covered in these courses (Table 12.1). This outline is intended not to illustrate how a speech outline would look but only to illustrate coordination and subordination.

Coordination   Focus first on the two major headings: psychology and sociology. In the outline in Table 12.1, they are equal and parallel. They are coordinate items. Within the psychology heading there are other coordinate items. Learning and motivation are coordinate; they represent two specific courses taught in psychology departments. The course in learning covers classical conditioning and operant conditioning, again coordinate items. Development

---

TABLE 12.1   **An Outline Illustrating Coordination and Subordination**

I. Psychology
  A. Learning
    1. Classical conditioning
      a. Development
      b. Current status
    2. Operant conditioning
      a. Development
      b. Current status
  B. Motivation
    1. Cognitive theories
      a. Development
      b. Current status
    2. Instinct theories
      a. Development
      b. Current status

II. Sociology
  A. Prejudice
    1. Instinct theories
      a. Development
      b. Current status
    2. Learning theories
      a. Development
      b. Current status
  B. Crime
    1. Instinct theories
      a. Development
      b. Current status
    2. Learning theories
      a. Development
      b. Current status

Create an outline illustrating coordination and subordination for one of the following topics: (1) exercise, (2) food, (3) drinks, (4) animals, and (5) college courses.

and current status are likewise coordinate; they are two topics covered in each of the different theories. The same is true of the sociology outline.

Note that the coordinate items of psychology and sociology are both given roman numerals (I and II); the major courses, capital letters (A and B); and the specific theories, arabic numerals (1 and 2).

Subordination   Two items of information are subordinate when they are related in such a way that one item is a part of, supports, or amplifies the other. For example, learning and motivation are two courses that are part of psychology and hence are subordinate to psychology. Classical conditioning and operant conditioning are types of learning and as such are subordinate to learning. Similarly, cognitive and instinct theories are subordinate to motivation in the same way that prejudice and crime are subordinate to sociology.

Note that items that are immediately subordinate to another item are given symbols of one order lower: Items subordinate to roman numeral items are given capital letters; items subordinate to arabic numeral items are given small letters; and so on. There is nothing magical about the hierarchy of this symbol system; it is simply the customary, agreed-on system.

Select any unit in this book. What are the coordinate items in the unit? What items are immediately subordinate to the unit title? How are coordination and subordination illustrated visually in this text?

ORGANIZATIONAL PATTERNS

Once you have identified the major propositions you wish to include in your speech, you need to devote attention to how you will arrange these propositions in the body of your speech. When you follow a clearly identified organizational pattern, your listeners will be able to see your speech as a whole and will be able to see more clearly the connections and relationships among your various pieces of information. Should they have a momentary lapse in attention—as they surely will at some point in just about every speech—they will be able to refocus their attention and not lose your entire train of thought.

Consider each pattern in terms of the topics to which it is most applicable and the ways in which you can arrange your main points and supporting materials. The introduction, conclusion, and transitions are considered in depth in Unit 13. The mechanical aspects of outlining and additional guidance in preparing the outline are presented in Unit 14.

Temporal Pattern

Organizing your propositions on the basis of some temporal (time) relationship is a popular and easy-to-use organizational pattern. It is also a pattern that listeners will find easy to follow. Generally, when you use this pattern you organize your speech into two, three, or four major parts, beginning with the past and working up to the present or the future, or beginning with the present or the future and working back to the past.

The temporal (sometimes called "chronological") pattern is especially appropriate for informative speeches in which you wish to describe events or processes that occur over time. It is also useful when you wish to demonstrate how something works or how to do something.

How would you organize a speech on "the ideal exercise plan," using at least three different organizational patterns discussed in this unit? How would you organize a speech on "Should the United States reduce defense spending," using at least three organizational patterns discussed here?

A speech on the development of language in the child might be organized in a temporal pattern and could be divided something like this:

The Development of Language

   I. Babbling occurs around the fifth month.

  II. Lallation occurs around the sixth month.

 III. Echolalia occurs around the ninth month.

 IV. "Communication" occurs around the twelfth month.

Here you would cover each of the events in a time sequence beginning with the earliest stage and working up to the final stage—in this case the stage of true communication.

Most historical topics lend themselves to organization by time. The events leading up to the Civil War, the steps toward a college education, and the history of writing would all be appropriate for temporal patterning. A time pattern would also be appropriate in describing the essential steps in a multistep process in which temporal order is especially important. The steps involved in making interpersonal contact with another person might look something like this:

Making Interpersonal Contact

   I. Spot the person you want to make contact with.

  II. Make eye contact.

 III. Give some positive nonverbal sign.

 IV. Make verbal contact.

How would you organize a speech to your class on the fall of communism in the Soviet Union? A speech on the major beliefs in traditional communism? What would your major propositions be?

Spatial Pattern

How would you organize a speech explaining the layout of a football field? A speech on the rules of football? What would your major propositions be?

You can also organize your main points on the basis of space. This pattern is especially useful when you wish to describe objects or places. Like the temporal pattern, it is an organizational pattern that listeners will find easy to follow as you progress, from top to bottom, left to right, inside to outside, or east to west, for example. The structure of a place, object, or even animal is easily placed into a spatial pattern. You might describe the layout of a hospital, school, or skyscraper or perhaps even the structure of a dinosaur with a spatial pattern of organization. Here is an example of an outline describing the structure of the traditional townhouse and using a spatial pattern:

The Townhouse

I. The first floor is the kitchen.

II. The second floor is the living and dining rooms.

III. The third floor is the master bedroom suite.

IV. The fourth floor is the children's rooms.

V. The fifth floor is the maid's rooms.

Note that this outline violates the general rule to use no more than four major points. Was it logical to break this rule in this case? What alternatives might have been used?

Topical Pattern

Perhaps the most popular pattern for organizing informative speeches is the topical pattern. When your topic conveniently divides itself into subdivisions, each of which is clear and approximately equal in importance, this pattern is most useful. A speech on principal cities of the world might be organized into a topical pattern, as might speeches on problems facing the college graduate, great works of literature, the world's major religions, and the like. Each of these topics would have several subtopics or divisions of approximately equal importance; consequently, a topical pattern seems most appropriate. For example, the topical pattern is an obvious one for organizing a speech on the powers of the government. The topic itself divides into three parts: legislative, executive, and judicial. A sample outline might look like this:

How would you organize a speech on the forms of communication? On computer software? On library holdings?

The Powers of Government

I. The legislative branch is controlled by Congress.

II. The executive branch is controlled by the president.

III. The judicial branch is controlled by the courts.

Problem-Solution Pattern

The problem-solution pattern is especially useful in persuasive speeches where you want to convince the audience that a problem exists and your solution would solve or lessen it.

Let's say you believe that jury awards for damages have gotten out of hand. You might want to persuade your audience, then, that jury awards for damages should be limited. A problem-solution pattern might be appropriate here. In this first part of your speech, you would identify the problem(s) created by these large awards, and in the second part, the solution. A sample outline for such a speech might look something like this:

I. Jury awards for damages are out of control. [the general problem]
   A. These awards increase insurance rates. [a specific problem]
   B. These awards increase medical costs. [a second specific problem]
   C. These awards place unfair burdens on business. [a third specific problem]

II. Jury awards need to be limited. [the general solution]
   A. Greater evidence should be required before a case can be brought to trial. [a specific solution]
   B. Part of the award should be turned over to the state. [a second specific solution]
   C. Realistic estimates of financial damage should be used. [a third specific solution]

Cause-Effect/Effect-Cause Pattern

Similar to the problem-solution pattern is the cause-effect or effect-cause pattern. This pattern is useful in persuasive speeches in which you want to convince your audience of the causal connection existing between two events or elements. In the cause-effect pattern you divide the speech into two major sections, causes and effects. For example, a speech on the reasons for highway accidents or birth defects might lend itself to a cause-effect pattern. Here you might consider first, say, the causes of highway accidents or birth defects and then some of the effects, for example, the number of deaths, the number of accidents, and so on.

Let's say you want to demonstrate the causes for the increase in AIDS in your state. You might use an effect-cause pattern that looks something like this:

I. AIDS is increasing in our state. [general effect]
   A. AIDS is increasing among teenagers. [a specific effect]
   B. AIDS is increasing among IV drug users. [a second specific effect]
   C. AIDS is increasing among women. [a third specific effect]

II. Three factors contribute to this increase. [general causal statement]
   A. Teenagers are ignorant about how the HIV virus is transmitted. [a specific cause]
   B. IV drug users exchange tainted needles. [a second specific cause]
   C. Women are not practicing safe sex. [a third specific cause]

As you can see from this example, this type of speech is often combined with the problem-solution type. For instance, after identifying the causes the speaker might then treat the causes as problems and offer solutions for each

How would you organize a speech in which you argue in favor of the need for comprehensive national health insurance? In which you argue that the vice-president of the United States should be elected separately? What would your major propositions be?

How would you organize a speech designed to persuade an audience that sports stars' salaries are damaging professional sports?

problem/cause (for example, education programs for teens, free needle exchange, and education programs for men and women).

The Motivated Sequence

Developed by Alan H. Monroe in the 1930s and widely used in all sorts of oral and written communications, the motivated sequence is a pattern of arranging your information so as to motivate your audience to respond positively to your purpose (Gronbeck, McKerrow, Ehninger, & Monroe 1994). In fact, it can be reasonably argued that all effective communications follow this basic pattern whether it is called the motivated sequence or given some other name.

As you will see, the motivated sequence is especially appropriate for speeches designed to move an audience to action (to persuade your listeners to do something). However, it is also useful for a wide variety of informative speeches.

Whereas the organizational patterns discussed previously provide ways of organizing the main ideas in the body of the speech, the motivated sequence is a pattern for organizing the entire speech. Here the speech (introduction, body, and conclusion) is divided into five parts or steps: (1) attention, (2) need, (3) satisfaction, (4) visualization, and (5) action.

Step 1. Gain Attention   The attention step makes the audience give you their undivided attention. If you execute this step effectively, your audience should be eager and ready to hear what you have to say. You can gain audience attention through a variety of means (more fully identified in Unit 13):

In what ways do television commercials gain your attention? Might these techniques prove effective in public speaking? If so, how?

What organizational pattern do most of the speeches you hear follow? What patterns do most of the college lectures you hear follow? What advice would you give your instructors on organizing college lectures?

1. Ask a question (rhetorical or actual).
2. Make reference to audience members.
3. Make reference to recent happenings.
4. Use humor.
5. Use an illustration or dramatic story.
6. Stress the importance of the topic to this specific audience.
7. Use audiovisual aids, tell the audience to pay attention, use a quotation, refer to yourself, refer directly to your thesis or purpose, make reference to a little-known fact or statistic.

 How might you gain attention in a speech to your class on "Five Guidelines in Finding a Job"?

Step 2. Establish Need   In the second part of your speech, you would demonstrate that a need exists. The audience should feel that something has to be learned or something has to be done because of this demonstrated need. Monroe suggests that need be established in four parts:

1. State the need or problem as it exists or will exist.
2. Illustrate the need with specific examples.
3. Further support the existence of the need with additional illustrations, statistics, testimony, and other forms of support (identified in Units 8, 9, 21–23).
4. Show how this need affects your specific listeners, for example, how it affects their financial status, their career goals, or their individual happiness.

Step 3. Satisfy the Need   Present the "answer" or the "solution" to satisfying the need that you demonstrated in Step 2. On the basis of this satisfaction step, the audience should now believe that what you are informing them about or persuading them to do will effectively satisfy the need. In this step you answer the question, "How will the need be satisfied by what I am asking the audience to learn, to believe, to do?" This satisfaction step usually involves:

1. A statement (with examples and illustrations, if necessary) of what you want the audience to learn, believe, or do.
2. A statement of how or why what you are asking them to learn, believe, or do will lead to satisfying the need identified in Step 2.

Step 4. Visualize the Need Satisfied   Visualization intensifies the audience's feelings or beliefs. In this step you take the audience beyond the present time and place and enable them to imagine the situation as it would be if the need were satisfied as you suggested in Step 3. There are two basic ways of doing this:

1. Demonstrate the benefits the audience will receive if your ideas are put into operation.
2. Demonstrate the negative effects the audience will suffer if your plan is not put into operation.

Of course, you could combine these two methods and demonstrate both the benefits of your plan and the negative consequences of the existing plan or of some alternative plan.

> ### TIPS
> *From Professional Speakers*
>
> Explain very carefully *how* they [the audience] can apply the information you have presented. For instance, if you have been convincing them they *should* give blood, tell them *where*. And make it sound easy to get there! The enthusiasm of the audience frequently fades quickly, and your stimulus is most important.
>
> **Frank Snell,** advertising executive and teacher. *How to Stand Up and Speak Well in Business* (New York: Simon & Schuster/Cornerstone, 1974), p. 135.

Bring what you feel is a particularly effective print ad to class. Does the ad contain all the elements considered in the motivated sequence?

Step 5. Ask for Action   Tell the audience what they should do to ensure that the need (as demonstrated in Step 2) is satisfied (as stated in Step 3). That is, what should the audience do to satisfy the need? Here you want to move the audience in a particular direction, for example, to speak in favor of additional research funding for AIDS or against cigarette advertising, to attend the next student government meeting, or to contribute free time to read for the blind. You can accomplish this step by stating exactly what the audience members should do, using an emotional appeal, or giving the audience guidelines for future action. These and other methods of concluding and motivating an audience are covered in depth in Units 13 and 22.

Here is a much-abbreviated example of how these five steps would look in a speech designed to inform an audience about the workings of home computers.

[Attention]

> *By the time we graduate, there will be more home computers than automobiles. [You might then go on to explain the phenomenal growth of computers in education until you have the complete attention of your audience revolving around the importance and growth of computers.]*

[Need]

> *Much as it is now impossible to get around without a car, it will be impossible to get around the enormous amount of information without a home computer. [You might then go on to explain how knowledge is expanding so rapidly that, without computer technology, it will be extremely difficult to keep up with any field.]*

[Satisfaction]

> *Learning a few basic principles of home computers will enable us to process our work more efficiently, in less time, and more enjoyably. [You might then explain the various steps your listeners could take to satisfy the needs you have already identified.]*

[Visualization]

> *With these basic principles firmly in mind—and with a home computer— you'll be able to stay at home and do your library research for your next speech by just punching in the correct codes. [You might then go through in more or less detail the speech research process so that your listeners will be able to visualize exactly what the advantages of computer research will be.]*

[Action]

> *These few principles should be supplemented by further study. Probably the best way to further your study is to enroll in a computer course. Another useful way is to read the brief paperback* The Home Computer

FOCUS **O**N

Additional Organizational Patterns

The six patterns just considered are the most common and the most useful for organizing most public speeches. But there are other patterns that might be appropriate for different topics.

Structure-Function

The structure-function pattern is useful in informative speeches in which you want to discuss how something is constructed (its structural aspects) and what it does (its functional aspects). This pattern might be useful, for example, in a speech given to explain what an organization is and what it does, the parts of a university and how they operate, or the sensory systems of the body and their various functions. This pattern might also be useful in discussing the nature of a living organism: its anatomy (that is, its structures) and its physiology (that is, its functions).

Comparison and Contrast

Arranging your material in a comparison-and-contrast pattern is useful in informative speeches in which you want to analyze two different theories, proposals, departments, or products in terms of their similarities and differences. In this type of speech you not only would be concerned with explaining each theory or proposal but also would focus primarily on how they are similar and how they are different.

Pro and Con, Advantages-Disadvantages

The pro-and-con pattern, sometimes called the advantages-disadvantages pattern, is useful in informative speeches in which you want to explain objectively the advantages (the pros) and the disadvantages (the cons) of each plan, method, or product.

Both the comparison-and-contrast and the pro-and-con patterns might be developed by focusing on the several qualities or aspects of each plan or product. For example, if you were comparing two health plans your major propositions might center on such topics as costs to the worker, hospital benefits, and sick leave. Under each of these major propositions, you would show what Health Plan No. 1 provides and then what Health Plan No. 2 provides.

Both of these patterns are also useful in persuasive speeches where you wish to highlight the weaknesses of one plan or product and the strengths of another, much like advertisers do when they compare their product with Brand X.

Claim and Proof

The claim-and-proof pattern is especially useful in a persuasive speech in which you want to prove the truth or usefulness of a particular proposition. It is the pattern that you see frequently in trials where the claim made by the prosecution is that the defendant is guilty and the proof is the varied evidence: The defendant had a motive; the defendant had the opportunity; the defendant had no alibi. In this pattern your speech would consist of two major parts. In the first part you would explain your claim (tuition must not be raised, library hours must be expanded, courses in AIDS education must be instituted). In the second part you would offer your evidence or proof (as to why tuition must not be raised, for example).

Multiple Definition

The multiple definition pattern is useful for informative speeches in which you want to explain the nature of a concept (What is a born-again Christian? What is a scholar? What is multiculturalism?). In this pattern each major heading would consist of a different type of definition or way of looking at the concept. A variety of definition types are discussed in Unit 19.

Who? What? Why? Where? When?

The 5W pattern—who, what, why, where, when—is the pattern of the journalist and is useful in informative speeches when you wish to report or explain an event, for example, a robbery, political coup, war, or trial. Here you would have five major parts to your speech, each dealing with the answers to one of these five questions.

What organizational pattern do most of the speeches you hear follow? What patterns do most of the college lectures follow? What advice would you give your instructors on organizing college lectures?

for the College Student. *[You might then identify the several computer courses that are available and that would be appropriate for a beginning student. Further, you might identify a few other books or perhaps distribute a brief list of books that would be appropriate reading for the beginning student.]*

Notice that in an informative speech you could have stopped after the satisfaction step because you would have accomplished your goal of informing the audience about some principles of home computers. But in some cases you may feel it helpful to complete the steps to emphasize your point in detail.

In a persuasive speech, on the other hand, you must go at least as far as visualization (if your purpose is limited to strengthening or changing attitudes or beliefs) or to the action step (if you are attempting to motivate behavior).

Because your organizational pattern serves primarily to help your listeners follow your speech, you might want to tell your listeners (in your introduction or as a transition between the introduction and the body of your speech) what pattern you will be following. Here are just a few examples:

In explaining the layout of the townhouse, we'll start at the bottom and go to the top.

I'll first explain the problems with jury awards and then propose three workable solutions.

First we'll look at the increase in AIDS, and then we'll look at three of the causes.

STRATEGIES OF INTERNAL ORGANIZATION

In addition to organizing your main ideas in terms of easy-to-follow patterns, consider the strategies of internal organization. For example, should you state your conclusion first and then give your evidence or should you first present your evidence? Should you put your strongest argument first, last, or in the middle? Where do you put your weakest argument? To answer these questions, consider the evidence on (1) climax and anticlimax orders and (2) primacy and recency.

Would you use climax or anticlimax order if you were giving a speech advocating expanding an abortion clinic to a group of right-to-lifers? Advocating dismantling an abortion clinic to a group of prochoice advocates? Why?

Climax and Anticlimax

Climax and anticlimax orders refer to the use of inductive (beginning with specifics and working up to a generalization) or deductive approaches (beginning with a generalization and from it deriving a series of specifics).

In climax order you first present your evidence (your specifics) and then climax it with your conclusion or thesis. For example, you might say to a college class:

The athletic program will have to be cut because of inadequate funds; the student union, which operates at a loss each year, will have to be closed; and class size will have to be increased 40 percent because insufficient funds will result in a number of faculty being fired.

You would then climax these bits of information with the main issue: Tuition must be raised.

In anticlimax order you would start out with the thesis that tuition must be raised (your general statement or conclusion) and then give your reasons (the specifics). Whether you choose the climax or the anticlimax order depends a great deal on the attitudes and viewpoints of your audience. Here are some suggestions:

- Lead with the information the audience will object to least.
- If you anticipate great objection to your thesis, present your arguments and somehow soften the blow that is soon to come.
- If you anticipate little or no objection to your thesis or if your audience already supports it, lead with it and present the reasons or support for it later.

Primacy and Recency

The rule of primacy states that what you hear first will be remembered best and will have the greatest effect. The rule of recency states that what you hear last or most recently will be remembered best and will have the greatest effect.

Research findings on this controversy offer a few useful conclusions.

- What is in the middle is remembered least and has the least general effect. Thus, if you have a speech with three points, put the weakest one in the middle.
- If your listeners are relatively neutral and have no real conviction either way, lead with your best argument and in this way get the listeners on your side early.
- With an audience that is favorable to your point of view, lead with your best argument.
- If you are faced with a hostile audience or with an audience that holds very different views from yours, put your most powerful argument last and work up to it gradually, assuming that you can count on the listeners staying with you until the end.

Research on memory tells us that the audience will remember very little of what you say in a speech. Interesting as your speech may be, listeners will forget most of what you say. Therefore, repeat your main assertions—whether you put them first or last in your speech—in your conclusion.

Intercultural researchers have argued that North Americans are largely deductive, whereas Koreans are largely inductive, in their reasoning (Samovar & Porter 1991, p. 93). How would you structure your speech if you were addressing an audience of all North Americans? Of all Koreans? Of half North Americans and half Koreans?

Would you use primacy or recency order if you were giving a speech arguing in favor of increasing tuition to a group of first-year college students? Supporting an increase in athletic scholarships to a group of physical education instructors? Why?

8. Make (Do not make) the death penalty mandatory for those convicted of selling drugs to minors.
9. Reinstate (Do not reinstate) the draft.
10. Eliminate (Expand) affirmative action programs.
11. Give (Do not give) political asylum to women who have been abused.
12. Elected political officials should (not) be allowed to serve as lobbyists at any time after their term of office has expired.
13. Courses on women's issues should (not) be required for all students at this college.
14. Expand (Reduce, Eliminate) ROTC programs.
15. Abolish (Expand, Reduce) intercollegiate athletic competition.
16. Legalize (Do not legalize) soft drugs.
17. Build (Do not build) houses for the homeless.
18. Become (Do not become) computer literate.
19. Support (Do not support) mandatory instruction in AIDS prevention in all elementary and high schools.
20. Grant (Do not grant) full equality to gay men and lesbians in the military.

UNIT 13

Introductions, Conclusions, and Transitions

Unit Objectives

After completing this unit, you should be able to:

1. Explain the methods for gaining audience attention; establishing a connection among speaker, audience, and topic; and orienting the audience

2. Identify four common faults of introductions

3. Explain the methods for summarizing, motivating your audience, and closing the speech

4. Identify three common faults of conclusions

5. Explain the recommendations made for speaking "before the introduction" and "after the conclusion"

6. Explain the types and functions of transitions and internal summaries

*N*ow that you have the body of your speech organized, you need to devote attention to your introduction, your conclusion, and the transitions that will hold the parts of your speech together.

INTRODUCTIONS

Although you obviously will deliver the introduction to your speech first, you should construct it only after you have constructed the rest of the speech (body and conclusion).

Begin collecting suitable material for your introduction as you prepare the entire speech, but wait until all the other parts are completed before you put the pieces together. In this way you will be better able to determine which elements should be included and which should be eliminated.

Together with your general appearance and your nonverbal messages, the introduction gives your audience its first impression of you and your speech. And as you know, first impressions are very resistant to change. Because of this, it is an especially important part of the speech. Your introduction sets the tone for the rest of the speech; it tells your listeners what kind of speech they will hear.

Your introduction should serve three functions: gain attention, establish a speaker-audience-topic connection, and orient the audience as to what is to follow. Let's look at each of these functions and at the ways you can serve these functions.

Gain Attention

In your introduction, gain the attention of your audience and focus it on your speech topic. And, of course, maintain that attention throughout your speech. You can secure attention in a number of ways; here are just a few.

Ask a Question   Questions are effective because they are a change from declarative statements and we automatically pay attention to change. Rhetorical questions, questions to which you don't expect an answer, are especially helpful in focusing the audience's attention on your subject: "Do you want to live a happy life?" "Do you want to succeed in college?" "Do you want to meet the love of your life?" Also useful are polling-type questions, questions that ask the audience for a show of hands: "How many of you have suffered through a boring lecture?" "How many of you intend to continue school after graduating from college?" "How many of you have suffered from loneliness?"

Refer to Audience Members   Reference to the audience makes them perk up and pay attention, because you are involving them directly in your talk. Harvey C. Jacobs (1985) gains attention by referring to members of the audience (and complimenting them) in his introduction:

> *Winston Churchill once gave this advice to public speakers: "One, never walk up a wall that's leaning against you; two, never try to kiss a person*

How do you gain attention interpersonally? Does this have any counterparts in the public speaking situation?

who's leaning away from you; and, three, never speak to a group that knows more about the subject than you do." You work much closer to the readers than I do. You know readers very well, I'm sure. Editors are often referred to as the ivory tower crowd, while circulation people are out in the trenches trying to peddle the product we editors and reporters create.

Refer to Recent Happenings   Referring to a previous speech, recent event, or prominent person currently making news helps gain attention because the audience is familiar with this and will pay attention to see how you are going to connect it to your speech topic. Soon after the financial problems of Orange County came to light, Arthur Levitt (1995, p. 194), chair of the U.S. Securities and Exchange Commission, in a speech on consumer protection, referred to recent events in his introduction:

> *This visit was scheduled well before a problem erupted in Orange County. It is a significant problem, and it may cause grief and loss to many. But our markets have been tested before—and they will surely be tested again. Problems will be dealt with, risk will be spread, plans will be developed to recoup losses. No other market in the world could have absorbed such a shock.*

Use Humor   A clever (and appropriate) anecdote is often useful in holding attention. Humor is also risky; if it falls flat, it can make the audience (and the speaker) uncomfortable. If you feel uncomfortable telling humorous stories or jokes in a public speaking situation, avoid this method. Similarly, avoid humor if you feel your joke or story will make any members of your audience uncomfortable or ill at ease. Further, make sure your humor is integral to your speech topic. Use humor only if it relates directly to your specific speech topic. Unit 15 discusses suggestions for using humor.

Use an Illustration or Dramatic Story   Much as people are drawn to soap operas, so too are they drawn to illustrations and stories about other people. Here is an example from a speech by Todd Prins (Schnoor 1994, p. 73):

> *An eight-year-old boy became just another victim when his mother turned unintentionally away from him for just a few seconds, unaware that there was a real danger present in her home. This was enough time for her child to be burned on over half of his body. Because of the injuries he received, he was hospitalized for sixteen days before he died.*

Do be sure to make the connection between your opening illustration and the topic and purpose of your speech. Don't expect the audience to make the connection themselves. They may not do so, and your great illustration will have had no effect.

Stress Importance of Topic   People pay attention to what they feel is important to them and ignore what seems unimportant and irrelevant. For example, in addition to telling your audience that budget cuts will hurt education in the

You have to be careful with humor. It should be appropriate to the audience and to the subject. It can serve to warm up the speaker or the audience, or it can be pointed. But be careful of how sharp the point is. Sarcasm, literally "flesh rending," can backfire, creating sympathy for the opposite point of view. Or, though appropriate for the immediate audience, it may generate bad publicity.

Henry Ehrlich, business and political speechwriter. *Writing Effective Speeches* (New York: Paragon House, 1992), p. 62.

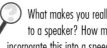 What makes you really want to listen to a speaker? How might you incorporate this into a speech introduction?

So, as you can see . . .

It follows, then, that . . .

To alert the audience to your introducing a qualification or exception:

But, . . .

One exception to this . . .

However, also consider . . .

To remind listeners of what has just been said and that it is connected with another issue that will now be considered:

In contrast to . . . , consider also . . .

Not only . . . , but also . . .

In addition to . . . , we also need to look at . . .

Not only should we . . . , but we should also . . .

To signal the part of your speech that you are approaching:

By way of introduction . . .

In conclusion . . .

Now, let's discuss why we are here today . . .

So, what's the solution? What should we do?

You can enhance your transitions by pausing between your transition and the next part of your speech. This will help the audience see that a new part of your speech is coming. You might also take a step forward or to the side after saying your transition. This will also help to reinforce the movement from one part of your speech to another.

Internal Summaries

Closely related to the transition (and in some cases a special type of transition) is the internal summary. An internal summary is a statement that summarizes what you have already discussed. It is a statement that usually summarizes some major subdivision of your speech. Incorporate a number of internal summaries into your speech—perhaps working them into the transitions connecting, say, the major arguments or issues.

An internal summary that is also a transition might look something like this:

The three arguments advanced here were (1) . . . , (2) . . . , (3) . . . Now, what can we do about them? I think we can do two things. First, . . .

Another example:

Inadequate recreational facilities, poor schooling, and a lack of adequate role models seem to be the major problems facing our youngsters. Each of these, however, can be remedied and even eliminated. Here is what we can do.

Note that these brief passages remind the listeners of what they have just heard and preview for them what they will hear next. The clear connection in their minds will fill in any gaps that may have been created through inattention, noise, and the like.

How important are transitions in the lectures you hear in college? Would you like to see lecturers use more transitions or less? Are internal summaries used?

UNIT IN BRIEF

Introductions	■ Purposes: to gain attention; establish a connection among speaker, audience, and topic; and orient the audience
	■ Avoid the major problems of apologizing (generally), pretending, making hollow promises, relying on gimmicks, and prefacing your introduction
Conclusions	■ Purposes: to summarize your speech or some aspect of it, motivate your audience, and provide crisp closure
	■ Avoid the common problems of introducing new material, diluting the strength of your position, and dragging out the conclusion
Transitions and internal summaries	■ Purposes: to connect the parts of your speech and give your listeners guides to help them follow your speech
	■ Use them between the introduction and the body, between the major propositions, and between the body and the conclusion

PRACTICALLY SPEAKING

Short Speech Technique

Prepare and deliver a two-minute speech in which you:

1. explain how a particular television commercial attempts to get your attention
2. explain how a television news program tries to maintain your attention throughout
3. describe the introductions and conclusions used on television talk shows
4. describe the introductions and conclusions used on television news programs
5. construct a connection among the speaker, audience, and topic for one of these situations: (a) college recruiter addressing your class on coming to work for a large corporation, (b) Peace Corps volunteer addressing your class on the value of becoming a Peace Corps volunteer, (c) candidate for college president addressing your class on why you should vote for him or her

13.1   Constructing Introductions

Prepare an introduction to one of the topics listed, making sure that you (1) secure the audience's attention and interest; (2) establish a connection among speaker, audience, and topic; and (3) orient the audience as to what is to follow. Be prepared to explain the methods you used to accomplish each of these aims.

1. College is not for everyone.
2. It is better never to love than to love and lose.
3. Maximum sentences should be imposed even for first offenders of the drug laws.
4. All alcoholic beverages should be banned from campus.
5. Abortion should be declared illegal.
6. Contribute to the Olympics.
7. Donate your organs to medicine after your death.
8. Switch to the new spreadsheet program.
9. Earn an M.B.A. degree.
10. Laws restricting Sunday shopping should be abolished.

13.2   Constructing Conclusions

Prepare a conclusion to a hypothetical speech on one of the topics listed, making sure that you (1) summarize the speech's main points, (2) motivate the audience, and (3) provide closure. Be prepared to explain the methods you used to accomplish each of these functions.

1. Children should be raised and educated by the state.
2. All wild-animal killing should be declared illegal.
3. Properties owned by churches and charitable institutions should be taxed in the same way as any other properties are taxed.
4. Suicide and its assistance by others should be legalized.
5. Teachers—at all levels—should be prevented from going on strike.
6. Gambling should be legalized in all states.
7. College athletics should be abolished.
8. Same-sex marriages should be legalized.
9. Divorce should be granted immediately when there is mutual agreement.
10. Privatization of elementary and high schools should be encouraged.

UNIT 14

Outlining the Speech

Unit Objectives

After completing this unit, you should be able to:

1. Identify two functions that outlines serve

2. Identify two major types of outlines

3. Explain four suggestions concerning the mechanics of outlining

4. Describe the characteristics of an effective delivery outline

The outline is a blueprint for your speech; it lays out the elements of the speech and their relationship to each other. With this blueprint in front of you, you can see at a glance all the elements of organization considered in the previous units—coordination and subordination, the functions of the introduction and conclusion, the transitions, the major propositions and their relationship to the thesis and purpose, and the adequacy of the supporting materials. And like a blueprint for a building, the outline enables you to spot weaknesses that might otherwise go undetected.

Begin outlining at the time you begin constructing your speech. Do not wait until you have collected all your material, but begin outlining as you are collecting material, organizing it, and styling it. In this way you will take the best advantage of one of the major functions of an outline—to tell you where change is needed. The outline should be changed and altered as necessary at every stage of the speech construction process.

Many students who are required to write outlines actually write them after they have written the corresponding English composition or speech. Why is this ineffective?

FUNCTIONS AND TYPES OF OUTLINES

Outlines will serve several important functions and may be of different types.

Functions of Outlines

An outline will help you to organize your speech. As you outline the speech, you clarify the central points, the major supporting materials, and the transitions. Once these can be easily examined visually, you may see, for example, if your assertions are properly coordinated or if your supporting materials do in fact support your assertions. If you are using a temporal or a spatial organizational pattern, for example, you can quickly see from the outline if the temporal or spatial progression is in fact clear or is in need of further development.

What advantages does a speaker who uses an outline have over the speaker who doesn't use an outline? What advantages does the speaker without an outline have?

Speech outlines provide an efficient way to assess the strengths and weaknesses of the speech as it is being constructed. Let's say you are preparing a speech on censorship and your major points concern sex and violence. Your outline will tell you at a glance if your supporting materials are adequately and evenly distributed between the two points. The outline may tell you that more material has to be collected on the sex issue, or that your speech is almost totally devoted to statistical information and you need a human interest element, and so on. In short, the outline can guide your collection of information.

The outline, when it is constructed from the beginning of the speech preparation process, helps you check the speech as a whole (or at least as much as you have constructed so far). When you work for a long time on a speech and when each part is constructed over a long period, it becomes difficult to "see the forest for the trees." The outline enables you to stand back and examine the entire forest.

 What other functions might an outline serve?

Types of Outlines

Outlines may be extremely detailed or extremely general. Since you are now in a learning environment where the objective is to make you a more proficient public speaker, your instructor may wish to suggest one type of outline over another. And, of course, just as the type of outline will depend on the specific speaker, the type of outline that proves best for instructional purposes will vary with the instructor. Personally, I prefer that students construct rather detailed outlines, but I recognize that this is for instructional purposes and that once students have learned the art of public speaking, they will adjust the outlining procedures to what fits them best.

The more detail you put into the outline, the easier it will be to examine the parts of the speech for all the qualities and characteristics that were discussed in the previous units. Consequently, I suggest that, at least in the beginning, you outline your speeches in detail and in complete sentences. The usefulness of an instructor's criticism will often depend on the detail of the outline.

With these factors in mind, then, I suggest that you do the following, especially in your beginning speeches.

- Begin constructing the outline as soon as you get the topic clearly in mind.
- Revise it constantly. Every new idea, every new bit of information, will result in some alteration of basic structure. At this point keep the outline brief and perhaps in the form of key words or phrases.
- Once you feel pretty confident that you are near completion, construct an outline in detail—using complete sentences—and follow the procedures and principles discussed in the next sections of this unit.
- Use this outline to test your organizational structure.

TIPS
From Professional Speakers

Your presentation structure, to be of any use whatsoever, must be simple enough to be remembered. It must be simple enough so that you'll remember what you want to say, and your audience will have no difficulty remembering what you told them.

Ron Hoff, leading speaker and advertising and marketing director. "*I Can See You Naked*": A Fearless Guide to Making Great Presentations (Kansas City, MO: Andrews & McMeel, 1988), p. 144.

CONSTRUCTING THE OUTLINE

After you have completed your research and have an organizational plan for your speech mapped out, put this plan (this blueprint) on paper. That is, construct what is called a "preparation outline" of your speech, using the following guidelines.

What identifying data does your instructor want prefaced to the outline?

Preface the Outline with Identifying Data

Before you begin the outline proper, identify the general and specific purposes as well as your thesis. This prefatory material should look something like this:

GENERAL PURPOSE: to inform

SPECIFIC PURPOSE: to inform my audience of four major functions of the mass media

THESIS: the mass media serve four major functions

These identifying notes are not part of your speech proper. They are not, for example, mentioned in your oral presentation. Rather, they are guides to the preparation of the speech and the outline. They are like road signs to keep you going in the right direction and to signal when you have gone off course.

One additional bit of identifying data should preface the preface: the title of your speech.

Outline the Introduction, Body, and Conclusion as Separate Units

Each of the three parts of the speech—introduction, body, and conclusion—although intimately connected should be labeled separately and be kept distinct in your outline. Like the identifying data above, these labels are not spoken to the audience but are further guides to your preparation.

By keeping the introduction, body, and conclusion separate, you will be able to see at a glance if they do in fact serve the functions you want them to serve. You will be able to see where further amplification and support are needed. In short, you will be able to see where problems exist and where repair is necessary.

At the same time, do make sure that you examine and see the speech as a whole—where the introduction leads to the body and the conclusion summarizes your propositions and brings your speech to a close.

Some textbooks suggest that the introduction, body, and conclusion should be outlined not as separate units but as one continuous sequence of speech parts. What advantages and disadvantages do you see in each recommendation?

Insert Transitions and Internal Summaries

Insert—using square brackets ([])—transitions between the introduction and the body, the body and the conclusion, the major propositions of the body, and wherever else you think they might be useful.

Insert your internal summaries (if these are not integrated with your transitions) wherever you feel they will help your audience to understand and remember your ideas.

Append a List of References

Some instructors require that you append a list of references to your speeches. If this is requested, then do so at the end of the outline or on a separate page. Some instructors require that only sources cited in the speech be included in the list of references, whereas others require that the full list of sources consulted be provided (those mentioned in the speech as well as those not mentioned).

Whatever the specific requirements, remember that these sources will prove most effective with your audience if you carefully integrate them into the speech. It will count for little if you consulted the latest works by the greatest authorities but never mention this to your audience. So, when appropriate, weave into your speech the source materials you consulted. In your outline refer to the source material by author's name, date, and page in parentheses and then provide the complete citation in your list of references.

In your actual speech it might prove more effective to include the source with your statement. It might be phrased something like this:

> *According to John Naisbitt, author of the nationwide best-seller* Megatrends, *the bellwether states are California, Florida, Washington, Colorado, and Connecticut.*

Regardless of what specific system is required (find out before you prepare your outline), make certain to include all sources of information, not just written materials. Information derived from personal interviews, course lectures, television programs, or the Internet should all be included in your list of references.

SOME MECHANICS OF OUTLINING

Assuming that the outline you construct for your early speeches will be relatively complete, here are a few guidelines concerning the mechanics of outlining.

Can you identify the mechanical principles governing the outlining of a unit or chapter in one of your textbooks?

Use a Consistent Set of Symbols

The following is the standard, accepted sequence of symbols for outlining:

I.
  A.
    1.
      a.
        (1)
          (a)

Begin the introduction, the body, and the conclusion with Roman numeral I. Treat each of the three major parts as a complete unit.

Not This:	This:
Introduction	Introduction
I.	I.
II.	II.
Body	Body
III.	I.
IV.	II.
V.	III.
Conclusion	Conclusion
VI.	I.
VII.	II.

Use Visual Aspects to Reflect the Organizational Pattern

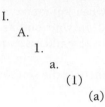 How does this textbook or any textbook use visual aspects to reflect the book's organizational structure?

Use proper and clear indentation. This will help to set off visually coordinate and subordinate relationships.

NOT THIS:

  I. Television caters to the lowest possible intelligence.

  II. Talk shows illustrate this.

  III. *General Hospital*.

THIS:

  I. Television caters to the lowest possible intelligence.
    A. Talk shows illustrate this.
      1. *Geraldo*
      2. *Ricki Lake*
      3. *Richard Bey*
    B. Soap operas illustrate this.
      1. *As the World Turns*
      2. *General Hospital*
      3. *The Young and the Restless*

Use One Discrete Idea Per Symbol

If your outline is to reflect the organizational pattern among the various items of information, use just one discrete idea per symbol. Compound sentences are sure giveaways that you have not limited each item to a single idea. Also, be sure that each item is discrete, that is, that it does not overlap with any other item.

NOT THIS:

I. Education might be improved if teachers were better trained and if students were better motivated.

THIS:

I. Education would be improved if teachers were better trained.

II. Education would be improved if students were better motivated.

Note that in THIS items I and II are single ideas but in NOT THIS they are combined.

NOT THIS:

I. Teachers are not adequately prepared to teach.
   A. Teacher education programs are inadequate.
   B. Course syllabi are dated.

THIS:

I. Teachers are not adequately prepared to teach.
   A. Teacher education programs are inadequate.
      1. Support for A
      2. Support for A
   B. In-service programs are inadequate.
      1. Support for B
      2. Support for B

Note that A and B are discrete in THIS but overlap in NOT THIS. In NOT THIS B is actually a part of A (one of the inadequacies of teacher education programs is that course syllabi are dated).

Use Complete Declarative Sentences

Phrase your ideas in the outline in complete declarative sentences rather than as questions or phrases. It is much easier, for example, to see if one item of information supports another if both are phrased in the declarative mode. If one is a question and one is a statement, essential relationships will be more difficult to see.

 What's wrong with the proposition, "Wasteful spending and the power of special interest groups would be reduced if term limits for politicians were instituted." How would you recast this proposition?

NOT THIS:

   I. Who should raise children?

  II. Should the state raise children?
     A. Equality for children
     B. Parents released for work.

THIS:

   I. Children should be raised by the state.
     A. All children treated equally.
     B. Parents released to work.

Note that in THIS all items are phrased as complete declarative sentences and their relationship is therefore brought out clearly. In NOT THIS, on the other hand, a mixture of question, sentence, and phrase obscures the important relationships among the items in the outline.

▬ A SAMPLE OUTLINE WITH ANNOTATIONS

Here is a relatively detailed outline similar to the ones you might prepare in constructing your speeches. The sidenotes should clarify both the content and the format of a full-sentence outline.

Generally, the title, thesis, and general and specific purposes of the speech are prefaced to the outline. When the outline is an assignment that is to be handed in, additional information may be requested.	**Have You Ever Been Culture-Shocked?**
	THESIS: Culture shock can be described in four stages.
Note the general format for the outline; note that the headings are clearly labeled and that the indenting helps you to see clearly the relationship that one item bears to the other. For example, in Introduction II, the outline format helps you to see that A and B are explanations (amplification, support) for II.	GENERAL PURPOSE: To inform
	SPECIFIC PURPOSE: To inform my audience of the four phases of culture shock
Note that the introduction, body, and conclusion are clearly labeled and separated visually.	## Introduction

The speaker assumes that the audience knows the general nature of culture shock and so does not go into detail as to its definition. But just in case some audience members do not know and to refresh the memory of others, the speaker includes a brief definition.	I. Many of you have or will experience culture shock.
	  A. Many people experience culture shock, that reaction to being in a culture very different from what you were used to.
	  B. By understanding culture shock, you'll be in a better position to deal with it if and when it comes.

Here the speaker attempts to connect the speaker, audience, and topic by stressing intercultural experiences and an abiding interest in the topic. Also, the	II. I've lived in four different cultures myself. A. I've always been interested in the way in which people adapt to different cultures.

B. With our own campus becoming more culturally diverse every semester, the process of culture shock becomes important for us all.

III. Culture shock occurs in four stages (Oberg 1960).
A. The honeymoon occurs first.
B. The crisis occurs second.
C. The recovery occurs third.
D. The adjustment occurs fourth.

[Let's follow the order in which these four stages occur and begin with the first stage, the honeymoon.]

Body

I. The honeymoon occurs first.
A. The honeymoon is the period of fascination with the new people and culture.
B. You enjoy the people and the culture.
1. You love the people.
a. For example, the people in Zaire spend their time very differently from the way New Yorkers do.
b. For example, my first 18 years living on a farm was very different from life in a college dorm.
2. You love the culture.
a. The great number of different religions in India fascinated me.
b. Eating was an especially great experience.

[But, like many relationships, life is not all honeymoon; soon there comes a crisis.]

II. The crisis occurs second.
A. The crisis is the period when you begin to experience problems.
1. One-third of American workers abroad fail because of culture shock (Samovar & Porter 1991, p. 232).
2. The personal difficulties are also great.
B. Life becomes difficult in the new culture.
1. Communication is difficult.
2. It's easy to offend people without realizing it.

[As you gain control over the crises, you begin to recover.]

III. The recovery occurs third.
A. The recovery is the period where you learn how to cope.
B. You begin to learn intercultural competence (Lustig & Koester 1996).
1. You learn how to communicate.

speaker makes the topic important to the audience by referring to their everyday surroundings.

Note that references are integrated throughout the outline just in a term paper. In the speech you might say, "Anthropologist Kalervo Oberg said it occurs in four stages."

The introduction serves the three functions noted: It gains attention; connects the speaker, audience, and topic; and orients the audience to what follows.

This transition cues the audience into a four-part presentation. Also, the numbers repeated throughout the outline will further aid the audience in keeping track of where you are in the speech. The transition also tells the audience that the speech follows a temporal pattern.

Notice the parallel structure throughout the outline. For example, note that I, II, III, and IV in the body are all phrased in exactly the same way. Although this may seem unnecessarily redundant, it will help your audience follow your speech more closely and will also help you in logically structuring your thoughts.

Notice that there are lots of examples throughout this speech. These examples are identified only briefly in the outline and would naturally be elaborated on in the speech.

Notice too the internal organization of each major point. Each main assertion in the body contains a definition of the stage (IA, IIA, IIIA, and IVA) and examples (IB, IIB, IIIB, and IVB) to illustrate the stage.

Because this is a specific fact, some style manuals require that the page number *should* be included.

Note that each statement in the outline is a complete sentence. You can easily convert this outline into a phrase or key-word outline for use in delivery. The full sentences, however, will help you see more clearly relationships among items.

4. explain how you would outline a speech on why members should contribute to UNICEF
5. explain how the author outlined a chapter in any one of your textbooks

14.1   Organizing a Scrambled Outline

This exercise provides an opportunity to work actively with the principles of organization and outlining discussed in the previous units. Your task is to unscramble the following statements from the outline on "culture shock" presented earlier and fit them into a coherent and logical outline consisting of an introduction, a body, and a conclusion. Don't look back at the outline until you've completed your unscrambling.

1. Culture shock occurs in four stages.
2. The crisis occurs second.
3. Many of you have experienced or will experience culture shock.
4. The adjustment occurs fourth.
5. The honeymoon occurs first.
6. Culture shock is a fascinating process; you may want to explore it more fully.
7. By knowing the four stages, you can better understand the culture shock you may now be experiencing on the job, at school, or in your private life.
8. I've lived in four different cultures myself.
9. The recovery occurs third.
10. Culture shock can be described in four stages.

If that was too easy, try this next one on friendship. Like the above, it contains the major statements from a speech outline. Try unscrambling these. One possible organizational pattern for the friendship outline (outline) is provided on page 263, so don't look until you've worked on this awhile.

1. We develop an acquaintanceship.
2. Friendship is an interpersonal relationship between two persons that is characterized by mutual positive regard.
3. We meet.
4. To understand friendships, we need to see what a friendship is and what its stages of development are.
5. Friendship is one of the most important of our interpersonal relationships.
6. We develop an intimate relationship.
7. Friendships develop through various stages.
8. Friendships do not develop full-blown but rather go through various stages—from the initial meeting to intimate friendship.
9. We develop a casual friendship.
10. By understanding friendship, we will be in a better position to develop and maintain productive and enjoyable friendships.
11. Friendship—an interpersonal relationship characterized by mutual positive regard—is one of our most important assets.
12. We develop a close relationship.
13. Friendship is vital to all of us.

Unscrambled Outline on Friendship

Here is one way—there may be others—in which these statements could have been arranged into a coherent outline:

Introduction

I. Friendship is one of the most important of our interpersonal relationships. (5)

II. Friendship is vital to all of us. (13)

III. To understand friendships, we need to see what a friendship is and what its stages of development are. (4)

Body

I. Friendship is an interpersonal relationship between two persons that is characterized by mutual positive regard. (2)

II. Friendships develop through various stages. (7)

A. We meet. (3)

B. We develop an acquaintanceship. (1)

C. We develop a casual friendship. (9)

D. We develop a close relationship. (12)

E. We develop an intimate relationship. (6)

Conclusion

I. Friendship—an interpersonal relationship characterized by mutual positive regard—is one of our most important assets. (11)

II. Friendships do not develop full-blown but rather go through various stages—from the initial meeting to intimate friendship. (8)

III. By understanding friendship, we will be in a better position to develop and maintain productive and enjoyable friendships. (10)

PART FOUR

Elements of Style and Delivery

UNIT 15

Characteristics of Style

Unit Objectives

After completing this unit, you should be able to:

1. Define *directness, abstraction, objectivity, formality,* and *accuracy* as they apply to style in public speaking

2. Define *denotation* and *connotation*

3. Explain the five thinking errors

4. Explain the major differences between oral and written style, as produced and as received

5. Identify the functions of humor in public speaking

6. Explain the guidelines for using humor in public speaking

Y *ou are a successful public speaker when your listeners create in their minds the meanings you want them to create. You are successful when your listeners adopt the attitudes and behaviors you want them to adopt. The language choices you make—for example, the words you select and the sentences you form—will greatly influence what meanings your listeners receive and thus how successful you are.*

▬ HOW LANGUAGE WORKS

Directness, abstraction, objectivity, formality, and accuracy are five aspects of language that relate directly to successful public speaking. Your ability to manipulate these five qualities of language will influence your ability to inform or persuade an audience.

Language Varies in Directness

Consider the following sentences:

1a. We should all vote for Halliwell in the next election.
1b. Vote for Halliwell in the next election.

2a. It should be apparent that we should abandon the present system.
2b. Abandon the present system.

3a. Many people would like to go to Xanadu.
3b. How many of you would like to go to Xanadu?

 How might indirect language actually help the speaker achieve her or his purpose?

The B-sentences are clearly more direct than the A-sentences. Note, for example, that the B-sentences address the audience directly. The A-sentences are more distant, more indirect. Indirect sentences address only an abstract, unidentified mass of individuals. The sentences might as well address just anyone. When you use direct sentences, you address your specific and clearly defined audience.

An audience's preference for directness or indirectness is influenced greatly by its culture, so be sure to take culture into consideration in choosing your words and sentences. Recall especially the discussion of high- and low-context cultures in Unit 12.

If you want to achieve directness, use active rather than passive sentences. Say "The professor invented the serum" rather than "The serum was invented by the professor." Use personal pronouns and personal references. Refer to your audience as "you" rather than "the audience" or "my listeners."

As noted in Unit 12, cultures differ in the degree of directness preferred. How would you assess your public speaking class on this characteristic of style?

Language Varies in Abstraction

Consider the following list of terms:

- entertainment
- film
- American film
- financially successful American film
- *Jurassic Park*

In what communication situations might abstract language prove more effective than concrete language?

At the top is the general or abstract *entertainment*. Note that *entertainment* includes all the other items on the list, plus various other items—television, novels, drama, comics, and so on. *Film* is more specific and concrete. It includes all of the items below it, as well as various other items, such as Indian film or Russian film. It excludes, however, all entertainment that is not film. *American film* is again more specific than *film* and excludes all films that are not American. *Financially successful American film* further limits *American film* to those that made money. *Jurassic Park* specifies concretely the one item to which reference is made.

Choose words from a wide range of abstractions. At times a general term may suit your needs best; at other times a more specific term may serve better. Generally, the specific term is the better choice.

The more general term—in this case, *entertainment*—conjures up a number of different images. One person in the audience may focus on television, another on music, another on comic books, and still another on radio. To some, *film* may bring to mind the early silent films. To others, it brings to mind postwar Italian films. To still others, it recalls Disney's animated cartoons. As you get more specific—less abstract—you more effectively guide the images that come to your listeners' minds. Specific rather than abstract language will aid you in both your informative and your persuasive goals.

Language Varies in Objectivity

The best way to explain how language varies in objectivity is to introduce two new terms: *denotation* and *connotation*.

Denotation   The denotative meaning of a term is its objective meaning. This is the meaning you would find in a dictionary. This meaning points to specific references. Thus, the denotation of the word *book,* for example, is the actual book, a collection of pages bound together between two covers. The denotative meaning of *dog* is a four-legged canine; the denotative meaning of the verb *kiss* is, according to the *Random House Dictionary,* "to touch or press with the lips slightly pursed in token of greeting, affection, reverence, etc."

Connotation   Connotative meaning, however, is different. The connotative meaning is our affective—our emotional meaning—for a term. The word *book* may signify boredom or excitement. It may recall the novel you have to read or perhaps this textbook that you are reading right now. Connotatively, *dog* may mean friendliness, warmth, and affection. The verb *kiss* may, connotatively, mean warmth, good feeling, and happiness.

Using Denotative-Connotative Meanings   All words (other than function words such as prepositions, conjunctions, and articles) have both denotative and connotative meaning. The relevance of this to you, as a public speaker, is considerable. Seldom do listeners misunderstand the denotative meaning of a term. When you use a term with which the audience is unfamiliar, you define it and thus make sure the term is understood. Similarly, arguments seldom center on denotation. Differences in denotative meaning are pretty easy to handle.

Differences in connotative meanings, however, pose difficulties. You may, for example, use the term *neighbor* and wish thereby to communicate security and friendliness. To some of your listeners, however, the term may connote unwanted intrusions, sneakiness, and nosiness. Notice that, both you and your listeners would surely agree that denotatively, *neighbor* means one who lives near another. What you and they disagree on—and what then leads to misunderstanding—is the connotation of the term.

Consider such terms as *politician, jock, lady, police, sex, religion, professor,* and *education*. You can easily appreciate the varied connotative meanings an audience may have for these terms. In public speaking, remember that your connotative meaning for a term is not necessarily the same as that of your audience. Select words with your audience's meanings in mind.

Cultural Differences in Meaning   Cultural differences add to the complexity and difficulty in accurately communicating meaning. The meaning of the word *dog* will obviously differ greatly for the person from the United States, where *dog* signifies a beloved pet, and for the person from a culture where *dog* signifies an eating delicacy. *Beef* to a person from Kansas or Texas, where cattle provide much of the state's wealth, will mean something very different from what it does to a person from India, where the cow is a sacred animal.

As a speaker, consider the audience's evaluation of key terms before using them in your speech. When you are part of the audience, as in a public speaking class, you often already know (generally, at least) the meanings members have for various terms. When you address an audience very different from yourself, however, this prior investigation becomes crucial. When there is any doubt, select another word or qualify the word to make clear exactly what you wish to communicate.

Language Varies in Formality

Language varies from formal to informal or colloquial. Linguist Mario Pei (1956), for example, identified five levels of formality. He illustrates these (from the most formal to the most informal) with the "same" sentence:

1. Those individuals do not possess any.
2. Those men haven't any.
3. Those men haven't got any.
4. Those guys haven't/ain't got any.
5. Dem guys ain't got none.

Formal style is the style of written prose and the style of strangers speaking in a formal context. As the above examples illustrate, formal style uses big words (*individuals* rather than *men*) and infrequently used words (*possess* rather than *have* or *got*).

In formal style, the sentences often contain written-language expressions such as *the former, the latter,* and *the aforementioned*. When you are reading, you can easily locate what *the former* or *the latter* refers to by simply looking back at the previous sentence. When listening to a speech, however, you can't go back and relisten to the previous sentence. You would have to pause to discover which item was the former and which the latter. In the process you would probably lose attention and miss much of what the speaker is saying.

No single guideline for selecting an appropriate level of formality-informality can be offered. As a general rule, however, speak at a level a bit more

TIPS
From Professional Speakers

Fancy, sesquipedalian words—like the six-shooter I've just fired off—should be avoided by speakers on nine out of ten occasions. This is a member of the Buckley clan telling you to keep your vocabulary simple when you are delivering a talk.

Every speaker is inherently in the business of education, true, but the field is not semantics, nor philology, nor etymology. Leave that to literary types. You want to be down to earth. You want your audience to understand just exactly what it is you wish to put across.

Reid Buckley, prominent lecturer and director of the Buckley School of Public Speaking in Camden, South Carolina. *Speaking in Public* (New York: HarperCollins, 1988), pp. 144–145.

In what types of situations would formal language be more effective than informal, conversational language?

formal than the conversational level of the audience. Therefore, use common words but avoid slang. Use informal constructions (for example, contractions and personal pronouns), but avoid forms your audience would consider incorrect (for example, "ain't got none").

Cultural Differences in Formality   Also note that the expected level of formality will vary greatly with the culture of the individuals. For example, it has been shown that Bahamian students expect public speakers to be more formal than most students in the United States do (Masterson, Watson, & Chichon 1991). Generally, it seems fair to say that Africans, Europeans, and Asians expect a greater degree of formality than people from, say, Canada and the United States do. In the accompanying TIPS the author offers a number of generalizations about formality. Does your own experience support or contradict these generalizations?

Language Varies in Accuracy

Language can reflect reality faithfully or unfaithfully. It can describe reality (as science tells us it exists) with great accuracy or distortion. For example, we can use language to describe the many degrees that exist in, say, wealth, or we can describe it inaccurately in terms of two values, rich and poor. We can discuss these ways in which language may vary in terms of the five thinking errors, central to the area of language study known as "General Semantics" (Korsybski 1933; DeVito 1974; Hayakawa & Hayakawa 1989) and now a significant part of critical thinking instruction (Kenneth G. Johnson 1991).

Polarization   Polarization refers to the tendency to look at the world in terms of opposites and to describe it in terms of extremes—good or bad, positive or negative, healthy or sick, intelligent or stupid, rich or poor, and so on. It is often referred to as the "fallacy of either-or." So destructive is either-or thinking that the American Psychiatric Association (1980) identifies it as one of the major behaviors characteristic of borderline personality disorder, a psychological disorder that lies between neurosis and psychosis and is characterized by unstable interpersonal relationships and confusion about one's own identity.

Most people, events, and objects, of course, exist somewhere between the extremes of good and bad, health and sickness, intelligence and stupidity,

" 'Alleged,' please, 'alleged.' "

Drawing by C. Barsotti; © 1993 The New Yorker Magazine, Inc.

wealth and poverty. Yet many have a strong tendency to view only the extremes and to categorize people, objects, and events in terms of these polar opposites.

Problems arise when polar opposites are used in inappropriate situations; for example, "The politician is either for us or against us." Note that these options do not include all possibilities. The politician may be for us in some things and against us in other things, or may be neutral. Beware of speakers implying and believing that two extreme classes include all possible classes—that an individual must be pro–rebel forces or anti–rebel forces, with no other alternatives.

Fact-Inference Confusion   You can make statements about the world you observe, and you can make statements about what you have not observed. In form or structure these statements are similar and cannot be distinguished by any grammatical analysis. For example, you can say, "This proposal contains 17 pages," as well as "This proposal contains the seeds of self-destruction." Both sentences look similar in form, yet they are very different types of statements. You can observe the 17 pages, but how do you observe "the seeds of self-destruction"? Obviously, this is not a descriptive but an inferential statement, a statement you make on the basis of not only what you observe but what you conclude.

You may wish at this point to test your ability to distinguish facts from inferences by taking the fact-inference test based on similar tests by Haney (1973) on the next page.

There is nothing wrong with making inferential statements. You must make them to talk about much that is meaningful. The problem arises in acting as if those inferential statements were factual statements. When you hear inferential statements, treat them as inferential and not as factual. Recognize that such statements may prove to be wrong, and be aware of that possibility.

Allness   Because the world is infinitely complex, we can never know all or say all about anything—at least, we cannot logically say all about anything. Beware of speakers who present information as if it were all there is or as if it were all you need to know to make up your mind. Disraeli once said that "to be conscious that you are ignorant is a great step toward knowledge." That observation is an excellent example of a nonallness attitude. If, as a critical listener, you recognize that you have more to learn, more to see, and more to hear, you will treat what the speaker says as part of the total picture, not the whole, not the final word.

Static Evaluation   Often when you form an abstraction of something or someone—when you formulate a verbal statement about an event or person—that statement remains static and unchanging. But the object or person to whom it refers has changed. Everything is in a constant state of change.

As critical listeners, respond to the statements of speakers as if they contained a tag that identifies the time frame to which they refer. Visualize each such statement as containing a date. Look at that date and ask yourself if the statement is still true today. Thus, when a speaker says that 10 percent of the population now lives at or below the poverty level, ask yourself about the date to which that statement applies. When was the statistic compiled? Does the poverty level determined at that time adequately reflect current conditions?

> Write down three statements you consider factual. Share these with others. Do these other people agree that these are factual?

Self Test

Can You Distinguish Facts from Inferences?

Carefully read the following report and the observations based on it. Indicate whether you think the observations are true, false, or doubtful on the basis of the information presented in the report. Write *T* if the observation is definitely true, *F* if the observation is definitely false, and *?* if the observation may be either true or false. Judge each observation in order. Do not reread the observations after you have indicated your judgment, and do not change any of your answers.

A well-liked college instructor had just completed making up the final examinations and had turned off the lights in the office. Just then a tall, broad figure with dark glasses appeared and demanded the examination. The professor opened the drawer. Everything in the drawer was picked up and the individual ran down the corridor. The president was notified immediately.

___ 1. The thief was tall, broad, and wore dark glasses.
___ 2. The professor turned off the lights.
___ 3. A tall figure demanded the examination.
___ 4. The examination was picked up by someone.
___ 5. The examination was picked up by the professor.
___ 6. A tall, broad figure appeared after the professor turned off the lights in the office.
___ 7. The man who opened the drawer was the professor.
___ 8. The professor ran down the corridor.
___ 9. The drawer was never actually opened.
___10. Three persons are referred to in this report.

Thinking Critically about Facts and Inferences

No. 3 is true, No. 9 is false, and all the rest are *?* Review your answers by referring back to the story. To get you started, note that the "instructor" and the "professor" need not be the same person. Also, there might not have been a thief; the dean may have demanded to see the instructor's examination.

 How many of the thinking errors (polarization, fact-inference confusion, allness, static evaluation, and indiscrimination) can you identify in one evening of prime-time television (comedies and hour dramas usually contain numerous examples)?

Indiscrimination   Nature seems to abhor sameness at least as much as vacuums. Nowhere in the universe can we find two things that are identical. Everything is unique—everything is unlike anything else. Our language, however, provides us with common nouns (such as *teacher, student, friend, enemy, war, politician,* and *liberal*) that lead us to focus on similarities. Such nouns lead us to group all teachers together, all students together, and all politicians together. These words divert attention away from the uniqueness of each individual, each object, and each event. The misevaluation of indiscrimination, then, is one in which the focus is on classes of individuals, objects, or events, rather than on the unique individual, object, or event.

There is nothing wrong with classifying. No one would argue that classifying is unhealthy or immoral. It is, on the contrary, an extremely useful method of dealing with any complex matter. Classifying helps us to deal with complexity. It puts order into our thinking. The problem arises from applying some evaluative label to that class and then using that label as an "adequate" map for each individual in the group. Put differently, indiscrimination is a denial of uniqueness.

Beware, therefore, of speakers who group large numbers of unique individuals under the same label. Beware of speakers who tell you that "Democrats are . . . ," that "Catholics believe . . . ," that "Mexicans are . . ." Ask yourself, "Which Democrats?" "How many Catholics?" "Which Mexicans?" And so on.

Can you recall any of the thinking errors in the speeches you've heard this semester?

ORAL STYLE

Oral style is a quality of spoken language that differentiates it from written language. You do not speak as you write. The words and sentences you use differ. The major reason for this difference is that you compose speech instantly. You select your words and construct your sentences as you think your thoughts. There is very little time in between the thought and the utterance. When you write, however, you compose your thoughts after considerable reflection. Even then, you probably often rewrite and edit as you go along. Because of this, written language has a more formal tone. Spoken language is more informal, more colloquial.

Generally, spoken language consists of shorter, simpler, and more familiar words than written language does. There is more qualification in speech than in writing. For example, when speaking you probably make greater use of such

Political campaign speaking—although extremely important to the welfare of the community and the country—is often quite boring. What stylistic suggestions would you offer a political candidate giving a campaign speech to your public speaking class?

expressions as *although, however,* and *perhaps.* When writing, you probably edit these out.

In addition, spoken language has a greater number of self-reference terms—terms that refer to the speaker herself or himself—than written language does. *I, me, our, us,* and *you* are examples of such terms. Spoken language also has a greater number of "allness" terms, such as *all, none, every, always,* and *never.* You are probably more careful when you write to edit out such terms after you realize they are not very descriptive of reality.

Further, spoken language has more pseudoquantifying terms (for example, *many, much, very,* and *lots*) and terms that include the speaker as part of the observation (for example, *it seems to me that . . .* or *as I see it . . .*). Speech also contains more verbs and adverbs; writing contains more nouns and adjectives.

Spoken language and written language not only do but should differ. The main reason why they should differ is that the listener hears a speech only once; therefore, speech must be instantly intelligible. The reader, on the other hand, can reread an essay or look up an unfamiliar word. The reader can spend as much time as he or she wishes with the written page. The listener, however, must move at the pace set by the speaker.

For the most part, it is wise to use "oral style" in your public speeches. The public speech, however, is composed much like a written essay. Both involve considerable thought and deliberation and much editing and restyling. Consequently, you will need to devote special effort to retaining and polishing your oral style. In the following unit specific suggestions for achieving this goal are presented.

To further clarify the differences, examine the contrasting examples of "Oral and Written Style" in the accompanying box.

What other differences can you identify between oral language and written language?

◼◼ THE HUMOROUS STYLE

It is important to understand the role of humor in public speaking as a speaker (to use it more effectively), as a listener (to better appreciate the speaker's strategies), and as a critic (to better evaluate and judge the speech). Although humor is an important element in some public speeches, it is not a necessary element; nor is it always desirable. It is effective in some situations, with some speakers, and with some audiences. Analyze each specific speaking situation, then make a judgment as to whether or not to try humor. It is extremely difficult to use humor effectively. At the same time, it may be extremely effective in the right situation. With this disclaimer, consider humor—its role in public speaking and some guidelines for its effective use.

Some writers would suggest that humor is more appropriate in some cultures than in others, that certain cultures have a sense of humor and others do not. Humor is probably a universal in all cultures, but each culture may have different rules as to when and where humor is appropriate. At business meetings in some cultures, humor *may* be inappropriate, but at Microsoft or Apple it *may* be both appropriate and expected. Questions about the cultural appropriateness of humor should probably be resolved by omitting it. You can err less by not using humor than by using it inappropriately. So, when in doubt, leave it out.

FOCUS **O**N

Oral and Written Style: A Comparative Example

To distinguish more clearly the characteristics of oral and written style, two excerpts—one in written style and one in oral style—are presented below. Read each carefully and note as many differences as you can.

Written Style

Three major ways of lying have been identified. The omission of information that is true is referred to as concealment. An example of this type of lie would occur when one answered one's parents' question "What did you do last night?" with the phrase "Listened to records," but without any reference to drinking. To present false information as if it were the truth would be considered an instance of falsification. An example of this latter type of lie would occur when an individual who owed money said, "The check is in the mail" when it really was not. Misidentifying the causes of an emotion, as in saying, "I'm not crying; I just got something in my eye," would be considered an example of misdirection.

Oral Style

We can identify three major ways of lying: concealment, falsification, and misidentification. First, concealment involves omitting true information. A good example of this occurs when your parents ask, "What did you do last night?" If you answer, "Listened to records" but omit drinking, then you've lied by concealment. Second, falsification involves presenting false information as if it were true. A popular example of falsification is when your friend who borrowed money tells you, "The check is in the mail" when it isn't. Third, misdirection involves misidentifying the causes of an emotion. For example, let's say you don't want others to know you're crying. You might lie by misdirection and say, "No, I'm not crying; I just got something in my eye."

Note some of the differences between these two styles. The oral-style version uses the active voice; the written style version relies on the more indirect passive voice. In the oral-style version we included a preview of the three types of lies to help the audience follow the discussion. No such preview is presented in the written-style version, largely because the reader can easily glance ahead or back for orientation. In the oral version the sentences are shorter, and guide phrases are included to help the listener follow the discussion (for example, *First, Second, Third*).

The language in the oral version is more informal and more personal; it makes use of personal pronouns (*we, you*) and contractions (*you've, isn't, you're*). It also involves the listener in the examples (*your parents, your friend who borrowed money, you don't want others to know you are crying*).

The written version depersonalizes the examples and makes use of written-style expressions such as *one, an individual,* and *latter.* Note too that in the oral version the key terms (*concealment, falsification,* and *misdirection*) are repeated to help the audience remember and follow the examples. Further, the oral version uses parallel structure. Consider these three sentences:

1. First, concealment involves omitting true information.
2. Second, falsification involves presenting false information as if it were true.
3. Third, misdirection involves misidentifying the causes of an emotion.

Notice, for example, that (1) guide phrases begin each sentence; (2) key terms are introduced next; (3) the verb *involves* is used in all three sentences; and (4) the gerund (the *-ing* form of the verb) is used to begin the defining phrase.

How would you characterize the humor of your favorite humorist?

What common mistakes do you observe when people use humor? Can you use these mistakes to help you formulate general principles for using humor effectively?

Humor can serve a number of important purposes, however. In a speech that is long and somber, humor breaks up the mood and lightens the tone. At times, humor serves as a creative and useful transition. Humor is excellent support material. It can help you emphasize a point, crystallize an idea, or rebut an opposing argument.

Some of you are probably excellent humorists. You can look at a situation, find the humor in it, and convey this humor to an audience easily and clearly. Others are probably ineffective humorists. In between these extremes lie most of us. All of us, however, could probably improve the humor in our communications. Effective humor in public speaking is relevant, brief, spontaneous, tasteful, and appropriate.

Relevance

Like any other type of supporting material, the humorous anecdote or story must be germane to your topic and your purpose. If it is not, don't use it. If you must go to exceptional lengths to make the story fit or if you have to distort seriously the proposition it should support, then reconsider your material. Here is an example of humor that is especially relevant for a speech on relationship communication (Hensley 1992, p. 115):

A woman went to an attorney and said, "I want to divorce my husband." Lawyer: Do you have any grounds? Woman: About 10 acres. Lawyer: Do you have a grudge? Woman: No, just a carport. Lawyer: Does your hus-

band beat you up? Woman: No, I get up about an hour before he does every morning. Lawyer: Why do you want a divorce? Woman: We just can't seem to communicate.

Brevity

Humor works best in public speaking when it is brief. If it occupies too great a portion of your speech, the audience may question your sincerity or seriousness. Humor in special occasion speeches, however, may logically occupy a greater part of the entire speech than in informative or persuasive speeches. Here David Awl (Boaz & Brey 1988), a student from Bradley University, uses humor (very briefly) in an after-dinner speech to introduce his topic:

> *What is it about so many of the great technological breakthroughs of the Twentieth Century, like Eggzilla, that are leaving us with the feeling that time is running out. Well, there's a name for this problem. No, not Olivia de Havilland. The good names are always taken. It's called time sickness, and it's sapping the enjoyment out of our lives.*

Spontaneity

Humor works best when it seems spontaneous. If humor appears studied or too well practiced, it may lose its effectiveness. In telling a humorous anecdote, for example, always keep your eyes on the audience, not on your notes. Never, never read your punch line. At the same time that humor should appear spontaneous, recognize the difficulty of getting a laugh. So, test your humor on your friends or family first to gauge their reactions and improve your delivery.

Don't telegraph your humorous material by long prefaces or by telling the audience that you are going to tell a funny story—you'll be lost if it fails to get the expected laugh. Let the humor of the story speak for itself.

Try also to develop a spontaneous retort just in case your humorous story turns out to be a dud. Don't look surprised, hurt, or as though you've lost control of yourself and your material. Instead develop a clever response. Stand-up comedians are masters of these rejoinders, which are often more humorous than even their best jokes.

Tastefulness

Humor should be tasteful. Reject vulgar and "off-color" expressions. Coarseness is never a substitute for wit. If there is even the smallest possibility that your humor might make your listeners uncomfortable, then eliminate it. Avoid poking fun at any group, race, religion, nationality, sex, sexual minority, occupation, or age-group. Especially avoid ethnic jokes; they have no place in a public speech.

At the same time, be careful of telling jokes at your own expense, of poking too much fun at yourself. Although we are often our own best foils, in a public speaking situation poking fun at yourself can damage your credibility. The audience may see you as a clown rather than as a responsible advocate.

In which situations is humor welcomed by members of your culture? In which situations would humor be frowned upon? How did you learn your culture's rules for the use of humor?

TIPS

From Professional Speakers

- Don't embarrass other people (unless it is a formal roast).
- Don't use ethnic or racial jokes.
- Don't use dialects.
- Don't make jokes about religion.
- Avoid any scatological or profane language.

Roger E. Axtell, professional speaker and intercultural communication expert. *Do's and Taboos of Public Speaking: How to Get Those Butterflies Flying in Formation* (New York: Wiley, 1992), p. 86.

Avoid sarcasm and ridicule. These are rarely humorous, and it is often difficult to predict how an audience will respond. Your listeners may well wonder when your sarcasm or ridicule will be directed at them.

Appropriateness

Like all forms of support, humor must be appropriate to you as the speaker. Tell jokes in your own style—not in the style of Roseanne or Jay Leno. Invest time in developing a style that is your own and with which you are comfortable.

Similarly, use humor that is appropriate to your audience and to the occasion. Jokes about babies or anecdotes about the singles' scene are not likely to prove effective with a group of retired teamsters. The topic of the joke and its implications must be relevant and appropriate to all elements of the public speaking act.

Although each politician has his or her own unique speaking style, there are generalizations that some theorists claim characterize "political speaking" in general. What are some of these generalizations? Can you give examples to support or refute such generalizations?

UNIT IN BRIEF

Language varies on five main dimensions:	■ direct and indirect ■ abstract and specific ■ objective and subjective ■ formal and informal ■ accurate and inaccurate (polarization, fact-inference confusion, allness, static evaluation, and indiscrimination)
Compared to written style, oral style is characterized by:	■ shorter, simpler, and more familiar words ■ more self-reference and "allness" terms ■ more pseudoquantifying terms and terms that include the speaker ■ more verbs and adverbs ■ oral style can be achieved by incorporating the above characteristics and by using short sentences, guide phrases, informal terms, sentences that involve the listener, and parallel structure
Humor in a public speech is most effective when it is:	■ relevant to your topic and your purpose ■ brief ■ spontaneous or seemingly spontaneous ■ tasteful rather than vulgar, off-color, or sarcastic ■ appropriate to you as a speaker, to your audience, to the topic, and to the occasion

PRACTICALLY SPEAKING

Short Speech Technique

Prepare and deliver a two-minute speech in which you:

1. tell a humorous story
2. describe an object in highly abstract and then highly concrete language
3. describe the language of a noted personality (from television, politics, arts, and so on)
4. describe an incident in highly objective and highly subjective language
5. describe the humorous style of a particular comedian or style of comedy

15.1   Making Concepts Specific

One of the major skills in public speaking is learning to make your ideas specific so that your listeners will understand exactly what you want them to understand. Here are 15 sentences. Rewrite each of them making the italicized terms more specific.

1. The *woman* walked up the *hill* with her *children.*
2. The *teacher* was *discussing economics.*
3. The *player scored.*
4. The *teenager* was *listening* to a *record.*
5. No one in the *city* thought the *mayor* was right.
6. The *girl* and the *boy* each received *lots* of *presents.*
7. I read the *review* of the *movie.*
8. The *couple* rented a *great car.*
9. The *detective* wasn't much help in solving the *crime.*
10. The *children* were playing an old *game.*
11. The *dinosaur approached* the *baby.*
12. He *walked* up the *steep hill.*
13. *They* played *games.*
14. The *cat climbed* the *fence.*
15. The *large house* is in the *valley.*

UNIT 16

Effective Style in Public Speaking

Unit Objectives

After completing this unit, you should be able to:

1. Define the five qualities of effective style

2. Identify the suggestions for achieving clarity, vividness, appropriateness, a personal style, and forcefulness

3. Identify the specific suggestions for constructing effective sentences

4. Define *parallel, antithetical,* and *periodic sentences* and give an example of each

5. Explain the principles for making your speech easy to remember

N ow that the general principles of language and style are understood, specific suggestions can be identified for improving your speech style—choosing words, phrasing sentences, and making your speech easy to remember.

CHOOSING WORDS

Choose carefully the words you use in your public speeches. Choose words to achieve clarity, vividness, appropriateness, a personal style, and forcefulness.

Clarity

Clarity in speaking style should be your primary goal. Here are some guidelines to help you make your speech clear.

Be Economical   Don't waste words. Two of the most important ways to achieve economy are to avoid redundancies and to avoid meaningless words. Notice the redundancies in the following expressions:

at 9:00 A.M. *in the morning*

we *first* began the discussion

the full *and complete* report

I *myself personally*

blue *in color*

*over*exaggerate

you, *members of the audience*

clearly unambiguous

about *approximately* ten inches *or so*

cash *money*

By withholding the italicized terms, you eliminate unnecessary words. You thus move closer to a more economical and clearer style.

Use Specific Terms and Numbers   Picture these items:

- bracelet
- gold bracelet
- gold bracelet with a diamond clasp
- braided gold bracelet with a diamond clasp

Notice that as we get more and more specific, we get a clearer and more detailed picture. Be specific. Don't say *dog* when you want your listeners to picture a *St. Bernard*. Don't say *car* when you want them to picture a *limousine*. Don't say *movie* when you want them to think of *Dumb and Dumber*.

 Why is clarity even more important in a public speech than it is in a written composition or book?

Can you identify some situations where a speaker might wish to make her or his message ambiguous?

The same is true of numbers. Don't say *earned a good salary* if you mean *earned $90,000 a year*. Don't say *taxes will go up* when you mean *taxes will increase 22 percent*. Don't say *the defense budget was enormous* when you mean *the defense budget was $17 billion*.

Use Guide Phrases   Listening to a public speech is difficult work. Assist your listeners by using guide phrases to help them see that you are moving from one idea to another. Use phrases such as *Now that we have seen how . . . , let us consider how . . .* , and *My next argument . . .* Terms such as *first, second, and also, although,* and *however* will help your audience follow your line of thinking.

Guide phrases are especially useful when speaking to listeners who are unfamiliar with the language you, as a native speaker, are speaking. And, of course, guide phrases will also prove valuable if you are speaking in a language that you have not fully mastered. The guide phrases will help compensate for the lack of language and speech similarity between speaker and audience.

Are you impressed by speakers who use words you don't understand? If so, would you suggest revising what is said about using short, familiar, and commonly used terms?

Use Short, Familiar Terms   Generally, favor the short word over the long one. Favor the familiar word over the unfamiliar word. Favor the more commonly used term over the rarely used term. Here are a few examples:

Poor Choices	Better Choices
innocuous	harmless
elucidate	clarify
utilize	use
ascertain	find out
erstwhile	former
eschew	avoid
expenditure	cost or expense

How might unfamiliar, foreign, or technical terms actually increase the speaker's likelihood of persuading certain audiences in certain situations?

Use Repetition and Restatement   Repetition, restatement, and internal summaries will all help to make your speech clearer. Repetition means repeating something in exactly the same way. Restatement means rephrasing an idea or statement in different words. Internal summaries are periodic summary statements or reviews of subsections of your speech. All will help listeners to follow what you are saying.

Distinguish Between Commonly Confused Words   Many words, because they sound alike or are used in similar situations, are commonly confused. Learn these terms and avoid such confusions. Here are ten of the most frequently confused words:

- Use *accept* to mean "to receive" and *except* to mean "with the exclusion of" (*She accepted the award and thanked everyone except the producer*).
- Use *affect* to mean "to have an effect or to influence" and *effect* to mean "to produce a result" (*The teacher affected his students greatly and will now effect an entirely new curriculum*).
- Use *between* when referring to two items (*It is between this one and that one*) and *among* when referring to more than two items (*I want to choose from among these five items*).

Although clarity is considered an essential stylistic feature in all public speaking textbooks, might an unclear or ambiguous style ever be appropriate? In what situations might such a style be more persuasive?

■ Use *can* to refer to ability and *may* to refer to permission (*I can scale the mountain, but I may not reveal its hidden path*).

■ Use *cheap* to refer to something that is inferior and *inexpensive* to something that costs little (*Inexpensive items are usually but not always cheap*).

■ Use *discover* to refer to the act of finding something out or of learning something previously unknown and use *invent* to refer to the act of originating something new (*We discover unknown lands, but we invent time machines*).

■ Use *explicit* to mean "specific" and *implicit* to mean "the act of expressing something without actually stating it" (*He was explicit in his denial of the crime but was implicit concerning his whereabouts*).

■ Use *imply* to mean "to state indirectly" and *infer* to mean "to draw a conclusion" (*She implied that she would seek a divorce; we can only infer her reasons*).

■ Use *tasteful* to refer to one's good taste and use *tasty* to refer to something that tastes good (*The wedding was tasteful and the food most tasty*).

■ Use *uninterested* to mean "a lack of interest" and use *disinterested* to mean "objective or unbiased" (*The student seemed uninterested in the lecture. The teacher was disinterested in who received what grades*).

Carefully Assess Culture-Specific Language   Much everyday language consists of idioms, expressions that are unique to a specific language or culture and whose meaning cannot be deduced from the individual words used. Expressions such as *kick the bucket, doesn't have a leg to stand on*, and, as in the accompanying cartoon, "*heads will roll*" are idioms. You either know the meaning of the expression or you don't; you can't figure it out from only a knowledge of the individual words.

The positive side of idioms is that they give your speech a casual and informal style; they make your speech sound like speech and not like a written essay.

"It's amazing. I just found out that in some countries 'heads will roll' is only a figure of speech."

Charles Barsotti for Barron's

TIPS

From Professional Speakers

Of all the language problems in international communication, idiomatic usage ranks almost at the top of the list. *Idioms are words and expressions peculiar to a language. They often have a meaning that differs from their logical or grammatical meaning and—here's the worse part—can't be translated literally into another language without confusing or losing the meaning. You know what that means, right? Don't use idioms.*

Mary A. DeVries, international communications expert. *Internationally Yours: Writing and Communicating Successfully in Today's Global Marketplace* (Boston: Houghton Mifflin, 1994), p. 83.

 How might you make more vivid such bland sentences as *The children played in the yard, The soldiers took the hill,* and *The singer sang three songs?*

The negative side of idioms is that they create problems for listeners who are not native speakers of your language. Many will simply not understand the meaning of your idioms. This problem is especially important because audiences are becoming increasingly intercultural and because the number of idioms we use is extremely high. If you are not convinced of this, read through any of the speeches in this text, especially in an intercultural group, and underline all idioms. You will no doubt have underlined a great deal more than most people would have suspected.

Vividness

Select words to make your ideas vivid and come alive in the minds of your listeners.

Use Active Verbs   Favor verbs that communicate activity rather than passivity. The verb *to be,* in all its forms—*is, are, was, were, will be*—is relatively inactive. Try using verbs of action instead. Rather than saying *The teacher was in the middle of the crowd,* say *The teacher stood in the middle of the crowd.* Instead of saying *The report was on the president's desk for three days,* try *The report rested [or slept] on the president's desk for three days.* Instead of saying *Management will be here tomorrow,* consider *Management will descend on us tomorrow* or *Management jets in tomorrow.*

Use Strong Verbs   The verb is the strongest part of your sentence. Choose verbs carefully, and choose them so they accomplish a lot. Instead of saying *He walked through the forest,* consider such terms as *wandered, prowled, rambled,* or *roamed.* Consider whether one of these might not better suit your intended meaning. Consult a thesaurus for any verb you suspect might be weak.

A good guide to identifying weak verbs is to look at your use of adverbs. If you use lots of adverbs, you may be using them to strengthen weak verbs. Consider cutting out the adverbs and substituting stronger verbs.

Use Figures of Speech   Figures of speech help achieve vividness. Figures of speech are stylistic devices that have been a part of rhetoric since ancient times. Table 16.1 contains ten figures you might use in your speech, along with definitions and examples.

TABLE 16.1	Figures of Speech	
Type	**Definition**	**Example**
Alliteration	Repetition of the same initial sound in two or more words	Fifty famous flavors; the cool, calculating leader.
Antithesis	Presentation of contrary ideas in parallel form	My loves are many; my enemies are few; "It was the best of times, it was the worst of times" (Dickens).
Climax	Arrangement of individual phrases or sentences in ascending order of force-fulness	As a child he lied, as a youth he stole, as a man he killed.
Hyperbole	Use of extreme exaggeration	He cried like a faucet; your obedient and humble servant; I'm so hungry I could eat a whale.
Irony	Use of a word or sentence whose literal meaning is the opposite of that which is intended	A teacher handing back failing examinations might say, "So pleased to see how many of you studied so hard."
Metaphor	Comparison of two unlike things	She's a lion when she wakes up; all nature is science; he's a real bulldozer.
Metonymy	Substitution of a name for a title with which it is closely associated	"City Hall issued the following news release," where *City Hall* is used instead of *the mayor* or the *city council*.
Personification	Attribution of human characteristics to inanimate objects	This room cries for activity; my car is tired and wants a drink.
Rhetorical question	Use of a question to make a statement or to produce a desired effect rather than secure an answer	Do you want to be popular? Do you want to get well?
Simile	Comparison of two unlike objects by using *like* or *as*	He takes charge like a bull; the manager is as gentle as a lamb.

How might you rephrase these sentences to make them more dramatic and vivid: *Medicare looks like it will be reduced, Vote,* and *Reductions in education will never be accepted by the citizens of Rowley.*

Use Imagery Appeal to the senses, especially our visual, auditory, and tactile senses. Make us see, hear, and feel what you are talking about.

Visual Imagery. In describing people or objects, create images your listeners can see. When appropriate, describe such visual qualities as height, weight, color, size, shape, length, contour. Let your audience see the sweat pouring down the faces of the coal miners; let them see the short, overweight executive in a pin-striped suit smoking a cigar.

Here Stephanie Kaplan (Reynolds & Schnoor 1991), a student from the University of Wisconsin, uses visual imagery to describe the AIDS Quilt:

> *The Names Project is quite simply a quilt. Larger than 10 football fields, and composed of over 9,000 unique 3-feet by 6-feet panels each bearing a name of an individual who has died of AIDS. The panels have been made in homes across the country by the friends, lovers, and families of AIDS victims.*

Auditory Imagery. Appeal to our sense of hearing by using terms that describe sounds. Let your listeners hear the car screeching, the wind whistling, the bells chiming, the angry professor roaring.

Tactile Imagery. Use terms referring to temperature, texture, and touch to create tactile imagery. Let your listeners feel the cool water running over their bodies and the punch of the fighter; let them feel the smooth skin of the newborn baby.

The above suggestions for using imagery are offered as aids to making your speech more vivid than it would normally be in, say, conversation. However, some evidence indicates that too many visual images may actually make your speech less memorable and less persuasive than it would be without these vivid images (Frey & Eagly 1993). When images are too vivid, they divert the brain from following a logically presented series of thoughts or arguments. The brain focuses on these extremely vivid images and loses the speaker's train of thought. The advice, therefore, is to use vividness when it adds clarity to your ideas. When you suspect your listeners may concentrate on the imagery rather than the idea, drop the imagery.

How can you use imagery in developing these propositions: (1) homelessness has reached epidemic proportions in this city, and (2) exercise builds hard bodies?

Appropriateness

Use language that is appropriate to you as the speaker. Also, use language that is appropriate to your audience, the occasion, and the speech topic. Here are some general guidelines to help you achieve this quality.

Speak on the Appropriate Level of Formality The most effective public speaking style is less formal than the written essay but more formal than conversation. One way to achieve an informal style is to use contractions. Say *don't* instead of *do not*, *I'll* instead of *I shall*, and *wouldn't* instead of *would not*. Contractions give a public speech the sound and rhythm of conversation, a quality most listeners react to favorably.

Use personal pronouns rather than impersonal expressions. Say *I found* instead of *It has been found*, or *I will present three arguments* instead of *Three arguments will be presented*.

Do remember, as noted in the previous unit, that the expected and desirable level of formality will vary greatly from one culture to another.

Avoid Unfamiliar Terms   Avoid using terms the audience does not know. Avoid foreign and technical terms unless you are certain the audience is familiar with them. Similarly, avoid jargon (the technical vocabulary of a specialized field) unless you are sure the meanings are clear to your listeners. Some acronyms (*NATO, UN, NOW*, and *CORE*) are probably familiar to most audiences; most such abbreviations, however, are not. When you wish to use any of these types of expressions, explain their meaning fully to the audience.

Avoid Slang   Avoid offending your audience with language that embarrasses them or makes them think you have little respect for them. Although your listeners may themselves use such expressions, they often resent their use by public speakers.

Avoid Racist, Sexist, and Heterosexist Terms   According to Andrea Rich (1974), "any language that, through a conscious or unconscious attempt by the user, places a particular racial or ethnic group in an inferior position is racist." Racist language expresses racist attitudes. Racist language emphasizes differences rather than similarities and separates rather than unites members of different cultures.

Avoid referring to culturally different groups with terms that carry negative connotations or picturing them in stereotypical and negative ways. At the same time, avoid slighting members who may represent only a minority of your audience. Include references in fairness to all groups in, for example, your examples and illustrations.

Use nonsexist language. Use *human* instead of *man* to include both sexes; use *she or he* instead of *he*; use *police officer* instead of *policeman* and *firefighter* instead of *fireman*.

Avoid sex-role stereotyping. Avoid, for example, making the hypothetical elementary school teacher female and the college professor male. Avoid referring to doctors as male and nurses as female. Avoid noting the sex of a professional with terms such as *female doctor* or *male nurse*. When you are referring to a specific doctor or nurse, the person's sex will become clear when you use the appropriate pronoun.

Avoid heterosexist language, language that disparages gay men and lesbians. As with racist language, we see heterosexism in the derogatory terms used for lesbians and gay men as well as in more subtle forms of language usage. For example, when you qualify a reference to a professional—as in *gay athlete* or *lesbian doctor*—you are in effect stating that athletes and doctors are not normally gay or lesbian.

Still another instance of heterosexism is the presumption of heterosexuality. Usually, people assume the person they are talking to or about is heterosexual. Usually, they are correct, since the majority of the population is heterosexual. At the same time, however, note that this practice denies the lesbian and gay identity an appropriate legitimacy. The practice is similar to the

Would you be offended by slang and vulgar expressions if you overheard strangers in the street using them? If your instructor used them? If students gave speeches using them? Under what, if any, circumstances would it be acceptable to use these expressions?

What alternatives can you offer for such terms as *mankind, countryman, man-made, the common man, manpower, repairman, doorman, stewardess, waitress, salesman, mailman,* and *actress*?

Why are such expressions as *female physicist* and *gay doctor* offensive? What do such expressions imply? What impression do you get of a speaker who uses such expressions?

TIPS

From Professional Speakers
·············

Avoid showy language. Speak the way you talk in everyday conversation. Your everyday speech is spontaneous, new, like freshly baked bread. Speech is alive. It has music to it. In one of his speeches, F. D. Roosevelt changed "We are endeavoring to construct a more inclusive society" to the way it would be spoken: "We're going to make a country where no one is left out." Say it the easy way, "trippingly on the tongue."

Elayne Snyder, corporate consultant and speech coach. *Persuasive Business Speaking* (New York: American Management Association, 1990), p. 145.

Personal style is not always the most effective style to use. When might a more formal, impersonal style be more effective?

presumption of whiteness and maleness that we have made significant inroads in eliminating.

Once brought to awareness, most people recognize the moral legitimacy of using language that is inclusive, language that is nonracist, nonsexist, and nonheterosexist. There are also rhetorical reasons for avoiding exclusionary language:

- It is likely to offend a significant part of your audience.
- It is likely to draw attention to itself and away from what you are saying.
- It is likely to reflect negatively on your credibility.

Personal Style

Audiences favor speakers who speak in a personal rather than an impersonal style, who speak with them rather than at them.

Use Personal Pronouns   Say *I* and *me* and *he or she* and *you*. Avoid such impersonal expressions as *one* (as in *One is led to believe . . .*), *this speaker*, and *you, the listeners*. These expressions distance the audience and create barriers rather than bridges.

Use Questions   Ask the audience questions to involve them. With a small audience, you might even briefly entertain responses. With larger audiences, you might ask the question, pause to allow the audience time to consider their responses, and then move on. When you direct questions to your listeners, they feel a part of the public speaking transaction.

Create Immediacy   Immediacy is a connectedness, a relatedness with one's listeners. *Immediacy* is the opposite of *disconnected* and *separated*. Here are some suggestions for creating immediacy through language:

- Use personal examples
- Use terms that include both you and the audience, for example, *we* and *our*
- Address the audience directly; say *you* rather than *students*, say *you'll enjoy reading . . .* instead of *everyone will enjoy reading*, and *I want you to see . . .* instead of *I want people to see . . .*
- Use specific names of audience members when appropriate
- Express concern for the audience members
- Reinforce or compliment the audience
- Refer directly to commonalities between you and the audience, for example, *We are all children of immigrants* or *We all want to see our team in the playoffs*
- Refer to shared experiences and goals, for example, *We all want, we all need, a more responsive PTA*
- Recognize audience feedback and refer to it in your speech; say, for example, *I can see from your expressions that we're all eager to get to our immediate problem*

Forcefulness/Power

Forceful or powerful language will help you achieve your purpose, whether it be informative or persuasive. Forceful language enables you to direct the audience's attention, thoughts, and feelings.

Eliminate Weakeners   Delete phrases that weaken your sentences. Among the major weakeners are uncertainty expressions and weak modifiers. Uncertainty expressions such as *I'm not sure of this but . . .* , *perhaps it might . . .* , and *maybe it works this way* communicate a lack of commitment and conviction and will make your audience wonder if you're worth listening to. Weak modifiers such as "It works *pretty* well," "It's *kind of like . . .* ," and "It *may be* the one we want" make you seem unsure and indefinite about what you are saying.

Cut out any unnecessary phrases that reduce the impact of your meaning. Instead of saying *There are lots of things we can do to help*, say *We can do lots of things to help*. Instead of saying *I'm sorry to be so graphic, but Senator Bingsley's proposal . . .* , say *We need to be graphic. Senator Bingsley's proposal . . .* Instead of saying *It should be observed in this connection that, all things considered, money is not productive of happiness*, say *Money does not bring happiness*. Consider the suggestions in Table 16.2 for achieving more powerful language.

Listen to a good network anchorperson. How forceful or powerful is her or his language? Can you identify specific examples of powerful and powerless language?

TABLE 16.2	Suggestions for More Powerful Speech	
Suggestions	**Examples**	**Comments**
Avoid hesitations	I, er, want to say that, ah, this one is, er, the best, you know.	Hesitations make you sound unprepared and uncertain
Avoid too many intensifiers	Really, this was the greatest; it was truly phenomenal.	Too many intensifiers make all your speeches sound the same and do not allow for intensifying what should be emphasized
Avoid tag questions	I'll review the report now, OK? That's a great proposal, don't you think?	Tag questions ask for another's agreement and therefore signal your need for approval and your own uncertainty or lack of conviction
Avoid self-critical statements	I'm not very good at this. This is my first speech.	Self-critical statements signal a lack of confidence and make public your inadequacies
Avoid slang or vulgar expressions	!!#//***. No problem.	Slang and vulgarity signal a low social class and hence little power; they may also communicate a lack of respect for your audience

How many powerful and powerless aspects are part of your general conversational style? What is the one stylistic aspect you might target for change? How will you go about effecting this change?

These suggestions are not limited in application to public speaking; they relate as well to interpersonal and small-group communication.

Vary Intensity as Appropriate   Much as you can vary your voice in intensity, so too can you phrase your ideas with different degrees of stylistic intensity. You can, for example, refer to an action as *failing to support our position* or as *stabbing us in the back*; you can say that a new proposal will *endanger our goals* or *destroy us completely*; you can refer to a child's behavior as *playful*, *creative*, or *destructive*.

Vary your language to express different degrees of intensity—from mild through neutral to extremely intense.

Avoid Bromides and Clichés   Bromides are sentences that are worn out because of constant usage. When we hear them, we recognize them as unoriginal and uninspired. Here are some examples:

- She's as pretty as a picture.
- Honesty is the best policy.
- If I can't do it well, I won't do it at all.
- I don't understand modern art, but I know what I like.

Clichés are phrases that have lost their novelty and part of their meaning through overuse. Clichés call attention to themselves because of their overuse. Here are some clichés to avoid:

the whole ball of wax	by hook or by crook
in this day and age	sweet as sugar
happy as a lark	tell it like it is
free as a bird	in the pink
no sooner said than done	tried and true
with bated breath	for all intents and purposes
it goes without saying	few and far between
he's a quick study	over the hill
no news is good news	mind over matter
the life of the party	keep your shirt on
a horse of a different color	down in the mouth

Review any one of the speeches contained in this text for each of the characteristics of language discussed in this unit: clarity, vividness, appropriateness, personal style, and forcefulness. Can you find specific examples of each?

PHRASING SENTENCES

Give the same careful consideration that you give to words to your sentences as well. Some guidelines follow.

Use Short Sentences   Short sentences are more forceful and economical than long sentences. They are easier to comprehend. They are easier to remember. Listeners have neither the time nor the inclination to unravel long and complex sentences. Help them to listen more efficiently. Use short rather than long sentences.

Use Direct Sentences   Direct sentences are easier to understand than indirect sentences. They are also more forceful. Instead of saying *I want to tell you of the three main reasons why we should not adopt Program A*, say *We should not adopt Program A. There are three main reasons.*

Use Active Sentences   Active sentences are easier to understand than passive sentences. They also make your speech seem livelier and more vivid. Instead of saying *The lower court's decision was reversed by the Supreme Court*, say *The Supreme Court reversed the lower court's decision.* Instead of saying *The proposal was favored by management*, say *Management favored the proposal.*

Use Positive Sentences   Positive sentences are easier to comprehend and remember than negative sentences. Notice how sentences (a) and (c) are easier to understand than sentences (b) and (d).

  a. The committee rejected the proposal.
  b. The committee did not accept the proposal.
  c. This committee works outside the normal company hierarchy.
  d. This committee does not work within the normal company hierarchy.

Vary the Types of Sentences   The advice to use short, direct, active, and positive sentences is valid most of the time. Yet too many sentences of the same type or length will make your speech sound boring. Use variety while following (generally) the preceding advice.

How would you adjust your style if your next speech was to be given to an audience such as that pictured here? What if it was to be given to a small group of, say, five or six?

Review any one of the speeches contained in this text for examples of effective sentences. Do you find direct and indirect sentences? Active and passive sentences? Positive and negative sentences? Can you find examples of parallel sentences, antithetical sentences, and periodic sentences? Which types of sentences seem to work best?

Here are a few special types of sentences that should prove useful, especially for adding variety, vividness, and forcefulness to your speech.

Parallel Sentences.   Phrase your ideas in parallel (similar, matching) style for ease of comprehension and memory. Note the parallelism in (a) and (c) and its absence in (b) and (d).

a. The professor prepared the lecture, graded the examination, and read the notices.
b. The professor prepared the lecture, the examination was graded, and she read the notices.
c. Love needs two people to flourish. Jealousy needs but one.
d. Love needs two people. Just one can create jealousy.

Antithetical Sentences.   Antithetical sentences juxtapose contrasting ideas in parallel fashion. John Kennedy used antithetical sentences when he said:

If a free society cannot help the many who are poor, it cannot save the few who are rich.

In his inaugural speech, President Kennedy phrased one of his most often quoted lines in antithetical structure:

Ask not what your country can do for you; ask what you can do for your country.

Listen carefully to the sentences used by an effective speaker or lecturer. Does this person follow the advice given here for phrasing sentences?

Periodic Sentences.   In periodic sentences, you reserve the key word until the end of the sentence. In fact, the sentence is not grammatically complete until you say this last word. For example, in *Looking longingly into his eyes, the old woman fainted*, the sentence doesn't make sense until the last word is spoken.

MAKING YOUR SPEECH EASY TO REMEMBER

If your aim is to communicate information and argument to a listener, then surely part of your job is to ensure that your listeners remember what you say. Here are a few techniques you might use in helping your audience remember your speech.

Stress Interest and Relevance

We learn easier and remember better that which is interesting and relevant to our own lives, because we give it greater attention. Almost automatically, we relate this new information to our own lives and to what we already know. This association of the new with the old helps us to remember the information.

Listeners will also think more about material they find interesting and relevant. This "active rehearsal" significantly aids all kinds of memorization. You would probably have little trouble remembering the address for a job interview that promises $1,500 per week to start; nor are you likely to forget the amount of money being offered. You might, however, have difficulty learning a complex set of numbers if they bore no relevance to your immediate life.

Create Connections

In trying to get someone to remember anything, associate it with what is already known. If a new theory resembles a theory the audience is familiar with, mention this and then point out its differences. If, for example, feedback in communication works like feedback in a thermostat (with which the audience is already familiar), mention that.

Pattern Your Messages

Things are more easily remembered if they are presented in an organized pattern. Consider this experiment. College students tried to memorize a list of words shown to them one at a time. Without any pattern, they had great difficulty. One group, however, was told that they should organize the words alphabetically. Each word began with a different letter. In recalling the list, the experimenters advised, they should go through the alphabet, recalling first the *A*-word, then the *B*-word, and so on. Not surprisingly, the group working with a pattern, in this case the alphabet, did significantly better. The pattern or organizational scheme helped the students to structure the information and thus increased their ability to remember the words. Use this insight and likewise assist listeners to remember what you say in your speech.

> *What other suggestions might you offer for making your speech easy to remember?*

The organizational patterns considered in the discussion of organization and outlining (Units 12, 13, and 14) help you to present the listeners with patterns to aid their memory. Time sequences and spatial sequences, for example, are obvious examples of using known organizational patterns to assist memory. A useful aid to assist remembering is the mnemonic device, discussed in the accompanying box.

Ⓕ O C U S Ⓞ N

Mnemonic Devices

A widely used memory system is the mnemonic device. (The word *mnemonic* comes from the Greek goddess of memory, Mnemosyne.) For example, if I were to ask how many days there are in November, you might go through the mnemonic rhyme "Thirty days hath September, April, June, and November."

A useful mnemonic device is the mediated associate. I remember the spelling distinction between *angle* and *angel* by recalling that the sequence *el* goes up physically, as do angels. I remember the 12 cranial nerves from college physiology because of the sentence "On old Olympus towering top a fine and gentle vision stands high." The initial letters in this sentence remind me of the first letter of each of the cranial nerves. Similarly, I remember the seven primary colors (red, orange, yellow, green, blue, indigo, and violet) by the name "Roy G. Biv."

You might consider coining a mnemonic to help your audience remember the points of your speech. But as you can see, this technique can appear overly contrived if carried too far. Use such devices sparingly and with originality.

Focus Audience Attention

The best way to focus the listeners' attention is to tell them to focus their attention. Simply say, "I want you to focus on three points that I will make in this speech. First, . . ." Then repeat at least once again (but preferably two or three times) these very same points. With experience in public speaking, you will be able to do this with just the right combination of subtlety and directness.

UNIT IN BRIEF

Choose your words to achieve an effective public speaking style	■ **Clarity:** Be economical; be specific; use guide phrases; use short, familiar terms; use repetition and restatement; avoid misusing commonly confused words ■ **Vividness:** Use active verbs; use strong verbs; use figures of speech; use imagery ■ **Appropriateness:** Speak on the appropriate level of formality; avoid unfamiliar terms; avoid slang and vulgar terms; avoid racist, sexist, and heterosexist expressions ■ **Personal style:** Use personal pronouns; ask questions; create immediacy ■ **Forcefulness:** Eliminate weakeners; vary intensity as appropriate; avoid bromides and clichés
Construct sentences to achieve clarity and forcefulness	■ Use short rather than long sentences ■ Use direct rather than indirect sentences ■ Use active rather than passive sentences ■ Use positive rather than negative sentences ■ Vary the types and lengths of sentences, making use of parallel, antithetical, and periodic sentences
Make your speech easy to remember	■ Make your material interesting and relevant to your audience ■ Connect what the audience knows with what you are talking about ■ Give your listeners an organization or pattern to follow ■ Focus your listeners' attention on the main points of your speech

PRACTICALLY SPEAKING

Short Speech Technique

Prepare and deliver a two-minute speech in which you:

1. analyze an advertisement in terms of clarity, vividness, appropriateness, personal style, or forcefulness (choose one or two)
2. describe the language of a person you consider forceful or weak
3. describe an object in the room, using visual, auditory, and tactile imagery
4. explain the meaning of some popular idioms

16.1   Rephrasing Clichés

Clichés are expressions whose meaning has become worn out from excessive usage. Many clichés are also idioms, expressions whose meanings are not easily deduced from the individual words but that must be understood as a single linguistic unit, much like a single word. Thus, in using clichés you betray a lack of originality and, when they are idioms, can easily create special problems for nonnative speakers of the language. The clichés and idioms listed below will provide a useful opportunity to practice your abilities to use language effectively. Rephrase each of these clichés/idioms, so that they are—following the guidelines for language given in this unit—clear, vivid, appropriate, personal, and forceful.

- Heads will roll.
- It's a blessing in disguise.
- You have to take the bitter with the sweet.
- Her problem was that she burned the candle at both ends.
- What can I add? That's the way the cookie crumbles.
- He meant well, but he drove everyone up the wall.
- So, I told her: Either fish or cut bait.
- He just has to get his act together.
- She has a heart of gold.
- I talked and talked, but it was in one ear and out the other.
- Lighten up! Keep your shirt on!
- He let it slip through his fingers.
- That Stephen King movie will make your hair stand on end.
- Well, it's easy being a Monday-morning quarterback.
- Don't put all your eggs in one basket.
- It's just water over the dam.
- He ran out with his tail between his legs.
- They gave the detective a real snow job.
- It was fun, but it wasn't what it was cracked up to be.
- I was so excited that I had my heart in my mouth.
- Wow, you're touchy. You get up on the wrong side of the bed?

U NIT 17

Characteristics of Delivery

Unit Objectives

After completing this unit, you should be able to:

1. Define the four methods of delivery in public speaking and explain their advantages and disadvantages

2. Explain the characteristics of effective delivery

3. Explain the principles that should govern the public speaker's appearance

4. Explain at least three general guidelines for using notes during the public speaking transaction

I f you are like my own students, delivery probably creates more anxiety for you than any other aspect of public speaking. Few speakers worry about organization or audience analysis or style. Many, however, worry about delivery—and so you have a lot of company.

This unit examines the general methods and principles that make for effectiveness in delivery. You can then adapt them to your own personality. The next unit offers specific suggestions for effective delivery.

METHODS OF DELIVERY

Speakers vary widely in their methods of delivery: Some speak "off-the-cuff," with no apparent preparation; others read their speeches from manuscript; some memorize their speeches word for word; others construct a detailed outline and actualize the speech itself at the moment of delivery. Speakers use all four of these general methods of delivery: impromptu, manuscript, memorized, and extemporaneous. Each has advantages and disadvantages.

Speaking Impromptu

When you speak impromptu, you speak without any specific preparation. You and the topic meet for the first time, and immediately the speech begins.

On some occasions you will not be able to avoid speaking impromptu. In a classroom, after someone has spoken, you might comment on the speaker and the speech you just heard—this requires a brief impromptu speech of evaluation. In asking or answering questions in an interview situation, you are giving impromptu speeches, albeit extremely short ones. At meetings, you may find yourself explaining a proposal or defending a plan of action; these too are impromptu speeches. The ability to speak impromptu effectively depends on your general public speaking ability. The more proficient a speaker you are, the better you will be able to function impromptu. Suggestions unique for speaking impromptu are offered in the accompanying TIPS and in Practically Speaking 17.1.

Have you ever had to speak impromptu? What one principle did you learn from the experience?

Advantages   The impromptu experience provides excellent training in the different aspects of public speaking, for example, maintaining eye contact, responding to audience feedback, and gesturing. The impromptu speech experience can also provide practice in basic organization and in development of examples, arguments, and appeals.

Disadvantages   The major disadvantage is that it focuses on appearances. The aim is often to *appear* to give an effective and well-thought-out speech. Another disadvantage is that it does not permit attention to the details of public speaking, such as audience adaptation, research, and style. Because of this inadequacy, the audience is likely to get bored. This in turn may make the speaker feel uncomfortable.

 How effective is the president in speaking from manuscript (through a TelePrompTer)?

Speaking from Manuscript

In the manuscript method, you read the entire speech. The speech is constructed in the same way you would any speech. After you have constructed the detailed preparation outline, you would write out the entire speech, exactly as you want it to be heard by your audience. You would then read this speech to the audience.

Advantages The major advantage of a manuscript speech is that you can control the timing precisely. This is particularly important when delivering a recorded speech, for example, on television. You don't want your conclusion cut off so the fifty-ninth rerun of *Roseanne* can go on as scheduled. Also, there is no danger of forgetting, no danger of being unable to find the right word. Everything is there for you on paper, so you probably will be less anxious.

Still another advantage is that the method allows you to use the exact wording you (or a team of speechwriters) want. In the political arena, this is often crucial; an ambiguous phrase that might prove insulting or belligerent could cause serious problems. The manuscript speech also has the advantage of being already written out, so you can distribute copies and thereby reduce the likelihood of being misquoted.

Disadvantages The most obvious disadvantage is that it is difficult to read a speech and sound natural and nonmechanical. Reading material from the printed page (or even from a TelePrompTer) with liveliness and naturalness is itself a skill that is difficult to achieve without considerable practice. Audiences do not like speakers to read their speeches. They prefer speakers who speak with them.

Reading a manuscript makes it difficult (even impossible) to respond to feedback from your listeners. With a manuscript, you are committed to the speech word for word and cannot make adjustments on the basis of audience feedback.

When the manuscript is on a stationary lectern, as it most often is, it is impossible for you to move around. You have to stay in one place. The speech controls your movement or, rather, your lack of movement.

Still another disadvantage is that it takes lots of time to write out a speech word for word, time that is much better spent working on the substance of your speech.

Speaking from Memory

The memorized method involves writing out the speech word for word (as does the manuscript speech), but instead of reading it, you would commit it to memory and recite it or "act it out."

Advantages The memorized method allows you to devote careful attention to style. As in the manuscript speech, you can carefully review the exact word, phrase, or sentence and eliminate any potential problems in advance. In politically sensitive cases or in cases where media impose restrictions, the memorized method may prove useful.

One of the reasons the memorized delivery is popular is that it has all the advantages of the manuscript method; at the same time, however, it allows you freedom to move about and otherwise concentrate on delivery.

Disadvantages   The major disadvantage, of course, is that you might forget your speech. In a memorized speech each sentence cues the recall of the following sentence. Thus, when you forget one sentence, you may forget the rest of the speech. This danger, along with the natural nervousness that speakers feel, makes this method a poor choice in most situations.

Another disadvantage is that the memorized method is even more time-consuming than the manuscript method, since it involves additional time for memorization. When you recognize that you may easily forget the speech, even after spending hours memorizing it, it hardly seems worth the effort.

Still another disadvantage is that the memorized method does not allow for ease in adjusting to feedback. In fact, there is even less opportunity to adjust to listener feedback than in the manuscript method. And if you are not going to adjust to feedback, you lose the main advantage of face-to-face contact.

Speaking Extemporaneously

Extemporaneous delivery involves thorough preparation and a commitment to memory of the main ideas and their order. It may also involve a commitment to memory of the first and last few sentences of the speech. There is, however, no commitment to exact wording for the remaining parts of the speech.

Advantages   The extemporaneous method is useful in most speaking situations. Good college lecturers use the extemporaneous method. They prepare thoroughly and know what they want to say and in what order they want to say it, but they have given no commitment to exact wording.

This method allows you to respond easily to feedback. Should a point need clarification, you can elaborate on it when it will be most effective to do so. This method makes it easy to be natural because you are being yourself. It is the method that comes closest to conversation or, as some theorists have put it, enlarged conversation. With the extemporaneous method, you can move about and interact with the audience.

Disadvantages   The major disadvantage is that you may stumble and grope for words. If you have rehearsed the speech a number of times, however, this is not likely to happen. Another disadvantage is that you cannot give the speech the attention to style that you can with other methods. You can get around this disadvantage too by memorizing those phrases you want to say exactly. There is nothing in the extemporaneous method that prevents your committing to memory selected phrases, sentences, or quotations.

What one general principle of extemporaneous speaking do most of your instructors follow? Violate?

Guidelines for Speaking Extemporaneously   Having stated a clear preference for the extemporaneous method, I do suggest that you memorize three parts of such a speech. Memorize your opening lines (perhaps the first few sentences), your closing lines (perhaps the last few sentences), and your major propositions and the order in which you will present them.

What are your personal reactions to someone who gives an impromptu speech? From manuscript? From memory? Extemporaneously?

Can you identify cultural differences in the way in which speakers are expected to address an audience? Do certain cultures expect impromptu speaking but frown on manuscript speaking, for example?

Memorizing the opening and closing lines will help you to focus your complete attention on the audience and will also put you more at ease. Once you know exactly what you will say in opening and closing the speech, you will feel more in control. Memorizing the main ideas will free you from relying on your notes and will make you feel more in control of the speech and the speech-making situation.

CHARACTERISTICS OF EFFECTIVE DELIVERY

Strive for a delivery that is natural, reinforces the message, is varied, and is conversational.

Effective Delivery Is Natural

Do men and women deliver public speeches differently? Do you expect men and women to deliver speeches differently? If so, in what way?

Listeners will enjoy and believe you more if you speak naturally, as if you were conversing with a small group of people. Don't allow your delivery to call attention to itself. Your ultimate aim should be to deliver the speech so naturally that the audience won't even notice your delivery. This will take some practice, but you can do it. When voice or bodily action is so prominent that it is distracting, the audience concentrates on the delivery and will fail to attend to your speech.

Effective Delivery Reinforces the Message

Effective delivery should aid instant intelligibility. Your main objective is to make your ideas understandable to an audience. A voice that listeners have to strain to hear, a decrease in volume at the ends of sentences, and slurred diction will obviously hinder comprehension.

When you give a public speech, everything about you communicates. You cannot prevent yourself from sending messages to others.

The way in which you dress is no exception. In fact, your attire will figure significantly in the way your audience assess your credibility and even the extent to which they will give you attention. In short, it will influence your effectiveness in all forms of persuasive and informative speaking. Unfortunately, there are no rules that will apply to all situations for all speakers. Thus, only general guidelines are offered below. Modify and tailor these for yourself and for each unique situation.

- Avoid extremes: Don't allow your clothes to detract attention from what you are saying
- Dress comfortably: Be both physically and psychologically comfortable with your appearance so that you can concentrate your energies on what you are saying
- Dress appropriately: Your appearance should be consistent with the specific public speaking occasion

Effective Delivery Is Varied

Listening to a speech is hard work. Flexible and varied delivery relieves this difficulty. Be especially careful to avoid monotonous and predictable patterns.

What characteristics of delivery do you want to improve most? What characteristics do you feel you have mastered sufficiently?

Monotonous Patterns   Speakers who are monotonous keep their voices at the same pitch, volume, and rate throughout the speech. The monotonous speaker maintains one level from the introduction to the conclusion. Like the drone of a motor, it easily puts the audience to sleep. Vary your pitch levels, your volume, and your rate of speaking.

Similarly, avoid monotony in bodily action. Avoid standing in exactly the same position throughout the speech. Use your body to express your ideas, to communicate to the audience what is going on in your head.

Predictable Patterns   A predictable vocal pattern is one in which, for example, the volume levels vary but always do so in the same pattern. Through repetition, the pattern soon becomes predictable. For example, each sentence may begin at a loud volume and then decline to a barely audible volume at the sentence end. In bodily action, the predictable speaker repeatedly uses the same movements or gestures. For example, a speaker may scan the audience from left to right to left to right throughout the entire speech. If the audience can predict the pattern of your voice or your bodily action, it will draw their attention away from what you are saying to this patterned and predictable delivery.

Effective Delivery Is Conversational

Although more formal than conversation, delivery in public speaking should have some of the most important features of conversation. These qualities are immediacy, eye contact, expressiveness, and responsiveness to feedback.

Immediacy   Just as you can create a sense of immediacy through language, so too can you create it with delivery. Make your listeners feel that you are talking

What public figure's style of delivery comes closest to your ideal?

Most public speaking textbooks advocate a conversational style of delivery. In what kinds of situations might a more formal, less conversational style be more effective?

directly and individually to each of them. You can communicate immediacy through delivery in a number of ways:

- Maintain appropriate eye contact with the audience members
- Maintain a physical closeness that reinforces a psychological closeness; don't stand behind the desk or lectern
- Smile
- Move around a bit; avoid the appearance of being too scared to move
- Stand with a direct and open body posture
- Talk directly to your audience and not to your notes or your visual aid

Eye Contact   Maintaining eye contact, in addition to communicating immediacy, makes the public speaking interaction more conversational. When giving a speech, look directly into your listeners' eyes. Make a special effort to establish eye contact. Lock eyes with different audience members for short periods.

Expressiveness   When you are expressive, you communicate genuine involvement in the public speaking situation. You can communicate this quality of expressiveness, of involvement, in several ways:

- Express responsibility for your own thoughts and feelings
- Vary your vocal rate, pitch, volume, and rhythm to communicate involvement and interest in the audience and the topic
- Allow your facial muscles and your entire body to reflect and echo this inner involvement
- Use gestures to communicate involvement—too few gestures may signal lack of interest, too many may communicate uneasiness, awkwardness, or anxiety

Responsiveness to Feedback   Read carefully the feedback signals sent by your audience. Then respond to these signals with verbal, vocal, and bodily adjustments. For example, respond to audience feedback signals communicating lack of comprehension or inability to hear with added explanation or increased volume.

TIPS
From Professional Speakers

Engage your audience by reaching out to them. As you speak, think that all who sit in front of you are your friends, with whom you will share something useful, valuable, or at least sufficiently attractive to absorb their attention for a few moments. If you are successful, you will have imparted a message that will be understood, retained, and even acted on.

Jack Valenti, president of the Motion Picture Association of America and former speechwriter to President Lyndon Johnson. *Speak Up with Confidence: How to Prepare, Learn, and Deliver Effective Speech* (New York: William Morrow, 1982), pp. 75–76.

USING NOTES

For many speeches it may be helpful to use notes. A few simple guidelines may help you avoid some of the common errors made in using notes.

Keep Notes to a Minimum

The fewer notes you take with you, the better off you will be. The reason so many speakers bring notes with them is that they want to avoid the face-to-face interaction required. With experience, however, you should find this face-to-face interaction the best part of the public speaking experience.

Resist the normal temptation to bring with you the entire speech outline. You may rely on it too heavily and lose the direct contact with the audience. Instead, compose a delivery outline (see p. 260), using only key words. Bring this to the lectern with you—one side of an index card or at most an 8½-by-11-inch page should be sufficient. This will relieve anxiety over the possibility of your forgetting your speech but will not be so extensive as to interfere with direct contact with your audience.

Use Notes with "Open Subtlety"

Do not make your notes more obvious than necessary; at the same time, don't try to hide them. Do not gesture with your notes and thus make them more obvious than they need to be; at the same time, do not turn away from the audience to steal a glance at them. Use your notes openly and honestly but gracefully, with "open subtlety." To do this effectively, you'll have to know your notes intimately. Rehearse at least twice with the same notes that you will take with you to the speaker's stand.

Can you offer any additional advice on using notes?

Do Not Allow Your Notes to Prevent Directness

When referring to your notes, pause to examine them. Then regain eye contact with the audience and continue your speech. Do not read from your notes— just take cues from them. The one exception to this is an extensive quotation or complex set of statistics that you have to read; then, almost immediately, resume direct eye contact with the audience.

What is the single most common error that speakers make in using their notes? What advice would you offer them?

Can you identify public speaking situations in which notes would be considered inappropriate?

UNIT IN BRIEF

Methods for delivering public speeches	■ **Impromptu:** speaking without preparation; useful in training in certain aspects of public speaking
	■ **Manuscript:** reading from a written text; useful when exact timing and wording are essential
	■ **Memorized:** acting out a memorized text; useful when exact timing and wording are required
	■ **Extemporaneous:** speaking after thorough preparation and memorization of the main ideas; useful in most public speaking situations
Characteristics of effective delivery	■ **Natural:** appears genuine, does not call attention to itself
	■ **Reinforces the message:** aids audience comprehension
	■ **Varied:** avoids monotony and predictable patterns of voice and bodily action
	■ **Conversational:** possesses some of the essential qualities of effective conversation: immediacy, eye contact, expressiveness, and responsiveness to feedback
Guidelines for using notes	■ Use few notes—the fewer the better
	■ Use notes with "open subtlety," neither obviously nor secretly; be so familiar with your notes that you will be able to concentrate on your audience
	■ Do not allow your notes to interfere with maintaining direct contact with your audience

PRACTICALLY SPEAKING

Short Speech Technique

Prepare and deliver a two-minute speech in which you:

1. describe the delivery of some noted personality (real or fictional)
2. compare the delivery styles of any two television personalities
3. describe the delivery styles of men and women
4. introduce an excerpt from literature and read the excerpt as you might a manuscript speech

17.1   Developing the Impromptu Speech

The following experience may prove useful as an exercise in delivery. Write an impromptu speech topic on each of three index cards. Select topics that are familiar but not clichés, worthwhile and substantive, and neither too simplistic nor too complex. Place all cards face down on a table. A speaker, chosen through some random process, selects two cards, reads the topics, selects one of them and takes approximately one or two minutes to prepare a two- to three-minute impromptu speech. A few guidelines may prove helpful.

1. Do not apologize. Everyone will have difficulty with this assignment, so there is no need to emphasize any problems you may have.
2. Do not express verbally or nonverbally any displeasure with or negative responses to the experience, the topic, the audience, or even yourself. Approach the entire task with a positive attitude and a positive appearance. Doing so will help make the experience more enjoyable for both you and your audience.
3. When you select the topic, jot down two or three subtopics you will cover and perhaps two or three bits of supporting material you will use in amplifying these two or three subtopics.
4. Develop your conclusion. It will probably be best to use a simple summary conclusion in which you restate your main topic and the subordinate topics you discussed.
5. Develop an introduction. Here it will probably be best simply to identify your topic and orient the audience by telling them the two or three subtopics you will cover.

UNIT 18

Effective Speech Delivery

Unit Objectives

After completing this unit, you should be able to:

1 Define *volume, rate,* and *pitch* and explain the major problems associated with each

2 Explain the major problems associated with articulation and pronunciation

3 Identify the values of pauses in a public speech

4 Explain how the public speaker may deal effectively with each of these aspects of bodily action: eye contact, facial expression, posture, gestures, movement, and proxemics

5 Describe the suggested rehearsal procedures

W hat specifically can you do to improve your delivery, your voice, and your bodily action? This unit answers that important question and also offers some suggestions for rehearsing your speech and for undertaking a long-term improvement program.

VOICE

Three dimensions of voice are especially significant to the public speaker: volume, rate, and pitch. Your manipulation of these elements will enable you to control your voice to maximum advantage.

Before reading further in this unit, try to describe your own speaking voice in terms of volume, rate, pitch, and quality. Which aspects are you pleased with? Which aspects do you feel need work?

Volume

Volume refers to the relative intensity of the voice. Loudness, on the other hand, refers to the perception of that relative intensity. In an adequately controlled voice, volume will vary according to a number of factors. For example, the distance between speaker and listener, the competing noise, and the emphasis the speaker wishes to give an idea will all influence volume.

The problems with volume are easy to identify in others, though difficult to recognize in ourselves. One obvious problem is a voice that is too soft. When speech is so soft that listeners have to strain to hear, they will soon tire of expending so much energy. On the other hand, a voice that is too loud will prove disturbing because it intrudes on our psychological space. However, it is interesting to note that a voice louder than normal communicates assertiveness (Page & Balloun 1978) and will lead people to pay greater attention to you (Robinson & McArthur 1982). On the other hand, it can also communicate aggressiveness and give others the impression that you would be difficult to get along with.

The most common problem is too little volume variation. A related problem is a volume pattern that, although varied, varies in an easily predictable pattern. If the audience can predict the pattern of volume changes, they will focus on it and not on what you are saying.

Fading away at the end of sentences is particularly disturbing. Here the speaker uses a volume that is appropriate, but ends sentences speaking the last few words at an extremely low volume. Be particularly careful when finishing sentences; make sure the audience is able to hear these at an appropriate volume.

If you are using a microphone, test it first. Whether its a microphone that clips around your neck, one you hold in your hand, or one that is stationed to the podium, try it out first. Some speakers—talk-show host Montel Williams is a good example—use the hand microphone as a prop and flip it in the air or from hand to hand as they emphasize a particular point. For your beginning speeches, it is probably best to avoid such techniques and to use the microphone as unobtrusively as you can.

From Professional Speakers

Speaking a little faster than usual certainly beats talking too slow. Fast-paced talking requires keener listening and will make the audience pay more attention. It also gives them the subliminal message that this speech is not going to go on all day and all night. You don't want to sound like an auctioneer, but pick up the pace a little more than your regular conversational speech. . . .

Another benefit of a fast-paced dialogue is that when you do slow down, or stop dead, the audience is alerted to the fact that "this must be important." It's a great way to emphasize.

Don Aslett, writer and professional speaker. *Is There a Speech Inside You?* (Cincinnati, OH: Writer's Digest Books, 1989), p. 70.

Rate

Rate refers to the speed at which you speak. About 150 words per minute seems average for speaking, as well as for reading aloud. The problems of rate are speaking too fast or too slow, or with too little variation or too predictable a pattern. If you talk too fast, you deprive your listeners of time they need to understand and digest what you are saying. If the rate is extreme, the listeners will simply not spend the time and energy needed to understand your speech.

If your rate is too slow, it will encourage your listeners to wander to matters unrelated to your speech. Be careful, therefore, not to bore the audience by presenting information at too slow a rate; yet do not give them information at a pace that is too rapid for listeners to absorb. Strike a happy medium. Speak at a pace that engages the listeners and allows them time for reflection but does not bore them.

Like volume, rate variations can be underused or totally absent. If you speak at the same rate throughout the entire speech, you are not making use of this important speech asset. Use variations in rate to call attention to certain points and to add variety. If you speak, for example, of the dull routine of an assembly-line worker in a rapid and varied pace or of the wonder of a circus in a pace with absolutely no variation, you are surely misusing this important vocal dimension. Again, if you are interested in and conscious of what you are saying, your rate variations should flow naturally and effectively. Too predictable a rate pattern is sometimes as bad as no variation at all. If the audience can predict—consciously or unconsciously—your rate pattern, you are in a vocal rut. You are communicating not ideas but words that you have memorized.

Pitch

Pitch refers to the relative highness or lowness of your voice as perceived by your listener. More technically, pitch results from the rate at which your vocal folds vibrate. If the folds vibrate rapidly, listeners will perceive your voice as having a high pitch. If the folds vibrate slowly, listeners will perceive your voice as having a low pitch.

Pitch changes often signal changes in the meanings of many sentences. The most obvious is the difference between a statement and a question. Thus, the difference between the declarative sentence "So this is the proposal you want me to support" and the question "So this is the proposal you want me to support?" is inflection or pitch. This, of course, is obvious. But note that, depending on where the inflectional change is placed, the meaning of the sentence changes drastically. Note also that all of the following questions contain exactly the same words, but they each ask a different question when you emphasize different words:

- Is *this* the proposal you want me to support?
- Is this the *proposal* you want me to support?
- Is this the proposal you want *me* to support?
- Is this the proposal you want me to *support?*

What voice problems do you hear most often in your college instructors? How might these be remedied?

How much does the voice contribute to the overall effect of a speech?

The obvious problems of pitch are levels that are too high, too low, and too patterned. Neither of the first two problems is common in speakers with otherwise normal voices, and with practice, you can correct a pitch pattern that is too predictable or monotonous. With increased speaking experience, pitch changes will come naturally from the sense of what you are saying. Because each sentence is somewhat different from every other sentence, there should be a normal variation—one that results not from some predetermined pattern but rather from the meanings you wish to convey to the audience.

ARTICULATION AND PRONUNCIATION

Articulation and pronunciation are similar in that they both refer to enunciation, the way in which we produce sounds and words. They differ, however, in a technical sense. Articulation refers to the movements the speech organs make as they modify and interrupt the air stream you send from the lungs. Different movements of these speech organs (for example, the tongue, lips, teeth, palate, and vocal cords) produce different sounds. Pronunciation refers to the production of syllables or words according to some accepted standard, identified in any good dictionary.

Our concern here is with identifying and correcting some of the most common problems associated with faulty articulation and pronunciation.

Articulation Problems

The three major articulation problems are omission, substitution, and addition of sounds or syllables. These problems are seen in both native speakers of English as well as in second-language English speakers. Fortunately, they can be easily corrected with informed practice.

Errors of Omission   Omitting sounds or even syllables is a major articulation problem but is one we can easily overcome with concentration and practice. Here are some examples:

Not This	This
gov-a-ment	gov-ern-ment
hi-stry	hi-story
wanna	want to
fishin	fishing
studyin	studying
a-lum-num	a-lum-i-num
hon-orble	hon-or-able
comp-ny	comp-a-ny
vul-ner-bil-ity	vul-ner-a-bil-ity

TIPS
From Professional Speakers

In every sentence, one word or phrase is more important than the rest. Read this sentence out loud: "The company was forced to ask him for his resignation." If you were a company spokesperson, you might consider "forced" to be the most important word. If you were a colleague of the person told to resign, you might consider "resignation" to be the key word.

Whatever your choice, you want to emphasize that word or phrase to make your point to your audience. This technique is called "punching" it. Speech writers underline the words they want the speaker to hit. You can do the same on your outline.

Marjorie Brody & **Shawn Kent,** communication consultants and trainers. *Power Presentations: How to Connect with Your Audience and Sell Your Ideas* (New York: Wiley, 1993), p. 31.

Errors of Substitution   Substituting an incorrect sound for the correct one is another easily remedied problem. Among the most popular are substituting *d* for *t* and *d* for *th*, illustrated by the first five examples.

Not This	This
wader	waiter
dese	these
ax	ask
undoubtebly	undoubtedly
beder	better
ekcetera	et cetera
ramark	remark
lenth	length

What is the Reverend W. A. Spooner (from whose name we get the word spoonerism: the interchanging of initial with sounds in other parts of the word) trying to say? "Sir, you have tasted two whole worms; you have hissed all my mystery lectures and have been caught fighting a liar in the quad; you will leave by the next town drain"?

Errors of Addition   When we make errors of addition, we add sounds where they do not belong. Some examples include:

Not This	This
acrost	across
athalete	athlete
Americer	America
idear	idea
filim	film
lore	law

If you make any of these errors, you can easily correct them by following these steps:

- Become conscious of your own articulation patterns (and the specific errors you might be making)
- Listen carefully to the articulation of prominent speakers (for example, broadcasters)
- Practice the correct patterns until they become part of your normal speech behavior

Pronunciation Problems

Among the most popular pronunciation problems are accenting the wrong syllable and pronouncing sounds that should remain silent.

Errors of Accent   Here are some common examples of accenting words incorrectly:

Not This	This
New Orleáns	New Órleans
ínsurance	insúrance
orátor	órator

Errors of Adding Sounds   Another common error is to pronounce sounds that should not be pronounced. For example, in the first four examples presented below, the error consists of pronouncing letters that should remain silent. In the last three examples the error consists of adding sounds that are not part of the word.

Not This	This
often	offen
homage	omage
Illinois	Illinoi
evening	evning
burgalar	burglar
athalete	athlete
airaplane	airplane

The best way to deal with pronunciation problems is to look up in a good dictionary any words whose pronunciation you are not sure of. Learn to read the pronunciation key in your dictionary, and make it a practice to look up words you hear others use that seem to be pronounced incorrectly or that you wish to use yourself but are not sure how to pronounce.

 PAUSES

Pauses come in two basic types: filled and unfilled. Filled pauses are pauses in the stream of speech that we fill with vocalizations such as *er*, *um*, and *ah*. Even expressions such as *well* and *you know*, when used just to fill up silence, are called filled pauses. These pauses are ineffective and weaken the strength of your message. They will make you appear hesitant, unprepared, and unsure of yourself.

Unfilled pauses are silences interjected into the normally fluent stream of speech. Unfilled pauses can be especially effective if used correctly. Here are just a few examples of places where unfilled pauses—silences of a few seconds—should prove effective.

1. Pause at transitional points. This will signal that you are moving from one part of the speech to another or from one idea to another. It will help the listeners separate the main issues you are discussing.

TIPS
From Professional Speakers

Violin virtuoso Isaac Stern was once asked how it was that all professional musicians could play the right notes in the right order, but some made beautiful music while others did not. He replied, "The important thing is not the notes. It's the intervals between the notes." Just as the best musicians add an extra shade of meaning—the difference between good music and great music—by spacing their notes, the best speakers know the value of pausing for effect.

Sandy Linver, communication consultant and president, Speakeasy, Inc. *Speak and Get Results: The Complete Guide to Speeches and Presentations That Work in Any Business Situation,* revised and updated. (New York: Simon & Schuster/Fireside, 1994), p. 139.

2. Pause at the end of an important assertion. This will allow the audience time to think about the significance of what you are saying.
3. Pause after asking a rhetorical question. This will provide the necessary time so the audience can think of how they would answer the question.
4. Pause before an important idea. This will help signal that what comes next is especially significant.

In addition, pauses are helpful before beginning your speech and after you have concluded your speech. Do not start speaking as soon as you get to the front of the room; rather, pause to scan the audience and to gather your thoughts. Also, do not leave the podium as you speak your last word; pause to allow your speech to sink in and avoid giving the audience the impression that you are eager to leave them.

Like most good things, pauses can be overdone. Used in moderation, however, they can be powerful aids to comprehension and persuasion.

What happens in the minds of listeners when speakers fail to pause sufficiently? What happens when speakers pause too often or for too long a time?

BODILY ACTION

Your body is a powerful instrument in your speech. You speak with your body as well as with your mouth. The total effect of the speech depends not only on what you say but also on the way you present it. It depends on your movements, gestures, and facial expressions as well as on your words.

Six aspects of bodily action are especially important in public speaking: eye contact, facial expression, posture, gestures, movement, and proxemics.

Eye Contact

The single most important aspect of bodily communication is eye contact. Do realize, however, that cultures differ widely on the amount and intensity of eye contact they consider appropriate. In some cultures, eye contact that is too intense may be considered offensive. In most of the United States audiences want and expect to be looked at rather directly. Not surprisingly, then, the two major problems with eye contact are not enough eye contact and eye contact that does not cover the audience fairly. Speakers who do not maintain enough eye contact appear distant, unconcerned, and less trustworthy than speakers who look directly at their audience. And, of course, without eye contact, you will not be able to secure that all-important audience feedback. Maintain eye contact with the entire audience. Involve all listeners in the public speaking transaction. Communicate equally with the members on the left and on the right, in both the back and the front.

Use eye contact to secure audience feedback. Are they interested? Bored? Puzzled? In agreement? In disagreement? Use your eyes to communicate your commitment to and interest in what you're saying. Communicate your confidence and commitment by making direct eye contact; avoid staring blankly through your audience or glancing over their heads, at the floor, or out the window.

TIPS
From Professional Speakers

Within many cultures around the world, it is believed that the eyes are the windows to the soul. In public speaking, since we usually want to arouse both spirit and soul, the eyes becomes the most important physical equipment of all.

Start by thinking about one-on-one conversations. Have you ever conversed with someone who kept looking away constantly, avoiding eye contact? This behavior often illustrates discomfort or dishonesty. Conversely, the person who maintains good eye contact is displaying sincerity, attention, and respect.

Roger E. Axtell, *Do's and Taboos of Public Speaking: How to Get Those Butterflies Flying in Formation* (New York: Wiley, 1992), p. 67.

What do you feel are the most common problems with the bodily action of public speakers? What one suggestion would you offer them?

Facial Expression

Facial expressions are especially important in communicating emotions—your anger and fear, boredom and excitement, doubt and surprise. If you feel committed to and believe in your thesis, you will probably display your meanings appropriately and effectively.

Nervousness and anxiety, however, may at times prevent you from relaxing enough so that your emotions come through. Fortunately, time and practice will allow you to relax, and the emotions you feel will reveal themselves appropriately and automatically.

Generally, members of one culture will be able to recognize the emotion displayed facially by members of other cultures. But there are differences in what each culture considers appropriate to display. Each culture has its own "display rules" (Ekman 1972). For example, Japanese Americans watching a stress-inducing film spontaneously displayed the same facial emotions as did other Americans when they thought they were unobserved. But when an observer was present, the Japanese Americans masked (tried to hide) their emotional expressions more than the Americans did (Ekman & Friesen 1971; Lustig & Koester 1996).

How would you describe the bodily action of talk-show hosts like Phil Donahue, Oprah Winfrey, Jay Leno, Sally Jesse Raphael, and Geraldo Rivera? How would you describe your own bodily action when speaking?

Can eye contact or facial expressions ever be used too extensively and actually work against the speaker? If so, how?

Posture

When delivering your speech, stand straight but not stiff. Try to communicate a command of the situation without communicating the discomfort that is actually quite common for beginning speakers.

Avoid the common mistakes of posture: Avoid putting your hands in your pockets, and avoid leaning on the desk, the podium, or the chalkboard. With practice, you will come to feel more at ease and will communicate this by the way you stand before the audience.

Gestures

You use gestures regularly and without thinking about them in conversation. For example, when saying "come here," you probably move your head, hands, arms, and perhaps your entire body to motion the listener in your direction. Both your body and your verbal message say "come here." These conversational gestures help illustrate and reinforce your verbal message. Gestures function the same way in public speaking. Use them to help make your verbal message clearer and more persuasive.

Effective bodily action is spontaneous and natural to you as the speaker, to your audience, and to your speech. If it seems planned or rehearsed, it will appear phony and insincere. As a general rule, don't do anything with your hands that doesn't feel right for you; the audience will recognize it as unnatural. If you feel relaxed and comfortable with yourself and your audience, you will generate natural bodily action without conscious and studied attention.

Avoid using your hands to preen, for example, fixing your hair or adjusting your clothing. Avoid fidgeting with your watch, ring, or jewelry. Avoid keeping your hands in your pockets or clasped in front of you or behind your back.

Is delivery (voice and bodily action) more important in informative speaking or in persuasive speaking?

Movement

Movement refers here to your large bodily movements. It helps to move around a bit. It keeps both the audience and you more alert. Even when speaking behind a lectern, you can give the illusion of movement. You can step backward or forward or flex your upper body so it appears that you are moving more than you are.

Use gross movements to emphasize transitions and to introduce new and important assertions. Thus, when making a transition you might take a step forward to signal that something new is coming. Similarly, this type of movement may signal the introduction of an important assumption, bit of evidence, or closely reasoned argument.

Avoid these three problems of movement: too little, too much, and too patterned movement. Speakers who move too little often appear strapped to the podium, afraid of the audience, or too uninterested to involve themselves fully. With too much movement, the audience begins to concentrate on the movement itself, wondering where the speaker will wind up next. With too patterned a movement, the audience may become bored—too steady and predictable a rhythm quickly becomes tiring. The audience will often view the speaker as nonspontaneous and uninvolved.

How would you describe the voice and bodily action of a specific prominent politician? A specific actor?

Proxemics

Proxemics refers to the way you use space in communication. In public speaking the space between you and your listeners and among the listeners themselves is often a crucial factor. If you stand too close to the audience, they might feel uncomfortable, as if their personal space is being violated. If you stand too far away from your audience, you might be perceived as uninvolved, uninterested, and uncomfortable. Watch where your instructor and other speakers stand and adjust your own position accordingly.

If you are using a lectern, you may wish to signal transitions by stepping to the side or in front of it and then behind it again as you move from one point to another. Generally, it is best to avoid the extremes; too much movement around the lectern and no movement are both to be avoided. You may wish to lean over it when, say, posing a question to your listeners or when advancing a particularly important argument. But never lean on the lectern; never use it as support.

REHEARSAL: PRACTICING AND IMPROVING DELIVERY

Effective public speaking delivery does not come naturally—it takes practice. Learn now how to use your practice time most effectively and efficiently.

The goal of practice is to develop a delivery that will help you achieve the purposes of your speech. Rehearsal should enable you to see how the speech will flow as a whole and to make any changes and improvements you think necessary. Through practice, you will learn the speech effectively and determine how best to present it to your audience.

The following procedures should assist you in using your time most effectively. A suggested long-term delivery improvement program appears in the accompanying box.

Rehearse the Speech as a Whole

Rehearse the speech from beginning to end. Do not rehearse the speech in parts. Rehearse it from getting out of your seat, through delivering the introduction, body, and conclusion, to returning to your seat. Be sure to rehearse

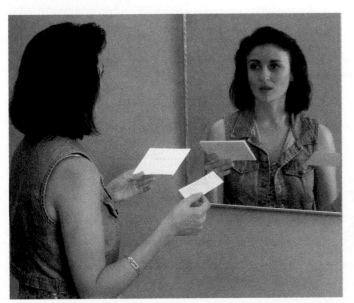

Beginning speakers often "rehearse" mentally; they review what they will say in their mind. How does this kind of "rehearsal" compare with rehearsal that more closely approximates the actual public speaking situation, for example, rehearsal that involves presenting the speech aloud while standing in front of a mirror or in front of a few friends?

the speech with all the examples and illustrations (and audiovisual aids, if any) included. This will enable you to connect the parts of the speech and to see how they interact with each other.

Time the Speech

Time the speech during each rehearsal. Make the necessary adjustments on the basis of this timing.

Approximate the Actual Speech Situation

Rehearse the speech under conditions as close as possible to those under which you will deliver it. If possible, rehearse the speech in the same room in which you will present it. If this is impossible, try to simulate the actual conditions as close as you can—in your living room or even bathroom. If possible, rehearse the speech in front of a few supportive listeners. It is always helpful (but especially for your beginning speeches) that your listeners be supportive rather than too critical. Merely having listeners present during your rehearsal will further simulate the conditions under which you will eventually speak. Get together with two or three other students in an empty classroom where you can each serve as speaker and listener.

See Yourself as a Speaker

Rehearse the speech in front of a full-length mirror. This will enable you to see yourself and to see how you will appear to the audience. This may be extremely difficult at first, and you may have to force yourself to watch. After a few attempts, however, you will begin to see the value of this experience. Practice your eye contact, your movements, and your gestures in front of the mirror.

Incorporate Changes and Make Delivery Notes

Have you discovered any useful rehearsal suggestions that might be of value to others?

Between rehearsals, make any changes in the speech that seem appropriate. Do not interrupt your rehearsal to make notes or changes; if you do, you may never experience the entire speech from beginning to end. While making these changes, note too any words whose pronunciation or articulation you wish to check. Also, insert pause notations ("slow down" warnings, and other delivery suggestions) into your outline.

If possible, record your speech (ideally, on videotape) so you can hear exactly what your listeners will hear: your volume, rate, pitch, articulation and pronunciation, and pauses. You will thus be in a better position to improve these qualities.

Rehearse Often

Rehearse the speech as often as seems necessary. Two useful guides are (1) rehearse the speech at least three or four times (less than this is sure to be too little) and (2) rehearse the speech as long as your rehearsals result in improvements in the speech or in your delivery. Some suggestions for a long-term delivery improvement program are provided in the accompanying box.

A Long-Term Delivery Improvement Program

Approach your long-term delivery program with positive thinking. This will help a great deal in setting up an attitude that will contribute to making you a truly effective public speaker. Tell yourself that you can do it and that you will do it.

1. Seek feedback from someone whose opinion and insight you respect. Your public speaking instructor may be a logical choice, but someone majoring in communication or working in a communication field might also be appropriate. Get an honest and thorough appraisal of both your voice and your bodily action.

2. Learn to hear, see, and feel the differences between effective and ineffective patterns. Learn to hear, for example, the patterned nature of your pitch or your overly loud volume. A tape recorder will be very helpful. Learn to see your gestures and your gross bodily movement. A full-length mirror will prove helpful though a video will provide even greater insight. Learn to feel your rigid posture or your lack of arm and hand gestures. Once you have perceived these differences, concentrate on learning more effective patterns. Practice a few minutes each day. Avoid becoming too conscious of any source of ineffectiveness. Just try to increase your awareness and work on one problem at a time. Do not try to change all your patterns at once.

3. Seek additional feedback on the changes. Make certain listeners agree that the new patterns you are practicing are really more effective. Remember that you hear yourself through air transmission as well as through bone conduction. Others hear you only through air transmission. So, what you hear and what others hear will be different.

4. For voice improvement, consult a book on voice and diction for practice exercises and for additional information on the nature of volume, rate, pitch, and quality.

5. If any of these difficulties persist, see a professional. For voice problems, see a speech clinician. Most campuses have a speech clinic. You can easily avail yourself of its services. For bodily action difficulties, talk with your public speaking instructor.

6. Seek professional help if you are psychologically uncomfortable with any aspect of your voice or your bodily action. It may be that all you have to do is to hear yourself or see yourself on a videotape—as others see and hear you—to convince yourself that you sound and look just fine. Regardless of what is causing this discomfort, however, if you are uncomfortable, do something about it. In a college community there is more assistance available to you at no cost than you will ever experience again. Make use of it.

What aspects of bodily action do you feel you need to improve? How will you go about improving these aspects?

UNIT IN BRIEF

Voice problems	■ **Volume:** overly soft, loud, or unvaried; fading away at ends of sentences ■ **Rate:** too rapid, too slow, too little variation; too predictable a pattern ■ **Pitch:** overly high, low, or monotonous; too predictable a pattern
Problems in articulation and pronunciation	■ **Errors of articulation:** (1) omission, (2) substitution, and (3) addition ■ **Errors of pronunciation:** (1) accent and (2) adding sounds
The functions of pauses	■ Signal a transition between major parts of the speech ■ Give the audience time to think ■ Allow listeners to ponder a rhetorical question ■ Signal the approach of an important idea
Effective bodily action	■ Maintain **eye contact** ■ Allow **facial expressions** to convey thoughts and feelings ■ Use **posture** to communicate command of the speech experience ■ **Gesture** naturally ■ **Move around** a bit ■ **Position** yourself neither too close nor too far from the audience
Rehearsal procedures	■ Rehearse the speech as a whole ■ Time the speech ■ Approximate the actual speech situation ■ See yourself as a speaker ■ Incorporate changes and delivery notes ■ Rehearse often

PRACTICALLY SPEAKING

Short Speech Technique

Prepare and deliver a two-minute speech in which you:

1. describe your growth as a public speaker over the last several months
2. describe the delivery of a speaker you consider effective or ineffective

3. outline the steps you intend to take to continue your learning of communication skills
4. compare the delivery styles of any two prominent people from the arts or politics
5. describe the delivery style of a prominent comedian or compare the delivery styles of any two comedians

18.1   Communicating Vocally But Nonverbally

This exercise is designed to give you practice in communicating effectively with your voice and body. In this exercise you recite the alphabet, attempting to communicate each of the following emotions: anger, nervousness, fear, pride, happiness, sadness, jealousy, satisfaction, love, and sympathy.

You may begin the alphabet at any point and may omit and repeat sounds, but you may use only the names of the letters of the alphabet to communicate these feelings.

You might first number the emotions in random order so that you will have a set order to follow that is not known to the audience, whose task it will be to guess the emotions you express.

As a variation, try going through the entire list of emotions twice: once facing the audience and employing any nonverbal signals desired, and once with your back to the audience without employing any additional signals. Are there differences in the number of correct guesses, depending on which method is used? If so, why?

After the exercise is completed, consider some or all of the following questions:

1. What vocal cues are used to communicate the various emotions?
2. Are some cues useful for communicating some emotions and not useful (or even detrimental) for communicating others? Explain.
3. What bodily cues are useful in communicating these various emotions?
4. Are some bodily cues useful for communicating some emotions and not useful for others? Explain.
5. Are there significant gender differences for effectively communicating these emotions? That is, should men and women use different cues in communicating these emotions?

PART FIVE

Elements of Public Speeches

Unit 19

The Informative Speech

Unit Objectives

After completing this unit, you should be able to:

 1   Explain the principles of informative speaking

 2   Explain description, definition, and demonstration as ways of communicating information

 3   Identify the major strategies to use in describing, defining, and demonstrating

*I*n this unit we look at the informative speech. First, a series of general principles useful for all informative speaking are presented, and second, the three
types of informative speeches are explained.

PRINCIPLES OF INFORMATIVE SPEAKING

When you communicate "information," you tell your listeners something they
do not know, something new. You may tell them of a new way of looking at old
things or an old way of looking at new things. You may discuss a theory not
previously heard of or a familiar one not fully understood. You may talk about
events the audience may be unaware of or have misconceptions about.
Regardless of what type of informative speech you intend to give, the following
principles should help.

Limit the Amount of Information

There is a limit to the amount of information a listener can take in at one time.
Resist the temptation to overload your listeners with information. Limit the
amount of information you communicate, and instead, expand its presentation. It is better to present two new items of information and explain these
with examples, illustrations, and descriptions than to present five items without this needed amplification.

Here, for example, is the type of thing you should avoid:

*In this speech I want to discuss the differences between women and men. I'm
going to focus on the physiological, psychological, social, and linguistic
differences.*

Clearly, the speaker is trying to cover too much. The speaker is going to be
forced to cover these four areas only superficially, with the result that little new
information will be communicated. Instead, select one area and develop it in
depth:

*In this speech I want to discuss some of the linguistic differences between
women and men. I'm going to focus on two linguistic differences: differences
in language development and differences in language problems. Let's look
first at the way in which girls and boys develop language.*

In this speech the speaker now has the opportunity to cover an area in
depth. As a result, the listeners are more likely to learn something.

Adjust the Level of Complexity

As you know from attending college classes, information can be presented in a
very simplified form or in an extremely complex form. The level of complexity
at which you communicate your information should depend on the wide

Of the speeches you've heard so far
in this course, what percentage
violated this principle?

In terms of complexity, how would you evaluate the average college lecture? The average textbook unit or chapter? The average newscast?

variety of factors considered throughout: the level of knowledge your audience has, the time you have available, the breadth of your purpose, the topic on which you are speaking, and so on. If you simplify a topic too much, you risk boring or, even worse, insulting your audience. If your talk is too complex, you risk confusing your audience and failing to communicate the desired information.

Generally, however, beginning speakers err on the side of being too complex and not realizing that a five- or ten-minute speech is not a very long format in which to make an audience understand sophisticated concepts or complicated processes. At least in your beginning speeches, try to keep it simple rather than complex. For example, make sure the words you use are familiar to your audience or, if not, explain and define them as you use them. Remember too that jargon and technical vocabulary familiar to the computer hacker may not be familiar to the person who still uses a typewriter. Always see your topic from the point of view of the audience; ask yourself how much they know about your topic and its language.

Another useful general principle is to talk in concrete rather than abstract terms. (Lots of suggestions for using specific language are provided in Unit 16.)

Stress Relevance and Usefulness

Listeners will remember your information best when they see it as relevant and useful to their own needs or goals. Notice that as a listener, you follow this principle all the time. For example, in a communication class you might attend to and remember the stages in the development of language in children simply because you will be tested on the information and you want to earn a high grade.

If you want the audience to listen to your speech, be sure to relate your information to their needs, wants, or goals. Throughout your speech, make

Can you develop another principle that would be useful for informative speaking?

sure the audience knows the information is relevant and useful to them. For example, you might say something like:

> We all want financial security. We all want to be able to buy those luxuries we read so much about in magazines and see every evening on television. Wouldn't it be nice to be able to buy a car without worrying about where you're going to get the down payment or how you'll be able to make the monthly payments? Actually, that is not an unrealistic goal, as I'll demonstrate in this speech. In fact, I will show you several methods for investing your money that will enable you to increase your income by at least 20 percent.

In recent studies on relevance, communication researchers investigated what students felt made their college lectures relevant to their personal and professionals goals (Frymier & Shulman 1995). They found that the greater the relevance of the lecture, the more the students were motivated to study. It seems reasonable to extend these findings to argue that the more relevant a speech, the more listeners will be motivated to listen and even to pursue further this new interest. Here, stated in the form of suggestions for informative speaking, are a few of the most frequently noted ways the researchers found for stressing relevance:

- Use examples that make content relevant
- Use exercises or explanations to show the content's importance to your listeners
- Explain how the content is related to your listeners' career goals
- Stimulate your listeners' thinking about how the content applies to their goals
- Use your own or your listeners' experiences to stress the importance of the content of your talk
- Relate current events to the content of your talk

Relate New Information to Old

Listeners will learn information more easily and retain it longer when you relate it to what they already know. So, relate the new to the old, the unfamiliar to the familiar, the unseen to the seen, the untasted to the tasted. Here, for example, Betsy Heffernan, a student from the University of Wisconsin (Reynolds & Schnoor 1991), relates the problem of sewage to a familiar historical event:

> During our nation's struggle for independence, the citizens of Boston were hailed as heroes for dumping tea into Boston Harbor. But not to be outdone, many modern day Bostonians are also dumping things into the harbor. Five-thousand gallons of human waste every second. The New England Aquarium of Boston states that since 1900, Bostonians have dumped enough human sewage into the harbor to cover the entire state of Massachusetts chest deep in sludge. Unfortunately, Boston isn't alone. All over the country, bays, rivers and lakes are literally becoming cesspools.

TIPS

From Professional Speakers

To introduce new material to an audience, you must allow their brains to hook into old, well-known, comfortable information-processing systems. To absorb new material or make sense of any material, your audience needs for you to follow a logical progression. In real life "A" does truly come before "B" and "C." So it must in your presentation. Start at the beginning.

Sonya Hamlin, communication consultant. *How to Talk So People Listen: The Real Key to Job Success* (New York: Harper & Row, 1988), p. 99.

How might you use the principle of relating new information to old if you wanted to describe a compact disc to someone who had never heard of one? Electricity to someone from the fifteenth century? Computers to someone from the nineteenth century?

Vary the Levels of Abstraction

You can talk about freedom of the press in the abstract by talking about the importance of getting information to the public, by referring to the Bill of Rights, and by relating a free press to the preservation of democracy. That is, you can talk about the topic on a relatively high level of abstraction. But you can also talk about freedom of the press by citing specific examples: how a local newspaper was prevented from running a story critical of the town council or how Lucy Rinaldo was fired from the *Accord Sentinel* after she wrote a story critical of the mayor. You can talk about the topic on a relatively low level of abstraction, a level that is specific and concrete.

Combining the high abstraction and the specific seems to work best. Too many high abstractions without the specifics or too many specifics without the high abstractions will generally prove less effective than the combination of abstract and specific.

Here, for example, is an excerpt from a speech on the homeless. Note that in the first paragraph, we have a relatively abstract description of homelessness. In the second paragraph, we get into specifics. In the last paragraph, the abstract and the concrete are connected.

> *Homelessness is a serious problem for all metropolitan areas throughout the country. It is estimated that there are now more than 200,000 homeless in New York City alone. But what is homelessness really about? Let me tell you what it's about.*
>
> *It's about a young man. He must be 25 or 30, although he looks a lot older. He lives in a cardboard box on the side of my apartment house. We call him Tom, although we really don't know his name. All his possessions are stored in this huge box. I think it was a box from a refrigerator. Actually, he doesn't have very much and what he does have easily fits in this box.*
>
> *There are some blankets my neighbor threw out, some plastic bottles Tom puts water in, and some Styrofoam containers he picked up from the garbage bin at Burger King. He uses these to store whatever food he finds.*
>
> *What is homelessness about? It's about Tom and 200,000 other "Toms" in New York and thousands of others throughout the rest of the country. And not all of them even have boxes to live in.*

Now that the general principles are clear, we can look at the three main types of informative speeches: description, definition, and demonstration.

THE SPEECH OF DESCRIPTION

When you describe, you are concerned with explaining an object or person or with explaining an event or process. Here are a few examples:

Describing an Object or Person

- the structure of the brain
- the contributions of Thomas Edison
- the gifted child
- the parts of a telephone

Do the speakers and lecturers you prefer follow these principles for informative speaking? Can you give specific examples of how they follow these rules?

Select an advertisement (television or print) and examine how closely it follows the principles of informative speaking identified here. Which principle is most important to the success of an advertisement? Why?

- the structure of Taj Mahal
- the layout of the Alamo
- the hierarchy of a corporation
- the human body
- the Internet
- the components of a computer system

Describing an Event or Process

- the bombing in Oklahoma City
- the development of consumerism
- the events leading to World War II
- organizing a bodybuilding contest
- the breakdown of Russian communism
- how a newspaper is printed
- the events leading to the *Exxon Valdez* oil spill
- the process of buying a house
- purchasing stock
- how e-mail works

Strategies for Describing

Here are some suggestions for describing objects and people, events and processes.

Select an Appropriate Organizational Pattern   Consider using a spatial or a topical organization when describing objects and people. Consider using a temporal pattern when describing events and processes. For example, if you were to describe the layout of Philadelphia, you might start from the north and work down to the south, using a spatial pattern. If you were to describe the contributions of Thomas Edison, you might select the three or four major contributions and discuss each of these equally, using a topical pattern.

If you were describing the events leading up to World War II, you might use a temporal pattern and start with the earliest and work up to the latest. A temporal pattern would also be appropriate for describing how a hurricane develops or how a parade is put together.

Use a Variety of Descriptive Categories   Describe the object or event with lots of descriptive categories. Use physical categories and ask yourself questions such as these:

- What color is it?
- How big is it?
- What is its texture?
- What is it shaped like?
- How high is it?
- How flexible is it?
- How much does it weigh?
- How long or short is it?
- What is its volume?
- How attractive/unattractive is it?

What descriptive categories might you use to describe this textbook? Does the book have psychological as well as physical characteristics that might be useful in describing it?

What categories might you use in describing a football? A forest? A house? An infant? A movie?

Also, consider social, psychological, and economic categories. In describing a person, for example, consider such categories as friendly/unfriendly, warm/cold, rich/poor, aggressive/meek, and pleasant/unpleasant.

Consider Using Audiovisual Aids   Audiovisual aids will help you describe almost anything. Use them if you possibly can. In describing an object or person, show your listeners a picture. Show them pictures of the brain, the inside of a telephone, the skeleton of the body. In describing an event or process, create a diagram or flowchart to illustrate the various stages or steps. Show your listeners a flowchart representing the stages in buying stock, in publishing a newspaper, in putting a parade together.

Consider *Who? What? Where? When?* and *Why?*   The 5W categories are especially useful when you want to describe an event or process. For example, if you are going to describe how to purchase a house, you might want to consider the people involved (*who?*), the steps you have to go through (*what?*), the places you will have to go (*where?*), the time or sequence in which each of the steps has to take place (*when?*), and the advantages and disadvantages of buying the house (*why?*).

Developing the Speech of Description

Here are two examples of how you might go about constructing a speech of description. In this first example, the speaker, following a temporal sequence, describes four suggestions for increasing assertiveness. Notice that the steps follow the order one would follow in becoming more assertive.

How might you go about describing the registration process at your school? What would your major propositions be?

GENERAL PURPOSE: to inform
SPECIFIC PURPOSE: to describe how we can become more assertive
THESIS: assertiveness can be increased (How can assertiveness be increased?)

  I. Analyze assertive behaviors.

 II. Record your own assertive behaviors.

III. Rehearse assertive behaviors.

IV. Act assertively.

In this second example, the speaker, using a topical pattern, describes the way in which fear works in intercultural communication:

GENERAL PURPOSE: to inform
SPECIFIC PURPOSE: to describe the way fear works in intercultural communication
THESIS: fear influences intercultural communication (How does fear influence intercultural communication?)

  I. We fear disapproval.

 II. We fear embarrassing ourselves.

III. We fear being harmed.

In delivering such a speech, a speaker might begin by saying:

There are three major fears that interfere with intercultural communication. First, there is the fear of disapproval—from members of our own group as well as from members of the other person's group. Second, we fear embarrassing ourselves, even making fools of ourselves, by saying the wrong thing or appearing insensitive. And third, we may fear being harmed—our stereotypes of the other group may lead us to see their members as dangerous or potentially harmful to us.

Let's look at each of these fears in more detail and we'll be able to see how they influence our own intercultural communication behavior.

Consider, first, the fear of disapproval.

THE SPEECH OF DEFINITION

What is leadership? What is a born-again Christian? What is the difference between sociology and psychology? What is a cultural anthropologist? What is safe sex? These are all topics for informative speeches of definition.

A definition is a statement of the meaning or significance of a concept or term. Use definitions when you wish to explain difficult or unfamiliar concepts or want to make a concept more vivid or forceful.

In defining a term or giving an entire speech of definition, you may focus on a specific term, a system or theory, or the similarities and/or differences among terms or systems. It may be a subject new to the audience or one familiar to them but presented in a new and different way.

Here are some examples:

Defining a Term

- What is multiculturalism?
- What is machismo?
- What is drug addiction?
- What is creativity?
- What is censorship?
- What is affirmative action?
- What is political correctness?
- What is a balanced budget?
- What is braille writing?
- What is classism?

Defining a System or Theory

- What is the classical theory of public speaking?
- What is the theory of cultural evolution?
- What are the parts of a generative grammar?
- What is expressionism?
- What are the major beliefs of Confucianism?
- What is futurism?

 How would you organize a speech to define "the ideal military leader"?

- What is the "play theory" of mass communication?
- What is religious fundamentalism?
- What is the philosophy of Greenpeace?
- What is cold fusion?

Defining Similar and Dissimilar Terms or Systems

- Communism and socialism: some similarities and differences
- What do Christians and Muslims have in common?
- Genetics and heredity
- Oedipus and Electra: How do they differ?
- Love and infatuation: their similarities
- Freshwater and saltwater fishing
- Ballet and square dancing
- Differences between critical and creative thinking
- Animal and human communication systems
- Snail mail and e-mail

Strategies for Defining

In giving a speech of definition, consider the following suggestions.

Use a Variety of Definitions   When explaining a concept, it is helpful to define it in a number of different ways. Here are some of the most important ways to define a term.

How many different types of definitions could you use to define wealth? Happiness? Entertainment? Economic hardship? Love? Anarchy?

Define by Etymology.   In defining the word *communication*, you might note that it comes from the Latin *communis*, meaning "common"; in *communicating*, you seek to establish a commonness, a sameness, a similarity with another individual. And *woman* comes from the Anglo-Saxon *wifman*, meaning literally a "wife man," where the word *man* was applied to both sexes. Through phonetic change, *wifman* became *woman*. Most larger dictionaries and, of course, etymological dictionaries will help you find useful etymological definitions.

Define by Authority.   You might, for example, define lateral thinking by authority and say that Edward deBono, who developed lateral thinking in 1966, has noted that "lateral thinking involves moving sideways to look at things in a different way. Instead of fixing on one particular approach and then working forward from that, the lateral thinker tries to find other approaches."

Or you might use the authority of cynic and satirist Ambrose Bierce and define love as nothing but "a temporary insanity curable by marriage" and friendship as "a ship big enough to carry two in fair weather, but only one in foul."

Define by Negation.   You might also define a term by noting what the term is not, that is, defining by negation. "A wife," you might say, "is not a cook, a cleaning person, a baby-sitter, a seamstress, a sex partner. A wife is . . ."

or "A teacher is not someone who tells you what you should know but rather one who . . ." Here Michael Marien (1992) defines futurists first negatively and then positively:

> *Futurists do not use crystal balls. Indeed, they are generally loath to make firm predictions of what will happen. Rather, they make forecasts of what is probable, sketch scenarios of what is possible, and/or point to desirable futures—what is preferable and what strategies we should pursue to get there.*

Define by Direct Symbolization.   You might also define a term by direct symbolization, by showing the actual thing or a picture or model of it. For example, a sales representative explaining a new computer keyboard would obviously use an actual keyboard in the speech. Similarly, a designer explaining the new magazine layout or types of fabrics would include actual layout pages or fabric samples.

What other types of definition can you identify?

Use Definitions to Add Clarity   If the purpose of the definition is to clarify, then it must do just that. This would be too obvious to mention except that so many speakers, perhaps for want of something to say, define terms that do not need extended definitions. Some speakers use definitions that do not clarify but in fact complicate an already complex concept. Make sure your definitions define only what needs defining.

Use Credible Sources   When you use an authority to define a term, make sure the person is in fact an authority. Tell the audience who the authority is and what the basis for the individual's expertise is. In the following excerpt, note how Russell Peterson (1985) uses the expertise of Robert McNamara in his definition:

> *When Robert McNamara was president of the World Bank, he coined the term "absolute poverty" to characterize a condition of life so degraded by malnutrition, illiteracy, violence, disease and squalor, to be beneath any reasonable definition of human decency. In 1980, the World Bank estimated that 780 million persons in the developing countries lived in absolute poverty. That's about three times as many people as live in the entire United States.*

Proceed from the Known to the Unknown   Start with what your audience knows and work up to what is new or unfamiliar. Let's say you wish to explain the concept of phonemics (with which your audience is totally unfamiliar). The specific idea you wish to get across is that each phoneme stands for a unique sound. You might proceed from the known to the unknown and begin your definition with something like this:

> *We all know that in the written language, each letter of the alphabet stands for a unit of the written language. Each letter is different from every other letter. A t is different from a g, and a g is different from a b, and so on. Each letter is called a "grapheme." In English we know we have 26 such letters.*

We can look at the spoken language in much the same way. Each sound is different from every other sound. A t sound is different from a d sound, and a d sound is different from a k sound, and so on. Each individual sound is called a "phoneme."

Now, let me explain in a little more detail what I mean by a "phoneme."

In this way, you will build on what the audience already knows, a procedure that is useful in all learning.

Developing the Speech of Definition

Here are two examples of how you might go about constructing a speech of definition. In this first example, the speaker explains the parts of a résumé and follows a spatial order, going from the top to the bottom of the page.

GENERAL PURPOSE: to inform
SPECIFIC PURPOSE: to define the essential parts of a résumé
THESIS: there are four major parts to a résumé (What are the four major parts of a résumé?)

I. Identify your career goals.

II. Identify your educational background.

III. Identify your work experience.

IV. Identify your special competencies.

In this second example, the speaker selects three major types of lying for discussion and arranges these in a topical pattern:

GENERAL PURPOSE: to inform
SPECIFIC PURPOSE: to define lying by explaining the major types of lying
THESIS: there are three major kinds of lying (What are the three major kinds of lying?)

I. Concealment is the process of hiding the truth.

II. Falsification is the process of presenting false information as if it were true.

III. Misdirection is the process of acknowledging a feeling but misidentifying its cause.

In delivering such a speech, a speaker might begin the speech by saying:

A lie is a lie is a lie. True? Well, not exactly. Actually, there are a number of different ways we can lie. We can lie by concealing the truth. We can lie by falsification, by presenting false information as if it were true. And we can lie by misdirection, by acknowledging a feeling but misidentifying its cause. Let's look at the first type of lie—the lie of concealment.

Most lies are lies of concealment. Most of the time, when we lie, we simply conceal the truth. We don't actually make any false statements. Rather, we simply don't reveal the truth. Let me give you some examples I overheard recently.

THE SPEECH OF DEMONSTRATION

In using demonstration (or in a speech devoted entirely to demonstration), you would explain how to do something or how something operates.

Here are some examples:

Demonstrating How to Do Something

- how to give mouth-to-mouth resuscitation
- how to balance a checkbook
- how to pilot a plane
- how to drive defensively
- how to mix colors
- how to say "no"
- how to develop your body
- how to prevent burnout
- how to ask for a raise
- how to fireproof your house

Demonstrating How Something Operates

- how the body maintains homeostasis
- how perception works
- the workings of a thermostat
- how information increases
- how a heart bypass operation is performed
- how the Internet works
- how divorce laws work
- how exercise helps the body
- how probate works
- how a hurricane works

Can you think of five or ten topics appropriate to a speech of demonstration?

Strategies for Demonstrating

In demonstrating how to do something or how something operates, consider the following guidelines.

Use Temporal Organization   In most cases a temporal pattern will work best in speeches of demonstration. Demonstrate each step in the sequence in which it is to be performed. In this way you will avoid one of the major difficulties in demonstrating a process, backtracking. Do not skip steps, even if you think they are familiar to the audience. They may not be. Connect each step to the other with appropriate transitions. For example, in explaining the Heimlich maneuver you might say:

> *Now that you have your arms around the choking victim's chest, your next step is to . . .*

Assist your listeners by labeling the steps clearly—"the first step," "the second step," and so on.

How does the speaker orient the audience? What organizational structure is signaled by this orientation? How else might this have been presented?

Does the speaker draw you into the topic and make it interesting to you? If so, how?

Are you convinced that the accusation of Stephen Cook against Cardinal Bernardin was a case of false memory syndrome? If not, what evidence would you want?

What level of credibility do you ascribe to the *Skeptical Inquirer?* How might the speaker have ensured that you would have a high level of credibility for this publication?

Syndrome as their cover stories during the week of November 29, 1993. Considering the sheer number of Americans in counseling or therapy today, the reality is that anyone of us could either be manipulated into developing our own false memories or be accused of abuse or other crimes based on someone else's false memories. In order to realize how we can protect ourselves from this phenomenon, we first need to investigate how False Memory Syndrome is destroying the lives of both the accused as well as the accuser. Then, we'll come to see how the psychological and legal communities are perpetuating this syndrome. And finally, we'll pursue solutions to ensure that none of us are wrongly accused of childhood sexual abuse based solely on someone's false memories.

There is little question, given the number of cases throughout the country, that False Memory Syndrome both exists and is devastating individuals. The Gannett News Service on March 16, 1994, reported that the False Memory Syndrome Foundation, headquartered in Philadelphia, fielded calls from over 11,000 individuals who were either therapy patients persuaded to believe they were victims of sexual abuse or by individuals accused of abusing someone in the past. Through therapy, memories of abuse are "discovered," and given current legal trends, are then used to potentially convict the accused. States the *Skeptical Inquirer* of Summer 1993, juries today are finding patients guilty with no evidence except therapist-induced memories.

The result, as described by Dr. Richard Ofshe in *Society* of March/April 1993, is that "because the memories implicate family and community members of horrible crimes, the trauma of this therapy radiates outward to involve often dozens of innocent people. . . . Thousands of families have already been shattered. The possibilities for fracturing family groups are all being realized: the accused spouse is divorced; siblings are forced to choose sides; grandparents are denied access to their grandchildren; grandchildren lose contact with their grandparents and so on."

Unfortunately, False Memory Syndrome does not only harm the accused, for the therapy patients themselves are also victimized. The November 29, 1993, issue of *Time* magazine relates the story of 39-year-old Melody Gavigan. She had checked herself into a local psychiatric hospital for depression. There, her counselor suggested incest. Through a therapist, she recovered extensive memories of molestation from ages one through five. She became so convinced of the memories that she confronted her father, severed all ties with him and formed an incest survivors group. Once away from therapy, Melody realized that her memories were simply not true. She is currently seeking to repair her familial relationships and is suing the hospital for malpractice. The devastation for Ms. Gavigan, as well as all victims of False Memory Syndrome, was expressed by Psychiatrist John J. Cannell in the *Missoulian* of

February 21, 1993. "[But] there is no healing if someone relies on something that is false to explain their problems. The pain is still there. People won't get well unless you search for the real causes of their pain." Clearly, our society's attempts to aid the true victims of childhood sexual abuse have left us with extensive and destructive problems.

With this devastation in mind, let's try to understand how and why false memories are created. Three critical underlying factors are responsible, for false memories are created through hypnosis and sustained because of a profit motive and current laws.

In examining how false memories are created, it is important to keep in mind that repressed memories themselves are not the problem, but rather how those memories are uncovered. The *U.S. News & World Report* of November 29, 1993, reports that the American Medical Association has repeatedly cited hypnosis as the critical underlying factor in current cases of False Memory Syndrome. Though hypnosis can be effective for a variety of needs, memory recall is not one of them. Dr. George Ganway explains in the May 17, 1993, *New Yorker* that memories recovered in hypnosis are more likely to contain a mixture of fact and fantasy.

By convincing patients that they were abused and should prosecute, the therapist is creating a source of income for years to come. *Newsweek* of December 13, 1993, reported that therapists justify legal action as a legitimate way to pay for the cost of therapy. Dr. Michael Yapko, a Psychologist and Expert of suggestive therapies, claims, "in essence, therapists create the problem they have to treat."

Finally, the third institution that fuels the production of false memories is our current legal system. Two recent legal trends in the United States are responsible for false memories entering the courtroom. First, according to *Society* of March/April, 1993, within the last two years, 15 states have decided to allow therapy-induced memories to serve as actual evidence in childhood sexual abuse cases. What we must understand is that under current law, once we are accused, we have virtually no way of defending ourselves against the testimony of the alleged victim and their therapist. The memories, whether real or false, can serve as grounds to convict us. Additionally, states the *Minneapolis Star and Tribune* of October 10, 1993, 23 states have enacted laws extending the statute of limitations for sexual abuse cases from three to nine years after the memory is recalled. This opens the door for more therapy patients to act on the suggestions of their therapists, filling our courtrooms with cases that consist of no more than fabricated evidence.

With the precedent toward hypnosis, combined with a legal system that drives therapists' profits, the stage is set for intense victimization of families. In order to end the needless destruction of American families, three steps need to be taken.

How effective was the story of Melody Gavigan?

How effective is this transition?

How effectively are the three underlying factors stated? How might they have been stated differently?

How effectively does the speaker establish the profit motive as one of the factors underlying false memory syndrome? What else might the speaker have said?

How effectively does the speaker establish that the current laws are a factor in false memory syndrome?

How effective is this internal summary and transition? Would you have preferred to have a brief preview of the three steps? Would this have helped you follow the remainder of the speech?

Did the speaker effectively make the case for "ending the injustice through legislation"? What else might have been included?

Eleanor Goldstein in her 1992 book, *Confabulations*, argues that the first step to ending the injustice is through legislation. The *New York Times* of March 27, 1994, reported that Illinois has recently introduced a bill "to protect people from lawsuits based on psychological quackery." This bill will reduce the statute of limitations for sexual abuse cases based on therapy-induced memories. Furthermore, the 15 states that currently allow therapy-induced memories to serve as evidence need to rescind their laws. The remaining states that have no legislation dealing with these issues need to pass laws that do not allow therapy-induced memories into the courtroom. Therefore, the only way we can protect ourselves from being wrongly accused or even imprisoned is by insisting that these laws are changed in each of our own states.

Second, the psychiatric community needs regulations regarding the use of hypnosis as a treatment for sexual abuse. As a model for our own personal advocacy, we can turn to the state of Ohio. According to the June 20, 1993, issue of the *Athens, Ohio "Messenger,"* a citizen group asked the State Board of Psychology to establish guidelines pertaining to therapy for patients who may have been abused or molested. We must confront our own State Boards of Psychology and demand that rigorous regulations be placed on counselors and therapists, declaring hypnosis and memory-induced therapies unethical.

Are you convinced that the psychiatric community needs to be regulated in its use of hypnosis in treating sexual abuse cases?

What do you think of the speaker's recommendations for taking charge of our own lives when, for example, seeking a therapist?

Third, and most importantly, we must be willing to take the time to protect ourselves. Before seeing a therapist of any kind for any reason, there are two things you need to ask your potential therapist: first, ask what percentage of the therapist's patients have been diagnosed as victims of childhood sexual abuse. If the number is unusually high and makes you uncomfortable, ask a second question. Find out what types of therapy the therapist tends to rely on. If the answer is hypnosis or suggestive therapy, seek out another therapist. Only by questioning our potential therapists can we ensure that our problems are accurately and fairly diagnosed.

What percentage of patients diagnosed as victims of childhood sexual abuse would you consider high? 10 percent? 25 percent? 40 percent? 55 percent? 70 percent? 85 percent? How would you have handled this if you were the speaker?

Was the type of evidence appropriate to the speech and topic? How effectively did the speaker integrate the research?

By better understanding the problems created by False Memory Syndrome, how and why false memories are created and how we can protect ourselves, it is clear that reliance on memory is far from foolproof. As more of us turn to the aid of therapy to understand our problems, it is essential that the advice we receive is accurate and, ultimately, healing. By allowing false memories to be created, we undermine the very point of mental health. Our alarm must produce change. Change that will protect not only the legitimate victims of abuse, but more importantly, the truly innocent.

What functions does the conclusion serve? Is the conclusion effective?

What effect did the speech have on you? Did it inform? Did it strengthen or change your attitudes and beliefs about false memory syndrome? Will it move you to any specific action (perhaps at a later date)?

SOURCE: This speech was given by Cindy Weisenbeck, a student at the University of Wisconsin–Eau Claire, Wisconsin. She was coached by Tom Glauner. The speech is reprinted from *Winning Orations of the Interstate Oratorical Association*, Larry G. Schnoor, ed. (1994), with permission of the Interstate Oratorical Association.

UNIT 20

The Persuasive Speech

Unit Objectives

After completing this unit, you should be able to:

1. Define *attitude*, *belief*, and *behavior* as used in persuasion

2. Explain the following principles of persuasion: the credibility principle, the selective exposure principle, the cultural difference principle, the audience participation principle, the inoculation principle, and the magnitude of change principle

3. Explain the foot-in-the-door and the door-in-the-face techniques

4. Explain the two types of persuasive speeches and the strategies for achieving each goal

*M*ost of the speeches you hear are persuasive. The speeches of politicians, advertisers, and religious leaders are clear examples. In most of your own speeches, you too will aim at persuasion. You will try to change your listeners' attitudes and beliefs or perhaps get them to do something. In school you might try to persuade others to (or not to) expand the core curriculum, use a plus/minus or a pass/fail grading system, disband the basketball team, allocate increased student funds for the school newspaper, establish competitive majors, or eliminate fraternity initiation rituals. On your job you may be called upon to speak in favor of (or against) unionization, a wage increase proposal, a health benefit package, or the election of a new shop steward.

In this unit we focus on the nature of attitudes, beliefs, and behaviors; the principles for making these speeches more effective; and the types of persuasive speeches.

Do you agree with culture critic Barbara Grizzuti Harrison's warning "Beware of people carrying ideas. Beware of ideas carrying people"?

ATTITUDES, BELIEFS, AND BEHAVIORS

In your persuasive speeches you might want to strengthen or change the attitudes or beliefs of your listeners. Or you might want to get them to do something; that is, you might want to influence their behaviors. Let's define more specifically what is meant by attitudes, beliefs, and behaviors.

Think of an attitude as a tendency to behave in a certain way. For example, if you have a favorable attitude toward chemistry, you will be more apt to elect chemistry courses, read about chemistry, talk about chemistry, and conduct chemistry experiments. If you have an unfavorable attitude toward chemistry, you will avoid chemistry courses, not read about chemistry, and so on. If you have a negative attitude toward horror films, you will resist going to see them and might try to discourage your friends or family from seeing them as well.

A belief is a conviction in the existence or reality of something or in the truth of some assertion. You may believe that there is justice in the world or that there is life after death. You may believe that democracy (or socialism or communism) is the preferred system of government or that children should be seen and not heard. You may believe that censorship is wrong, that power corrupts, or that television contributes to teenage violence.

Behavior in persuasion refers to overt, observable actions: Voting for Tania for class president, buying a Ford, reading to a student who is blind, studying for an economics final, and saying "Yes, I will marry you" are all examples of behaviors. They are all actions, and you can observe each of them.

How might you apply in your next public speech Lord Chesterfield's advice to his son "To please people is the greatest step toward persuading them"?

PRINCIPLES OF PERSUASION

Your success in strengthening or changing attitudes or beliefs and in moving your listeners to action will depend on your use of the principles of persuasion. These principles will be useful to you in all your attempts at persuasion.

The Credibility Principle

You will be more persuasive if your listeners see you as credible. You may wish to look at Unit 23, Speaker Credibility, for more specifies on how you can enhance your own credibility. If your listeners see you as competent, knowledgeable, of good character, and charismatic or dynamic, they will think you credible. As a result, you will be more effective in changing their attitudes or moving them to do something.

 On what topics would you be a credible spokesperson? Why?

Here, for instance, Willard C. Butcher (1987) establishes his credibility by referring to his commitment to and association with high ethical standards:

> For example, my own company, like most others, has a Corporate Code of Conduct—a blueprint that spells out the value standards we expect our employees to live up to. But having a written document is no guarantee that decisions will be made in an ethical way.
>
> We must constantly work at making our Code of Conduct a "living document" and the practice of corporate ethics, a "living spirit" throughout the Chase organization.
>
> Stated another way, "Church on Sunday, Sin on Monday" ethics will not cut it. We must practice what we preach and incorporate ethics into every decision we make.

The Selective Exposure Principle

Your listeners (in fact, all audiences) follow the "law of selective exposure." It has at least two parts:

1. Listeners will actively seek out information that supports their opinions, beliefs, values, decisions, and behaviors.
2. Listeners will actively avoid information that contradicts their existing opinions, beliefs, attitudes, values, and behaviors.

Walter Cronkite has enjoyed enormous credibility. Can you name five or six people who enjoy high credibility in your own mind? Why do you ascribe such high credibility to these people?

Of course, if you are very sure that your opinions and attitudes are logical and valid, then you might not bother to seek out supporting information. And you may not actively avoid nonsupportive messages. People exercise selective exposure most often when their confidence in their opinions and beliefs is weak.

Some Implications of Selective Exposure   This principle of selective exposure suggests a number of implications. For example, if you want to persuade an audience that holds very different attitudes from your own, anticipate selective exposure operating and proceed inductively; that is, hold back on your thesis until you have given the audience your evidence and argument. Only then relate this evidence and argument to your initially contrary thesis.

If you were to present listeners with your thesis first, they might tune you out without giving your position a fair hearing. So, become thoroughly familiar with the attitudes of your audience if you want to succeed in making these necessary adjustments and adaptations.

Let's say you are giving a speech on the need to reduce spending on college athletic programs. If your audience was composed of listeners who agreed with you and wanted to cut athletic spending, you might lead with your thesis. Your introduction might go something like this:

> *Our college athletic program is absorbing money that we can more profitably use for the library, science labs, and language labs. Let me explain how the money now going to unnecessary athletic programs could be better spent in these other areas.*

On the other hand, let's say you were addressing alumni who strongly favored the existing athletic programs. In this case you might want to lead with your evidence and hold off stating your thesis until the end of your speech.

The Cultural Difference Principle

Members of different cultures respond very differently to persuasive attempts (Lustig & Koester 1996; Dodd 1995). In some cultures, for example, the credibility of religious leaders is extremely influential in persuasion—if a religious leader says something, it is taken as true and therefore believed. In other cultures, a religious leader's credibility is assessed individually—not all religious leaders are equally believable. In still other cultures, a religious leader's credibility is assessed negatively.

Schools in the United States teach students to demand logical and reliable evidence before believing something. The critical thinking emphasis throughout contemporary education and in this text provides a good example of this concern with logic, argument, and evidence. Other cultures give much less importance to these forms of persuasion.

Some audiences favor a deductive pattern of reasoning. They expect to hear the general principle first and the evidence, examples, and argument second. Other audiences favor a more inductive pattern (Asian audiences are often cited as examples), where the examples and illustrations are given first and the general principle or conclusion is given second.

Do men and women respond similarly to persuasive appeals? Do men and women speakers use similar persuasive appeals?

Still other cultures expect a very clear statement of the speaker's conclusion. Low-context cultures (the United States, Germany, and Sweden, for example) generally expect an explicit statement of both the speaker's position and what he or she wants the audience to do. Low-context cultures prefer to leave as little as possible unspoken. High-context cultures (Japanese, Chinese, and Arabic, for example) prefer a less explicit statement and prefer to be led indirectly to the speaker's conclusion. An explicit statement ("Vote for Smith" or "Buy Viterall") may be interpreted as too direct and even insulting.

The Audience Participation Principle

Persuasion is greatest when the audience participates actively in your presentation. In experimental tests the same speech is delivered to different audiences. The attitudes of each audience are measured before and after the speech. The difference between the audience's attitudes before and after the speech is taken as a measure of the speech's effectiveness. For one audience the sequence consists of (1) pretest of attitudes, (2) presentation of the persuasive speech, and (3) posttest of attitudes. For another audience the sequence consists of (1) pretest of attitudes, (2) presentation of the persuasive speech, (3) audience paraphrasing or summarizing of the speech, and (4) posttest of attitudes. Researchers consistently find that those listeners who participate actively (as in paraphrasing or summarizing) are more persuaded than those who receive the message passively. Demagogues and propagandists who succeed in arousing huge crowds often have the crowds chant slogans, repeat catchphrases, and otherwise participate actively in the persuasive experience.

How might you use the audience participation principle in your classroom persuasive speeches?

The implication here is simple: Persuasion is a transactional process. It involves both speaker and listeners. You will be more effective if you can get the audience to participate actively in the process.

The Inoculation Principle

The principle of inoculation can be explained with the biological analogy on which it is based. Suppose that you lived in a germ-free environment. Upon leaving this germ-free environment and being exposed to germs, you would be particularly susceptible to infection, because your body had not built up an immunity—it would have no resistance. Resistance, the ability to fight off germs, might be achieved by the body, if not naturally, then through some form of inoculation. You could, for example, be injected with a weakened dose of the germ so that your body began to fight the germ by building up antibodies that created an "immunity" to this type of infection. Your body, because of the antibodies it produced, would be able to fight off even powerful doses of this germ.

The situation in persuasion is similar to this biological process. Some of your attitudes and beliefs have existed in a "germ-free" environment—they have never been attacked or challenged. For example, many of us have lived in an environment in which the values of a democratic form of government, the importance of education, and the traditional family structure have not been challenged. Consequently, we have not been "immunized" against attacks on these values and beliefs. We have no counterarguments (antibodies) prepared

Can you give a personal example of how the inoculation principle operates in your own life?

to fight off these attacks on our beliefs, so if someone were to come along with strong arguments against these beliefs, we might easily be persuaded.

Contrast these "germ-free" beliefs with issues that have been attacked and for which we have a ready arsenal of counterarguments. Our attitudes on the draft, nuclear weapons, college athletics, and thousands of other issues have been challenged in the press, on television, and in our interpersonal interactions. As a result of this exposure, we have counterarguments ready for any attacks on our beliefs concerning these issues. We have been inoculated and immunized against attacks should someone attempt to change our attitudes or beliefs.

Some Implications of Inoculation   If you are addressing an inoculated audience, take into consideration the fact that they have a ready arsenal of counterarguments to fight your persuasive assault. For example, if you are addressing heavy smokers on the need to stop smoking or alcoholics on the need to stop drinking, you might assume that these people have already heard your arguments and that they have already inoculated themselves against the major arguments. In such situations, be prepared, therefore, to achieve only small gains. Don't try to reverse totally the beliefs of a well-inoculated audience. For example, it would be asking too much to get the smokers or the alcoholics to quit their present behaviors as a result of one speech. But it might not be too much to ask to get them—at least some of them—to attend a meeting of a smoking clinic or Alcoholics Anonymous.

If you are trying to persuade an uninoculated audience, your task is often much simpler, since you do not have to penetrate a fully developed immunization shield. For example, it might be relatively easy to persuade a group of high school seniors about the values of a college core curriculum, since they probably have not thought much about the issue and probably do not have arguments against the core curriculum at their ready disposal.

Do recognize, however, that even when audiences have not immunized themselves, they often take certain beliefs to be self-evident. As a result, they may well tune out any attacks on such cherished beliefs or values. This might be the case, for example, if you try to persuade a devotedly religious audience that there is no God. Although they may not have counterarguments ready, they may accept their religious beliefs as so fundamental that they simply will not listen to attacks on such beliefs.

Whenever trying to change fundamental beliefs, proceed slowly and be content with small gains. Further, an inductive approach would suit your purposes better here. Attacking cherished beliefs directly creates impenetrable resistance. Instead, build your case by first presenting your arguments and evidence and then gradually work up to your conclusion.

If you try to strengthen an audience's belief, give them the "antibodies" they will need if ever under attack. Consider raising counterarguments to this belief and then demolishing them. Much as the injection of a small amount of a germ will enable the body to build an immunization response, presenting counterarguments and then refuting them will enable your listeners to immunize themselves against future attacks on these values and beliefs. This procedure results in greater and longer-lasting resistance to strong attacks than merely providing the audience with an arsenal of supporting arguments.

What principle of persuasion can you formulate from Mark Twain's observation "Habits can't be thrown out the upstairs window. They have to be coaxed down the stairs one step at a time"?

The Magnitude of Change Principle

The greater and more important the change you want to produce in your audience, the more difficult will be your task. The reason is simple: We normally demand a greater number of reasons and lots more evidence before we make important decisions—changing careers, moving our families to another state, or investing our life savings in certain stocks.

On the other hand, we may be more easily persuaded (and demand less evidence) on relatively minor issues—whether to take a course in "Small-Group Communication" rather than "Persuasion," or to give to the United Heart Fund instead of the American Heart Fund.

People change gradually, in small degrees over a long period. And although there are cases of sudden conversions, this general principle holds true more often than not. Persuasion is therefore most effective when it strives for small changes and works over a considerable period. For example, a persuasive speech stands a better chance when it tries to get the alcoholic to attend just one AA meeting rather than to give up alcohol for life. If you try to convince your audience to change their attitudes radically or to engage in behaviors to which they are initially opposed, your attempts may backfire. In this type of situation, the audience may tune you out, closing their ears to even the best and most logical arguments.

When you have the opportunity to try to persuade your audience on several occasions (rather than simply delivering one speech), two strategies will prove relevant: the foot-in-the-door and the door-in-the-face techniques.

Foot-in-the-Door Technique   As its name implies, the foot-in-the-door technique involves getting your foot in the door first. That is, you first request something small, something your audience will easily comply with. Once this compliance has been achieved, you then make your real request (Freedman & Fraser 1966; Dejong 1979; Cialdini 1984; Pratkanis & Aronson 1991). Research shows that people are more apt to comply with a large request after they have complied with a similar but much smaller request. For example, in **one** study the objective was to get people to put a "Drive Carefully" sign on **their** lawn (a large request). When this (large) request was made first, only about 17 percent of the people were willing to comply. However, when this request was preceded by a much smaller request (to sign a petition), between 50 and 76 percent granted permission to install the sign. The smaller request and its compliance paved the way for the larger request and put the audience into an agreement mode.

In using this strategy, be sure that your first request is small enough to gain compliance. If it isn't, then you miss the chance ever to gain compliance with your desired and larger request.

Door-in-the-Face Technique   This technique is the opposite of foot-in-the-door (Cialdini & Ascani 1976; Cialdini 1984). With this strategy, you first make a large request that you know will be refused (for example, "We're asking most people to donate $100 for new school computers"). Later you make a more moderate request, the one you really want your listeners to comply with (for example, "Might you be willing to contribute $10?"). In changing from the

What persuasion principles would be of most value to you if you were trying to persuade your class that government must do more for the homeless? That class members should give blood during the upcoming blood drive?

large to the more moderate request, you demonstrate to your listeners both your willingness to compromise and your sensitivity. The general idea here is that your listeners will feel that since you have made concessions, they will also make concessions and at least contribute something. Listeners will probably also feel that $10 is actually quite little, considering the initial request, and, research shows, are more likely to comply and will donate the $10.

In using this technique, be sure that your first request is significantly larger than your desired request but not so large as to seem absurd and be rejected out of hand.

THE SPEECH TO STRENGTHEN OR CHANGE ATTITUDES OR BELIEFS

Many speeches seek to strengthen existing attitudes or beliefs. Much religious and political speaking, for example, tries to strengthen attitudes and beliefs. Usually, people who listen to religious speeches are already believers, so these speeches strive to strengthen the attitudes and beliefs they already hold. Here the audience is already favorable to the speaker's purpose and is willing to listen.

Speeches designed to change attitudes or beliefs are more difficult to construct. Most people resist change. When you attempt to get people to change their beliefs or attitudes, you are fighting an uphill (but not impossible) battle.

Speeches designed to strengthen or change attitudes or beliefs come in many forms. Depending on the initial position of the audience, you can view the following examples as topics for speeches to strengthen or change attitudes or beliefs.

- Marijuana should be legalized.
- General education requirements should be abolished.
- College athletic programs should be expanded.
- History is a useless study.
- Television shows are mindless.
- CDs and tapes should be rated for excessive sex and violence.
- Free syringes should be given to drug users.
- Puerto Rico should become the fifty-first state.
- Gambling should be legalized throughout the United States.
- The United States should expand its famine relief program.

Strategies for Strengthening or Changing Attitudes and Beliefs

When you attempt to strengthen or change your listeners' attitudes and beliefs, consider the following principles.

Estimate Listeners' Attitudes and Beliefs   Carefully estimate—as best you can—the current state of your listeners' attitudes and beliefs. If your goal is to strengthen these attitudes and beliefs, then you can state your thesis and your objectives as early in your speech as you wish. Since your listeners are in basic

Why is it generally easier to strengthen attitudes and beliefs than to change them? In what kinds of situations might the reverse be true?

TIPS

From Professional Speakers

Know exactly what response you hope to evoke. This should be thought through and determined in advance. Are you in the spotlight to motivate your audience, to rouse them, to produce or sell more, to educate, share information, raise their morale, or challenge them? You should know specifically what you want to accomplish and organize your thoughts, material, and delivery to that end.

Buck Rogers, former vice-president of marketing at IBM and, according to *USA Today*, one of the most requested speakers in America. *Getting the Best Out of Yourself and Others* (New York: HarperCollins, 1987), pp. 203–204.

How would you estimate the attitudes and beliefs of members of your public speaking class on such topics as these: (1) Abortion should (not) be legal; (2) the government should (not) control pharmaceutical prices; (3) assisted suicide should (not) be made legal; (4) the death penalty should (not) be declared illegal; (5) term limits for politicians should (not) be mandated.

agreement with you, your statement of your thesis will enable you to create a bond of agreement between you.

You might say, for example:

Like you, I am deeply committed to the fight against abortion. Tonight I'd like to explain some new evidence that has recently come to light and that we must know if we are to be effective in our fight against legalized abortion.

If, however, you are in basic disagreement and you wish to change listeners' attitudes, then reserve your statement of your thesis until you have provided them with your evidence and argument. Get listeners on your side first by stressing as many similarities between you and your audience members as you can. Only after this should you try to change their attitudes and beliefs. Continuing with the abortion example (but this time with an audience that is opposed to your antiabortion stance), you might say:

We are all concerned with protecting the rights of the individual. No one wants to infringe on the rights of anyone. And it is from this point of view—from the point of view of the inalienable rights of the individual—that I want to examine the abortion issue.

In this way you stress your similarity with the audience before you state your antiabortion position to this proabortion audience.

Seek Small Changes   When addressing an audience whose members are opposed to your position and your goal is to change their attitudes and beliefs, seek change in small increments. Let's say, for example, that your ultimate goal is to get an antiabortion group to favor abortion on demand. Obviously, this goal is too great to achieve in one speech. Therefore, strive for small changes. Here, for example, is an excerpt in which the speaker attempts to get an antiabortion audience to agree that some abortions should be legalized. The speaker begins as follows:

> *One of the great lessons I learned in college is that most extreme positions are wrong. Most of the important truths lie somewhere between the extreme opposites. And today I want to talk with you about one of these truths. I want to talk with you about rape and the problems faced by the mother carrying a child conceived in this most violent of all the violent crimes we can imagine.*

Notice that the speaker does not state a totally proabortion position but instead focuses on one area of abortion and attempts to get the audience to agree that in some cases abortion should be legalized.

Demonstrate Your Credibility   Show the audience that you are knowledgeable about the topic, have their own best interests at heart, and are willing and ready to speak out in favor of these important concerns. More specific ways of demonstrating credibility are covered in Unit 23.

Give Listeners Good Reasons   Give your audience good reasons for believing what you want them to believe. Give them hard evidence and arguments. Show them how such attitudes and beliefs relate directly to their goals, their motives. (Evidence and argument are covered in Unit 21 and motivational appeals in Unit 22.)

Developing the Speech to Strengthen or Change Attitudes and Beliefs

Here are some examples to clarify the nature of this type of persuasive speech. These examples present the specific purpose, the thesis, and the question asked of the thesis to help identify the major propositions of the speech.

This first example deals with birth control and uses a topical organizational pattern:

GENERAL PURPOSE: to persuade (to strengthen or change attitudes and beliefs)
SPECIFIC PURPOSE: to persuade my audience that advertisements for birth control devices should be allowed in all media
THESIS: media advertising of birth control devices is desirable (Why is media advertising desirable?)

   I. Birth control information is needed.
      A. Birth control information is needed to prevent disease.
      B. Birth control information is needed to prevent unwanted pregnancies.

  II. Birth control information is not available to the very people who need it most.

 III. Birth control information can best be disseminated through the media.

Why are the principles of persuasion more difficult to apply to large audiences than they are to small audiences?

Can you identify any additional strategies that might prove useful in strengthening or changing attitudes or beliefs?

In this second example, the speaker uses a problem-solution organizational pattern, first presenting the problems created by cigarette smoking, and then the solution:

GENERAL PURPOSE: to persuade (to strengthen or change attitudes and beliefs)
SPECIFIC PURPOSE: to persuade my audience that cigarette advertising should be banned from all media
THESIS: cigarette advertising should be abolished (Why should cigarette advertising be abolished?)

I. Cigarette smoking is a national problem.
   A. Cigarette smoking causes lung cancer.
   B. Cigarette smoking pollutes the air.
   C. Cigarette smoking raises the cost of health care.

II. Cigarette smoking will be lessened if advertisements are prohibited.
   A. Fewer people will start to smoke.
   B. Smokers will smoke less.

In delivering such a speech, a speaker might begin like this:

I think we all realize that cigarette smoking is a national problem that affects each and every one of us. No one escapes the problems caused by cigarette smoking—not the smoker and not the nonsmoker. Cigarette smoking causes lung cancer. Cigarette smoking pollutes the air. And cigarette smoking raises the cost of health care for everyone.

Let's look first at the most publicized of all smoking problems: lung cancer. There can be no doubt—the scientific evidence is overwhelming—that cigarette smoking is a direct cause of lung cancer. Research conducted by the American Cancer Institute and by research institutes throughout the world all come to the same conclusion: Cigarette smoking causes lung cancer. Consider some of the specific evidence. A recent study—reported in the November 1989 issue of the . . .

THE SPEECH TO STIMULATE ACTION

Speeches designed to stimulate the audience to take action or to engage in some specific behavior are referred to as speeches to actuate. The persuasive speech addressed to motivating a specific behavior may focus on just about any behavior imaginable. Here are some possible topics:

- Vote in the next election.
- Vote for Smith.
- Do not vote for Smith.
- Contribute to the book sale.
- Buy a ticket to the football game.
- Listen to *20/20.*

 How would you develop a speech to persuade your audience that ads for birth control devices should *not* be allowed on television?

TIPS
From Professional Speakers

In preparing your speech, isolate the most important points and make sure you present them in the most dynamic and positive way possible. Don't bury them among a hodgepodge of thought or sandwich them between your laughs. Give them the kind of attention you'd expect from an advertising agency—that is, make sure that the most important points are distinguishable and as memorable as possible.

Buck Rogers, former vice-president of marketing at IBM and, according to *USA Today,* one of the most requested speakers in America. *Getting the Best Out of Yourself and Others* (New York: HarperCollins, 1987), p. 204.

- Major in economics.
- Take a course in computer science.
- Buy a Pontiac.
- Write a living will.

Strategies for Stimulating Listeners to Action

When designing a speech to get listeners to do something, keep the following principles in mind.

Be Realistic   Set reasonable goals for what you want the audience to do. Remember, you have only 10 or 15 minutes, and in that time you cannot move the proverbial mountain. So, ask for small, easily performed behaviors—signing a petition, voting in the next election, donating a small amount of money.

Demonstrate Your Own Compliance   As a general rule, never ask the audience to do what you have not done yourself. So, demonstrate your own willingness to do what you want the audience to do. If you don't, the audience will rightfully ask, "Why haven't *you* done it?" In addition to your having done what you want them to do, show them that you are pleased to have done so. Tell them of the satisfaction you derived from donating blood or from reading to blind students.

Stress Specific Advantages   Stress the specific advantages of these behaviors to your specific audience. Don't ask your audience to engage in behaviors solely for abstract reasons. Give them concrete, specific reasons why they will benefit from the actions you want them to engage in. Instead of telling your listeners that they should devote time to reading to blind students because it is the right thing to do, show them how much they will enjoy the experience and how much they will personally benefit from it.

Can you identify any additional strategies that might be useful in stimulating listeners to action?

Developing the Speech to Stimulate Action

Here are two examples of the speech to actuate. The first example is a speech on devoting time to helping people with disabilities. In the speech the speaker asks for a change in the way most people spend their leisure time. The speech utilizes a topical organizational pattern; each of the subtopics is treated about equally.

GENERAL PURPOSE: to persuade (to stimulate action)
SPECIFIC PURPOSE: to persuade my audience to devote some of their leisure time to helping people with disabilities
THESIS: leisure time can be well used in helping people with disabilities (How can leisure time be spent helping people with disabilities? or What can we do to help people with disabilities?)

   I. Read for the blind.
       A. Read to a blind student.
       B. Make a recording of a textbook for blind students.

  II. Run errands for students confined to wheelchairs.

III. Type for students who can't use their hands,

In this second example, the speaker tries to persuade the audience—composed of parents and teachers—to see the advantages of the new multicultural curriculum at the town's high school and stresses two major issues:

GENERAL PURPOSE: to persuade (to strengthen and change attitudes)
SPECIFIC PURPOSE: to persuade my audience to believe that the multicultural curriculum should be adopted
THESIS: the multicultural curriculum is beneficial (Why is the multicultural curriculum beneficial?)

I. The multicultural curriculum will teach tolerance.

II. The multicultural curriculum will raise all students' self-esteem.

In delivering the speech, the speaker might say:

We've all heard about the new multicultural curriculum proposed for the high schools in our county. After years of research, we now know about the effects of multicultural education on students. And what we know is that multicultural education—such as that presented in the curriculum before you—teaches tolerance for all people and all groups and, equally important, raises the self-esteem of all our sons and daughters. Let me explain how this curriculum teaches tolerance.

How would you develop a speech to move an audience to action if your specific purpose was to persuade listeners to enroll in a course on AIDS education? To persuade listeners to believe that the multicultural curriculum should *not* be adopted?

UNIT IN BRIEF

Principles of persuasion	■ **Credibility:** demonstrate competence, character, and charisma
	■ **Selective exposure:** (1) proceed inductively if you anticipate resistance; (2) analyze your audience's attitudes and beliefs; and (3) deal with potential counterarguments to your thesis
	■ **Cultural difference:** take into consideration (1) the different emphases that different cultures place on persuasive appeals and (2) the patterns for presenting these appeals
	■ **Audience participation:** actively involve the audience
	■ **Inoculation:** (1) try for small gains with an inoculated audience; (2) proceed inductively when attacking any uninoculated, long-held belief; and (3) refute counterarguments when strengthening an audience's beliefs

■ **Magnitude of change**: strive for small changes in short speeches or when advocating significant changes

    Foot-in-the-door (request something small; follow with the request)

    Door-in-the-face (request something large; follow with the request)

Strategies of persuasion to strengthen or change attitudes and beliefs	■ Estimate the current status of your listeners' attitudes and beliefs ■ Seek change in small increments ■ Demonstrate your own credibility ■ Give your listeners both logical and motivational reasons
Strategies of persuasion to stimulate action	■ Be realistic in what you ask listeners to do ■ Demonstrate your own willingness to do as you want your listeners to do ■ Stress the specific (rather than the general or abstract) advantages of this behavior

PRACTICALLY SPEAKING

Short Speech Technique

Prepare and deliver a two-minute speech in which you:

1. explain an interesting attitude or belief you have come across
2. explain how a speech strengthened or changed one of your attitudes or beliefs
3. explain an advertisement in terms of the principles of persuasion
4. explain cultural differences in popularly held beliefs regarding such concepts as God, life, death, family, happiness, education, law, or men and women

20.1   Points of View: Cultural Issues and Persuasion

The objective of this exercise is to stimulate you to think about persuasive strategies for a variety of contemporary cultural situations. It may be completed individually, in small groups, or with the entire class.

What persuasive strategies would you use to convince your class of the validity of either side in any of these points of view? For example, what persuasive strategies would you use to persuade your class members that interracial adoption should be encouraged or discouraged? Do realize that these "points of view" are simplified for purposes of this exercise and should not be taken as complete descriptions of these complex issues.

Point of View: Interracial Adoption. Those in favor of interracial adoption argue that the welfare of the child—who might not get adopted if not by someone of another race—must be considered first. Adoption (regardless of race) is good for the child and therefore is a positive social process. Those opposed to interracial adoption argue that children need to be raised by those of the same race if the child is to develop self-esteem and become a functioning member of his or her own race. Interracial adoption is therefore a negative social process.

Point of View: Women and the Church. Many women (and men)—both Catholic and non-Catholic—believe that women should be allowed to become priests and advance in the hierarchy of the Catholic Church just like a man does. The sexes are equal and therefore should have equal opportunities, and that includes in the church. The Catholic Church rejects this idea and refuses to ordain women as priests; its argument is basically that Jesus (to whom the Catholic Church traces itself) established a church with only men as its priests and that's the way it must remain.

Point of View: Gays and Lesbians and the Military. Regardless of the status of the current law, a large group within the U.S. military are opposed to gay men and lesbians in the military. The gay and lesbian communities argue that gay men and lesbians should be accorded exactly the same rights and privileges as heterosexuals—no more, no less. Those opposed argue that gay men and lesbians will undermine the image of the military and will make heterosexuals uncomfortable.

Point of View: Interracial Marriage. Those in favor of interracial marriage argue that everyone has the right to make his or her own decision and if a person falls in love with someone of a different race, his or her decision is a personal one, not a social one. Those opposed to interracial marriage argue that it dilutes the purity of the races (with the minority races suffering the most) and even threatens the continuance of the race. Given our current society, it also makes life difficult for the children.

Point of View: Affirmative Action. Those in favor of affirmative action argue that because of the injustices in the way certain groups (racial, national, gender) were once treated, they should now be given preferential treatment to correct the imbalance caused by the social injustices. Those opposed to affirmative action argue that merit must be the sole criterion for promotion, jobs, entrance to graduate schools, and so forth, and that affirmative action is just reverse racism or sexism; one form of injustice cannot correct another form of injustice.

20.2   Analyzing a Persuasive Speech

This exercise is designed to help you further identify the major parts of a speech and the ways in which they fit together and to see the principles of persuasion in an actual speech. First, carefully read the following speech, by William Fort, without looking at the questions to the side. Then reread the speech while considering and responding to each of the Critical Thinking questions.

How effective is the opening quotation? Does it gain attention? Does it introduce the importance of the topic?

How would members of your class respond to this topic? Would they see it as important? As relevant to their everyday lives?

How might you relate this topic to members of your class?

What method does Fort use to orient his listerners? How effective is this?

What is the thesis? How would members of your class respond to this thesis?

Sick Building Syndrome

What is so terrible as war? I will tell you what is ten times and ten thousand times more terrible than war— outraged nature. I see that three persons out of every four are utterly unaware of the general causes of their own ill-health, and that is to stupid neglect, or what is just as bad, stupid ignorance."

In 1859, Reverend Charles Kingsley used these powerful words to address the cholera epidemic. Which created a 40 percent infant mortality rate in England, simply because of a lack of sanitation. Today we face a similar situation. There is a problem that most are unaware of, which is causing influenza, smallpox, pneumonia, tuberculosis, meningitis, airborne lead poisoning, and most fatally, Legionnaires' disease. This problem? Sick Building Syndrome. Sick Building Syndrome describes any building with actual or potential health hazards due to contaminated air. The incidence of SBS is rising, partially because buildings have been planned with maximum energy savings in mind since the energy crisis of the 1970s. Dr. Tony Pickering, who is currently studying SBS, states in the May 1987 issue of *World Press Review* that "SBS affects 90 percent of supersealed buildings, and in some cases sickens up to 70 percent of the building occupants." Supersealed buildings describe any building which uses mechanical ventilation. In basic terms, a building whose windows cannot open or close.

SBS is a serious problem that we need to become aware of, because if we don't do something to cure this disease today, then like England in the 1860s, thousands of Americans will die in the 1990s. So today we will investigate SBS by first examining the general causes of the problem, then looking at the symptoms of SBS, and finally, we will find ways to end the outraged nature of SBS.

There are three majors causes of SBS. The first is that buildings are using ineffective heating, ventilation, and air conditioning systems, also known as HVAC systems. Architect William Heineman describes these systems in the December

1985 issue of *National Safety and Health News*: "Once we enter these air-tight buildings, we are completely dependent upon their support systems for survival. The quality and quantity of air we breathe are totally contained within the system."

Not only do these systems pick up fungus and bacteria and recirculate it throughout a system, but also airborne viruses, germs from co-workers, and cigarette smoke. "Microbiological health hazards are the most widespread of the many hazards in mechanically ventilated buildings," declares environmentalist Sandy Moretz in the February 1988 issue of *Occupational Hazards* magazine. Ms. Moretz goes on to state, "The vast majority of this microbial growth is caused by stagnant water and dirt build-up in air filters, and condensation drainage trays that are not regularly cleaned." Or, in Kingsley's words, "stupid neglect" and "stupid ignorance."

The third major cause of SBS is the lack of governmental support. The Environmental Protection Agency's Eileen Claussen states in the June 6, 1988, issue of *Time* magazine that "Some Americans spend an estimated 90 percent of their time indoors, however no specific federal regulations have been adopted for control of air in offices, even though the air in some buildings is 100 times as polluted as the air outside the buildings."

Ineffective HVAC systems, lack of maintenance on existing systems, and no governmental support all perpetuate the problems associated with Sick Building Syndrome. And those problems are significant. The symptoms of SBS don't start out with your building throwing up or your elevator doors getting a fever, rather as minor annoyances such as a dry throat, headaches, or drowsiness. In fact, the May 1987 issue of *Occupational Health and Safety* printed a survey of over 1,000 office workers, half of which worked in naturally ventilated buildings, and half worked in mechanically ventilated buildings. The results showed that while only 15.7 percent of those in naturally ventilated buildings had frequent headaches, 37.4 percent of those in mechanically ventilated buildings did. When it comes to drowsiness, 13.8 percent in naturally ventilated buildings, and 51.4 percent, four times as many in mechanically ventilated buildings were frequently drowsy on the job.

These lopsided figures translate into a monetary loss by building owners. James Repace, an indoor air specialist with the EPA, states in the January 1989 issue of *Discover* magazine, "The millions of workdays lost each year (due to SBS) translate into billions of dollars in medical expense, diminished productivity, and compensation claims." In May 1988, 70 workers boycotted their office building, claiming that the air inside the building was so contaminated it caused frequent headaches, dizziness, eye irritation, chest pains, and breathing difficulties. The Washington, D.C., building is the National Headquarters of the Environmental Protection Agency.

What is the specific purpose? Was the purpose sufficiently limited?

Does the speaker effectively weave in relevant research? Is the research appropriate? Sufficient? What additional research would you have wanted in order to be convinced of the importance of this topic?

Does the speaker use sufficient guide phrases or transitions to help listeners follow his development? How effective is this internal summary?

Are these statistics convincing to you? Would you want additional information before accepting the importance of SBS?

How important would this argument be to members of your class?

How might the speaker have made these deaths more dramatic?

How effectively does the speaker use humor? Is this appropriate?

Note that the speaker discussed the causes of SBS before identifying the problems it creates. Is this pattern effective? How would you have arranged this speech?

Are these calls to action effective? Should the speaker have been more specific (less specific) in his recommendations? If you heard this speech would you be willing to do as requested? Why?

What organizational pattern does the speaker use? Is this pattern effective, given the speaker's specific purpose?

Although usually the symptoms of SBS are the ones I've previously mentioned, sometimes just one visit into any super-sealed building can be fatal. In May 1985, 37 men, women and children who stayed on the fourth floor of Stafford General Hospital mysteriously died. Later the cause was found to be Legionnaires' disease, a harmful bacterium which originated in an air conditioning system which blew the deadly disease through the air ducts right into the unsuspecting patients' rooms. The HVAC system hadn't been cleaned in over a year. This incident, outlined in the *Air Conditioning, Heating and Refrigeration News*, is not an isolated one. In fact, the September 2, 1985, issue of *U.S. News & World Report* says "'Legionnaires' disease strikes 25 to 50,000 Americans a year, and about 15 percent of the victims die." Translating these figures, we can see that the outraged nature of SBS causes around 5,000 deaths annually.

Hospitals, hotels, the Environmental Protection Agency, and school buildings are places where we should be able to go and feel safe and secure. However until we, as individuals and as a nation, do something to stop the enraged nature of Sick Building Syndrome, then each and every trip into a super-sealed building will be potentially life threatening.

On an individual level, the one sure-fire way to prevent becoming a victim of SBS is to wear a gas mask at all times. But since gas masks are uncomfortable, hard to find—and let's face it—unattractive, I'll recommend other means of survival. First, we need to become aware of general causes of our own ill health in these buildings. Realize that if you have frequent headaches, dry throat, drowsiness, eye irritation, chest pains, or breathing difficulties inside a building, that it probably is a sick building.

Once this awareness is achieved, please act. Pick up the phone and call your local building inspector and ask him or her to examine your sick building, and let you and the building owner know what actual or potential health hazards are there due to contaminated air. Another practical step we can all take is to tell others about the problem so they can also help find these sick buildings and pressure building owners to start a preventative program against SBS.

On a larger level, we can see the need to attack the number one cause of SBS, which is microbial growth in HVAC systems. David Custer, the Vice-President of Environmental Management Systems, says in the February 1987 issue of *Buildings*, "Microbiological health hazards are the most preventable of the many hazards in supersealed buildings. They can be virtually eliminated through simple maintenance." The types of simple maintenance which Mr. Custer speaks of include replacing all dirty air filters, emptying all condensation drainage trays, and treating the entire system with an inexpensive antimicrobial solution. By spending a few dollars today, they can save millions tomorrow, and end their stupid neglect. This is a simple, and logical, solution which will be easy and inexpensive to implement.

Finally, federal legislation which a) requires building owners to use certain types of tested, effective HVAC systems, and b) which requires them to clean and maintain their existing systems, would be a great help in calming the outraged nature of SBS.

In 1859, one of England's major problems was a cholera epidemic which created a 40 percent infant mortality rate. This could have been solved by taking simple preventative measures and being more sanitary. Unfortunately, most ignored Reverend Kingsley, and because of it, hundreds of thousands needlessly died. Research scientist Michael McCawley said in the June 6, 1988, issue of *Time* that "unless we realize the severity of the problem today, Sick Building Syndrome will be one of the major problems in the 1990s." If we follow the simple steps which I've outlined, we can learn from the English mistakes of the 1860s, and end the stupid neglect, stupid ignorance, and outraged nature associated with SBS, and in the process we can all play doctor and save the thousands of lives lost each year to SBS.

Do you believe that "Sick Building Syndrome will be one of the major problems in the 1990s" and that we can save thousands of lives lost each year to SBS? If not, what might the speaker have done to make you believe these statements?

How effective was the conclusion? Did the speaker summarize his major points? Did he bring the speech to a definite close?

SOURCE: This speech, given by William Fort, a student from California State University at Chico, was presented at the 1989 Championship Debates and Speeches. Reprinted by permission of the American Forensic Association.

UNIT 21

Developing Arguments

Unit Objectives

After completing this unit, you should be able to:

1. Define *argument* and *evidence* and explain the three general tests for reasoning

2. Explain the nature of reasoning from specific instances to a generalization and from a generalization to specific instances, the major tests, and the guidelines to follow in using these forms of reasoning effectively

3. Explain the nature of reasoning from analogy, the major tests, and the guidelines to follow in using reasoning from analogy effectively

4. Explain the nature of cause-effect reasoning, the major tests, and the guidelines to follow in using cause-effect reasoning effectively

5. Explain the nature of reasoning by sign, the major tests, and the guidelines to follow in using reasoning by sign effectively

T his unit is the first of a three-unit sequence dealing with proof, the ways to persuade an audience to think or do as you wish. This three-part division, developed in the classical rhetorics of ancient Greece and Rome, consists of logic, argument, and evidence; motivational appeals; and appeals based on the credibility of the speaker. In this unit we begin with the logical part and consider how to develop and evaluate arguments. Units 22 and 23 focus on motivational appeals and speaker credibility.

ARGUMENT AND EVIDENCE

An argument consists of evidence (for example, facts) and a conclusion. Evidence plus the conclusion that the evidence supports equals an argument. Reasoning is the process you go through in forming conclusions on the basis of evidence. For example, you might reason that since college graduates earn more money than nongraduates (evidence), Jack and Jill should go to college if they wish to earn more money (conclusion).

When you present an argument in a public speech, you attempt to prove something to your listeners. You want to prove that what you say is true, practical, or worth pursuing. In the vast majority of cases, you cannot prove in any objective sense that, say, marijuana should or should not be legalized or that the death penalty benefits or harms society. Rather, you seek, as a speaker, to establish the probability of your conclusions in the minds of the listeners. Thus, the process is in part a logical one of demonstrating that what you say is probably true. The process is also, however, a psychological one of persuading your listeners to accept the conclusions as you have drawn them.

Select two or three advertisements from a newspaper or magazine. What is their main argument? What form of reasoning did the advertiser use to support the argument?

"In the interest of streamlining the judicial process, we'll skip the evidence and go directly to sentencing."

Drawing by Handelsman; © 1995 The New Yorker Magazine, Inc.

Here political activist and filmmaker Oliver Stone delivers a speech. Can you identify five or six ways in which films are similar to public speeches?

The information presented here applies to the speaker in constructing the speech, to the listener in receiving and responding to the speech, and to the speech critic or analyst in analyzing and evaluating the speech. A poorly reasoned argument, inadequate evidence, and stereotypical thinking, for example, need to be avoided by the speaker, recognized and responded to by the listener, and negatively evaluated by the critic.

Argument and Evidence in Cultural Perspective

Before getting to the specific forms of argument, recall the general tests of support applicable to all forms of argument that we introduced in Unit 7 as tests of research. And specifically recall these from a multicultural perspective.

Is the Support Recent? Recency is especially important in technologically advanced societies because technology and all it influences change so rapidly. In some agrarian cultures of Africa and Asia, recency is much less important. In matters of soil cultivation, for example, the recency of a technique may make people suspicious.

Is There Corroborative Support? In collectivist cultures members are expected to share responsibility and blame and to protect other members. They are expected to provide corroboration for the ideas and behaviors of colleagues or friends. This practice is built into the culture's rules for communication. For example, when colleagues publicly agree with an individual, they offer no evidence; instead, colleagues offer respect and show that they are being polite and are following the rules of etiquette. This practice is much less common in individualistic cultures, where competition is emphasized and colleague support is not written into the rules of etiquette.

Are the Sources Unbiased? In American courts of law, for example, eyewitness testimony from an unbiased source is extremely powerful evidence and counts heavily in the minds of both judge and jury. In certain African cultures, however, an eyewitness's testimony does not count as evidence,

In what cases would the recency of support be irrelevant to the validity of your argument?

What kind of evidence would you want before believing such assertions as these:
a. Women are better judges of people than men are.
b. As a group, college professors are happier than lawyers or medical doctors.
c. Unemployment will increase over the next five years.

because the people believe that if you speak up, you obviously have something to gain (Lustig & Koester 1993, p. 224).

In evaluating the evidence of others as listeners and critics and in using these forms of reasoning, remember that different people see things differently—even in matters of logic, argument, and evidence.

REASONING FROM SPECIFIC INSTANCES AND GENERALIZATIONS

In reasoning from specific instances (or examples), you examine several specific instances and then conclude something about the whole. This form of reasoning, known as induction, is useful when you want to develop a general principle or conclusion but cannot examine the whole. For example, you sample a few communication courses and conclude something about communication courses in general; you visit several Scandinavian cities and conclude something about the whole of Scandinavia.

You probably follow this same general process in dealing with another person. For example, you see Samantha in several situations and conclude something about Samantha's behavior in general; you date Pat a few times, or maybe even for a period of several months, and on that basis draw a general conclusion about Pat's suitability as a spouse.

Here Karen Bowers, a student from Bradley University (Schnoor 1994, p. 61), uses specific instances to support the generalization that the work environment can be dangerous:

> *"141 Men and Girls Die in Triangle Shirtwaist Factory Fire; Street Strewn with Bodies; Piles of Dead Inside," reported the headline of* The New York Times *on March 26, 1911. Today, we generally view this "ancient history" as a tragedy of the industrial era. Is it? "25 employees die in Hamlet, North Carolina, Imperial Food Product Plant Fire," reported* Time *magazine on September 16, 1991. There was little chance for escape because most emergency exits had been locked. The 11-year-old plant had never been inspected. Unfortunately, this is not unusual. The January 28, 1991, edition of* The Nation *notes, "Work kills more people than die from drugs, AIDS, or car accidents."*

Technically, you may also argue in the other direction—namely, from a general principle to some specific instance. That is, you begin with some general statement or axiom that is accepted as true by the audience and argue that since something is true of the entire class, it must also be true of the specific instance, which is a member of that class.

Reasoning from general principles—actually, more a way of presenting your argument than a type of reasoning—is useful when you wish to argue that some unexamined instance has certain characteristics. You would, for example, note the general class or category and show that an unexamined instance or item is a member of that general class. You would then draw the conclusion that therefore the item also possesses the qualities possessed by the whole (or covered by the general principle).

What do you think of novelist Virginia Woolf's often quoted observation "When a subject is highly controversial, one cannot hope to tell the truth. One can only show how one came to hold whatever opinion one does hold. One can only give one's audience the chance of drawing their own conclusions as they observe the limitations, the prejudices, the idiosyncrasies of the speaker"?

How would you reason from specific instances to support the proposition that "tenure for college teachers should be abolished" or that "tenure for college teachers should be continued"?

Note in this excerpt from Ken Lonnquist's speech "Ghosts" how he argues against abortion from the general principle that one does not have control over the body of another (Linkugel, Allen, & Johannesen 1978):

> We say that it is our right to control our bodies, and this is true. But there is a distinction that needs to be made, and that distinction is this: Preventing a pregnancy is controlling a body—controlling your body. But preventing the continuance of a human life that is not your own is murder. If you attempt to control the body of another in that fashion, you become as a slave master was—controlling the lives and the bodies of his slaves—chopping off their feet when they ran away, or murdering them if it pleased him. This was not his right; it is not our right.

Critically Evaluating Reasoning from Specific Instances to a Generalization

Apply these tests in reasoning from specific instances.

1. *Are enough specific instances examined?* Obviously, there will be a limit to the number of specific instances you can examine. After all, your time, energy, and resources are limited. Yet it is important that you examine enough instances to justify your conclusion. Exactly how much is enough will vary from one situation to another. You cannot spend three days in a foreign country and conclude something about the entire country. You cannot interact with three Ethniquians and conclude something about all Ethniquians.

Two general guidelines might prove helpful in determining how much is enough. First, the larger the group you wish covered by your conclusion, the greater the number of specific instances you should examine. If you wish to draw conclusions about a class of 75 million Martians, you will have to examine a considerable number of Martians before drawing any valid conclusions. On the other hand, if you are attempting to draw a conclusion about a bushel of 100 apples, sampling a few is probably sufficient.

Second, the greater the diversity of items in the class, the more specific instances you will have to examine. Some classes or groups of items are relatively homogeneous, whereas others are more heterogeneous; this will influence how many specific instances constitute a sufficient number. Pieces of spaghetti in boiling water are all about the same; thus, sampling one usually tells you something about all the others. On the other hand, communication courses can be very different from each other, so valid conclusions about the entire group of communication courses will require a much larger sample.

2. *Are the specific instances representative?* Specific instances must be representative. If you wish to draw conclusions about the entire class, examine specific instances coming from all areas or subclasses within the major class. If, for example, you wanted to draw conclusions about the student body of your school, you could not simply examine communication majors or physics majors or art majors. Rather, you would have to examine a representative sample. Similarly, you could not survey only members of one culture and conclude something about members of other cultures. To draw conclusions about the whole, be sure to examine all significant parts of that whole.

What *specific* sampling procedures should a reporter writing an article on the students of your college follow? How many students should be interviewed? How could the reporter ensure representativeness?

3. *Are there significant exceptions?* When you examine specific instances and attempt to draw a conclusion about the whole, take into consideration the exceptions. Thus, if you examine the GPA of astrology majors and discover that 70 percent have GPAs above 3.5, you might be tempted to draw the conclusion that astrology majors are especially bright. But what about the 30 percent who have lower GPAs? How much lower are these scores? This may be a significant exception that must be taken into account when drawing your conclusion and that necessitates qualifying your conclusion in important ways. Exactly how many exceptions will constitute "significant exceptions" will depend on the unique situation.

As a speaker, you should disclose significant exceptions to your listeners. To hide these would be dishonest and also usually ineffective from a persuasive point of view because, more often than not, the audience either has heard or will hear of these exceptions. If you have not mentioned them, the audience will become suspicious of your overall honesty, and your credibility will quickly decline.

Do advertisers follow this principle? Can you cite specific examples in which advertisers violated this injunction to disclose significant exceptions?

Critically Evaluating Reasoning from a Generalization to Specific Instances

In testing reasoning from general principles to specific instances, apply these two tests.

1. *Is the general principle true or at least probably true?* Obviously, if the general principle is not true, it would be useless to apply it to any specific instance. In most situations you cannot know if a general principle is true, simply because you cannot examine all instances of the class. If you did examine all instances of the class, there would be no reason to use this form of reasoning, since you would already have examined the instance to which you wish to apply the general principle. For example, if you examine all the apples in the bushel, there is no reason to formulate the general conclusion that all the apples are rotten and to say that therefore one particular apple is rotten. In examining all the apples, you will have examined that specific apple. Consequently, what we are really dealing with is a general principle that seems to be "usually" and "probably" true. Thus, our conclusions about any specific instance will also be only "usually" or "probably" true.

2. *Is the unknown or the unexamined item clearly a specific member of the class?* If you want to draw a conclusion about a particular Atlantan and if you want to reason that this person is assertive because all Atlantans are assertive, you have to be certain that this person is in fact a member of the class of Atlantans.

Using Specific Instances and Generalizations

In reasoning from specific instances to general principle, stress that your specific instances are sufficient in number to warrant the conclusion you are drawing. Demonstrate that the specific instances are in fact representative of the whole. Show that there are no significant exceptions.

In using reasoning from general principle to specific instances, make certain that the audience accepts your general principle. This is especially important when your audience consists of members from different cultures. Depending on the cultures represented, you might not be able to assume that all members accept the idea that democracy is the best form of government, that capitalism is good, that state and church should be kept separate, or that men and women are equal. If the basic principle is not accepted by your audience, any attempt to use it as evidence concerning a specific instance will be doomed to failure. Conduct a thorough audience analysis before using this type of argument. The general principle must be accepted before you use it as a basis for a conclusion about an unexamined specific instance.

◼ REASONING FROM ANALOGY

In reasoning from analogy, you compare like things and conclude that since they are alike in so many respects, they are also alike in some as-yet-unknown or unexamined respect. For example, you reason that since the meat at Grand Union is fresh, the fish will be also. In this simple bit of reasoning, you compared two like things (the two foods, meat and fish) and concluded that what was known to be true about one item (that the meat was fresh) would also be true of the unknown item (the fish).

Analogies can be literal or figurative. In a literal analogy the items being compared are from the same class—foods, cars, people, countries, cities, or whatever. For example, in a literal analogy one might argue that (1) word processing, database, and desktop publishing software are all similar to tax preparation software—they are all popular, have been around for about the same number of years, and have been revised repeatedly; (2) these software packages have all been easy to learn and use; (3) therefore, tax preparation software will be easy to learn and use. Here, then, we have taken a number of like items belonging to the same class (types of computer software) and then reasoned that the similarity would also apply to the unexamined item (tax preparation software).

In a figurative analogy the items compared are from different classes. These analogies are useful for amplification but do not constitute logical proof. Here, for example, Richard Lidstad (1995, p. 560), vice-president of human resources for 3M, uses a sports analogy to illustrate the differences between the old and the new approach to management:

> *The old hierarchical corporation looked and acted like a football team. In football, there is narrow specialization of function. Each man plays only one position, and they all look to the quarterback or the coach for the next play. And when the play is executed, each person has a carefully defined job to execute.*
>
> *The new way to look at business is more like a hockey team. There is rapid, continuous action . . . and everyone must pass, shoot and play defense, even though each player may have a primary role.*

TIPS
From Professional Speakers

Analogies provide a change of pace and build in a sense of suspense. The audience looks forward to the end when the point of your story comes clear and they can see the connection with what you've been saying. Analogies can underline a basic truth with a seemingly light-hearted moment.

Using an example from daily life puts every member of the audience directly into the story, as well as humanizing you, the teller.

A word of caution: Think through your analogy to see how apt it is for making an instant connection between your point and the point of the story. Will everyone get the punch line? Does it really fit?

Sonya Hamlin, communication consultant and Emmy Award–winning television host, producer, and writer. *How to Talk So People Will Listen: The Real Key to Job Success* (New York: Harper & Row, 1988), p. 183. Reprinted by permission.

Teamwork is the most critical element in hockey, since individuals play multiple and often interchangeable roles. Success depends on how well those roles are blended.

As this example illustrates, the figurative analogy only creates an image. It does not prove anything and should not be used as evidence or as an argument. Its main purpose is to clarify, and it is particularly useful when you wish to clarify a complex process or, as in the above example, illustrate differences.

How would you use reasoning from analogy to support the proposition that "what goes around, comes around"?

Critically Evaluating Reasoning from Analogy

In testing the adequacy of an analogy—here of literal analogies—ask yourself two general questions:

1. *Are the two cases being compared alike in essential respects?* In the example of the tax preparation software, one significant difference was not noted: To use that software effectively, you really have to know the rules and regulations governing taxes. You can learn to use word processing software without going beyond the information contained in the manual; but to learn to use tax preparation software, you have to know what is in not only the manual but also the tax code.

2. *Do the differences make a difference?* In any analogy, regardless of how literal it is, the items being compared will be different: No two things are exactly the same. But in reasoning with analogies, ask yourself if the differences make a difference. Obviously, not all differences make a fundamental difference. The difference in the knowledge you need for the various software programs, however, is a substantial difference that needs to be considered.

Using Reasoning from Analogy

When reasoning from analogy, stress the numerous and significant similarities between the items being compared and minimize the differences between them. Mention differences that do exist and that the audience will think of, but show that these do not destroy the validity of your argument. If the audience knows there are differences but you do not squarely confront these, your argument is going to prove ineffective. The listeners will be wondering, "But what about the difference in . . . ?"

How would you use analogy to persuade your audience that college core requirements should be eliminated?

For example, let us say you are giving a speech in favor of instituting the honor system at your college. You might argue from the analogy of West Point and say something like:

The honor system has worked at other colleges. West Point is perhaps the most famous example. At West Point students take their examinations without any proctors. They are totally on their own honor.

But your audience may well reject this analogy and say to themselves (and perhaps in the question period) that West Point is a very different type of college. Therefore, you need to confront the difference between West Point and your school. You might begin by saying:

> *I know that many of you are thinking that West Point is a very different type of school from ours. But in matters that relate to the honor system, it is not different. Let me show why these two colleges are actually alike in all essential respects. First, both our schools enroll students of approximately the same academic abilities. SAT scores, for example, are almost identical, as are high school grades. Second, both schools . . .*

REASONING FROM CAUSES AND EFFECTS

In reasoning from causes and effects, you may go in either of two directions: from cause to effect (from observed cause to unobserved effect) or from effect to cause (from observed effect to unobserved cause).

Here, for example, a speaker (Ling 1993, p. 100) reasons from known causes (one of which is the growth of the aged population in Japan) to effects (health care problems for global corporations, the topic of the entire speech):

> *A second, related dynamic is a dramatic acceleration in the silvering of Japan.*
>
> *Over 30 percent of the health insurance costs in this country are for people over 70 years old.*
>
> *By the year 2000, 25 percent of the population will be over 65. Just for comparison, the aging of the Japanese population is advancing 5 times faster than France, and almost twice that of Germany and the U.K.*

In this excerpt the speaker (Orr 1993, p. 727) reasons in the other direction: from a known effect (loss of numerous corporations' status) to an unknown cause (single-minded focus):

> *Consider this: of the 43 companies listed as "excellent" in the 1982 best seller* In Search of Excellence, *less than half retained this status five years later. No doubt, many of those who slipped had become so focused on one set of circumstances that they couldn't adapt to change.*

Critically Evaluating Reasoning from Causes and Effects

In testing reasoning from cause to effect or from effect to cause, ask yourself the following questions.

1. *Might other causes be producing the observed effect?* If you observe a particular effect (say, high crime or student apathy), you need to ask if causes other than the one you are postulating might be producing this effect. Thus, you might postulate that poverty leads to high crime, but there might be other factors actually causing the high crime rate. Or poverty might be one cause, but it might not be the most important cause. Therefore, explore the possibility of other causes producing the observed effect.

TIPS

From Professional Speakers

Confusing sequence with cause and effect. A demanding controller joins the company August 1 as head of Max's department. Max resigns on August 31; therefore, Max left because he had difficulty working with the new controller. As in this case, chronology may have little or nothing to do with the result.

Dianna Booher, business communication consultant and president of Booher Consultants. *Communicate with Confidence!* (New York: McGraw-Hill, 1994), p. 119.

2.   *Is the causation in the direction postulated?* If two things occur together, it is often difficult to determine which is the cause and which is the effect. For example, a lack of interpersonal intimacy and a lack of self-confidence are often seen in the same person. The person who lacks self-confidence seldom has intimate relationships with others. But which is the cause and which is the effect? It might be that the lack of intimacy "causes" low self-confidence; it might also be, however, that low self-confidence "causes" a lack of intimacy. Of course, it might also be that some other previously unexamined cause (a history of negative criticism, for example) might be producing both the lack of intimacy and the low self-confidence.

3.   *Is there evidence for a causal rather than merely a time-sequence relationship?* Two things might vary together, but they may not be related in a cause-effect relationship. Divorce frequently results after repeated instances of infidelity, but infidelity itself may not be the cause of the divorce rate. Rather, some other factor may be leading to both infidelity and divorce. Thus, even though infidelity may precede divorce, it may not be the cause of it. When you assume that a temporal relationship implies a causal relationship, you are committing a fallacy of reasoning called *post hoc ergo propter hoc* ("after this, because of this").

Here, for example, Susumu Yoshida (1995, p. 304), president of Sumitomo Chemical America, uses cause to effect reasoning to explain why the Japanese communicate as they do and how this can create a major communication barrier between Japanese and American businesspeople:

> *Few people in America fully realize how great the communication barrier is for Japanese. There is a well-known Japanese phrase that essentially says, "If a nail sticks up, it will be hammered down." So it may sound strange to you, but it's almost a taboo for Japanese to have strong views different from the group. In fact, when we use our language, we often try to be ambiguous and use indirect expressions to reduce the risk of confrontation. While this is an integral part of Japanese tradition, trouble begins when what an American understood is often different from what his Japanese counterpart intended.*

Using Cause-Effect Reasoning

Stress the causal connection by pointing out that:

1. other causes are not significant and may for all practical purposes be ruled out
2. the causal connection is in the direction postulated, that is, that the cause is indeed the cause and the effect is indeed the effect
3. the evidence points to a causal connection—that the relationship is not merely related in time

Furthermore, depending on the specific purpose of your speech, make the audience realize that this causal connection can be altered to their advantage. Tell them that the effect may be strengthened (if the effect is desirable) or broken (if the effect is undesirable).

What do you think of using the position of the stars at the time of a person's birth as a sign that this person will have a particular Leo (or Aries or Virgo) personality?

How would you use reasoning from causes and effects to support the proposition that "soft drugs lead to hard drugs" or that "soft drugs do not lead to hard drugs"?

REASONING FROM SIGN

Some years ago I went to my doctor because of a minor skin irritation. Instead of looking at my skin, the doctor focused on my throat, noticed it was enlarged, felt around a bit, and began asking me a number of questions. Did I tire easily? Yes. Did I drink lots of liquid? Yes. Did I always feel thirsty? Yes. Did I eat a great deal without gaining any weight? Yes. She then had me stretch out my hand and try to hold it steady. I couldn't do it. These indicators were signs of a particular illness. Based on these signs, she made the preliminary diagnosis that I had a hyperthyroid condition. The results of blood and other tests confirmed the preliminary diagnosis. I was promptly treated, and the thyroid condition was corrected.

Medical diagnosis is a good example of reasoning by sign. The general procedure is simple. If a sign and an object, event, or condition are frequently paired, the presence of the sign is taken as proof of the presence of the object, event, or condition. Thus, the tiredness, extreme thirst, and overeating were taken as signs of hyperthyroidism because they frequently accompany the condition. When these signs disappeared after treatment, it was taken as a sign that the thyroid disease had been arrested. Further tests confirmed this as well.

Here is an example of the same form of reasoning as used in a speech. In this case the speaker (Rolland 1993, p. 524) reasons from a number of signs to the conclusion that Americans are willing to sacrifice to achieve health care reform:

> *For example, a nationwide* Wall Street Journal/NBC *poll in March found:*
> - *66 percent willing to pay higher taxes so everyone can get health insurance;*
> - *52 percent willing to accept limits on the right to choose their own doctor; and*
> - *46 percent even willing to accept higher insurance deductibles and copayments.*

Critically Evaluating Reasoning from Sign

In reasoning from sign, ask yourself these questions.

1. *Do the signs necessitate the conclusion drawn?* Given the extreme thirst, overeating, and the like, how certain can I be of the "hyperthyroid" conclusion? With most medical and legal matters, we can never be absolutely certain, but we can be certain beyond a reasonable doubt.

2. *Are there other signs that point to the same conclusion?* In the thyroid example, the extreme thirst could have been brought on by any number of factors. Similarly, the swollen throat and the overeating could have been attributed to other causes. Yet taken together, they seemed to point to only one reasonable diagnosis. This was later confirmed with additional and more sophisticated signs in the form of results from blood tests and thyroid scans. Generally, the more signs that point toward the conclusion, the more confidence we can have that it is valid.

3. *Are there contradictory signs?* Are there signs pointing toward contradictory conclusions? If, for example, "Higgins" had a motive and a history of violence

What form of reasoning would a good detective use most often? Can you give a hypothetical example of such reasoning, using such concepts as motive, prior history of similar criminal actions, and lack of alibi?

Student government debates, such as the one in which this speaker is engaged, rely heavily on logical arguments. What types of logical arguments (specific instances, analogy, cause-effect, and sign) would prove most effective in convincing an audience of your peers that (1) gays and lesbians should (not) be permitted in the U.S. military; (2) affirmative action should (not) be declared illegal; (3) condoms should (not) be distributed in schools; (4) school prayer should (not) be banned in public schools?

(signs supporting the conclusion that Higgins was the murderer) but also had an alibi for the time of the murder (a sign pointing to the conclusion of innocence), the conclusion of guilt would have to be reconsidered or discarded.

Using Reasoning from Sign

Stress the certainty of the connection between the sign and the conclusion. Make the audience see that because these signs are present, no other conclusion is likely. Let them see that for all practical purposes, all other conclusions are ruled out.

This is the procedure followed in law. The guilt of an individual must be established not conclusively but beyond all reasonable doubt. The audience should be made to see that your conclusion drawn from sign is the best—the most reasonable—conclusion possible.

Make the connection between the signs and the conclusions clear to the audience. If you, as a speaker, know of the connection between, say, enlarged eyes and hyperthyroidism, this does not mean that the audience knows it. State explicitly that enlarged eyes can be produced only by hyperthyroidism and that therefore the sign—enlarged eyes—can lead to only one reasonable conclusion: hyperthyroidism.

How would you use reasoning from sign to support the proposition that "foreign language mastery should be required of all college graduates"?

What types of logical arguments (specific instances, analogy, causes-effects, and sign) would prove most effective in convincing an audience of your peers that (1) gays and lesbians should (not) be permitted in the U.S. military, (2) abortion should be made legal (illegal) in all states, or (3) this college should (not) be declared smoke-free?

UNIT IN BRIEF

Reasoning from specific instances to generalizations	■ Examine a valid number of specific instances ■ Examine specific instances that are representative ■ Account for the significant exceptions
Reasoning from generalizations to specific instances	■ The principle should be generally true ■ The unexamined instance should be covered by the generalization ■ The principle should be accepted by the audience to be most effective ■ To be most effective, stress the sufficiency and representativeness of the sample and account for exceptions
Reasoning from analogies	■ Use cases that are alike in essential respects ■ Use cases in which the differences do not make a significant difference ■ To be most effective, stress similarities, minimize the importance of differences, and confront differences squarely
Reasoning from causes and effects	■ Be sure that other causes are not producing the observed effect ■ Be sure the causation is in the direction postulated ■ Be sure there is evidence for a causal rather than simply a temporal relationship ■ To be most effective, rule out other possible causes, be sure the causation is in the postulated direction, and be sure the relationship is causal (rather than just temporal)
Reasoning from sign	■ Use signs that clearly support the conclusion ■ Identify other signs that point in the same direction ■ Account for contradictory signs ■ To be most effective, stress the certainty of the connection between sign and conclusion, and answer the major counterarguments

PRACTICALLY SPEAKING

Short Speech Technique

Prepare and deliver a two-minute speech in which you:

1. develop an argument for or against the legalization of steroids
2. develop an argument from specific instances to support one of these generalizations: (1) Hard work leads to rewards, (2) people who agree with others become leaders, or (3) inflation will increase
3. develop an analogy to help explain one of the following concepts: teaching, research, parenting, happiness, philosophizing, or therapy
4. develop a cause-effect or effect-cause argument for any of the following propositions: (1) single-parent adoption should be encouraged (discouraged), (2) divorces should be made easier (more difficult) to obtain, or (3) open a retirement account now
5. develop an argument from sign to support any of the following conclusions: (1) The economic value of a college education has lessened over the last few decades, (2) exercise regularly, or (3) immigration policies need to be revised
6. select one newspaper feature (advice to the lovelorn, astrology, medical advice column, celebrity news, editorial, or letters to the editor, for example) and describe the types of evidence used

21.1   Evaluating the Adequacy of Reasoning

Here are, in brief, a few arguments. Read each of them carefully and (1) identify the type of reasoning used, (2) apply the tests of adequacy discussed in this unit, and (3) indicate what could be done to make the reasoning more logical and more persuasive.

1. Dr. Manchester should be denied tenure for being an ineffective teacher. Two of my friends are in Manchester's statistics course and they hate it; they haven't learned a thing. Manchester's student evaluation ratings are way below the department and college average, and the readings Manchester assigns are dull, difficult, and of little relevance to students.
2. The lack of success among the Martians who have settled on Earth is not difficult to explain. They simply have no ambition, no drive, no desire to excel. They're content to live on welfare, drink cheap wine, and smoke as much grass as they can get their hands on.
3. I went out with three people I met at clubs—they were all duds. In the club they were fine, but once we got outside I couldn't even talk with them. All they knew how to do was wear freaky clothes and dance. So when Pat asked me out, I said no. I decided it would be a waste of time.
4. One recent sociological report indicates some interesting facts about Theta Three. In Theta Three there are, as most of us know, few restrictions on premarital sexual relations. Unlike the case in this country, in Theta Three the permissive person is not looked down on. Social taboos in regard to

sex are few. Theta Three also has the highest suicide rate in the galaxy. Suicide is not infrequent among teenagers and young adults. This condition must be changed. But before it is changed, life must be accorded greater meaning and significance. Social, and perhaps legal, restrictions on premarital sexual relations must be instituted.

5. Pat and Chris are unhappy and should probably separate. The last time I visited, Pat told me they had just had a big fight and mentioned they now fight regularly. Chris spends more time with the kids than with Pat and frequently goes out after work with people from the office. Often, Chris has told me, they sit for hours without saying a word to each other.

21.2   Analyzing Arguments: The Toulmin Model

An excellent way to analyze arguments is with the model developed by Stephen Toulmin (Toulmin, Rieke, & Janick 1979), a British philosopher and logician. In Toulmin's model there are three essential parts and an additional three parts that may be used depending on the argument and the audience. The three essential parts are data, claim, and warrant.

The **data** are the facts and opinions—the evidence—used to support your claim. For example: *The college has recently incurred vast additional expenses.*

The **claim** is the conclusion you wish the audience to accept; it is the proposition you want the audience to believe is true, justified, or right. For example: *Tuition must be increased.*

The **warrant** is the connection leading from the data to the claim. The warrant is the principle or the reason why the data justify (or warrant) the claim. For example: *Tuition has been and is likely to continue being the principal means by which the college pays its expenses.*

The three optional elements that may or may not be present, depending on the type of argument advanced and the nature of the audience to be persuaded, are the backing, the qualifier, and the reservation.

The **backing** is the support for the warrant—the supporting material that backs up the principle or reason expressed in the warrant. Backing is especially important if the warrant is not accepted or believed by the audience. For example: *Over the last 40 years, each time the college incurred large expenses it raised tuition.*

The **qualifier** is the degree to which the claim is asserted; it is an attempt to modify the strength or certainty of the claim. The qualifier is used only when the claim is presented with less than total certainty. For example: *Probably.*

The **reservation** (or rebuttal) specifies those situations under which the claim might not be true. For example: *Unless the college manages to secure private donations from friends and alumni.*

Usually these six parts of an argument are laid out in diagrammatic form to further illustrate the important relationships. See Figure 21.1.

The main value of Toulmin's system is that it provides an excellent method for analyzing arguments, one especially appropriate to the public speaking situation. The following questions may also help you to analyze the validity and possible effectiveness of your arguments:

FIGURE 21.1
A diagram of the parts of an argument
in a Toulmin analysis.

Data
The college has recently incurred
vast additional expenses.

Claim
Tuition must be increased.

Warrant
Tuition has been and is
likely to continue being
the principal means by
which the college pays
its expenses.

Qualifier
Probably.

Reservation
Unless the college
manages to secure
private donations
from friends and
alumni.

Backing
Over the last 40 years,
each time the college
incurred large expenses
it raised tuition.

1. Are the data sufficient to justify the claim? If not, what additional data are needed?
2. Is the claim properly (logically) qualified? Is the claim presented with too much certainty?
3. Is the warrant adequate to justify the claim on the basis of the data? Does the audience accept the warrant, or will it need backing? What other warrants might be utilized?
4. Is the backing sufficient for accepting the warrant? Will the audience accept the backing? What further support for the warrant might be used?
5. Are the essential reservations stated? What other reservations might the audience think of that should be included here?

Test your understanding of these six elements of the Toulmin model by identifying which element each of the following statements represents. They are presented here in random order.

_____1. Cicero College must adopt a policy of training all its students in computer literacy.
_____2. Employers are demanding computer literacy for all positions.

_____3. This new emphasis must take place as soon as possible.

_____4. Colleges are obligated to prepare students for the job market.

_____5. Colleges that have failed to prepare students for the job market have found themselves without students.

_____6. Unless the job market changes drastically.

_____7. Unless Cicero becomes a college devoted solely to the fine arts.

_____8. Tawny Bay, Middlecenter, and Mt. Hill Colleges all neglected computer literacy and have declined 30 percent in enrollment.

_____9. All students should be trained in computer science, with the possible exception of those in the fine arts.

Answers: 1 = claim; 2 = data; 3 = qualifier; 4 = warrant; 5 = backing; 6 = reservation; 7 = reservation; 8 = backing; 9 = qualifier.

Now that the mechanics of this model are clear, select one of the "claims" that follow and construct and diagram an argument using Toulmin's system. Include all six parts of the argument: claim, data, warrant, backing, qualifier, and reservation. After you have constructed and diagrammed an argument, exchange your paper with another student. Then, in groups of five or six (or with the class as a whole), analyze the argument, evaluating its validity and its potential rhetorical effectiveness for an audience composed of students from your class. The five questions presented previously might provide a useful starting place.

Claims

1. Senator Smiley should be reelected.
2. College football should be abolished.
3. Everyone has ESP.
4. Take a course in critical thinking.
5. Reduce your stress.
6. Support the college athletic fund.
7. Keep a daily journal.
8. Express your opinions to your local representative.
9. Trace your family origins.
10. Visit India.

UNIT 22

Motivating Behavior

Unit Objectives

After completing this unit, you should be able to:

1. Explain the role of motivational appeals in persuasion

2. Describe Maslow's hierarchy of needs

3. Identify the principles of motivation and explain their relevance to public speaking

4. Identify the major motivational appeals and explain how they work

Motivational appeals—appeals to needs, desires, and wants—are the most powerful means of persuasion you possess. Because of their importance, this entire unit is devoted to explaining what motivational appeals are and how you can use them effectively.

When you use motivational appeals, you appeal to your listeners' needs and desires. You appeal to motives, to those forces that energize, move, or motivate a person to develop, change, or strengthen particular attitudes or ways of behaving. For example, one motive might be the desire for status. This motive might lead you to develop certain attitudes about what occupation to enter, the importance of saving and investing money, and so on.

One of the most useful analyses of motives is Abraham Maslow's (1970) five-fold classification, reproduced in Figure 22.1. One of the assumptions contained in it is that you would seek to fulfill first the need at the lowest level and only then the need at the next higher level. Thus, for example, if you were starving (that is, if your need for food had not been fulfilled), you would not concern yourself with the need for security or freedom from fear. Similarly, if your need for protection and security had not been fulfilled, you would not be concerned with the need for friendship. The implication for the speaker is clear: You must determine what needs of your audience have been satisfied and therefore what other needs you might use to motivate them.

How would you describe your own motives in terms of Maslow's hierarchy of needs? Which of these levels do you feel are generally satisfied in the lives of the members of your class?

Do you know people you would describe as "self-actualizers"? If so, how do they differ from most other people?

FIGURE 22.1
Maslow's "hierarchy of needs."

Self-Actualization Needs
Doing what one is fitted for doing
Self-fulfillment
Actualizing one's potential

Self-Esteem Needs
High self-evaluation, self-respect, self-esteem, esteem of others, strength, achievement, competency, reputation, prestige, status, fame, glory

Belonging and Love Needs
Friendship, affectional relationships, interpersonal acceptance

Safety Needs
Security, stability, protection, freedom from fear, freedom from anxiety, freedom from chaos, structure, order, law

Physiological Needs
Food, water, air

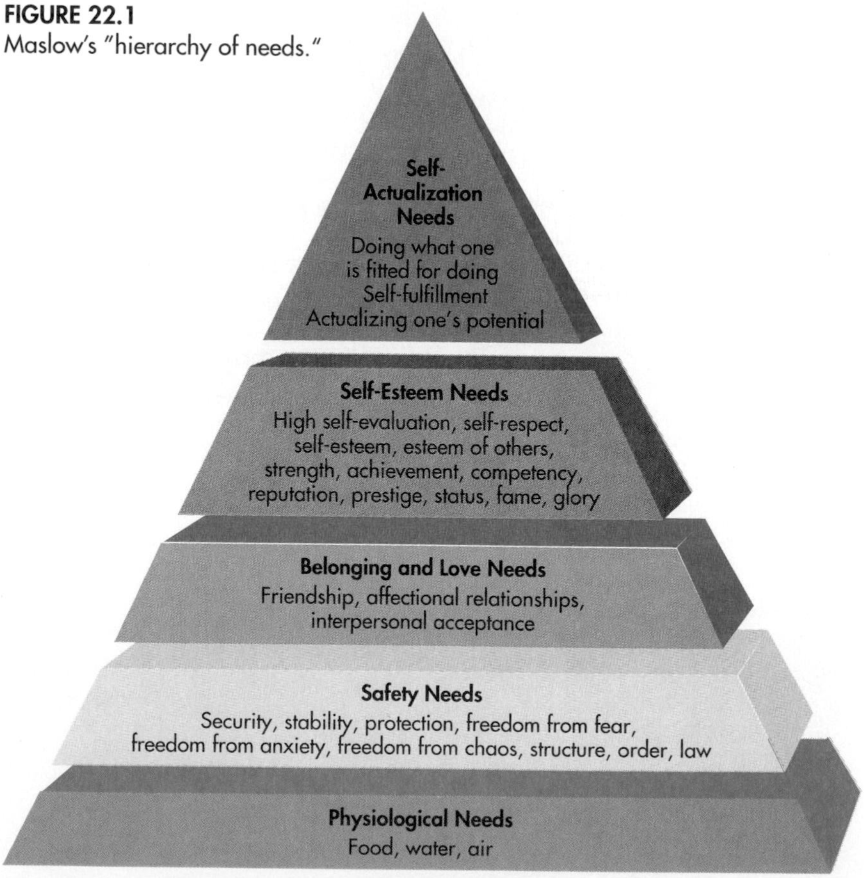

SOURCE: Based on Abraham Maslow, *Motivation and Personality*. New York: HarperCollins, 1970.

PRINCIPLES OF MOTIVATION

Let's consider some principles of motivation so that you will be able to use motivational appeals more effectively in your own speeches. A somewhat different perspective is provided by research on compliance-gaining strategies (as explained in the box on page 380).

Motives Differ

Motives are not static; nor do they operate in the same way with different people. Motives differ from one time to another and from one person to another.

Motives change with time. Think of the motives that are crucial to you at this time in your life and that motivate your current thinking and behavior. These motives may not, however, be significant in ten or even two years. They may fade and others may take their place. Now, for example, attractiveness may be one of the more dominant motives in your life; you have a strong need to be thought attractive by your peers. Later in life, this motive may be replaced by, for example, the desire for security, financial independence, or power.

Motives function differently with different people. This is simply a specific application of the general principle that people are different. Consequently, different people will respond differently to the very same motive.

Have your motives changed since you started college? If so, how?

Motives Are Ordered

Not all motives are equal in intensity. Some are powerful and exert a strong influence on behavior; others are less powerful and may influence behavior only slightly. Motives exist in varying degrees of intensity. Some motives are strong, some are weak, and the vast majority are somewhere in between. Since motives vary in intensity and strength, they vary in the influence they have on the individual. Determining which motives your audience holds strongly and which weakly may be one of your most difficult tasks. But if you can identify those motives that will strongly influence the audience, you need not waste time on motives that are ineffective in influencing behavior.

What motives influence you the most in regard to (a) attending college, (b) establishing interpersonal relationships, (c) selecting your occupational goals, and (d) planning your activities over the last weekend?

Further, motives may be ordered in terms of their degree of generality or specificity. Motives are general classes of needs and desires. For example, the status motive may include a host of specifics that, taken together, make up and define status for a particular person. But as you know, people are motivated by appeals not to abstract and general motives but rather to specific aspects of these motives. Thus, to appeal to status you would need to appeal to, for example, the desire to be recognized by others on the street, to have a job that is respected by family and friends, or to have a home in an exclusive part of town.

The more specific your appeal, the more effective your appeal will be in persuading your audience. Consider, for example, the difference between the teacher's appeal to read this book because it will help to make you an educated person versus the appeal to read this book because it will help you to pass this course or the next test.

Motives Interact

Do you have conflicting motives pulling you in different directions? If so, how do you think you will eventually resolve the conflict?

Motives rarely operate in isolation; usually a collection of motives operate together. Sometimes these motives operate in the same direction, all influencing behavior in the same way. At other times motives conflict with one another, each stimulating behavior in somewhat different directions.

In cases where a number of motives influence behavior in the same direction, your appeal should be directed to a number of motives rather than limited to just one. For example, if you want an audience to contribute money to AIDS research, appeal to a variety of influential motives—safety for oneself and one's family and friends, altruism, control over the environment, and so on.

In cases where motives conflict with one another, your task is more difficult. Let's say, for example, that humanitarian motives would lead your audience to give money to AIDS research, but their desire to use their money for personal luxuries would lead them not to donate funds. In this case you might propose that the humanitarian motives are more noble or perhaps that the amount of money involved is not so great that they would impoverish themselves.

How would you use any one of these strategies to persuade others and accomplish each of the following goals: (a) to persuade a friend to cut classes and go to the movies, (b) to persuade a group to vote in favor of building a senior citizen center, (c) to persuade audience members to reaffirm their faith in the government, (d) to persuade audience members to manage their time more efficiently, (e) to persuade audience members to change their telephone company to Expand-a-Phone.

F O C U S   O N

Compliance-Gaining Strategies

In addition to the motivational appeals detailed in this unit, there are lots of compliance-gaining strategies, techniques for getting others to do as you wish (Marwell & Schmitt 1967; Miller & Parks 1982). Here are several.

Promise. Promise the audience that they will receive some kind of reward if they do as you request: *The time you spend organizing your finances will be cut in half with this new computer program.*

Threat. Threaten the audience with some form of punishment if they do not do as you suggest: *If we don't elect Senator Underdog, you can kiss social security good-bye.*

Self-Feelings. Make the audience see that they will feel better about themselves if they do as you suggest (or will feel worse about themselves if they don't do as you suggest): *Charity helps not only those who need it, but also those who give.*

Altercasting. Cast your listeners in the role of the "good" person (or "bad" person) and argue that they should comply with your suggestion because a person with "good" qualities would comply (while a person with "bad" qualities would not): *Let's side with those who are trying to do something to help the homeless and not with the landlords and insurance companies who want the homeless to have no rights.*

Debt. Make the audience realize that they have a debt, an obligation, to do as you suggest: *Look at everything the school has done for us; it's time we did something for the school.*

Moral appeals. Make the audience see that what you are advocating is moral and right and that their moral responsibility is to do as you suggest (as it would be immoral to not do what you suggest): *It would be totally immoral to do nothing, to allow the homeless to be without shelter any longer. Building these shelters is the only moral alternative.*

What two or three motives will prove the most persuasive to members of your class? What evidence do you have for your choices?

Motives Are Culturally Influenced

Throughout this discussion, keep in mind that the listener's culture will greatly influence the motives to which he or she will be responsive. Members of highly individualistic cultures—the United States, Sweden, Germany, and Norway, for example—are more likely to be moved by appeals to status (which itself is an individualistic motive) than by appeals to the desire to conform. Members of highly collective cultures—such as Arabic, Japanese, Latin American, and Chinese cultures—are more likely to be moved by appeals to conformity than by appeals to status. To further complicate matters, members of collective cultures may think it inappropriate for a speaker to appeal to motives of status and self-reward.

Can you attribute any of your current motives to cultural training?

The motives discussed here are those that are judged potent in much of the United States. Researchers in communication and psychology, for example, find these motives operating in a variety of situations, and, of course, advertisers and the media appeal to these motives in designing their ads, their magazines, and their sitcoms. As you read the discussions herein, consider how these needs might work in other cultural situations.

MOTIVATIONAL APPEALS

In reviewing the motivational appeals described in this section, try to visualize how you would use each one in your next speech. If that's too easy, try visualizing how you would use these motives on broadly different audiences, for example, a group of college professors, members of the American Medical Association, or the local PTA. And try to apply these motives in speeches to groups composed of members from cultures differing widely from your own.

Polish leader Lech Walesa once said, "He who gives food to the people will win." What is the "food" for your audience in this class?

How do you respond to the fear appeals that are currently used in popular advertisements?

Altruism

Altruism, some argue, does not exist. It is said that all of our motives are selfish, and perhaps this is right. Any action, any belief, any attitude can usually be traced to a motive that might be regarded as selfish—to greed, to sensory pleasure, to personal power. But it is equally true that most of us want to believe that our motives are altruistic, at least sometimes. We want to do what we consider the right thing; we want to help others; we want to contribute to worthy causes. We want to help the weak, feed the hungry, cure the sick. The fact that we derive some kind of selfish pleasure from these actions does not militate against our viewing them as being motivated by altruism.

Appeals to altruism are most effective when done with moderation. If they are not moderate, they will seem unrealistic and out of touch with the way real people think in a world that is practical and difficult to survive in. Here is an especially good example of the use of the appeal to altruism. In this speech Charlotte Lunsford (1988) appeals to altruism but also to other motives. She effectively uses the principle of appealing to a wide variety of motives:

> *Volunteerism still combines the best and the most powerful values in our society—pride in the dignity of work, the opportunity to get involved in things that affect us, the freedom of choice and expression, the chance to put into practice an ethic of caring, and the realization that one person can make a difference.*
>
> *To these altruistic reasons for volunteering, we can add some very specific rewards for giving of one's time in the service of others:*
>
> - *a chance to do the things that one does best*
> - *working with a respected community organization*
> - *seeing the results of one's own work*
> - *the opportunity to make business and professional contacts—"networking"*
> - *the opportunity to develop social skills*
> - *and the chance to move to paid employment*

Fear and Safety

We are motivated in great part by a need to avoid fear. We fear the loss of those things we desire. We fear the loss of money, family, friends, love, attractiveness, health, job, and just about everything else we now have and value. We also fear punishment, rejection, failure. We fear the unknown, the uncertain, the unpredictable.

The use of fear in persuasion has been studied extensively, and the results show that strong amounts of fear work best (Allen & Preiss 1990). With low or even moderate levels of fear, the audience members are not motivated sufficiently to act; with high levels of fear, they perk up and begin to listen.

The other side of fear is safety. We all have a need for safety. Maslow (1970) put safety at the second level, just above the satisfaction of the physiological need for food and drink. We want to feel protected, to be free of fear. Sometimes the safety motive is seen in the individual's desire for order, structure, and organization. We fear what is unknown, and order and structure make things predictable and hence safe.

In this excerpt Edwin J. Feulner, Jr. (1995, p. 411), appeals to the desire for safety:

> *It is a false economy to withdraw any more of our 100,000 troops from Europe because Russia is not an immediate danger. To those who say, "Well, we'll just come back when Russia is a threat again," I say, "You mean like we did in 1944 on the beaches of Normandy?" And to those who ask "Why should America pay anything to defend Europe or East Asia?" I say, "We're not paying for Europe's defense or Japan's defense. We're paying for our defense."*

Individuality and Conformity

The two conflicting motives of individuality and conformity can be considered together because they are opposite sides of the same coin. Each pulls us in a different direction, and each lessens the effects of the other. Many people have a desire to be individuals but also to be one of the crowd. In individualistic cultures, the desire to stand out, to be one of a kind, is the stronger motive in most situations. In collectivist cultures, the desire to be one of a group, to conform to the group standards and rules, is the stronger motive in most situations.

Are you motivated by both the desire to be different and the desire to be one of a group? If so, does this create difficulties?

Power, Control, and Influence

We want power, control, and influence. First, we want power over ourselves—we want to be in control of our own destinies; we want to be responsible for our own successes. As Emerson put it, "Can anything be so elegant as to have few wants, and to serve them one's self?"

Can you identify one specific way in which you are influenced by the motives discussed here?

How might Jesse Jackson use the appeals discussed here when speaking, say, to the students at your college about affirmative action?

We also want control over other persons. We want to be influential. We want to be opinion leaders. We want others to come to us for advice, guidance, and instruction. Similarly, we want control over events and things in the world. We want to control our environment. You will motivate your listeners when you enable them to believe that they can increase their power, control, and influence as a result of their learning what you have to say or of their doing as you suggest.

Self-Esteem and Approval

"In his private heart," wrote Mark Twain, "no man much respects himself." And perhaps because of this, we have a need for a positive self-image, to see ourselves in the best possible light. We want to see ourselves as self-confident, as worthy and contributing human beings. Inspirational speeches, speeches of the "you are the greatest" type, never seem to lack receptive and suggestible audiences.

Self-esteem is, at least in part, attained by gaining the approval of others (something that is more important in collectivist cultures than it is in individualistic cultures). Most people are concerned with peer approval but also want approval from family, teachers, elders, and children. Somehow the approval of others makes us feel positive about ourselves. Approval from others also ensures the attainment of related goals. For example, if you have peer approval, you probably also have influence. If you have approval, you are likely to have status. In relating your propositions to your audience's desire for approval, avoid being too obvious. Few people want to be told that they need or desire approval.

Love and Affiliation

We are motivated to love and be loved. For most persons, love and its pursuit occupy a considerable amount of time and energy. If you can teach your audience how to be loved and how to love, you will have not only an attentive but also a grateful audience.

We also want affiliation—friendship and companionship. We desire to be a part of a group (an especially strong desire in collectivist cultures). Notice how advertisements for discos, singles bars, and dating services emphasize this need for affiliation. On this basis alone they successfully gain the attention, interest, and participation of thousands. Again, such affiliation seems to assure us that we are in fact worthy creatures. If we have friends and companions, surely we are people of some merit.

In this excerpt Leo Buscaglia (1988), noted author and lecturer, appeals to our desire for love and affiliation:

> *Relationships that are based on little more than a steamy attraction more often than not end by leaving us bewildered, wondering what went wrong when we find that we are no longer "happily-ever-aftering." We usually discover that it was the small conflicts, the petty peeves, the infantile rigidity and stubbornness, the disillusionment and the refusal to forgive.*
>
> *There is no simple formula for making us better lovers. At best we can base our love on certain tried-and-true rules that can make a positive beginning.*

Which single motive is the most influential in your life right now? Which is the least influential?

Achievement

We want to achieve in whatever we do. As a student, you want to be successful. As a teacher and writer, I too want to be successful. We want to achieve as friends, as parents, as lovers. This is why we read books and listen to speeches that purport to tell us how to be better achievers. We also want others to recognize our achievements as real and valuable. "Being successful in my work" is extremely important to most college students.

In using the achievement motive, be explicit in stating how your speech, ideas, and recommendations will contribute to the listeners' achievements. At the same time, recognize that different cultures will view achievement very differently. To some, achievement may be financial; to others, it may be group popularity; to still others, it may mean security.

In this speech Raymond W. Smith (1995, p. 360), CEO of Bell Atlantic, used the achievement motive in persuading his audience (Advertising Women of New York) of the importance of interactive advertising:

> *Barry Diller bought QVC at the very same time that Sears closed its franchise catalog business. Diller saw the future; Sears could only mourn the past.*
>
> *Which of you will be the pioneers of the new interactive medium? You'd better decide quick, because it won't be "new" very long. The leaders will establish themselves very fast. The rest will have trouble ever catching up.*
>
> *Yogi Berra once said, "When you come to a crossroads—take it!" I couldn't have said it better myself.*

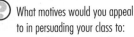 What motives would you appeal to in persuading your class to:
- support (do not support) Channel 1?
- vote for (against) affirmative action proposals?
- support (do not support) a multiculturalism requirement?
- support (do not support) the building of a homeless shelter in their neighborhood?

Financial Gain

Most people are motivated to some extent by the desire for financial gain—for what it can buy, for what it can do. We may be concerned with buying necessities, luxuries, or even time. Concerns for lower taxes, for higher salaries, for fringe benefits are all related to the money motive. Show the audience that what you are saying or advocating will make them money and they will listen with considerable interest, much as they read the current get-rich-quick books that are flooding the bookstores.

In a speech designed to motivate the audience to take action against certain proposed budget cuts, Cyril F. Brickfield (1985) appealed to the financial motive of his senior citizen audience:

> *Congress is now considering freezing Social Security COLA's [cost-of-living adjustments]. Congress is willing to force more than a half million of us into poverty. But the defense budget is exempt from any freeze.*
>
> *Ladies and gentlemen, let me ask you, is it fair that older Americans must lose their inflation protection while the Pentagon doesn't?*

What are your thoughts on George Bernard Shaw's observation "Money is the most important thing in the world. It represents health, strength, honor, generosity, and beauty as conspicuously as the want of it represents illness, weakness, disgrace, meanness, and ugliness. Not the least of its virtues is that it destroys base people as certainly as it fortifies and dignifies noble people"?

Status

One motive that accounts for a great deal of our behavior is our desire for status. In our society our status is measured by our occupation and wealth; often job and money are positively related.

But there are other kinds of status: the status that comes from competence on the athletic field, from excelling in the classroom, or from superiority on

What motives are used in popular television advertisements to sell soft drinks? Cosmetics? Automobiles? Diet products? Fast foods at chain restaurants? Breakfast cereals?

the dance floor. To be most effective, link your propositions with your specific audience's desire for status.

In this excerpt Kelly Zmak (Boaz & Brey 1987), a student from San Jose State University, appeals to the audience's desire for status and success:

> You know, as college people we all have something in common. We want to be successful. The levels of our success vary, but to be successful is something that we all strive for. Having an advantage in today's world is something none of us would mind. But having a disadvantage is something that none of us can afford. I would say that there are many of you here today that are not capitalizing on your potential, because you do not own a personal computer. And for those of you who do, listen up. Your computer may not have the power, the capabilities, and the features needed to give the home user, the student, and the businessperson an advantage in today's world.

Self-Actualization

According to Maslow (1970), the self-actualization motive influences attitudes and behaviors only after all other needs are satisfied. And since these other needs are very rarely all satisfied, the time spent appealing to self-actualization might be better spent on appealing to other motives. And yet it seems that regardless of how satisfied or unsatisfied our other desires are, we all have a desire to self-actualize, to become what we feel we are fit for. If we see ourselves as poets, we must write poetry. If we see ourselves as singers, we must sing. If we see ourselves as teachers, we must teach. Even if we do not pursue these as occupations, we nevertheless have a desire to write poetry, to sing, or to teach—even if only in our imaginations. Appeals to self-actualization encourage listeners to strive for their highest ideals and are always welcomed.

Here, for example, William Jackson (1985) appeals to self-actualization in his speech on happiness in life:

> One of the greatest wastes of our national resources is the number of young people who never achieve their potential. If you think you can't, you won't. If you think you can, there is an excellent chance you will. The cost of excellence is discipline. The cost of mediocrity is disappointment. Only a mediocre person is always at his best. There should be two goals in your life; one is to get what you want in life, and the other is to enjoy your successes. Only the wisest people achieve the latter.

CRITICALLY EVALUATING MOTIVATIONAL APPEALS

As shown, motivational appeals are all around us. People use them on us and we use them on others. In dealing with motivational appeals, whether as speaker or listener, ask yourself these questions:

1. *Are the motivational appeals being used instead of argument and evidence?* Especially ask yourself, "Are they being used to the exclusion of argument and

evidence?" If the speaker (or the advertisement) seeks to arouse our emotions so we forget the fact that there is no evidence to support his or her position, then we need to ask why.

Some ethicists claim that motivational appeals that "short circuit" the reasoning process are unethical (Haiman 1958; Johannesen 1990). Such appeals seek to get you to believe or do something purely on the basis of your emotional response and in fact discourage logical analysis and evaluation.

Do you agree that motivational appeals that divert attention from critical thinking and evaluation are unethical?

2. *Are the appeals to high or low motives?* It is often relevant to ask if the motives being appealed to are basically high or low. For example, in asking for a charitable donation an organization may appeal to such high or positive motives as your altruism or your desire to help those less fortunate than you. Or it can play on your lower or more base motives, such as guilt and, to some extent, pity. It can present images of children playing and learning as a result of your contributions, or it can present images of children eating garbage and dying of starvation with the clear message that your lack of contributions are causing this situation to continue.

A speaker can seek to arouse feelings of love and peace but also feelings of hatred and war. Speeches at rallies often run the gamut from emphasizing the positive emotions of companionship, faith, and love to stressing the negative emotions of prejudice, hatred, and divisiveness.

UNIT IN BRIEF

Principles of motivation	■ Motives differ from one person to another ■ Motives are ordered, varying in intensity and generality ■ Motives interact, sometimes in concert and sometimes in conflict ■ Motives are culturally influenced
Popular motivational appeals	■ Altruism ■ Fear ■ Individuality and conformity ■ Power, control, and influence ■ Self-esteem and approval ■ Love and affiliation ■ Achievement ■ Financial gain ■ Status ■ Self-Actualization
Thinking critically about motivational appeals	■ Are the appeals used instead of or to divert attention from the absence of logical appeals? ■ Are the appeals made to our better selves?

PRACTICALLY SPEAKING

Short Speech Technique

Prepare and deliver a two-minute speech in which you:

1. analyze a current print or television advertisement for its motivational appeals
2. explain how fear is used in education
3. analyze the appeals used on a typical cover of an issue of the *National Enquirer*, the *Star*, or the *Globe*
4. use at least three motivational appeals to support any of the following propositions: (1) Buy this used car, (2) give to AIDS research, (3) make meditation a part of your day, (4) buy generic, (5) join a gym

22.1 Constructing Motivational Appeals

Select any combination of specific "Purposes" and "Audiences" that follow and develop a motivational appeal based on one or more of the motivational appeals discussed in this unit. After constructing your appeal, share the results of your labors with others, either in a small group or in the class as a whole. In your discussion you may wish to consider some or all of the following questions.

1. Why did you select the specific motivational appeal you did?
2. Why did you assume that this appeal would prove effective with the topic and the audience selected?
3. How effective do you think such an appeal would be if actually presented to such an audience?
4. Might the appeal backfire and stimulate resentment in the audience? If so, why might such resentment develop? What precautions might be taken by the speaker to prevent such resentment from developing?
5. What are the ethical implications of using this motivational appeal?
6. Where in the speech do you think you would place this appeal? In the beginning? Middle? End? Why?

Purposes	Audiences
1. Marijuana should (not) be made legal for all those over 18 years of age	1. Senior citizens of Metropolis
2. Cigarette smoking should (not) be banned in all public places	2. Senior Club of DeWitt Clinton High School
3. Capital punishment should (not) be law in all states	3. Small Business Operators Club of Accord
4. Social security benefits should be increased (decreased) by at least one-third	4. American Society of Young Dentists

Purposes	Audiences
5. Retirement should (not) be mandatory at age 65 for all government employees	5. Council for Better Housing
6. Police personnel should (not) be permitted to strike	6. Veterans of Vietnam
7. National health insurance should (not) be instituted	7. Los Angeles Society of Interior Designers
8. Athletic scholarships should (not) be abolished	8. Catholic Women's Council
9. Domestic partnerships should (not) be accorded the same rights and privileges as marriages	9. National Council of African American Artists
10. Required courses in college should (not) be abolished	10. Parent-Teacher Association of New Orleans Elementary Schools
11. Teachers should (not) be paid according to performance rather than (but according to) seniority, degrees earned, or publications	11. Midwestern Council of Physical Education Instructors
12. Divorce should (not) be granted immediately when the parties request it	12. Society for the Rehabilitation of Ex-Offenders

Are any of your credibility judgments culture-related? That is, might you attribute high or low credibility ratings to people, products, or institutions because of their culture or the culture in which they were developed?

Are any of your credibility judgments gender-related? That is, do you attribute higher credibility to women on some issues and to men on others?

the most important factor might be the teacher's goodness or morality or perhaps the reputation of his or her family.

At the same time, each culture may define each of the characteristics of credibility differently. For example, "character" may to some mean following the rules of a specific religion and to others following one's individual conscience. The Koran, the Old Testament, and the New Testament will all have very different levels of credibility ascribed to them depending on the religious beliefs of the audience. And this will be true even when all three religious books say essentially the same thing.

Similarly, members of different cultures may perceive the credibility of the various media very differently. For example, members of a repressive society in which the government controls television news may come to attribute little credibility to such broadcasts. After all, these persons might reason, television news is simply what the government wants us to know. This may be hard to understand or even to recognize by someone raised in the United States, for example, where the media are free of such political control.

The recommendations that follow are based largely on persuasion research conducted in the United States. When dealing with multicultural audiences, adjust your appeals accordingly. A good example of this need for cultural adjustment is seen in the first recommendation made below, namely, to tell listeners of your competence. The recommendation is a generally good one for most audiences you'll encounter in the United States. In some cultures, however, to stress your own competence or that of your corporation may be

---

FOCUS **O**N

How We Form Credibility Impressions

We form a credibility impression of a speaker on the basis of two sources of information, as shown in the accompanying figure.

First, we assess the reputation of the speaker as we know it; this is initial, or what theorists call extrinsic, credibility. Second, we evaluate how that reputation is confirmed or refuted by what the speaker says and does during the speech. This is derived, or intrinsic, credibility. In other words, we combine what we know about the speaker's reputation with the more immediate information we get from present interactions. Information from these two sources—reputation and present encounters—interacts, and the audience forms some collective final assessment of credibility.

How we form credibility impressions.

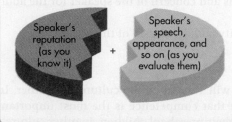

Speaker's reputation (as you know it) + Speaker's speech, appearance, and so on (as you evaluate them) = Final assessment of speaker's credibility (to you)

taken to mean that your audience members are inferior or that their corporations are not as good as yours. In other cultures, if you don't stress your competence your listeners may assume it's because you don't have any.

Before reading any further about credibility, you may wish to take the self-test "How Credible Are You?"

Self Test

How Credible Are You?

This test is designed to stimulate you to focus on yourself as a credible spokesperson. Respond to each of the following phrases as you think members of this class (your audience) see you when you deliver a public speech. Use the following scale:

7 = Very true
6 = Quite true
5 = Fairly true
4 = Neither true nor untrue
3 = Fairly untrue
2 = Quite untrue
1 = Very untrue

___ 1. Knowledgeable about the subject matter
___ 2. Experienced
___ 3. Confident
___ 4. Informed about broader related issues
___ 5. Fair in the presentation of material (evidence and argument)
___ 6. Concerned with the audience's needs
___ 7. Consistent over time on the issues addressed in the speech
___ 8. Similar to the audience in attitudes and values
___ 9. Positive rather than negative
___10. Assertive in personal style
___11. Enthusiastic about the topic and in general
___12. Active rather than passive

Thinking Critically About Your Credibility

The test focuses on the three qualities of credibility—competence, character, and charisma—and is based on a large body of research (for example, McCroskey 1982; Riggio 1987). Items 1–4 refer to your perceived competence: How competent or capable does the audience see you when you give a public speech? Items 5–8 refer to your perceived character: Does the audience see you as a person of good and moral character? Items 9–12 refer to your perceived charisma: Does the audience see you as dynamic and active rather than as static and passive? You may wish to consider what specific steps you can take to change any audience perception with which you may be unhappy.

What credibility do you attribute to the president of the United States? To the president of your college?

COMPETENCE

What aspects of your competence would you stress if you were giving a speech on how to succeed in college to a group of high school seniors? A speech on managing your time more effectively? A speech on how to make friends?

On a ten-point scale (10 being the highest), how would members of your class evaluate the competence of the following people speaking on the subjects indicated: Cher (contemporary music), Helen Gurley Brown (aging), and Al Gore (the environment)? What are your reasons?

Competence refers to the knowledge and expertise a speaker is thought to have. The more knowledge and expertise the audience sees you as having, the more likely the audience will be to believe you. For example, you are likely to believe a teacher or doctor to the extent that you think he or she is knowledgeable about the subject.

Competence is logically subject-specific. Usually, competence is limited to one specific field. A person may be competent in one subject and totally incompetent in another. Often, however, we do not make the distinction between areas of competence and incompetence; thus, we may perceive a person we think is competent in politics as competent in general. We will therefore perceive this person as credible in many fields. We refer to this as the halo effect—a phenomenon that occurs when listeners generalize their perception of competence to all areas. Listeners see the speaker's competence as a general trait of the individual.

This halo effect also has a counterpart—the reverse halo. Here the person, seen as incompetent in, say, mathematics, is perceived to be similarly incompe-

"My heartfelt thanks to Kitty Lundell for writing my speeches, and to Keith Donegan for delivering them."

Drawing by Weber; © 1992 The New Yorker Magazine, Inc.

How would you evaluate the competence of consumer advocate Ralph Nader speaking on, say, the reform of the judicial system? The legality of prostitution? Trade policy with countries that violate human rights? Prescription prices? Health warning labels on food products?

tent in most other areas as well. As a critic of public speaking, be particularly sensitive to competence being subject-specific. Be sensitive to both the halo effect and the reverse halo effect.

Demonstrate your competence to your audience. You want your audience to see you as knowledgeable and expert. Here are some methods you can use.

Tell Listeners of Your Competence

Let the audience know of your special experience or training that qualifies you to speak on this specific topic. If you are speaking on communal living and you have lived on a commune yourself, then indicate this in your speech. Tell the audience of your unique and personal experiences when these contribute to your credibility. Here, for example, G. J. Tankersley (1984) establishes his knowledge concerning educational issues:

> I've probably had more occasions than many other businessmen to consider these subjects over the years. This is largely because I've spent a good part of my own "extracurricular" time on education.
>
> Currently, I'm co-chairman of a drive to raise funds for Auburn University, which is my alma mater. I'm a member of the Business–Higher Education Forum, a group of about 80 business leaders and college presidents who concern themselves with some of the issues I'm going to discuss today. And I've been working at the University of Pittsburgh, where I'm a Vice Chairman of the Board of Trustees and Chairman of the Board of Visitors at the Business School.

Also, I used to teach. Just after World War II and before I started my career in the gas business, I taught thermodynamics for four years at Auburn's Engineering School.

Cite a Variety of Research Sources

Make it clear to your audience that you have thoroughly researched your topic. Do this by mentioning some of the books you have read, the persons you have interviewed, the articles you have consulted. Weave these mentions throughout your speech. Don't bunch them together at one time.

Look again at Jay Lane's speech on dust (Unit 2). Note that he cites several books, articles, and interviews. Because of these citations—neatly woven into the speech—we get the impression Lane is knowledgeable about the topic and has thoroughly researched it.

Stress the Competencies of Your Sources

If your audience is not aware of them, then emphasize the particular competencies of your sources. For example, saying simply, "Senator Smith thinks . . ." does nothing to establish the senator's credibility. Instead, consider saying something like:

> *Senator Smith, who headed the Finance Committee for three years and was formerly professor of economics at MIT, thinks . . .*
> *Senator Smith, who has fought in the last two wars and who knows firsthand what war is, has argued that . . .*

In this way it becomes clear to the audience that you have chosen your sources carefully and have done so with a view toward providing the most authoritative sources possible.

Demonstrate Confidence

If you followed the nine steps for preparing a public speech, you probably have considerable confidence in your speech. Communicate that confidence to the audience. Let them know you are comfortable and at ease speaking to them. If, for example, you are using visual aids, become so familiar with them that you know exactly what order they are in and exactly when in your presentation you will use each.

Avoid Apologizing

Do not needlessly call attention to your inadequacies as a spokesperson or to any gaps in your knowledge. No one can know everything. Your audience does not expect you to be the exception. Stress your competencies, not your inadequacies. Avoid such statements as:

> *I know I'm no expert in toxic waste, but . . .*

TIPS

From Professional Speakers

A businessperson in New York said that two of his contacts in Southeast Asia dropped him and his company before negotiations were barely warm. To this day, he's not completely sure why, but he now suspects that when he tried to convey his credentials and the qualifications of his company to supply the foreign firm with tools, his message came across as "Our companies are better than your companies." The wrong slant or one sentence too many can turn an honest attempt to convey information into unintentionally obnoxious boasting.

Mary A. DeVries, international communication expert. *Internationally Yours: Writing and Communicating Successfully in Today's Global Marketplace* (Boston: Houghton Mifflin, 1994), p. 193.

I really should have looked into this more carefully, but time was short. But I did, though, read . . .

I didn't read the opposing arguments, because I don't believe they can possibly be right.

CHARACTER

We perceive a speaker as credible if we perceive that speaker as having high moral character. Here our concern is with the individual's honesty and basic nature—we want to know if we can trust that person. We believe a speaker we can trust. An individual's motives or intentions are particularly important in judging character. When the audience perceives your intentions as good for them (rather than for your personal gain), they will think you credible and they will believe you.

As a speaker, demonstrate those qualities of character that will increase your credibility. Here are some suggestions for demonstrating character.

On a ten-point scale (10 being the highest), how would members of your class evaluate the character of the following people speaking on the subjects indicated: Newt Gingrich (welfare reform), Shirley MacLaine (the afterlife), and Bill Clinton (health care reform)? What are your reasons?

Stress Similarities

Emphasize the ways in which you are similar to your audience, particularly in beliefs, attitudes, values, and goals. We perceive as believable people who are like ourselves, especially in basic values. The more similar people are to ourselves, the more likely we are to perceive them as credible.

In this first example, Lee Teng-Hui (1995, p. 611), president of the Republic of China, stresses his similarity with the audience (primarily Cornell University students and staff) through his experiences at Cornell:

> *It has been a long and challenging journey, with many bumps in the road, yet my wife and I are indeed very happy to return to this beloved campus.*
>
> *This trip has allowed both of us to relive our dearest Cornell experiences. The long, exhausting evenings in the libraries, the soothing and reflective hours at church, the hurried shuttling between classrooms, the evening strolls, hand in hand—so many memories of the past have come to mind, filling my heart with joy and gratitude.*

What aspects of your character would you stress to an audience of senior citizens in a speech on the need for increased health care for pregnant teenagers?

In this second example, occurring later in the speech, President Teng-Hui (1995, p. 612) stresses similarities in values:

> *Today, the institutions of democracy are in place in the Republic of China; human rights are respected and protected to a very high degree. Democracy is thriving in my country. No speech or act allowed by law will be subject to any restriction or interference. Different and opposing views are heard every day in the news media, including harsh criticism of the President. The freedom of speech enjoyed by our people is in no way different from that enjoyed by people in the United States.*

Stress Fairness

If you are delivering a persuasive speech, stress that you have examined both sides of the issue (if indeed you have). If you are presenting both sides, make it clear that your presentation is accurate and fair. Be particularly careful not to omit any argument the audience may already have thought of—this is a sure sign that your presentation is not fair and balanced. Tell the audience you would not advocate a position did you not base it on a fair evaluation of the issues.

Demonstrate Long-Term Consistency

We feel more comfortable putting our trust in someone who has been consistent over time. We become leery of persons who flit from one issue to another or from one team to another. If you have been in favor of XYZ for the last three years, then tell the audience. For example:

> *I began working as a volunteer for the Drug Hotline when I first entered college, four years ago. Now that I'm ready to graduate, I want to tell you about the work the hotline is doing and why you should get involved in one of the most important projects I have ever worked on.*

Stress Concern for the Audience

Make it clear to the audience that you are interested in their welfare rather than seeking self-gain. If the audience feels that you are "out for yourself," they will justifiably downgrade your credibility. Make it clear that the audience's interests are foremost in your mind.

Stress Concern for Enduring Values

Can you cite any recent examples in which politicians sought to establish their character? What strategies did they use?

We view speakers who are concerned with small and insignificant issues as less credible than speakers who demonstrate a concern for lasting truths and general principles. Thus, make it clear to the audience that your position—your thesis—is related to higher-order values; show them exactly how this is true.

Notice in this example how John E. Jacob (1995, pp. 572–573), executive vice-president and chief communications officer of Anheuser-Busch Companies, stresses his concern for such enduring values as doing good for others and for yourself.

> *I am not asking you to live a life of selfless service, although some of you may choose to do so. I am not asking you to deny yourself the benefits of advancement in your chosen career. I am not urging you to take a vow of poverty.*
>
> *But I am asking you to recognize that dollars and cents are just one measure of an individual's worth, and not a very reliable one at that. Rather, the true test is what a person does for their community and for mankind.*
>
> *You can make your contribution in the board room . . . or the class room . . . or the court room. You can help make the world a better place as an engineer . . . as a health care professional . . . as an artist . . . or in any other of a wide range of fields. But in making the world a better place, you*

are also making yourself a better person. And that is one lesson you must never forget, if you are to be true to the idealism that has characterized Benedict College throughout its history.

CHARISMA

Charisma is a combination of the speaker's personality and dynamism as seen by the audience. We perceive as credible or believable speakers we like rather than speakers we do not like. We perceive as credible speakers who are friendly and pleasant rather than aloof and reserved. Similarly, we favor the dynamic speaker over the hesitant, nonassertive speaker. We perceive the shy, introverted, softspoken individual as less credible than the extroverted, forceful individual. The great leaders in history have been dynamic people. Perhaps we feel that the dynamic speaker is open and honest in presenting herself or himself. The shy, introverted individual may be seen as hiding something. As speakers, we can do much to increase our charisma and hence our perceived credibility.

Demonstrate a Positive Outlook

Show the audience that you have a positive orientation to the public speaking situation and to the entire speaker-audience encounter. We see positive and forward-looking people as more credible than we see negative and backward-looking people. Stress your pleasure at addressing the audience. Stress hope rather than despair; stress happiness rather than sadness. Note how Donald Ed Engen (1985) demonstrates a positive orientation in the following excerpt:

On a ten-point scale (10 being the highest), how would members of your class evaluate the charisma of the following people speaking on the subjects indicated: Coretta Scott King (civil rights), Elizabeth Taylor (AIDS research), and Boris Yeltsin (democratic reform)? What are your reasons?

Who do you feel are the most charismatic speakers today? What qualities do these speakers have that other speakers lack?

Sometimes . . . you have to work at uncovering why the material is important to you. Here are two helpful rules:

1. Learn everything you can about your subject. The more you know about it, the more excited and passionate you'll become.
2. As you learn, ask yourself, "How does this relate to me?" "Do I care?" "What does this mean to me?" For example: "The disease of muscular dystrophy, which I am discussing with this group, could it strike my little girl?" Or, "The beautiful car I am presenting to this customer, would it make my own family happy?"

Lilyan Wilder, communication consultant and coach. *Talk Your Way to Success* (New York: Simon & Schuster/Fireside, 1986), p. 60.

How would you stress your charisma to an audience of sports fans in a speech on supporting the Olympics?

Which of these three credibility characteristics would most influence you in buying a new car? In choosing a doctor? In selecting a graduate school? In choosing a relationship partner? Why?

This annual fly-in is truly one of the greatest events in aviation. It is a true reflection of the energy, excitement, sense of adventure, and triumph of technology in our society. As many of you know, I was an active member of EAA until I became FAA administrator.

I wouldn't miss the opportunity to return to Oshkosh each summer. Paul Poberezny, his wife, Audrey, and his son, Tom, make all of us feel at home here. EAA is truly a strong membership organization, with its many members sustaining aviation through both their activities and the ideas that they promote with aviation. As FAA administrator, I am grateful that I can count on EAA members who want to keep the fun and adventure in flying.

Act Assertively

Show the audience that you are a person who will stand up for your rights. Show them that you will not back off simply because the odds may be against you or because you are outnumbered.

Demonstrate Enthusiasm

The lethargic speaker, the speaker who somehow plods through the speech, is the very opposite of the charismatic speaker. Try viewing a film of Martin Luther King, Jr., or Billy Graham speaking—they are totally absorbed with the speech and with the audience. They are excellent examples of the enthusiasm that makes speakers charismatic. Lilyan Wilder, in the accompanying TIPS, provides some useful suggestions for developing this needed enthusiasm.

Be Emphatic

Use language that is emphatic rather than colorless and indecisive. Use gestures that are clear and decisive rather than random and hesitant. Demonstrate a firm commitment to the position you are advocating; the audience will be much more likely to agree with a speaker who believes firmly in the thesis of the speech.

Here is an excerpt from one of the most famous of all speeches designed to establish credibility, Richard Nixon's "Checkers" speech. How effectively does Nixon establish his credibility?

Then, in 1942, I went into the service. Let me say that my service record was not a particularly unusual one. I went to the South Pacific. I guess I'm entitled to a couple of battle stars. I got a couple of letters of commendation.

But I was just there when the bombs were falling. And then I returned to the United States, and in 1946 I ran for Congress.

When we came out of the war, Pat and I—Pat during the war had worked as a stenographer, and in a bank, and as an economist for a government agency, and when we came out, the total of our savings, from both my law practice, her teaching, and all the time I was in the war, the total for that entire period was just a little less than $10,000—every cent of that, incidentally, was in government bonds—well, that's where we start, when I got into politics.

GENERAL GUIDELINES

In addition to these specific suggestions for projecting competence, character, and charisma, here are four general guidelines for becoming a more credible speaker.

Develop Credibility Characteristics

Develop or strengthen the characteristics of competence, character, and charisma as a person as well as a speaker. This is easy to say but may be extremely difficult to put into practice; nevertheless, it is important to have these goals. The actual development of these qualities is the best insurance to make you credible in public speaking situations.

Demonstrate Credibility

Whether you introduce yourself or someone else does it, it is helpful to legitimize yourself to the audience, especially in the introduction. If you have a broad knowledge of the topic or firsthand experience, tell the audience as early as possible. For example, a speaker might say something like this:

> *I've just returned to the States after spending two years in the Peace Corps. I worked in Guatemala for 10 months and in Chile for 14 months. I taught the people about farming, irrigation, and crop rotation. In just the short time I was in these places, we managed to increase the vegetable crops by more than 300 percent. I want to apply some of that same information we used in Guatemala and Chile to the problems you are now facing on your own farms.*

If there is a formal introduction to your speech, you may have references integrated into this introduction to help establish your credibility. When teachers introduce themselves to their classes, they often establish their credibility. They might, for example, refer to their degrees, where they studied, or some research project on which they are working. At first glance this may seem immodest, but as long as the references are true, such credibility-establishing references allow the audience to better appreciate the information the teacher will communicate.

Use Varied Methods to Establish Credibility

Do not rely on the same few methods to build your credibility. Use a number of different methods. Be sure to consider all three components of credibility: competence, character, and charisma.

An excerpt from Senator Edward Kennedy's "Chappaquiddick" speech follows. How effectively does Kennedy establish his general credibility?

> *The people of this state, the state which sent John Quincy Adams and Daniel Webster and Charles Sumner and Henry Cabot Lodge and John Kennedy to the United State Senate, are entitled to representation in that*

Write a brief introduction (approximately one minute in length, or about 130 to 150 words) about yourself for someone else to use in introducing you and your next speech. What characteristics of credibility would you want stressed? How could this be done most effectively?

body by men who inspire their utmost confidence. For this reason, I would understand full well why some might think it right for me to resign. For me this will be a difficult decision to make.

It has been seven years since my first election to the Senate. You and I share many memories—some of them have been glorious, some have been very sad. The opportunity to work with you and serve Massachusetts has made my life worthwhile.

And so I ask you tonight, People of Massachusetts, to think this through with me. In facing this decision, I seek your advice and opinion. In making it, I seek your prayers. For this is a decision that I will have finally to make on my own.

CRITICALLY EVALUATING CREDIBILITY APPEALS

In using and in listening to credibility appeals, critically evaluate them. Here are three questions that will be helpful to ask:

1. *Is the dimension of credibility used relevant to the issue at hand?* For example, is the politician's family (nice as they may be) relevant to his or her position on gun control, social security, or immigration? Is the person's former military service or lack of it relevant to the issue being discussed?

2. *Are credibility appeals being used instead of argument and evidence?* Just as motivational appeals can be used instead of or to divert attention from logical reasons and evidence, so too can credibility appeals. You can see this regularly in the political debates and accusations and defenses that appear regularly in the news. Too frequently, the argument revolves around issues of credibility that often—though not always—are irrelevant to the issues.

3. *Are the credibility appeals true?* For example, should the actor who, dressed as a dentist in a dentist's office environment, advertises toothpaste be accorded credibility? Do you unconsciously associate credibility with the uniform? Is the advertiser justified in conveying this misleading image of the actor?

Here, for example, is an excerpt from Senator Bob Dole's (1995, p. 450) speech announcing his candidacy for the presidency of the United States. How effectively does Dole establish his competency, character, and charisma?

When I set off to war it was to defend a community of values unique in all the world. I came back sustained by the love and generosity of friends and neighbors who renewed my sense of life's responsibilities. Over the years they have given me opportunities for service which I can never hope to repay.

Because they restored my spirit in a time of trial I have dedicated myself to restoring the spirit of America. And so today, tempered by adversity, seasoned by experience, mindful of the world as it is—yet confident it can be made better—I have come home to Kansas with a grateful heart to declare that I am a candidate for the Presidency of the United States.

Of logical, motivational, and credibility appeals, which win political elections? Which type of advertising wins consumers?

UNIT IN BRIEF

Definitions of credibility	■ Credibility: the audience's perception of the speaker's believability ■ Extrinsic credibility: the speaker's reputation as seen by the audience ■ Derived, or intrinsic, credibility: the audience's impression derived from the speaker's speech
Components of credibility	■ **Competence**: the knowledge and expertise the speaker is thought to possess ■ **Character**: the honesty and integrity the speaker is seen to possess ■ **Charisma**: the personality and dynamism the speaker is seen to have
Critically evaluating credibility appeals	■ Is the appeal relevant? ■ Are credibility appeals used to divert attention from the argument and evidence? ■ Are the credibility appeals true?

PRACTICALLY SPEAKING

Short Speech Technique

Prepare and deliver a two-minute speech in which you:

1. explain why you think a particular person is credible or not credible
2. explain the credibility of a television personality such as Oprah Winfrey, Geraldo Rivera, Phil Donahue, Montel Williams, Sally Jesse Raphael, Jerry Springer, Ricki Lake, Richard Bey, Rolanda Watts, Regis Philbin, or Cathy Lee Gifford
3. explain why you think a particular person would be a great spokesperson for a particular product—consider playing the role of the advertising executive trying to convince your client to hire your choice for product spokesperson
4. explain how credibility operates in (a) dating, (b) meeting your partner's family, (c) teaching, (d) interviewing for a job, or (e) sales

23.1   Comparative Credibility Judgments

Credibility judgments are made both absolutely and comparatively. Thus, for example, you may judge the credibility of a witness at a trial, a newspaper reviewer, or a local religious leader on the basis of some absolute standards you may have. But even in making this absolute judgment, you are probably also comparing this person with similar others and are probably positioning this person somewhere on a scale along with these others. Similarly, you may make a comparison credibility judgment of the three candidates running for mayor and vote for the one to whom you attribute the highest credibility. So, your judgment for Senator Smith is made not just absolutely but also in comparison with the others in the race.

This exercise emphasizes the concept of comparative credibility judgments and asks you to rank-order the people, roles, and institutions listed below; use 3 for the highest credibility and 1 for the lowest.

After completing these ratings, consider, for example:

- What reasons did you use in constructing your rankings? What qualities of credibility did you consider in your rankings?
- Do any of your rankings illustrate the notion that credibility depends on the subject matter?
- Are there certain qualities that make you believe someone regardless of the subject matter?
- Which of the three major characteristics of credibility—competence, character, charisma—would you consider the most and the least important for (a) a family physician, (b) a college professor, (c) a divorce lawyer, (d) a romantic-life partner, (e) a best friend?
- Are any of your credibility judgments gender- or culture-related? That is, might you attribute high or low credibility ratings to people, products, or institutions because of their gender or culture?

1. Talk-show hosts on cultural differences

_____ Oprah Winfrey

_____ Montel Williams

_____ Sally Jesse Raphael

2. Talk-show hosts on men's reluctance to express themselves

_____ Montel Williams

_____ Cathy Lee Gifford

_____ Geraldo Rivera

3. Financial news periodicals

_____ *Money* magazine

_____ *Wall Street Journal*

_____ *Barron's*

4. Newscasters

_____ Diane Sawyer

_____ Dan Rather

_____ Peter Jennings

5. U.S. politicians on the role of the politician in today's world

_____ Bill Clinton

_____ Newt Gingrich

_____ Jesse Jackson

6. Speaker on leading a happy life

_____ professor

_____ physician

_____ lawyer

7. Institutions on community service

_____ bank

_____ insurance company

_____ hospital corporation

8. Authors of exercise books on the proper way to exercise

_____ Richard Simmons

_____ Jane Fonda

_____ Arnold Schwarzenegger

9. Sources of accurate and up-to-date information on film and television

_____ _Entertainment Tonight_

_____ _National Enquirer_

_____ _People Magazine_

10. Scholar on the meaning of life

_____ philosopher

_____ minister/priest/rabbi

_____ scientist

UNIT 24

The Special Occasion Speech

Unit Objectives

After completing this unit, you should be able to:

1. Explain the speech of introduction, the principles to follow and the pitfalls to avoid

2. Explain the speech of presentation or acceptance, the principles to follow and the pitfalls to avoid

3. Explain the speech to secure goodwill, the principles to follow and the pitfalls to avoid

4. Explain the speech of tribute, the principles to follow and the pitfalls to avoid

When you give a "special occasion" or "ceremonial" speech, you are giving a speech that is part information and part persuasion. These special occasion speeches are reviewed separately because their purposes are a bit more limited in scope. We discuss four special occasion speeches: (1) the speech of introduction, (2) the speech of presentation or acceptance, (3) the speech designed to create goodwill, and (4) the speech of tribute.

THE SPEECH OF INTRODUCTION

The speech of introduction is usually designed to introduce another speaker or to introduce a general topic area and a series of speakers. Often, for example, before a speaker addresses an audience, another speaker sets the stage by introducing both the speaker and the topic. At conventions where a series of speakers address an audience, a speech of introduction might introduce the general topic on which the speakers will focus and perhaps provide connecting links among the several presentations.

In giving a speech of introduction, your main purpose is to gain the attention and arouse the interest of the audience. Your speech should pave the way for favorable and attentive listening. It should seek to create an atmosphere conducive to achieving the particular speech purpose. The speech of introduction is basically informative and follows the general patterns already laid down for the informative speech. The main difference is that instead of discussing a topic's issues, you would discuss who the speaker is and what the speaker will talk about. In your speeches of introduction, follow these general principles.

Have you ever had an opportunity to give a special occasion speech? If so, how did it go?

Speeches at graduation are often of the "inspirational" type. What principles would you suggest the inspirational speaker follow? What pitfalls would you suggest this speaker avoid?

Establish the Significance of the Speech

Your major concern in introducing another speaker is to establish the importance of the speech for this specific audience. In this way you focus the audience's attention and interest on the main speaker.

Establish Relevant Connections

Establish a connection or relationship among the essential elements in the public speaking act. At a minimum, draw connections among the speaker, the topic, and the audience. Answer the implicit questions of the audience: Why should we listen to this speaker on this topic? Why is this speaker appropriate to speak on this topic? What do this speaker and this speech topic have to do with us, the audience?

If you can answer such questions satisfactorily, you will have done your job of establishing a ready and receptive audience for the speaker.

Stress the Speaker's Credibility

Establish the speaker's credibility. The speech of introduction is the ideal opportunity to present those accomplishments of the speaker that the speaker could not mention with modesty. Review the ways of establishing credibility (Unit 23) for some useful suggestions. The most general guideline is to try to answer the audience's question, What is there about this speaker that has earned her or him the right to speak on this topic, to this audience? In answering this question, you will inevitably establish the speaker's credibility.

Be Consistent with the Main Speech

Make your speech of introduction consistent in style and manner with the major speech. To introduce a speaker on terminal diseases in a humorous and flippant style would clearly be inappropriate. Conversely, to introduce a humorist in a somber and formal style would be equally inappropriate.

In judging style and manner, predict the tone the main speech will take. Just as you answer an invitation with the same degree of formality with which it is extended, so too would you introduce a speaker with the same degree of formality that will prevail during the actual speech. Otherwise, the speaker will have to counteract an inappropriate atmosphere created by the speech of introduction.

Be Brief

Remember that the audience has come to hear the main speaker, so be brief. In actual practice, speeches of introduction vary considerably in length—from "Ladies and gentlemen, the president" to pages and pages. You will have to judge how long is long enough. If the main speech is to be brief—say, 10 or 20 minutes—your speech of introduction should be no longer than 1 or 2 minutes. If, on the other hand, the main speech is to be an hour long, then your introduction might last 5 or 10 minutes or even longer. In estimating length, visualize yourself as a member of the audience listening to your own speech of introduction. How much would you want to hear?

What principles of the speech of introduction do talk-show hosts use when they introduce their guests? What would you like to hear them include more of?

Don't Cover the Speaker's Topic

Don't cover the substance of the topic or what the speaker will discuss. Clever stories, jokes, startling statistics, or historical analogies, which are often effective in speeches of introduction, will prove a liability if the guest speaker intended to use this same material. It is not uncommon to find a speaker suddenly lacking an introduction or a conclusion because the material was used in the speech of introduction. If you have any doubts, check with the speaker well in advance of the actual speech. In this way you will avoid duplicating the material and embarrassing the speaker and yourself.

Don't Oversell the Speaker

Speakers giving introductions have a tendency to oversell the guest speaker, the topic, or both. The speech of introduction should be complimentary but should not create an image impossible to live up to. To say, for example, that "Morso Osrom is not only the world's greatest living expert on baldness but a most fascinating, interesting, and humorous speaker as well" only adds difficulties to the speaker's task. It would be better to let the speaker demonstrate his or her own communicative abilities.

The same is true for the topic. To say that "This is the most important topic today" or "Without the information given here, we are sure to die paupers" will only encumber the speaker by setting unrealistic expectations for the audience.

What would an ideal speech of introduction sound like if it were introducing you to the class for your next speech?

Sample Speeches of Introduction

Here, for example, is the introductory speech, transcribed from television, given by Hal Bruno at the vice-presidential debates, October 13, 1992.

> *Good evening from Atlanta and welcome to the Vice-Presidential Debates, sponsored by the Nonpartisan Commission on Presidential Debates. It's being held here in the Theatre for the Arts on the campus of Georgia Tech. I'm Hal Bruno from ABC News and I'm going to be moderating tonight's debate.*
>
> *The participants are Republican Vice-President Dan Quayle, Democratic Senator Al Gore, and Retired Vice-Admiral James Stockdale, who is the Vice-Presidential nominee for independent candidate Ross Perot.*
>
> *Now, the ground rules for tonight's debate. Each candidate will have two minutes for an opening statement. I will then present the issues to be discussed. For each topic the candidates will have a minute and fifteen seconds to respond. Then this will be followed by a five-minute discussion period in which they can ask questions of each other if they so choose.*
>
> *Now, the order of response has been determined by a drawing and we'll rotate with each topic. At the end of the debate, each candidate will have two minutes for a closing statement. Our radio and TV audience should know that the candidates were given an equal allocation of auditorium seats for their supporters, so I'd like to ask the audience here in the theater to please refrain from applause or any partisan demonstration once the debate is under way because it takes time away from the candidates.*
>
> *So, with that plea from your moderator, let's get started and we'll turn first to Senator Gore for his opening statement.*

Most introductory speeches will be similar to that given above and will generally follow the rules already noted. Next, however, is an introductory speech of a very different type. In this speech Michael Greene, president of the National Academy of Recording Arts and Sciences, seeks not to introduce another speaker but rather to set the activities within a context. He seeks to put the proceedings—in this case the Grammy music awards—into a social perspective. The speech is one of "introduction" because it introduces a theme or point of view that is to pervade the entire award presentation. At the same time, the speech puts the academy's position on funding for the arts on record and gives this position extremely wide circulation. The speech is, however, primarily one of persuasion and seeks to strengthen the attitudes and beliefs of the immediate audience and to move the more remote audience (the viewers) to action.

Good evening. I'm pleased to welcome all of you, more than a billion viewers in 167 countries, to the 37th Annual Grammy Awards. The extraordinary artists and recordings we pay tribute to here tonight remind us of music's powerful influence in our lives. Music and the arts are a healing, therapeutic force that lifts our spirits and unites us as a culture.

But the fact is, our culture is at serious risk. Viewers around the world may not be aware that the funding necessary to ensure the survival of our proud legacy of jazz, blues and virtually all other forms of indigenous American music is being threatened. Our National Endowment for the Arts could have its budget slashed by forty percent next year, another forty percent the year after, finally "zeroed out" the year after that. And folks, National Public Radio and PBS will surely be next. We are here tonight on the brink of becoming the only industrialized nation in the world with no federal support for the arts.

THEY SAY IT'S A MATTER OF MONEY. Yet it costs taxpayers about a dollar a year to keep jazz, blues, folk, and classical music on the public radio airwaves, and for the Arts Endowment to bring theater, dance and music to communities across America.

Is it really about money? You know, if the Pentagon tried to operate on the Arts Endowment's annual budget, they'd have to shut down in just five hours.

The arts are an economic plus—second only to aerospace as our most lucrative national export. Despite all this, our Speaker of the House has yet to agree to meet with the chairman of the Arts Endowment. It's hard to imagine either the Secretary of Commerce or Defense being treated with such total disregard.

Since the Arts and Humanities Endowments were founded with bi-partisan support thirty years ago, they have enjoyed the support of every President, Republican or Democrat. Our leaders knew that politicizing America's arts agenda would cripple the accomplishments that make America a leading culture force.

We MUST NOT allow the arts to be politicized, privatized, commercialized, sanitized, neutralized or "zeroed out."

Artists by their very nature stretch the limits. Controversy is both part of the price and the VALUE of artistic freedom. Lest we forget, one of the

Endowment's most controversial grants was the funding of the Vietnam Veterans Memorial in Washington, D.C. Today it is the most heralded and visited tourist attraction in our nation's capital.

To see to it that the arts retain their proper place within our society, grab a pencil and I'll tell you what you can do.

On Tuesday, March 14, a campaign of unprecedented scope will be waged; It's called the National Call in Day for Arts and Culture. This campaign begins tonight by your calling 1-800-225-2007 for options that will see to it that your congressional representatives know that you support the continued funding for these vital programs.

When Winston Churchill was asked during World War II to cut the British Arts Council Budget, he didn't waste words. "Hell no," said Churchill, "what have we been fighting for?"

Folks, without arts education and the Arts Endowment, music and the love of it will no longer be a cultural treasure, but more a privilege tied to personal, family and class economics.

Lets join together tonight in a triumphant effort to keep the arts alive. Our very culture depends on it. Thank you.

THE SPEECH OF PRESENTATION OR ACCEPTANCE

We consider speeches of presentation and speeches of acceptance together because they frequently occur together and because the same general principles govern both types of speeches.

In a speech of presentation, you would seek to (1) place the award or honor in some kind of context and (2) give the award an extra air of dignity or status. A speech of presentation may focus on rewarding a colleague for an important accomplishment (Teacher of the Year) or recognizing a particularly impressive performance (Academy Award winner). It may honor an employee's service to a company or a student's outstanding grades or athletic abilities.

Before reading the suggestions, what do you think makes a good speech of presentation or acceptance?

The speech of acceptance is the counterpart to this honoring ceremony. Here the recipient accepts the award and also attempts to place it in some kind of context. At times the presentation and the acceptance speeches are rather informal and amount to a simple "You really deserve this" and an equally simple and direct "Thank you." At other times—as, for example, in the presentation and acceptance of a Nobel Prize—the speeches are formal and prepared in great detail and with great care. Such speeches are frequently reprinted in newspapers throughout the world.

Somewhere between these two extremes lies the average speech of presentation and acceptance. In your speeches of presentation, follow these two principles.

State the Reason for the Presentation

As the presenter, make clear why this particular award is being given to this particular person. If a scholarship is being awarded for the best athlete of the year, then say so. If a gold watch is being awarded for 30 years of faithful service, say this.

What would you say if you were presenting the Teacher of the Year Award?

State the Importance of the Award

The audience (as well as the group authorizing or sponsoring the award) will no doubt want to hear something about the importance of the award. You can state this in a number of different ways. For example, you might refer to the previous recipients (assuming they are well known to the audience), the status of the award (assuming that it is a prestigious award), or its influence on previous recipients.

A Sample Speech of Presentation

Here is a particularly effective speech of presentation given by Michael Greene, immediately after he gave the introductory speech reprinted earlier. Here Greene presents five Life Achievement and Trustees Awards, and in a relatively short speech succeeds in highlighting the careers and contributions of five outstanding recording artists.*

> *Just as the Grammy Awards represent the best in today's music, our Life Achievement and Trustees Awards recognize individuals whose careers and cumulative contributions have had a profound effect on our culture. This year's five recipients, through their artistry and vision, have both enriched and advanced the recording medium.*
>
> *Our first recipient is Barbra Streisand. She recorded her first album in 1962, and since then 50 albums have borne her artistic stamp, earning her eight Grammy Awards and a worldwide audience. A singer at heart, she's achieved unprecedented success as an actress, director, and producer as well. She is also a spokesperson for many humanitarian causes.*
>
> *Henry Mancini, a twenty-time Grammy winner, redefined the art of composing for film while carving out an equally enviable career as a conductor, instrumentalist, songwriter, and arranger. A tireless supporter of arts education—the recording industry and the academy are deeply in the debt of this extraordinary gentleman.*
>
> *Patsy Cline. The female country star who crossed over to pop and to timeless ballads. We lost Patsy far too soon, but her music continues to exert a powerful influence on several generations of country and pop artists.*
>
> *Curtis Mayfield. Singer, songwriter, producer, guitarist, and record executive. The Chicago-born pioneer of the soul era influenced attitudes and opinions around the world with his socially relevant songs. A Grammy legend, award winner last year—his energy and creativity continue to inspire us all.*
>
> *And Miss Peggy Lee. "Why Don't You Do Right" was the title of her first hit with Benny Goodman, and she's been doing right ever since—as a jazz and pop vocalist and songwriter. Forever identified with such classics as "Mañana," "Fever," and "Is That All There Is," Peggy is the embodiment of coolness, hipness, and sophistication.*
>
> *With us in the house this evening are two of our Life Achievement honorees. Please help me acknowledge Curtis Mayfield and Peggy Lee.*

*This speech, delivered March 1, 1995, was transcribed from the televised presentation.

In preparing and presenting your speech of acceptance, follow these three principles.

Express Thanks

Thank the people responsible for sponsoring and awarding you the award— the academy members, the board of directors, the student body, your fellow teammates.

Acknowledge Others Who Helped

Much as an author will thank those persons who helped her or him in the writing of a particular book (see, for example, the acknowledgments in the preface of this book), the award recipient should thank those instrumental in the achieving of the award. In thanking such people, be specific without boring the audience. It is not necessary to detail exactly what each person contributed, but it is interesting to the audience to learn, for example, that Pat Tarrington gave you your first role in a soap opera or that Chris Willis convinced you to play the role in the film that led to your first Academy Award.

What would you say in a speech of acceptance if you received the award for outstanding student of the year?

Convey Your Feelings

Put the award into personal perspective. Tell the audience what the award means to you right now and perhaps what it will mean to you in the future. Allow the audience a personal closeness to you that they might not otherwise experience.

Sample Speeches of Acceptance

Here is an exceptionally moving and provocative acceptance speech that clearly illustrates how closely tied together are the speaker, audience, and occasion. The speech was given by Elizabeth Taylor in acceptance of the Jean Hersholt Humanitarian Award, given for her great humanitarian work in behalf of people with AIDS. It was presented by Angela Lansbury for the Academy of Motion Picture Arts and Sciences on March 29, 1993. The speech was transcribed from television.

> *I have been on this stage many times as a presenter. I have sat in the audience as a loser. And I've had the thrill and the honor of standing here as a winner. But I never, ever, thought I would come out here to receive this award.*
>
> *It is the highest possible accolade I could receive from my peers. And for doing something I just have to do, that my passion must do.*
>
> *I am filled with pride and humility. I accept this award in honor of all the men, women, and children with AIDS who are waging incredibly valiant battles for their lives—those to whom I have given my commitment, the real heroes of the pandemic of AIDS.*
>
> *I am so proud of the work that people in Hollywood have done to help so many others, like dearest, gentle Audrey.* And while she is, I know, in heaven, forever guarding her beloved children, I will remain here as rowdy an activist as I have to be and, God willing, for as long as I have to be. [Applause]*
>
> *Tonight I am asking for your help. I call upon you to draw from the depths of your being, to prove that we are a human race, to prove that our love outweighs our need to hate, that our compassion is more compelling than our need to blame, that our sensitivity to those in need is stronger than our greed, that our ability to reason overcomes our fear, and that at the end of each of our lives we can look back and be proud that we have treated others with the kindness, dignity, and respect that every human being deserves.*
>
> *Thank you and God bless.*

Here is another brief speech of acceptance, given by an college professor upon receiving honorary membership in the Golden Key Honor Society for excellence in teaching:

What would you say if you were given the award for Outstanding U.S. College Student of the Year?

---

*Audrey Hepburn, who had been presented with a posthumous award for her humanitarian work, especially that for UNICEF.

I must confess that I was not aware that there was an organization—an honor society—so dedicated to excellence. And the more I thought about it, the more important I realized it was. And I thought it especially appropriate—though perhaps a bit embarrassing—that it was founded by students.

The great thing about Golden Key and about this award is that you help make excellence respectable, worthy of having as a goal, as a way of learning and a way of life—and a little bit less scary. You seek out excellence, reward it, and thereby provide useful models.

I hope that we will also—students and teachers—seek out and speak out when excellence does not prevail where it should prevail. The need for this is now, when our educational system (especially in places like New York City) seems to be growing more concerned with the numbers of students being graduated from high schools and colleges rather than with the quality of their education and where the curriculum we may or may not teach in elementary school is being dictated by ignorance and prejudice, instead of knowledge, fairness, and justice.

I thank the Golden Key for giving excellence such a prominent voice and I thank you for asking for excellence from me and for telling me that I'm on the right track. I'm honored, I'm flattered. I thank you.

How would you evaluate this speech of acceptance? Does it follow the principles considered in this section?

Here is an acceptance speech given by Mary Chapin Carpenter on receiving the Grammy for the best album of 1994, *Stones in the Road*. The speech was transcribed from television.

Thank you so much. This makes me very happy and very emotional.

This album means a lot to me, and I want to thank Columbia, my record company, for giving me all the time I needed to make it. Thank you.

My managers, Tom and John; Studio One; and everybody who works there.

My wonderful band; John Jennings, my coproducer and most necessary friend in the world.

I know I'm forgetting a lot of people, but I'm very happy to be a musician. Especially in this time, when the arts are being cut in so many ways, it's very important that we still really do what we do and speak out on behalf of that.

Thank you so very very much.

Here is an example of a most effective acceptance speech. William Faulkner, one of the leading American writers of the twentieth century, is the speaker. He was awarded the Nobel Prize in literature in 1949 and the Pulitzer Prize in 1955. Faulkner delivered the following Nobel Prize acceptance speech on December 10, 1950, in Stockholm, Sweden, reportedly in his first dress suit and before television cameras for the first time. The speech is one of the best acceptance speeches ever recorded. It is especially noteworthy for its clarity of style and purpose and for its universal theme.

I feel that this award was not made to me as a man, but to my work—a life's work in the agony and sweat of the human spirit, not for glory and least of all for profit, but to create out of the materials of the human spirit something which did not exist before. So this award is only mine in trust. It will not be difficult to find a dedication for the money part of it commensurate with the purpose and significance of its origin. But I would like to do the same with the acclaim too, by using this moment as a pinnacle from which I might be listened to by the young men and women already dedicated to the same anguish and travail, among whom is already that one who will someday stand here where I am standing.

Our tragedy today is a general and universal physical fear so long sustained by now that we can even bear it. There are no longer problems of the spirit. There is only the question: when will I be blown up? Because of this, the young man or woman writing today has forgotten the problems of the human heart in conflict with itself which alone can make good writing because only that is worth writing about, worth the agony and the sweat.

He must learn them again. He must teach himself that the basest of all things is to be afraid; and, teaching himself that, forget it forever, leaving no room in his workshop for anything but the old verities and truth of the heart, the old universal truths lacking which any story is ephemeral and doomed—love and honor and pity and pride and compassion and sacrifice. Until he does so, he labors under a curse. He writes not of love but of lust, of defeats in which nobody loses anything of value, of victories without hope, and, worst of all, without pity or compassion. His griefs grieve on no universal bones, leaving no scars. He writes not of the heart but of the glands.

Until he relearns these things, he will write as though he stood among and watched the end of man. I decline to accept the end of man. It is easy enough to say that man is immortal simply because he will endure; that when the last dingdong of doom has clanged and fades from the last worthless rock hanging tideless in the last red and dying evening, that even then there will still be one more sound. That of his puny inexhaustible voice, still talking. I refuse to accept this. I believe that man will not merely endure: he will prevail. He is immortal, not because he alone among creatures has an inexhaustible voice, but because he has a soul, a spirit capable of compassion and sacrifice and endurance. The poet's, the writer's, duty is to write about these things. It is his privilege to help man endure by lifting his heart, by reminding him of the courage and honor and hope and pride and compassion and pity and sacrifice which have been the glory of his past. The poet's voice need not merely by the record of man; it can be one of the props, the pillars, to help him endure and prevail.

What is the theme of this speech? Do you agree that the theme of this speech is universal?

Don't Misjudge the Importance of the Award

Neither underestimate nor overestimate the importance or significance of an award. Most speakers—rather like the presenter in the accompanying cartoon—err in the direction of exaggeration. When this is done, the presenter, the recipient, and the entire situation can appear ludicrous. Be realistic. A good guideline to follow is to ask yourself what this award will mean next year or five years from now to these very same people. Will they remember it? Will it have exerted a significant influence on their lives? Will the local or national news-

AND NOW THE AWARD FOR THE MOST AWESOME PERFORMANCE OF A DUDE CRASHING HIS BIKE THROUGH A PLATE-GLASS WINDOW, RUNNING THROUGH THE MALL SHOOTING AT OTHER DUDES, AND BEATING UP A WHOLE BUNCH OF **OTHER** DUDES ALL BY HIMSELF! GIMME THE ENVELOPE.

Drawing by M. Stevens; © 1992 The New Yorker Magazine, Inc.

papers report it? Is it a likely item for a television spot? Obviously, the more questions to which you answer yes, the less likelihood of your exaggerating. The more questions to which you answer no, the more reserved you need to be.

Don't Be Long-Winded

Few people want to hear long speeches of presentation or acceptance. Normally, awards are given at dinners or some other festive function, and people are generally eager to get on with other activities. If many awards are to be given on this same occasion, then you have added reason to be especially brief. We see this very commonsense principle violated yearly on the Academy Awards show. The story told by news correspondent Charles Osgood in the accompanying TIPS can be taken as a reminder (rather than as specific advice) against delivering an overly long speech of acceptance.

Generally, the length of the speech should be proportional to the importance of the award: Awards of lesser importance should be presented and accepted with short speeches; awards of greater significance may be presented and accepted with longer speeches. When acknowledging those who helped you, be selective. Do not include everyone you have ever known; select the most significant few and identify these. Everyone knows that there were others who influenced you, so it is unnecessary to state the obvious: "And there are many others, too numerous to mention, who helped me achieve this wonderful award."

Avoid Platitudes and Clichés

Platitudes and clichés abound in speeches of presentation and acceptance. Be especially careful not to include expressions that will lead your audience to

TIPS

From Professional Speakers

When Marlene Dietrich sent Mikhail Baryshnikov to pick up her award from the Council of Fashion Designers in New York, the great dancer asked her what she wanted him to say. She said, "Take the thing, look at it, thank them, and go." Mikhail said, "That's it?" and she said, "That's it! They don't have time to listen anyway."

Charles Osgood, CBS news correspondent and anchor of *CBS Sunday Night News. Osgood on Speaking: How to Think on Your Feet Without Falling on Your Face* (New York: Morrow, 1988), p. 39.

think this is a canned presentation and the entire ceremony is perfunctory. Obvious examples to avoid are these:

This award winner is so well known that no introduction is necessary.

I really don't deserve this award.

There is no one more deserving of this award than this year's recipient.

THE SPEECH TO SECURE GOODWILL

The speech to secure goodwill is a peculiar hybrid, part information and part persuasion. And it is difficult to determine where information ends and persuasion begins. In fact, the strength of the goodwill speech often depends on the extent to which the information and the persuasion are blurred in the minds of the audience.

On the surface, the speech to secure goodwill informs the audience about a product, company, profession, institution, way of life, or person. Beneath this surface, however, lies a more persuasive purpose: to heighten the image of a person, product, or company—to create a more positive attitude toward this person or thing.

Many speeches of goodwill have a still further persuasive purpose: to get the audience ultimately to change their behavior toward the person, product, or company. Such a speech functions to create goodwill but invariably also functions to alter behavior. The securing of goodwill and the changing of behavior are not, in reality, separable.

A special type of goodwill speech is the speech of self-justification, where the speaker seeks to justify his or her actions to the audience. Political figures do this frequently. Richard Nixon's "Checkers" speech, his Cambodia-bombing speeches, and, of course, his Watergate speeches are clear examples of self-justification. Edward Kennedy's Chappaquiddick speech, in which he attempted to justify what happened when Mary Jo Kopechne drowned, is another example. (Excerpts from these speeches are provided in Unit 23.)

Whenever there is a significant loss of credibility, the speaker will be called upon to offer a speech of self-justification. As any political leader's image goes down, the frequency of the self-justifying speeches goes up. In securing goodwill, whether for another person or for yourself, the following principles should prove helpful.

How do corporations secure goodwill in their newspaper and magazine advertisements?

Demonstrate the Contributions That Deserve Goodwill

Demonstrate how the audience may benefit from this company, product, or person. Or, at least (in the speech of self-justification), show how the audience has not been hurt or not been hurt willfully. Often this is accomplished obliquely. When IBM demonstrates it has accomplished a great deal through research, it also stresses implicitly and sometimes more directly that these developments make it easier to function in business or in the home. General Electric's "We bring good things to life" is designed to secure goodwill and to demonstrate that the company benefits the audience—with more free time, less hard labor, and more accessible and inexpensive entertainment.

Stress Uniqueness

In a world dominated by competition, the speech to secure goodwill must stress the uniqueness of the specific company, person, profession, and so on. Distinguish it clearly from all others; otherwise, any goodwill you secure will be spread over the entire field.

Establish Credibility

Speeches to secure goodwill must also establish credibility, thereby securing goodwill for the individual or commodity. To do so, concentrate on those dimensions of credibility discussed earlier (see Unit 23). Demonstrate that the subject is competent, of good intention, and of high moral character. Examine how Lee Iacocca does this in his speech on the odometer (p. 420). Who could not have goodwill toward such an individual, product, or business?

Don't Be Obvious

An ineffective goodwill speech is an obvious advertisement; an effective one is not. The effective goodwill speech looks, on the surface, very much like an objective informative speech. It will not appear to ask for goodwill, except on close analysis.

Don't Plead for Goodwill

Those who plead for goodwill may achieve some goals, but in the long run they seem to lose out. Few people want to go along with someone who appears weak. If you attempt to justify some action, justify it with logic and reason. Do not beg for goodwill—demonstrate that it is due you. Most audiences are composed of reasonable people who prefer to act out of logic, who recognize that not everyone is perfect, and who are ready to establish or reestablish goodwill toward an individual.

How would you build a speech designed to secure the goodwill of the community for your college?

Don't Overdo It

Overkill is ineffective. You will turn off your audience rather than secure their goodwill. Remember: Your perspective and the perspective of your audience are very different. Your acquaintance with the product may fully convince you of its greatness, but your audience does not have that acquaintance. Consequently, they will not appreciate too many superlatives.

A Sample Speech to Secure Goodwill

A particularly good example of the speech to secure goodwill is the following speech by Lee Iacocca, former CEO of Chrysler Corporation. Here Iacocca was presented with a particularly difficult problem: Chrysler was accused of disconnecting its odometers so that the cars would appear to be new, despite the 40 miles of road test. This was not a particularly horrible offense, since most car buyers know their cars are put through various tests, yet it presented Iacocca with a credibility problem. He met this head-on with a series of print and television advertisements in which he admitted the error and spelled out what he would do to correct this error of judgment.

Testing cars is a good idea. Disconnecting odometers is a lousy idea. That's a mistake we won't make again at Chrysler. Period.   —LEE IACOCCA

Let me set the record straight.

1. *For years, spot checking and road testing new cars and trucks that come off the assembly line with the odometers disengaged was standard industry practice. In our case, the average test mileage was 40 miles.*
2. *Even though the practice wasn't illegal, some companies began connecting their odometers. We didn't. In retrospect, that was dumb. Since October 1986, however, the odometer of every car and truck we've built has been connected, including those in the test program.*
3. *A few cars—and I mean a few—were damaged in testing badly enough that they should not have been fixed and sold as new. That was a mistake in an otherwise valid quality assurance program. And now we have to make it right.*

What we're doing to make things right.

1. *In all instances where our records show a vehicle was damaged in the test program and repaired and sold, we will offer to replace that vehicle with a brand new 1987 Chrysler Corporation model of comparable value. No ifs ands or buts.*
2. *We are sending letters to everyone our records show bought a vehicle that was in the test program and offering a free inspection. If anything is wrong because of a product deficiency, we will make it right.*
3. *Along with free inspection, we are extending their present 5 year or 50,000 mile protection plan on engine and powertrain to 7 years or 70,000 miles.*
4. *And to put their minds completely at ease, we are extending the 7 year or 70,000 mile protection to all major systems: brakes, suspension, air conditioning, electrical, and steering.*

The quality testing program is a good program. But there were mistakes and we were too slow in stopping them. Now they're stopped. Done. Finished. Over.

Personally, I'm proud of our products. Proud of the quality improvements we've made. So we're going to keep right on testing. Because without it we couldn't have given America 5 year 50,000 mile protection five years ahead of everyone else. Or maintained our warranty leadership with 7 years 70,000 mile protection. I'm proud, too, of our leadership in safety-related recalls.

But I'm not proud of this episode. Not at all. As Harry Truman once said, "The buck stops here." It just stopped. Period.

How would you evaluate this speech? If you were president of Chrysler, how would you have handled this situation?

THE SPEECH OF TRIBUTE

The speech of tribute encompasses a wide variety of speeches (also see the accompanying box, "More Special Occasion Speeches"). All are designed to pay some kind of tribute to a person or event. They include the commendation, praising some living person, and the commemoration of some particular event or happening. The general purpose of the speech of tribute is to inform the audience of some accomplishment or of the importance of some event. It should also heighten the audience's awareness of the occasion, accomplishment, or person; strengthen or create positive attitudes; and increase the audience's appreciation. On the surface, then, the purpose is informative; below the surface, it is persuasive. In the speech of tribute, these principles should prove effective.

Involve the Audience

Involve the audience in some way. This is not always easy. Some tributes seem only to involve the individual being praised and some abstraction such as history, posterity, or culture. Make any history, posterity, or culture relevant to this specific audience. For example, if you were giving a eulogy, you would relate the meaning and accomplishments of the individual being eulogized to the specific audience. You would, in other words, answer the listeners' question, "What did this person's life mean to me?"

State the Reason for the Tribute

It is frequently helpful to give the audience some idea of why you are making this tribute. Oftentimes it is obvious: The teacher praises the student; the president congratulates the employee; the student eulogizes the teacher; and so on. When the connections are clear as in these cases, do not belabor them. But when they are not obvious to the audience, then tell the audience why you are the person giving this tribute.

Be Consistent with the Occasion

Construct and present a speech that is consistent with the specific occasion. This does not mean that all eulogies must be somber or that all sports award presentations must be frivolous. It is to say only that the speech should not contradict the basic mood of the occasion.

Don't Go Overboard

The speech of tribute records the positive, and the speech should be positive. But don't go overboard and over-exaggerate the specific accomplishments of an individual. This is dishonest and usually ineffective. State the person's accomplishments realistically. With some eulogies, it is difficult to recognize the real person for all of the unrealistic and undeserved (and dishonest) praise.

TIPS
From Professional Speakers

When you sit back after a good dinner and listen to others speak, you tend to make very simple judgements of their performance:
- Do you like them?
- Can you hear them?
- Have they interested or amused you?
- Was it well presented?
- Were they relevant?
- Were they succinct?

   When you prepare a speech, if you try and see yourself as your audience will see you, then hopefully you can please them.

Martin Nicholls, frequent speaker and author. *After Dinner Speeches* (London: Ward Lock Limited, 1989), p. 11.

What main propositions would you seek to include in a speech of tribute to "bodybuilder of the year," "the world's happiest couple," or "the current Nobel Peace Prize winner"?

A Sample Speech of Tribute

Speeches at college graduation, as you'll discover, are often of the "inspirational" type. What principles would you suggest the inspirational speaker follow? What pitfalls would you suggest this speaker avoid?

In the following speech,* former President Ronald Reagan pays tribute to the astronauts who died in the shuttle *Challenger* explosion in 1986. The occasion was an extremely sad one. Most of the nation had watched the tragedy on television just hours before. The speech reflects this sadness and mourning and will surely become a classic of the genre.

Ladies and gentlemen, I planned to speak to you tonight to report on the State of the Union, but the events of earlier today have led me to change those plans. Today is a day for mourning and remembering. Nancy and I are pained to the core by the tragedy of the shuttle Challenger. *We know we share this pain with all of the people of our country. This is truly a national loss.*

Nineteen years ago, almost to the day, we lost three astronauts in a terrible accident on the ground, but we've never lost an astronaut in flight; we've never had a tragedy like this. And perhaps we've forgotten the courage it took for the crew of the shuttle but they, the Challenger *seven, were aware of the dangers and overcame them and did their jobs brilliantly.*

We mourn seven heroes: Michael Smith, Dick Scobee, Judith Resnik, Ronald McNair, Ellison Onizuka, Gregory Jarvis and Christa McAuliffe. We mourn their loss as a nation, together.

The families of the seven—we cannot bear, as you do, the full impact of this tragedy but we feel the loss and we're thinking about you so very much. Your loved ones were daring and brave and they had that special grace, that special spirit that says, "Give me a challenge and I'll meet it with joy." They had a hunger to explore the universe and discover its truths. They wished to serve and they did—they served all of us.

We've grown used to wonders in this century; it's hard to dazzle us. For 25 years the United States space program has been doing just that. We've grown used to the idea of space, and perhaps we forget that we've only just begun. We're still pioneers. They, the members of the Challenger *crew, were pioneers.*

And I want to say something to the schoolchildren of America who were watching the live coverage of the shuttle's takeoff. I know it's hard to understand that sometimes painful things like this happen. It's all part of the process of exploration and discovery; it's all part of taking a chance and expanding man's horizons. The future doesn't belong to the fainthearted. It belongs to the brave. The Challenger *crew was pulling us into the future, and we'll continue to follow them.*

I've always had great faith in and respect for our space program, and what happened today does nothing to diminish it. We don't hide our space program, we don't keep secrets and cover things up. We do it all up front and in public. That's the way freedom is and we wouldn't change it for a minute. We'll continue our quest in space. There will be more shuttle flights and more shuttle crews and, yes, more volunteers, more civilians, more teachers in space. Nothing ends here. Our hopes and our journeys continue.

*Reprinted from the *New York Times* (January 29, 1986), p. A9.

FOCUS **O**N

More Special Occasion Speeches

In speeches of **dedication,** you might aim to give some special meaning to, say, a new research lab, a store opening, or the start of the building of a bridge.

In **commencement** speeches, such as you'll hear at your own graduation, you aim to congratulate and inspire the recent graduates. The speech is intended as a kind of transition from school to the next stage in life.

In a **eulogy,** a type of speech of tribute, you seek to praise someone who died, to set their life and contributions in perspective and in a positive light.

In speeches of **farewell,** you say goodbye to a position or to colleagues. You're moving on, and you want to express your feelings to those you are leaving.

The **toast** aims to say hello or good luck in a relatively formal sense. Speeches at weddings, conferences, and banquets often include toasting the honorees.

Can you imagine situations in your own life where you might be called upon to give such special occasion speeches?

I want to add that I wish I could talk to every man and woman who works for NASA, or who worked on this mission, and tell them: "Your dedication and professionalism have moved and impressed us for decades, and we know of your anguish. We share it."

There's a coincidence today. On this day 390 years ago, the great explorer Sir Francis Drake died aboard ship off the coast of Panama. In his lifetime the great frontiers were the oceans, and a historian later said, "He lived by the sea, died on it, and was buried in it." Well, today we can say of the Challenger *crew, their dedication was, like Drake's, complete. The crew of the space shuttle* Challenger *honored us by the manner in which they lived their lives. We will never forget them nor the last time we saw them this morning as they prepared for their journey and waved goodbye and "slipped the surly bonds of earth to touch the face of God."*

Thank you.

These four general special occasion speech types (introduction, presentation/acceptance, goodwill, and tribute) are easily adapted to other types of speeches. The accompanying box identifies several of these additional special occasion speeches.

THE SPECIAL OCCASION SPEECH IN CULTURAL PERSPECTIVE

Like all forms of communication, the special occasion speech must be developed with a clear understanding of the influence of culture.

In the discussion of the speech of introduction the suggestion was made not to oversell the speaker and in the discussion of the speech of tribute the suggestion was made not to go overboard in praising the person. Excess exaggeration is generally evaluated negatively in much of the United States. On the other hand, it is often expected in, for example, some Latin cultures.

Culture will also influence the way in which an acceptance should be framed. Not surprisingly, collectivist cultures would suggest that you give lots of credit to the group whereas individualist cultures would suggest that taking self-credit (when it is due) is appropriate. Thus, if you were accepting an award for a performance in a play, a collectivist orientation would lead you to give greater praise to others involved in the play than would an individualistic orientation.

In the discussion of the speech of goodwill the suggestion was offered to present yourself as being worthy of the goodwill rather than as a supplicant begging for it. In some cultures, however, this attitude might be seen as arrogant and disrespectful to the audience. Pleading for goodwill in, for example, some Asian cultures would be seen as suitably modest and respectful of the audience.

In introducing or in paying tribute to someone, consider the extent to which you wish to focus on the person's contribution to the group or to individual achievement. An audience with a predominantly collectivist orientation will expect to hear group-centered achievements whereas an audience of predominantly individualistic orientation will expect to hear more individually focused achievements.

All this is not to say that you should simply give the audience what it wants or expects but rather that these expectations need to be considered as you develop your speech.

Can you think of other cultural differences that should be noted here?

UNIT IN BRIEF

The speech of introduction	■ Establishes a connection among speaker, topic, and audience
	■ Establishes the speaker's credibility
	■ Is consistent in style and manner with the major speech
	■ Is brief
	■ Avoids covering what the speaker intends to discuss
	■ Avoids overselling the speaker
The speech of presentation	■ States the reason for the presentation
	■ States the importance of the award
The speech of acceptance	■ Thanks those who gave the award
	■ Thanks those who helped
	■ States the meaning of the award to the speaker

	■ Speeches of presentation and acceptance are most effective when they (1) avoid misjudging the importance of the award, (2) are relatively brief, and (3) do not rely on platitudes and clichés
The speech to secure goodwill	■ Stresses the benefits the audience may derive ■ Stresses uniqueness ■ Establishes the speaker's credibility and the credibility of the subject ■ Avoids being obvious in securing goodwill ■ Avoids pleading for goodwill ■ Avoids overdoing the superlatives
The speech of tribute	■ Involves the audience ■ States the reason for the tribute ■ Is consistent with the occasion ■ Avoids disproportionate praise

PRACTICALLY SPEAKING

Short Speech Technique

Prepare and deliver a two-minute speech in which you:

1. introduce any speaker you wish, speaking to any audience you wish, on any subject you wish
2. present an award for the best speaker of the year, the best quarterback, the best actor, the best firefighter, the best police officer, or the best teacher
3. explain how an advertisement is like a speech to secure goodwill
4. toast your friend's new relationship commitment
5. say thanks for a group of your friends who just surprised you with a birthday party; they're all clapping and yelling "Speech, speech"
6. eulogize a person

24.1   Developing the Speech of Introduction

Prepare a speech of introduction approximately two minutes in length. For this experience, you can assume that the speaker you introduce will speak on any topic you wish. Do, however, assume a topic appropriate to the speaker and to your audience—your class. You may wish to select your introduction from one of the following suggestions:

1. Introduce a historical figure to the class
2. Introduce a contemporary religious, political, or social leader
3. Prepare a speech of introduction that someone might give to introduce you to your class
4. Introduce a famous media (film, television, radio, recording, writing) personality—alive or dead
5. Introduce a series of speeches debating the pros and cons of multicultural education

24.2   Developing the Speech of Presentation/Acceptance

Form pairs in which one person serves as the presenter and one as the recipient of a particular award or honor. You can select a situation from the list presented below or make one up yourselves. The presenter should prepare and present a two-minute speech in which you present one of the awards to the other person. The recipient should prepare and present a two-minute speech of acceptance.

1. Academy Award for best performance
2. Gold watch for service to the company
3. Ms. or Mr. America
4. Five million dollars for the college library
5. Award contributions to intercultural understanding
6. Book award
7. Mother (Father) of the Year award
8. Honorary Ph.D. in communication for outstanding contributions to the art and practice of effective communication
9. Award for outstanding achievement in architecture
10. Award for raising a prize hog

24.3   Developing the Speech to Secure Goodwill

Prepare a speech approximately three to five minutes in length in which you attempt to secure the goodwill of your audience toward one of the following:

1. Your college (visualize your audience as high school seniors)
2. A particular profession or way of life (teaching, religious life, nursing, law, medicine, bricklaying, truck driving, and so on)
3. This course (visualize your audience as college students who have not yet taken this course)
4. The policies of a particular foreign country now in the news
5. A specific multinational corporation

24.4   Developing the Speech of Tribute

Prepare a speech approximately three to five minutes in length in which you pay tribute to one of the following persons:

1. Politician for supporting AIDS research
2. Scientist for advances in cancer research
3. Visitor from another planet
4. Famous athlete for building a children's hospital
5. Consumer advocate for exposing fraud in advertising

UNIT 25

Speaking in Small Groups

Unit Objectives

After completing this unit, you should be able to:

1. Define the *small group* and explain the group as a culture

2. Describe problem-solving, idea generation, and information-sharing groups

3. Explain small group tasks of both members and leaders

4. Explain the panel, symposium and team presentations, symposium-forum, and oral and written reports as ways of presenting a group's thinking

*V*ery likely you are a member of several small groups. The family is the most obvious example, but you also function as a member of a team, a class, a collection of friends, a problem-solving workgroup, and so on. Some of your most important and most personally satisfying communications take place within small groups. In this unit we look into the role of speaking in small groups; specifically, we examine the nature of the small group, ways to communicate effectively in small groups, and guidelines for presenting a group's findings, conclusions, or recommendations.

What groups are you a member of? What needs do these groups serve for you?

THE SMALL GROUP

A small group is a relatively small collection of individuals (usually, around 5 to 12) who are related to each other by some common purpose and have some degree of organization among them. People on a bus would not constitute a group, since they are not working at some common purpose. Should the bus get stuck in a ditch, however, the riders may quickly become a group and work together to get the bus back on the road.

Before beginning your study of small group communication, examine how apprehensive you are in group discussions and in meetings by taking the self-test on page 430.

The Small Group as a Culture

Many groups—especially long-standing work groups—develop into small cultures with their own norms. These norms are the rules or standards of behavior, the rules that say which behaviors are appropriate (for example, willingness to take on added tasks, or conflict directed toward issues rather than

In what ways is your family a small group? Does it serve problem-solving, idea generation, or information-sharing functions? Might any of the principles and guidelines discussed in these units be useful in your family communication?

"I don't know how it started, either. All I know is that it's part of our corporate culture."

Drawing by M. Stevens; © 1994 The New Yorker Magazine, Inc.

How Apprehensive Are You in Group Discussions and Meetings?

Just as you have apprehension in public speaking and conversations (Unit 3), so too do you have some degree of apprehension in group discussions and in meetings. This brief test is designed to measure your apprehension in these small group situations.

This questionnaire consists of 12 statements concerning your feelings about communication in group discussions and meetings. Please indicate in the space provided the degree to which each statement applies to you, by marking whether you (1) Strongly Agree, (2) Agree, (3) Are Undecided, (4) Disagree, or (5) Strongly Disagree. There are no right or wrong answers. Some of the statements are similar to other statements. Do not be concerned about this. Work quickly; just record your first impression.

____ 1. I dislike participating in group discussions.

____ 2. Generally, I am comfortable while participating in group discussions.

____ 3. I am tense and nervous while participating in group discussions.

____ 4. I like to get involved in group discussions.

____ 5. Engaging in a group discussion with new people makes me tense and nervous.

____ 6. I am calm and relaxed while participating in group discussions.

____ 7. Generally, I am nervous when I have to participate in a meeting.

____ 8. Usually, I am calm and relaxed while participating in meetings.

____ 9. I am very calm and relaxed when I am called upon to express an opinion at a meeting.

____10. I am afraid to express myself at meetings.

____11. Communicating at meetings usually makes me uncomfortable.

____12. I am very relaxed when answering questions at a meeting.

SCORING: This test will enable you to obtain two subscores, one for group discussions and one for meetings. To obtain your scores, use the following formulas:

For Group Discussions
18 plus scores for items 2, 4, and 6 minus scores for items 1, 3, and 5

For Meetings
18 plus scores for items 8, 9, and 12 minus scores for items 7, 10, and 11

Scores above 18 show some degree of apprehension.

SOURCE: From James C. McCroskey, *An Introduction to Rhetorical Communication,* 6th ed. (Englewood Cliffs, N.J.: Prentice Hall, 1993).

In which type of group situation are you more apprehensive? Why?

toward people) and which are inappropriate (for example, coming late or not contributing actively). Sometimes these rules for appropriate behavior are explicitly stated in a company contract or policy: All members must attend department meetings. Sometimes rules are implicit: Members should be well groomed. Regardless of whether or not norms are spelled out, they are powerful regulators of members' behaviors.

Norms may apply to individual members as well as to the group as a whole and, of course, will differ from one group to another (Axtell 1990a, 1993). For example, in Japan and in many Arab countries it is customary to begin meetings with what many Americans would think is unnecessary socializing. While many Americans prefer to get right down to business, the Japanese, for example, prefer rather elaborate socializing before getting to the business at hand. They want first to experience confidence and trust (DeVries 1994).

In the United States, men and women in business are expected to interact when making business decisions as well as when socializing. In Muslim and Buddhist societies, however, religious restrictions prevent mixing the sexes. In the United States, Bangladesh, Australia, Germany, Finland, and Hong Kong, for example, punctuality for business meetings is very important. But in countries like Morocco, Italy, Brazil, Zambia, Ireland, and Panama, for instance, time is less highly regarded and being late is no great insult and is even expected. In the United States and in much of Asia and Europe, meetings are held between two groups. In many Persian Gulf nations, however, the business executive is likely to conduct meetings with several different people—sometimes dealing with totally different issues—at the same time. In this situation, you have to expect to share what in the United States would be "your time" with these other parties. In the United States, very little interpersonal touching goes on during business meetings; in Arab countries, however, touching (for example, handholding) is common and is a gesture of friendship.

Norms that regulate a particular member's behavior, called role expectations, identify what each person in an organization is expected to do; for example, Pat has a great computer setup and so should play the role of secretary.

You are more likely to accept the norms of your group when you (Napier & Gershenfeld 1989):

- want to continue your membership in the group
- feel your group membership is important
- are in a group that is cohesive, when you and the other members are closely connected
- are attracted to each other and depend on each other to meet your needs
- would be punished by negative reactions or exclusion from the group for violating the group norms

Cross-cultural studies show that members of different cultures have different tendencies to conform to group norms—even when these conflict with their own perceptions. For example, in a classic study a subject is seated with confederates of the experimenter who misjudge the length of a line shown on a screen (Asch 1946). Does the subject report what he or she really sees or go along with the majority? The answer is that many people do contradict their own perceptions to go along with the group, but it varies with the

Do men and women behave similarly as small group members? As small group leaders? Are men's and women's small group behaviors perceived similarly?

In what ways are cultural norms similar to (or different from) small group norms? Can you identify two or three cultural norms that influence your communication behavior in the classroom?

culture. For example (and contrary to popular stereotypes), German and Japanese respondents are less conformist than North Americans or Chinese respondents (Moghaddam, Taylor, & Wright 1993). It is also interesting to note that people are showing less conformity to group norms today than they did when the original studies were conducted in the 1940s (Moghaddam, Taylor, & Wright 1993).

TYPES OF SMALL GROUPS

Several group situations call for the skills of public speaking. Here three such groups are considered: the problem-solving group, the idea generation group, and the information-sharing group.

Problem-Solving Groups

A problem-solving group is a collection of individuals who meet to solve a problem or reach a decision. In one sense this is the most exacting kind of group to participate in. It requires not only a knowledge of small group communication techniques but a thorough knowledge of the particular problem. We look at this group first in terms of the classic and still popular problem-solving approach, whereby we identify the steps you would go through in solving a problem. (These steps are, in one sense, the group's agenda; they are the main activities of the group. The accompanying box explains the nature of the agenda in more detail.)

Another popular type of group is the personal growth group, which seeks to encourage its members to function more effectively, for example, becoming more assertive or dealing with an abusive relationship. Have you ever been in a personal growth group? How does a personal growth group differ from a problem-solving group?

F O C U S   O N

The Group Agenda

Most groups have an agenda. An agenda is simply a list of the tasks of the group. It is an itemized listing of what the group hopes to consider. Sometimes the agenda is prepared by the supervisor, consultant, or CEO and is simply presented to the group; the group is then expected to follow the agenda item by item. At other times the group will develop its own agenda, usually as its first or second order of business.

Generally, the more formal the group, the more important this agenda becomes. In informal groups, the agenda may simply be general ideas in the minds of the members (for example, "We'll review the class assignment and then make plans for the weekend"). In formal business groups, the agenda will be much more detailed and explicit. Some agendas specify not only the items that must be covered but also the order in which they should be covered and even the amount of time that should be devoted to each item.

The agenda must be agreed upon by the group members. If it is imposed by the CEO, for example, then there is little doubt that the group members will accept it and follow it. If it is one the group itself develops, then both leader and members must make sure members agree to follow it. At times it might be helpful to have a brief discussion of the agenda and a commitment from all members to follow it.

What types of small groups do you participate in now? What types are you likely to participate in as a regular part of your professional life? What skills will prove especially valuable to you as a participant in these groups?

The Problem-Solving Sequence   The problem-solving approach, which owes its formulation to the philosopher John Dewey's steps in reflective thinking, identifies six steps (see Figure 25.1). These steps are designed to make problem solving more efficient and effective.

Step 1. Define and Analyze the Problem.   Generally, it is best to define the problem as an open-ended question ("How can we improve the student newspaper?") rather than as a statement ("The student newspaper needs to be improved") or a yes/no question ("Does the student newspaper need improvement?"). The open-ended question allows for greater freedom of exploration.

Limit the problem so that it identifies a manageable area for discussion. A question such as "How can we improve the university?" is too broad and general. Rather, it would be more effective to limit the problem and to identify one subdivision of the university on which the group might focus—the student newspaper, student-faculty relationships, registration, examination scheduling, or student advisory services, for example.

Step 2. Establish Criteria for Evaluating Solutions.   Before any solutions are proposed, decide how to evaluate the solutions. Identify the standards or criteria you will use in evaluating the solutions or selecting one solution over another.

Consider both practical and value criteria. Focusing on the practical, you might decide that the solutions must not increase the budget, must lead to a higher number of advertisers, must increase the readership by at least 10 percent, and so on. In focusing on the value criteria, you might consider that the newspaper must be a learning experience for all those who work on it or that it must reflect attitudes consistent with the university's mission statement.

FIGURE 25.1
Steps in problem-solving discussion.

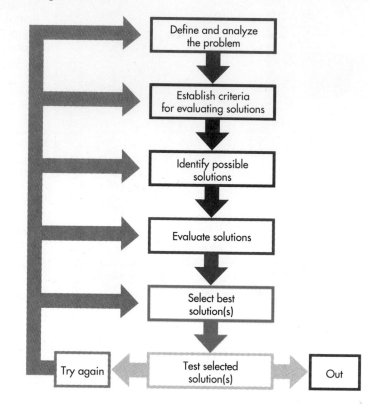

Step 3. Identify Possible Solutions. Identify as many solutions as possible. Focus on quantity rather than quality. Brainstorming may be particularly useful at this point (see the discussion of idea generation groups on p. 436). Solutions to the student newspaper problem might include incorporating reviews of faculty publications, student evaluations of specific courses, reviews of restaurants in the campus area, outlines for new courses, and employment information.

Step 4. Evaluate Solutions. After all the solutions have been proposed, go back and evaluate each according to the practical and value criteria already established. For example, to what extent does incorporating reviews of area restaurants meet the criteria for evaluating solutions? Would it increase the budget? Would it lead to an increase in advertising revenue? Match each potential solution against the criteria. A useful procedure in analyzing any kind of issue is provided by critical thinking pioneer Edward deBono (see "The Six Critical Thinking Hats Technique" box).

Step 5. Select the Best Solution(s). Select the best solution(s). Thus, for example, if "reviews of faculty publications" and "outlines for new courses" best met the criteria for evaluating solutions, the group might then decide that these are its solutions.

It's interesting to note the differences between groups in the United States and those in Japan. In the United States, groups are supposed to reach decisions relatively quickly; speed is always important. In Japan, groups are expected to be more deliberate and to make decisions after greater reflection. From even this seemingly simple difference, it is easy to see how people from the United States might view Japanese people as indecisive and unwilling to commit to a decision. Likewise, it is easy to see how those from Japan might view those from the United States as impulsive, thoughtless, and more interested in getting the job done than in thinking about it carefully and fully (Lustig & Koester 1993, Samovar & Porter, 1995).

Step 6. Test Selected Solution(s).   After one or more solutions are selected, the group might decide to put them into operation to test their effectiveness. For example, the group might decide to run the two new features in the next several months' issues. Then the group might, for example, poll students about the new newspaper or examine the number of copies purchased. Or the group might analyze the advertising revenue or see if reader-

---

F OCUS O N

The Six Critical Thinking Hats Technique

Critical thinking pioneer Edward deBono (1987) suggests that in defining and analyzing problems, you use six thinking hats. With each hat, you look at the problem from a different perspective. The technique provides a convenient and interesting way to further explore a problem from a variety of different angles.

The **fact hat** focuses attention on the data, the facts and figures that bear on the problem. For example, What are the relevant data on the newspaper? How can you get more information on the paper's history? How much does it cost to print? How much advertising revenue can you get?

The **feeling hat** focuses attention on your feelings, emotions, and intuitions concerning the problem: How do you feel about the newspaper and about making major changes?

The **negative argument hat** asks that you become the devil's advocate: Why might this proposal fail? What are the problems with publishing reviews of courses? What is the worst-case scenario?

The **positive benefits hat** asks that you look at the upside: What are the opportunities this new format will open up? What benefits will reviewing courses provide for the students? What would be the best thing that could happen?

The **creative new idea hat** focuses attention on new ways of looking at the problem and can be easily combined with the techniques of brainstorming discussed later in this unit: What other ways can you use to look at this problem? What other functions can a student newspaper serve that have not been thought of? Can the student paper provide a service to the nonacademic community as well?

The **control of thinking hat** helps you analyze what you have done and are doing. It asks that you reflect on your own thinking processes and synthesize the results of your thinking: Have you adequately defined the problem? Are you focusing too much on insignificant issues? Have you given enough attention to the possible negative effects?

Are there other perspectives from which you might profitably view a problem or a solution?

Groups may use different decision-making methods in deciding, for example, authority (the group discusses but the leader decides), majority rule (the decision is made by the largest numbers of members), and consensus (decisions are reached only when all group members agree). What are the advantages and disadvantages of each of these methods?

ship did increase 10 percent. If the feedback is positive, the group might then recommend these solutions as permanent changes.

If these solutions prove ineffective, the group would go back to one of the previous stages and repeat part of the process. Often this takes the form of selecting other solutions to test. But it may also involve going further back to, for example, a reanalysis of the problem, an identification of other solutions, or a restatement of criteria.

The Idea Generation Group

Many small groups exist solely to generate ideas and often follow a formula called brainstorming, a technique for bombarding a problem and generating as many ideas as possible (Osborn 1957, DeVito 1996). In this system the process occurs in two phases: (1) the brainstorming period proper and (2) the evaluation period.

In the brainstorming period, a problem is selected that is amenable to many possible solutions or ideas. Before the actual session, group members are informed of the problem to be brainstormed, so they can think about it. When the group meets, each person contributes as many ideas as possible. All ideas are recorded either in writing or on tape. During this idea-generating session, four general rules are followed.

Don't Criticize.   No criticism is allowed. All ideas are recorded. They are not evaluated; nor are they even discussed. Any negative criticism—whether verbal or nonverbal—is itself criticized by the leader or the members.

Work for Quantity.   The more ideas, the better. Somewhere in a large pile of ideas will be one or two good ones. The more ideas generated, the more effective the brainstorming session.

Combine and Extend Ideas.   While you may not criticize a particular idea, you may extend it or combine it in some way. The value of a particular idea may well be in the way it stimulates someone to combine or extend it.

Think Wild.   The wilder the idea, the better. It is easier to tone down an idea than to spice it up. A wild idea can easily be tempered, but it is not so easy to elaborate on a simple or conservative idea.

After all the ideas are generated—a period lasting no longer than 15 or 20 minutes—the entire list of ideas is evaluated. The ones that are unworkable are thrown out; the ones that show promise are retained and evaluated. During this phase, negative criticism is allowed.

Communicating New Ideas   If a group develops an idea, it will generally seek in some way to put this idea into operation. Often it's necessary to convince others that the idea is workable and cost-effective. Here are a few suggestions for communicating new ideas more effectively:

■ If possible, attach the new idea to an old one. People are more apt to understand and accept new ideas when they somehow resemble old and more comfortable ones. If it's a new rule, show how it's related to the old rule.

- Present the idea in a nonthreatening manner. New ideas often frighten people. If your ideas might lead people to feel insecure about their jobs, then alleviate these worries before you try to explain the idea in any detail. And generally, it is best to proceed slowly.
- Present new ideas tentatively. You may be taken with the flash of inspiration and not have reasoned out the practical implications of the idea. So, if you present your ideas tentatively and they are shown to be impractical or unworkable, you will be less hurt psychologically and—most important— will be more willing to try presenting new ideas again.
- In many instances, it will prove helpful to link changes and new ideas to perceived problems in the organization or relationship. If you are going to ask employees to complete extensive surveys, then show them how this extra work will correct a problem and benefit them and the organization.
- Say why you think the idea would work. Give the advantages of your plan over the existing situation and explain why you think this idea should be implemented. The patterns for organizing a public speech will prove helpful in accomplishing this.
- State the negatives (with most ideas, there usually are some) as you understand them and, of course, why you think the positives outweigh them.
- Relate the new ideas to the needs and interests of those on whom the innovation will have an impact.
- As persuasion research suggests, proceed inductively when you anticipate objections. When presenting ideas to a hostile or potentially hostile audience, give the benefits before introducing the new idea. Ideally, you'll move your audience into wanting the benefits and values of the new idea before they ever hear of the idea itself.

Listening to New Ideas   In responding to new ideas, be careful of groupthink, the tendency to be swayed by what the other members of the group or organization think (see p. 442 for a more detailed discussion of groupthink). Appropriate responses to creativity will often run counter to the majority opinion, if only because there seems a natural tendency to resist change. First focus on the idea; make sure you understand it and its implications. Then consider what others are saying.

A particularly good creative and critical thinking technique to use in responding to new ideas is PIP'N, a technique that derives from Carl Rogers's (1970) paraphrasing technique and Edward deBono's (1976) PMI (plus, minus, interesting) technique. It involves four steps:

> **P = Paraphrase.** State in your own words what you think the other person is saying. This will ensure that you and the person proposing the idea are talking about the same thing. Your paraphrase will also provide the other person with the opportunity to elaborate or clarify his or her ideas.

> **I = Interesting.** State something interesting that you find in the idea. Say why you think this idea might be interesting to you, to others, to the organization.

> **P = Positive.** Say something positive about the idea. What is good about it? How might it solve a problem or make a situation better?

In what situations might you use the brainstorming concepts intrapersonally? That is, is there a personal problem or issue that might be approached with the techniques of brainstorming?

N = **Negative.** State any negatives you think the idea might entail. Might it prove expensive? Difficult to implement? Is it directed at insignificant issues?

Information-Sharing Groups

The purpose of information-sharing groups is to acquire new information or skills through a sharing of knowledge. In most information-sharing groups, all members have something to teach and something to learn.

In information-sharing groups, the members pool their knowledge to the benefit of all. Members may follow a variety of discussion patterns based on the organizational patterns discussed for the body of the speech (Unit 12). For example, a historical topic might be developed chronologically, with the discussion progressing from the past into the present and perhaps predicting the future.

In addition to following the guidelines for members and leaders (presented below), here are a few additional guidelines to follow in participating in information-sharing groups:

■ Assume that everyone has something to contribute. Enter the group with the idea that you are in fact going to learn something.

■ Assume your fair share of the teaching. Know what you are going to contribute and review it for ease in discussion.

■ Try to spread the interaction among all members about evenly. Discourage those who might monopolize the discussion, and encourage those who might be more reticent in their contributions.

■ Make sure you understand another's contributions before taking issue with him or her. If appropriate, use the PIP'N technique, discussed above.

In what ways is your public speaking class similar to an information-sharing group?

▬ MEMBERS AND LEADERS IN SMALL GROUPS

In this section we consider the roles or functions of small group members and leaders. By gaining insight into the roles of both members and leaders, you will be in a better position to analyze your own small group behavior and to modify it as you wish.

Members in Small Groups

In this section we answer two main questions: What are the major roles that members serve in small group communication? How can you become a more effective participant in small groups?

Member Roles   Member roles can be divided into three general classes (Benne & Sheats 1948). These roles are, of course, frequently served by leaders as well. **Group task roles** are those that help the group focus more specifically on achieving its goals. For example, one person may almost always seek the opinions of others, whereas another may concentrate on elaborating details, another on evaluating suggestions, and still another on stimulating the group to greater activity. Usually, it is better for the roles to be spread about evenly among the members so that each may serve many group task roles.

Group building and maintenance roles focus not only on the task to be performed but also on interpersonal relationships among members. For example, members might positively reinforce others, try to resolve conflict, keep the channels of communication open, or mediate the differences between group members.

Individual roles are counterproductive. They hinder the group's achieving its goal and are individual- rather than group-oriented. Such roles, often termed dysfunctional, hinder the group's productivity and member satisfaction. Examples include expressing negative evaluation, trying to focus attention on oneself, trying to dominate the group, and pleading the case of some special group.

What roles do you normally serve in small groups? Are you satisfied or dissatisfied with your playing these roles? If dissatisfied, what might you do about it?

Member Participation   Another perspective on group membership can be gained from looking at the recommendations for effective participation in small group communication.

- *Be Group-Oriented.* In the small group, you are a member of a team, a larger whole. Your participation is of value to the extent that it advances the goals of the group and promotes member satisfaction. Your task is to pool your talents, knowledge, and insight so that the group may arrive at a better solution than any one person could have developed.
- *Center Conflict on Issues.* Conflict is a natural part of the small group process. It is particularly important in the small group to center conflict on issues rather than on personalities. When you disagree, make it clear that your disagreement is with the solution suggested or the ideas expressed, and not with the person who expressed them.
- *Be Critically Open-Minded.* Come to the group with a mind open to alternatives. Don't come with your mind already made up. When the latter happens, the small group process degenerates into a series of individual debates in which each person argues for his or her own position.

What are to you the most important qualities of a group leader? How might you cultivate such qualities in your own communications?

Three types of leadership styles are often distinguished: laissez-faire (the leader lets the group members do as they wish and offers information only when asked), democratic (the leader provides direction but allows the group to make its own decisions and progress the way its members wish), and authoritarian (the leader dominates the group and makes the decisions regardless of what the group members may want). Which type of leader would you find most difficult to work under in, say, a work team? Which style are you most likely to adopt with, say, subordinates at work?

- *Ensure Understanding.* Make sure your ideas are understood by all participants. If something is worth saying, it is worth saying clearly. Don't hesitate to ask if something you said was clear.

Leaders in Small Groups

In many small groups, one person serves as leader. In others, leadership may be shared by several persons. In some groups, a person may be appointed the leader or may serve as leader because of her or his position within the company or hierarchy. In other groups, the leader may emerge as the group proceeds in fulfilling its functions or may be voted as leader by the group members. In any case, the role of the leader(s) is vital to the well-being and effectiveness of the group. (Even in leaderless groups, where all members are equal, leadership functions must still be served.)

Before examining leadership any further, you should find it interesting to analyze your own views on and style of leadership by taking the accompanying self-test, "What Kind of Leader Are You?"

What situations seem to bring out the leader in you? What situations seem to inhibit your leadership emergence?

Self Test

What Kind of Leader Are You?

Instructions: Respond by indicating YES if the statement is a generally accurate description of your leadership style and NO if it is not.

____ 1. I would speak as a representative of the group.
____ 2. I would settle conflicts when they occur in the group.
____ 3. I would be reluctant to allow the others freedom of action.
____ 4. I would decide what should be done and how it should be done.
____ 5. I would refuse to explain my actions when questioned.
____ 6. I would allow members complete freedom in their work.
____ 7. I would permit the others to use their own judgment in solving problems.
____ 8. I would let the others do their work as they think best.
____ 9. I would allow the others a high degree of initiative.
____10. I would permit the group to set its own pace.

Thinking Critically About Leadership Style

These questions come from an extensive leadership test and should help you focus on some ways a leader can accomplish a task and ensure member satisfaction. Questions 1–5 are phrased so that a leader concerned with completing the group's task would answer YES. Questions 6–10 are phrased so that a leader concerned with ensuring that the group members are satisfied would answer YES. Think about your own style of leadership. Do you adjust your style on the basis of the group, or do you have one style that you use in all situations? Consider too the styles of leadership that you respond to best.

SOURCE: "T-P Leadership Questionnaire: An Assessment of Style," from J. W. Pfeiffer & J. E. Jones, *Structured Experiences for Human Relations Training.* Copyright 1969 by the American Educational Research Association. Reprinted by permission of the publisher.

Leaders need to be concerned with task and people, though each situation will call for a somewhat different combination of task and people concerns (Hersey & Blanchard 1988). For example, a group of scientists working on AIDS research would probably require a leader who provides them with the needed information to accomplish their task. They would be self-motivating and would probably need little in the way of social and emotional encouragement. On the other hand, a group of recovering alcoholics might require leadership that stresses the social and emotional needs of the members.

Leadership effectiveness depends on combining the concerns for task and people according to the specifics of the situation.

Leaders' Functions: Task and People   With this situational view of leadership, we can look at some of the major functions leaders serve. In relatively formal small group situations—as when politicians plan a strategy, advertisers discuss a campaign, or teachers consider educational methods—the leader has several specific functions.

The following functions are not the exclusive property of the leader. Nevertheless, when there is a specific leader, he or she is expected to perform them. Leadership functions are performed best when they are performed unobtrusively—in a natural manner.

- Activate group interaction. Perhaps the group is newly formed and the members feel a bit uneasy with one another. Don't expect diverse members to sit down and discuss a problem without becoming familiar with each other. As the group leader, stimulate the members to interact. Also serve this function when members act as individuals rather than as a group.
- Maintain effective interaction. Even after the group is stimulated to group interaction, see that members maintain effective interaction and that all members have an opportunity to express themselves. When the discussion begins to drag, prod the group to effective interaction: "Do we have any additional comments on the proposal?" "Would anyone like to add anything?"
- Keep members on track. As the leader keep all members reasonably on track by asking questions, interjecting internal summaries as the group goes along, or providing transitions so that the relationship of an issue just discussed to one about to be considered is clear.
- Ensure member satisfaction. In leading a group help it to meet not only its surface purposes but also its underlying or interpersonal purposes that motivated many of the members to come together in the first place.
- Encourage ongoing evaluation and improvement. Most groups encounter obstacles as they try to solve a problem, reach a decision, or generate ideas. Most groups could use some improvement. If the group is to improve, it must focus on itself. Along with trying to solve some external problem, it must try to solve its own internal problems as well—for example, personal conflicts, failure of members to meet on time, or members who come unprepared. As the leader, try to identify such difficulties and encourage and help the group to resolve them.
- Prepare members for the discussion. This may involve preparing the members for the small group interaction as well as for the discussion of a specific issue or problem. If members are to discuss a specific problem, it may be necessary to brief them. Or you might need to distribute certain

How will the skills of leadership figure into your professional life? If such skills will figure prominently, what do you intend to do to master leadership skills more fully?

Create an evaluation form for group membership or group leadership that includes what you consider the most important elements in evaluating the effectiveness of a group member or leader.

materials before the actual discussion or tell members to read certain materials or view a particular film or television show. Whatever the preparations, as the leader, organize and coordinate them.

Thinking Critically About Small Group Communication: Groupthink

An especially insightful perspective on thinking critically in the small group situation is the concept of groupthink. According to Irving Janis (1983), "groupthink" occurs when group members are more concerned with agreement than with careful analysis of a problem.

Many specific behaviors of group members can lead to groupthink. One of the most significant occurs when the group limits its discussion to only a few alternative solutions. Another occurs when despite indications of possible dangers, the group does not reexamine its decisions. Still another happens when the group spends little time discussing why certain initial alternatives were rejected. For example, if the group rejected a certain alternative because it was too costly, members will devote little if any time to ways to reduce the cost.

In groupthink, members are extremely selective in the information they consider seriously. While facts and opinions contrary to the group's position are generally ignored, those that support the group's position are readily and uncritically accepted. The following symptoms should help you recognize groupthink in groups you observe or participate in:

- Group members think the group and its members are invulnerable.
- Members create rationalizations to avoid dealing with warnings or threats.
- Members believe their group is moral.
- Those opposed to the group are perceived in simplistic, stereotyped ways.
- Group pressure is applied to any member who expresses doubts or questions the group's arguments or proposals.
- Members censor their own doubts.
- Group members believe all are in unanimous agreement, whether this is stated or not.
- Group members emerge whose function it is to guard the information that gets to other members, especially when it may create diversity of opinion.

Have you ever witnessed "groupthink"? If so, what were the consequences?

PRESENTING THE GROUP'S THINKING

The purpose of small group interaction is not completed when the group has reached its decisions. Rather, these decisions (findings, conclusions, recommendations) need to be presented to some larger group—the entire union membership, your class as a whole, the board of directors. There are lots of ways in which these decisions can be presented. Here is just a sampling.

The Panel

In the panel, the group members are cast in the role of "experts" and participate informally and without any set pattern of who speaks when. The procedure is similar to that of the regular small group interaction, except that the group is really discussing the issue to inform an audience who is present but does not participate in the actual discussion.

A variation is the two-panel format, with an expert panel and a lay panel. The expert panel is composed of the members who participated in the group and who, ideally, have information the lay panel members do not. The information is shared by the interaction between the lay and the expert panel.

Notice that this is the format followed by the multitude of television talk shows. In these cases the moderator is the host (Winfrey, Donahue). The "expert panel" is the group of guests (the dysfunctional family, the gossip columnists, the political activists). And the lay panel is the members of the studio audience who ask questions or offer comments. Another lay panel consists of the at-home audience, people who can often call in or who probably talk to others in the home or on the phone about the discussion.

Here are a few suggestions for making these presentations more effective:

 How effectively do talk-show hosts lead panel discussions? What host do you find most effective? Least effective?

- Always treat the questions and the questioners with respect. You'll notice this on the popular talk shows. No matter how stupid the question is, the moderator treats it seriously, though often restructuring it just a bit so that it makes more sense. Treat the questions objectively; don't try to bias the question or the answer through your verbal or nonverbal responses.
- Speak in short turns. The group's interaction should resemble a conversation, rather than individual public speeches. Resist the temptation to tell long stories or go into too much detail.
- Try to spread the conversation around the group. Generally, try to give each member the opportunity to speak about equally.

The Symposium and Team Presentation

In the symposium, each member delivers a prepared presentation, a public speech. All speeches are addressed to different aspects of a single topic. In the symposium, the leader introduces the speakers, provides transitions from one speaker to another, and may provide periodic summaries.

The team presentation is popular in business settings. In this type of presentation, two or three members of the group will report the group's findings to a larger group. In some situations, the team presentation may amount to "positive papers," in which the report of the majority and the minority are presented, as is done by the Supreme Court. Or if, say, the group has considered new scheduling systems, the team members might each present one of the proposed systems.

Here are a few suggestions for making these presentations more effective:

- Coordinate your presentations very carefully. Team presentations and symposia are extremely difficult to synchronize. Make sure everyone knows exactly what he or she is responsible for. Make sure there is no (or very little) overlap among the presentations.
- Much as you would rehearse a public speech, try to rehearse these presentations and their coordination. This is rarely possible to do in actual practice, but it's still a useful ideal.
- Select a strong leader to introduce the presentations and to manage audience questions.

TIPS
From Professional Speakers

The good ones [team presentations] are well organized, with each segment clearly tied to and supporting one overall main message, which itself is clearly and positively presented. Each segment is necessary, and no glaring gaps are evident. Coverage of each is appropriate to its importance. Segments of equivalent significance receive comparable treatment, that is, there is no inappropriate overkill or skimpy coverage.

Thomas Leech, consultant and teacher. *How to Prepare, Stage, and Deliver Winning Presentations* (New York: American Management Association, 1992), p. 335.

- Keep last-minute changes to a minimum. When they are unavoidable, make sure all members know about the changes.
- Adhere carefully to time limits. If you speak for more time than allotted, that time is deducted from that of a later speaker. As you can appreciate, violating time limits will severely damage the entire group's presentation.
- Provide clear transitions between the presentations. Internal summaries work especially well as connectives between one speech and the next: "Now that Judy has explained the general proposal, Peter and Margaretta will explain some of the advantages and disadvantages of the proposal. First we'll hear from Peter, with the advantages, and then from Margaretta, with the disadvantages."

The Symposium-Forum

The symposium-forum consists of two parts: a symposium, with prepared speeches (as just explained), and a forum, with questions from the audience and responses by the speakers. The leader introduces the speakers and moderates the question-and-answer session.

The suggestions for making these presentations more effective are essentially the same as for the panel and the symposium.

Oral and Written Reports

In many cases, the group leader will make a presentation of the group's findings, recommendations, or decisions to some other group—the class as a whole, the entire student body, the board of directors, the union membership, or the heads of departments.

 In what other ways might a group's thinking be communicated?

Depending upon the specific situation, these reports may be similar to speeches of information or speeches of persuasion. In some cases, your task might be to simply inform the other group of the recommendations of your committee—for example, recommendations on ways to increase morale, on new pension proposals, or on developments in competing organizations. In other cases, your report will be largely persuasive, for example, to convince the larger group to give you increased funding so that your group's decisions can be implemented.

In some situations, a brief oral report and a more extensive written report are required. A good example of this is the press conference. In this situation, your oral report would be delivered to members of the press, who would also receive a written report. After your oral report, the press would question you for further details. Here are a few suggestions for more effective oral and written reports:

- Write the written report as you would a term paper, and from that develop a summary of the report in the form of a public speech, following the ten steps explained throughout this text.
- Don't read the written report. Even though the oral and the written report may cover essentially the same content, they are totally different in development and presentation. The written report is meant to be read; the oral report is meant to be listened to.

■ In some instances, it is helpful to distribute the written report and use your oral report to highlight the most essential aspects of the report. Members may then refer to the report as you speak—a situation not recommended for most public speeches.

■ In very rare instances, you may choose to distribute the written report only after you have completed your oral report. Generally, people don't like this procedure; they prefer the option of thumbing through the report as they listen or of reserving reading until they have heard the oral report.

UNIT IN BRIEF

The small group	■ A small group is a collection of individuals and is small enough for all members to communicate with relative ease as both senders and receivers ■ The members are related to each other by some common purpose ■ Most small groups develop norms identifying what is considered appropriate
Types of groups	■ The problem-solving group attempts to solve a particular problem or at least to reach a decision ■ The idea generation group tries to generate as many ideas as possible ■ The information-sharing group attempts to acquire new information through a sharing of knowledge or insight
Members and leaders in groups	■ Members should be group-oriented, center conflict on issues, be critically open-minded, and ensure understanding ■ Leaders should seek to address the task and the interpersonal needs of members, and should activate the group interaction, maintain effective interaction, keep members on track, ensure member satisfaction, encourage ongoing evaluation, and prepare members for discussion

Presenting the group's thinking	■ Small groups make use of four major formats:
	   The panel
	   The symposium and team presentations
	   The symposium-forum
	   Oral and written reports

PRACTICALLY SPEAKING

Short Speech Technique

Prepare a two-minute speech in which you:

1. explain the functions of a group to which you belong
2. explain the leadership qualities of a person you know or have read about
3. explain your own leadership traits and abilities
4. illustrate how a problem might be solved by tracing the six stages in the problem-solving process
5. explain how you see decisions made by authority, majority rule, and consensus in the groups with which you are familiar
6. explain how a problem could be analyzed using the "Six Critical Thinking Hats Technique"

25.1   The Problem-Solving Group

Together with four, five, or six others, form a problem-solving group and discuss one of the following questions:

- What should we do about the homeless?
- What should we do to improve student morale?
- What should we do to better prepare ourselves for the job market?
- What should we do to improve student-faculty communication?
- What should be the college's responsibility concerning AIDS?

Before beginning the discussion, prepare a discussion outline, answering the following questions:

- What is the problem? How long has it existed? What caused it? What are its effects?
- What criteria should be used to evaluate possible solutions?
- What are some possible solutions?
- What are the advantages and disadvantages of each of these possible solutions?
- In light of the advantages and disadvantages, what solution seems best?
- How might we put this solution to a test?

After the group discussion, present the findings of the group using one of the following methods or some combination of them:

1. A panel discussion
2. A symposium
3. A two- or three-person team presentation
4. A symposium-forum
5. A simulated press conference
6. An oral report

Thinking Critically About Speeches

*H*ere are five very different speeches, all models of excellence.

Three speeches are by college students:

- *Rebecca Witte's "America's Youth in Crisis" explains teenage suicide and what can be done about it*
- *Maria Lucia R. Anton's "Sexual Assault Policy a Must" argues for the need for a sexual assault policy on campus*
- *Sara Mitchell's "Homosexuals and the Military" argues against restrictions based on affectional orientation*

Two speeches are by professional speakers:

- *Martin Luther King, Jr.'s "I Have a Dream," one of the best-known speeches of our time, focuses on civil rights*
- *William J. Banach's (1991) "Are You Too Busy to Think?" focuses on critical thinking and the need to raise questions even about widely held assumptions*

Along with each speech is a series of questions to provide some initial structure for thinking critically about speeches. The questions are numbered to make it easier to refer to these in small group or general class discussions. The questions focus on a variety of critical thinking skills:

- **Identification** *or* **discovery questions** *ask you to examine a portion of the speech and identify the means used by the speaker to accomplish some aim; for example, How did the speaker gain attention? What thought pattern did the speaker use? What forms of reasoning did the speaker rely on?*
- **Evaluation questions** *are both specific and general. Specific evaluation questions ask that you examine a particular section and evaluate how effectively the speaker handled a task; for example, How effectively did the speaker support an argument? How effective was the orientation? Did the speaker effectively relate the topic to the specific audience? General evaluation questions ask you to make an overall assessment of the speech; for example, Did the speaker accomplish his or her aim? Was the speech an effective one?*
- **Problem-solving** *or* **application questions** *ask that you place yourself in the role of the speaker and consider how you would deal with specific issues; for example, If this speech was addressed to your class, what changes would the*

speaker have to make in the examples used? Would the organizational pattern the speaker used prove effective with your class?

The following suggestions will help you get the most out of your reading-thinking:

1. *First, read the speech all the way through, ignoring the questions.*
2. *After you have read through the entire speech, quickly read through the questions to give yourself a broad overview of the areas focused on.*
3. *Read the speech in brief sections and respond to the questions keyed to these sections.*
4. *Think too about these general issues:*
   a. *What principle is the speaker following or violating?*
   b. *How might the speaker have accomplished his or her aim more effectively? What could the speaker have done better?*
   c. *What adjustments or changes would the speaker have had to make were he or she speaking to other audiences, for example, to your class?*
   d. *What rhetorical devices or techniques can you identify that might prove useful to you as a public speaker?*

Use these speeches as learning tools, as models. What can you learn from these speeches that will help you in your own public speaking?

America's Youth in Crisis—Rebecca Witte

(1) What does the title mean to you? Does it gain your attention?

(2) Do the opening lines gain your attention? Do they involve you in the speech by withholding the topic while you think of what this seven-letter word might be? (3) What other attention-gaining devices might the speaker have used?

(4) What other functions does the introduction serve?

(5) What effect do these statistics have on you?

(6) What is the specific purpose of this speech? The thesis? (7) Are they sufficiently narrowed and limited in scope?

I am a seven letter word. I destroy friends, families, neighborhoods and schools. I am the biggest killer among teenagers today. I am not alcohol. I am not cocaine. I am suicide.

According to the American Suicide Prevention Association, 85% of all teenagers between the ages of 15 and 18 consider committing suicide. Of that 85%, 50% of them will attempt and roughly 32% will succeed.

Obviously, suicide kills thousands of high school teenagers every year. In fact, the ASPA says that over 3,000 teenagers died in 1993 from suicide alone. Why is it then that the high schools aren't doing anything? Why is it that high schools do not have mandatory suicide prevention programs as a part of their everyday curriculum? Those are very good questions and that is why I am here today. First, we'll establish why teenagers commit suicide; next, we'll compare the schools who have a prevention program to those that do not; and finally, look at what we can do to help decrease the number of suicides every year.

According to Psychiatrist, Glenda Taber, in her book *Suicide: The Teenage Death Syndrome,* "Teens are under more stress today than ever before." This stress stems from such things as drugs, alcohol abuse, abusive parents and abusive boyfriend or girlfriend, pressure to have sex, failure, be it on the job or in school, even homosexuality. Taber says that when these teens are so low that they are actually considering suicide, they have what is known as tunnel vision, meaning that they can see no other option other than the one in front of them. They can't even see the light at the end of the tunnel. Dr. Michael Gleason, a Psychiatrist at Christian Northwest Hospital in St. Louis, Missouri, says that suicide is such an easy option for teenagers because they aren't taught the correct ways to deal with the stressors in their lives. So they don't. Instead, they continue to build up one stressor on top of another until they all come toppling over. Suicide then becomes an easy, permanent answer to a difficult, temporary situation. Dr. Gleason puts it this way, "Picture it. These teens are dealing with multitudes of problems every day, and one little thing promises to take it all away." A national organization called TREND, or Turning Reactional Excitement in New Directions, has published a pamphlet entitled "Getting Out or Getting Help." In this pamphlet it states that teens need to be taught that there are other options besides suicide. It goes on to say that every community across the United States has a suicide hotline number. Unfortunately, for these troubled teens the primary place for them to get this vital information is at school.

Then why is it that high schools refuse to do anything? TREND itself has given them two options of what to do: publish the suicide hotline number and teach teenagers other options besides suicide. What is holding them back? According to a study conducted by *Newsweek*, June, 1992, superintendents and principals seem to possess a fear of suicide. They interviewed over 2,000 high school principals. Only 22% of those interviewed claimed to discuss suicide in any way, shape or form. This includes prevention programs in class, assemblies, publication of the community's suicide hotline number and any advertisement that the school has suicide counseling available. That leaves 80% of the high school students in America to fend for themselves. One superintendent went so far as to say, "Hey if we discussed everything that affects teenagers today, we'd have to add on another month to the school year." What he doesn't understand is that unless he decides to face this problem he will lose many of his students before the year 2000.

This fear that high school authorities have of suicide often snowballs into disaster. According to the *St. Louis Post Dispatch*, August, 1992, a newspaper editor of a small school in St. Charles County, Missouri, wanted to publish an article about suicide in her school's paper. She dealt with the issues honestly and carefully, providing some statistics, some things to look for in friends and their community's suicide hotline

(8) Do you agree with the proposition that "teens are under more stress today than ever before"? If not, what would have convinced you?

(9) What credibility do you ascribe to TREND? To what sources would you attribute greater credibility?

(10) Are you surprised at the principals' attitude toward suicide information? What does it lead you to think about high school programs in suicide prevention?

(11) What effect did the *St. Louis Post Dispatch* article have on you? What does it lead you to think?

number. The principal, however, would not allow the article to be published, saying his school did not have a problem with suicide. The article went unpublished, as did the suicide hotline number. Later that year, the editor graduated. And two days after her graduation, her best friend shot himself in the head. Two weeks after that, an alum from the school from two years before shot himself in the head. And two weeks after that, the principal's son shot himself in the head. Three suicides from a school where "suicide is not a problem."

The real problem is that the story is true and is happening to schools all across the country. Another problem is that the story does not end here. The small community found out about the editor's article and demanded the principal's resignation, blaming him for the three deaths. He resigned and moved on to another high school, initiating a suicide prevention program there, and at the small school . . . well, suicide still isn't a problem. You see, even the communities are afraid of suicide. They are afraid that by admitting suicide is a problem, they're giving in to it.

(12) Does the *San Francisco Tribune* article convince you that suicide prevention programs work? What other evidence might you want?

Admittance is the first step. Unfortunately, most programs are not initiated until after the school has suffered great suicidal loss. According to the *San Francisco Tribune,* March, 1993, North High School in San Francisco had the highest suicide average in a ten-year period. Their average death rate was five deaths a year with an additional 15 attempts. A new principal came in and decided to stop the death and initiated a program. In the past three years their average death rate has dropped from five deaths a year to less than one and from 15 attempts to about three.

(13) Was the research adequate for a speech on this topic? What did you like about the research? How might it have been improved?

Obviously, these programs work. And they work for three reasons. The first is because most often these programs are interspliced with health class. Health class is a mandatory class every public high school student must take in order to graduate. By making it mandatory, the schools are guaranteeing these students will take the class. I mean, what student is going to pick "Death 101" over Home Ec or Shop? The second reason they work is because the books that deal with suicide do so in a down-to-earth personal manner. This appeals to teenagers, making them want to learn. So, they do. The final reason they work is because teenagers are able to take this new information throughout the rest of their lives. This is beneficial to you and me because these students are graduating with this vital information. They know the statistics, they know the signs to look for in friends and they know the community's suicide hotline number. They know what to do when suicide comes knocking not only at their doors, but at our doors as well.

(14) Would you want evidence that the books really do deal with suicide in a "down-to-earth personal manner"? If so, what kind of evidence would be especially effective to an audience such as your own class?

(15) What organizational pattern did the speaker use? What other organizational patterns would have been appropriate?

The programs work, but it takes a superintendent who is willing to face the issues. Without our help this could take years and many lives. So what can we do to help decrease the numbers of suicidal deaths? There are many things, but first and foremost, make sure every person you know knows your community's suicide hotline number. It's very easy to find; simply open up the yellow pages and look up "suicide." Secondly, check with the high schools in your area and see if they have a suicide prevention program. If they don't, make them. We all know that with enough arguing, enough petitioning, enough phone calls, something has to be done. Talk to the parents, talk to the students, talk to the school board if you have to, but do something to stop the death in your area. Remember, just because you don't hear about it, doesn't mean it doesn't happen.

Finally, because suicide does not just affect teenagers, because it affects every age group across the spectrum, check for some of these possible suicide signs in friends of yours as published in *Health* from Heath Publishing in 1993:

1. Severe depression
2. Giving away personal possessions
3. Buying a weapon
4. Talking about suicide
5. A decrease in energy
6. A sudden increased use of drugs or alcohol
7. Wanting to continually be alone

We all know why teens commit suicide. We all know what happens to the schools who do nothing compared to those that do. And now, we know what we can do to decrease the numbers of suicides every year. The next suicide victim could be someone you know. You may hold their life, their future, in the palm of your hands.

SOURCE: Speech given by Rebecca Witte, University of Missouri–St. Louis. She was coached by Sherry LaBoon and Tom Preston. Reprinted with permission of the Interstate Oratorial Association, *Winning Orations*, 1994, Larry Schnoor, editor.

(16) Are you going to comply with the speaker's recommendations—to look up the phone number and to check with the local high schools? If not, why not? What suggestions might you have been willing to follow?

(17) What functions did the conclusion serve?

(18) What kind of visual aid might you have used in this speech?

(19) What one thing did you like best about this speech?

(20) What one suggestion would you make to improve this speech?

Sexual Assault Policy a Must— Maria Lucia R. Anton

"If you want to take her blouse off, you have to ask. If you want to touch her breast, you have to ask. If you want to move your hand down to her genitals, you have to ask. If you want to put your finger inside her, you have to ask."

What I've just quoted is part of the freshman orientation at Antioch College in Ohio. In the sexual offense policy of this college, emphasis is given to three major points: (1) If you have a sexually transmitted disease, you must disclose it to a

(1) What effect do the opening lines of the speech have on you? Do they gain your attention?

potential partner; (2) To knowingly take advantage of some-one who is under the influence of alcohol, drugs and/or prescribed medication is not acceptable behavior in the Antioch community; (3) Obtaining consent is an on-going process in any sexual interaction. The request for consent must be specific to each act.

The policy is designed to create a "safe" campus environ-ment according to Antioch President Alan Guskin. For those who engage in sex, the goal is 100% consensual sex. It isn't enough to ask someone if they would like to have sex, you have to get verbal consent every step of the way.

This policy has been highly publicized and you may have heard it before. The policy addresses sexual offenses such as rape, which involves penetration, and sexual assault, which does not. In both instances, the respondent coerced or forced the primary witness to engage in non-consensual sexual conduct with the respondent or another.

Sexual assault has become a major problem on U.S. campuses today. However, in spite of increased sexual assaults on campuses, many still go without a policy to protect their students. The University of Guam, where I am a senior, is one example.

Sexual assault has become a reality on many campuses across the nation. Carleton College in Northfield, Minnesota, was sued for $800,000 in damages by four university women. The women charged that Carleton was negligent in protecting them against a known rapist. From the June 3, 1991, issue of *Time Magazine*:

> Amy had been on campus for just five weeks when she joined some friends to watch a video in the room of a senior. One by one the other students went away, leaving her alone with a student whose name she didn't even know. "It ended up with his hands around my throat," she recalls. In a lawsuit she has filed against the college, she charges that he locked the door and raped her again and again for the next four hours. "I didn't want him to kill me, I just kept trying not to cry." Only afterwards did he tell her, almost defiantly, his name. It was on top of the "castration list" posted on women's bathroom walls around campus to warn other students about college rapists. Amy's attacker was found guilty of sexual assault but was only suspended.
>
> Julie started dating a fellow cast member in a Carleton play. They had never slept together, she charges in a civil suit, until he came to her dorm room one night, uninvited, and raped her. She struggled to hold her life and education together, but finally could manage no longer and left school. Only later did Julie learn that her assailant was the same man who had attacked Amy.

(2) What effect does this extended quotation have? Might it have been more effective were the story told in the speaker's own words?

Ladies and gentlemen, the court held that the college knew this man was a rapist. The administration may have been able to prevent this from happening if they had expelled the attacker, but they didn't. My campus has no reports of sexual assault; is administration waiting for someone to be assaulted before they formulate a sexual assault policy? This mistake has been made elsewhere. We don't have to prove it again.

Perhaps some statistics will help you understand the magnitude of the problem. According to *New Statesman & Society,* June 21, 1991, issue:

■ A 1985 survey of sampled campuses by *Ms. Magazine* and the National Institute of Mental Health found that 1 in every 4 college women were victims of sexual assault. Seventy-four percent knew their attackers. Even worse, between 30 to 40 percent of male students indicated that they might force a woman to have sex if they knew they would escape punishment.

■ In just one year, from 1988 to 1989, reports of student rape at the University of California increased from 2 to 80.

These numbers are indeed disturbing. But more disturbing are the effects of sexual assault. A victim feeling the shock of why something this terrible was allowed to happen. Having intense fears that behind every dark corner could be an attacker ready to grab her, push her to the ground and sexually assault her. Many waking moments of anxiety and impaired concentration as she remembers the attack. Countless nights of reliving the traumatic incident in her sleep. Mood swings and depression as she tries to deal internally with the physical hurt and the emotional turmoil that this attack has caused.

Many campuses are open invitations for sexual assault. The absence of a policy is a grand invitation. I have never been sexually assaulted so why do I care so much about a policy? You know why, because I could be assaulted. I won't sit and wait to be among 1 out of every 4 women on my campus to be assaulted. The first step to keep myself out of the statistics is to push for a sexual assault policy on my campus. One way to do this is through a petition to the university.

Although the Antioch policy sounds a little far fetched and has been the target of criticism in comedy routines such as those on *Saturday Night Live,* although students feel this is unnatural, many campuses are taking heed and revising their own policies. Campuses like mine don't have a sexual policy to revisit. Does yours?

By far the most controversial policy today is that of Antioch. I'm not saying that we need one as specific as theirs, but every university has a responsibility to provide a safe

(3) What are the purpose and thesis of the speech? Note that these are not stated explicitly until the end of the speech. Should they have been stated earlier?

(4) How effectively does the speaker make the case that sexual assault on college campuses is a real problem? Assume the audience did not believe this was a real problem—would the speaker have convinced them?

(5) Does the speaker make the effects of sexual assault real to the audience? Would both men and women understand the speaker equally? How would you have made this point to members of your class?

(6) In what way does the speaker establish her credibility here?

environment for its students. Universities have an obligation to provide a sexual assault policy to protect their students.

The following points are fundamental to the safety of the students and need to be addressed by universities:

1. Every campus should have a sexual assault policy that is developed with input from the students, faculty, staff, and administration. The policy then needs to be publicized in the student handbook. The school newspaper should print and campus radio broadcast the policy periodically to heighten awareness.

2. Campuses must institute programs to educate students and other campus personnel. Examples of these include discussing the sexual assault policy during mandatory student orientation and conducting special workshops for faculty and other staff.

3. Outline a step-by-step written procedure to guarantee that sexual assault victims are assisted by the university. It is pertinent that they are not without support at this very critical time.

My vision is a campus where there is no place for any sexual assault. I want to leave my classroom at night knowing that my trip from the building to the car will not be one of fear for my personal safety.

You may be saying to yourself that there are laws to handle crimes like these. From *The Chronicle of Higher Education*, May 15, 1991, Jane McDonnell, a senior lecturer in women's studies at Carleton, says colleges cannot turn their backs on women. "We'd be abandoning victims if we merely sent them to the police," she says. "The wheels of justice tend to grind slowly and rape has one of the lowest conviction rates of any crime."

Without a policy, most institutions lack specific penalties for sexual assault and choose to prosecute offenders under the general student-conduct code. In cases such as Carleton College, Amy's attacker was allowed back on campus after his suspension and consequently he raped again.

Although the policy may not stop the actual assault, would-be offenders would think twice before committing sexual assault if they knew they would be punished. In addition, it guarantees justice for victims of sexual assault. We need to make it loud and clear that sexual assault will not be tolerated.

Yes, universities have a big task in the struggle to prevent sexual assault.

You and I can actively assist in this task and can make a giant contribution to move it forward. On my campus students

---

(7) How reasonable do you find the speaker's proposals?

(8) Does the speaker effectively answer the question of the audience member who says to himself or herself, "Why can't the police handle these cases?" Is this issue relevant to the speaker's specific purpose?

(9) How would you evaluate the adequacy of research for the speech? How would you evaluate its integration into the speech?

have not only voiced their concerns but we have also started a petition demanding that the university formulate a sexual assault policy.

The bottom line is, we need to prevent sexual assault on campus. The key to prevention is a sexual assault policy. If you don't have a policy, then you need to petition your administration to have one. I know I won't stop my advocacy until I see a policy on my campus.

SOURCE: This speech was given by Maria Lucia R. Anton, University of Guam. She was coached by Don R. Swanson. Reprinted with permission of the Interstate Oratorical Association, *Winning Orations*, 1994, Larry G. Schnoor, editor.

(10) What functions does the speaker's conclusion serve?

(11) What would you have titled this speech if you were delivering it to your class?

Homosexuals and the Military—Sara Mitchell

When I went home for the holidays last December, my cousin, Ellen, announced that she's in love and this time she thinks it's forever. Her lover's name is Linda. Twelve years after acknowledging to herself that she is a lesbian, Ellen decided to come out. She was tired of lying about who she is.

Gays and lesbians are our cousins, our brothers and sisters, sons and daughters, even mothers and fathers. A recent article in *Science* magazine estimates the homosexual population at between 4% and 10%. Odds are all of us have known numerous homosexuals, with or without being aware of it.

What is homosexuality? Until recently, most people believed it was a disease which could be cured or that it was willful immoral conduct. However, more and more recent studies suggest what most gays have long felt. Sexual orientation is not a choice. It is biologically determined and trying to change it would be like trying to change the color of your eyes.

This changing definition of homosexuality has resulted in a lot of controversy and has complicated the issue of whether homosexuals should be allowed to serve in the United States armed forces. This is the topic of my speech today: Homosexuals and the Military.

First, I would like to examine the current policy on gays in the military. Second, I will explore the rationale (or irrationality) behind it.

The current policy is the result of a compromise between the Clinton administration, Congress and the military leadership. It attempts to distinguish homosexuality from homosexual behavior. The policy states, "Homosexual orientation is

(1) Does the opening story gain your attention? Why or why not?

(2) Does the speaker make the topic relevant to the audience? What do you think of as the speaker stresses the topic's relevance?

(3) As you read the next few paragraphs, consider how the speaker seems to have estimated her audience's initial attitudes toward homosexuals in the military. What adaptations do you feel she may have made?

(4) Would you have liked supporting evidence for these statements?

(5) At this point, do you know the position the speaker will take? If so, what gives you the clues? If this speaker were delivering this speech to your class, how would you change this introduction?

(6) Is the orientation sufficiently clear?

(7) Is the distinction between homosexuality and homosexual behavior sufficiently clear?

not a bar to service . . . unless manifested by homosexual conduct."

What constitutes homosexual conduct? Sex with someone of the same gender, of course. But holding hands and same-sex dancing are also grounds for discharge. And statements interpreted by anyone as indicating homosexuality could launch an investigation.

Anthony Rotundo states in a March, 1993, issue of *The Chronicle of Higher Education* that many famous 19th century men such as Abraham Lincoln and Daniel Webster had romantic friendships with other men. Alexander Hamilton, while serving under George Washington, wrote to another man:

I wish [to] convince you that I love you. I shall only tell you that 'til you bade us adieu. I hardly knew the value you had taught my heart to set upon you.

Today, this letter, which is preserved in Hamilton's papers, would certainly cause an investigation and that investigation would probably end with Hamilton's discharge.

What about same-sex dancing? Does that mean all kinds of dancing? Is that slam-dancing or just slow-dancing? My sister and I went out not too long ago, and our dates didn't feel like dancing so we danced together. I guess that was an incestuous as well as a homosexual act.

John Money, professor emeritus of medical psychology at Johns Hopkins University, points out that during the Vietnam War draftees claimed homosexuality to avoid service. Suppose we became involved in another unpopular war? Simply holding hands with someone of the same gender could make anyone ineligible for service.

The wording of the policy is ridiculous at best and at worst could pose serious problems for the military.

Now I will discuss the rationale behind the policy on gays in the armed forces. As I said, it is the result of a compromise. Its stated intent is to allow homosexuals to serve their country—as long as they deny their homosexuality that is. Actually, its aim is to keep gays out of the military.

Those who vehemently insist that homosexuals should not be allowed to serve in the military have a multitude of reasons. For many it is a moral issue. Others fear the spread of AIDS or cite problems due to lack of privacy. Perhaps the strongest argument against allowing gays and lesbians to serve is that it will hurt morale and unit cohesion. These are all valid concerns and I will address each one separately.

Morality. We should respect and accommodate each other's moral beliefs as much as possible, but we should also respect each other's rights and personal freedom. Many people feel that extramarital sex of any kind is immoral, but no one is asking single heterosexual men and women to take vows of

---

(8) What effect does the example of Alexander Hamilton have on you? What do the letter and the investigation it would have caused have on your thinking about homosexuals and the military?

(9) At what point did this speech become persuasive? What is the earliest reference that this was a persuasive rather than an informative speech?

(10) In what other ways might the speaker have phrased her transition?

(11) Does the speaker select the most important issues for discussion?

(12) How effective is the argument used in this section on morality? What else might the speaker have said?

celibacy to serve their country. Behavior that does not cause harm to others should be at least tolerated if not condoned.

AIDS. most people seem to be unaware of the military's AIDS testing program. Every single recruit is tested and rejected if the results are positive. Once in the military, mandatory testing continues on a regular basis. The armed forces probably have a lower AIDS rate than any other segment of the population.

Lack of Privacy. Before I address this concern, I'd like to say that I am a veteran. I served four years in the Army and three in the Army Reserves, including seven months of active duty during the Gulf War. And, by the way, I'm straight. During my four years in the regular Army, I went to the field countless times and often lived in tents with the men in my platoon. During Desert Storm, I went to the Gulf with a combat engineering company of about 150 men and three women. We lived in the desert for six months. At one point, my whole battalion, 700 men and 30 women, lived together under one roof in a warehouse. We managed to live peacefully together and, with a little consideration, give each other necessary privacy. The few problems we did have were the result of attitudes not circumstances.

It could be argued that this is not the same as gays and straights living together. Heterosexual men seem particularly concerned about being the object of unwanted lust and sexual advances. Forgive me for enjoying that they are frightened of being in the same position women have always been in. The simple solution is absolute zero tolerance of sexual harassment of any kind.

And finally, morale. The current Department of Defense directive states that:

> The presence of [homosexuals] adversely affects the ability of military services to maintain discipline, good order and morale; to foster mutual trust and confidence among service-members.

General Schwarzkopf, testifying before the Senate Armed Forces Committee, said that introducing homosexuality into any military organization would destroy "the very bonding that is so important for the unit's survival in war." This stance ignores what James Burk, associate professor of sociology at Texas A&M University, points out is an "undisputed" fact. "Homosexuals have always served in the military (often with exemplary records) and will continue to do so." Homosexuality is not the problem. Homophobic attitudes are, and attitudes, unlike sexual orientation, can be changed.

I have discussed the ban on gays in the military and the reasons behind it. I have attempted to show why the ban is unacceptable and that the reasons for the ban are invalid. In

(13) Are you convinced that the armed forces have a lower AIDS rate than any other segment of the population? What evidence—in addition to the testing policy noted by the speaker—might have convinced you of this?

(14) What effect does this discussion have on your perception of the speaker as a credible spokesperson on this topic? Would it have been more effective if the speaker discussed this earlier in the speech?

(15) What effect did the discussion of the heterosexual male have on your perception of the speaker?

(16) How effectively does the speaker argue for the proposition that homophobic attitudes, not homosexuality, are the cause of the difficulties with homosexuals in the military?

(17) What functions did the conclusion serve? Were these functions served effectively?

(18) Was the evidence sufficient? Were the sources cited appropriate to the topic? What other evidence would you have used?

(19) How many transitions can you identify? In what other parts of the speech might transitions have

(20) What organizational changes would you have made in this speech?

(21) What other titles might have been appropriate? How would you title this speech for an audience that favors including homosexuals in the military? For an audience opposed to including homosexuals in the military?

conclusion, I'd like to say that all Americans who are willing to serve their country should be given that opportunity without having to deny their very nature. Let us respect each other's rights and let us respect each other.

SOURCE: This speech was given by Sara Mitchell, Tennessee Technological University. She was coached by Graham Kash. Reprinted with permission of the Interstate Oratorical Association, *Winning Orations*, 1994, Larry G. Schnoor, editor.

I Have a Dream—Martin Luther King, Jr.*

This is probably one of the most famous speeches of the twentieth century. Before reading the speech, examine what you know about it. What did you hear about it? Did you read it in elementary or high school or in college? If so, in what context? What image do you have of this speech?

I am happy to join with you today in what will go down in history as the greatest demonstration for freedom in the history of our nation.

Five score years ago, a great American, in whose symbolic shadow we stand today, signed the Emancipation Proclamation. This momentous decree came as a great beacon light of hope to millions of Negro slaves, who had been seared in the flames of withering injustice. It came as a joyous daybreak to end the long night of their captivity.

But one hundred years later, the Negro is still not free. One hundred years later, the life of the Negro is still sadly crippled by the manacles of segregation and the chains of discrimination. One hundred years later, the Negro lives on a lonely island of poverty in the midst of a vast ocean of material prosperity. One hundred years later, the Negro is still languished in the corners of American society and finds himself an exile in his own land. So we have come here today to dramatize a shameful condition.

One of the standards often used in evaluating speeches is universality (see Unit 5)—that is, the extent to which the speech addresses issues that are important for all time and for all people. This standard is much like the standard used in evaluating great literature. As you read this speech, keep this standard in mind. (1) How would you evaluate this speech using the standard of universality?

In a sense we've come to our nation's capital to cash a check. When the architects of our republic wrote the magnificent words of the Constitution and the Declaration of Independence, they were signing a promissory note to which every American was to fall heir. This note was a promise that all men—yes, black men as well as white men—would be guaranteed the unalienable rights of life, liberty, and the pursuit of happiness.

Speeches are addressed to specific audiences and are judged largely on the basis of how effectively the speaker adapts the topic and purpose to a specific audience. Yet there are often other audiences the speaker hopes to address. (2) To whom was King speaking? That is, whom did King see as his primary audience? What other audiences was King addressing?

It is obvious today that America has defaulted on this promissory note insofar as her citizens of color are concerned. Instead of honoring this sacred obligation, America has given the Negro people a bad check; a check which has come back

Notice that in this speech, neither an elaborate orientation nor any lengthy attention-getting devices are used in the introduction. (3) Given the circumstances of this speech (see footnote to speech), were King's rhetorical choices effective?

*The speaker, Martin Luther King, Jr. (1929–1968), was a Baptist minister and civil rights leader who won the Nobel Prize in 1964 for his nonviolent struggle for racial equality. This speech was delivered on August 28, 1963, at the Lincoln Memorial in Washington, D.C., to some 200,000 blacks and whites holding a demonstration. Some ten civil rights leaders—after meeting with President Kennedy—addressed the crowd. It was generally agreed that King's speech was the highlight of the demonstration.

marked "insufficient funds." But we refuse to believe that the bank of justice is bankrupt. We refuse to believe that there are insufficient funds in the great vaults of opportunity of this nation. So we've come to cash this check—a check that will give us upon demand the riches of freedom and the security of justice. We have also come to this hallowed spot to remind America of the fierce urgency of now. This is no time to engage in the luxury of cooling off or to take the tranquilizing drug of gradualism. Now is the time to make real the promises of Democracy. Now is the time to rise from the dark and desolate valley of segregation to the sunlight of racial justice. Now is the time to lift our nation from the quicksands of racial injustice to the solid rock of brotherhood. Now is the time to make justice a reality for all of God's children.

It would be fatal for the nation to overlook the urgency of the moment. This sweltering summer of the Negro's legitimate discontent will not pass until there is an invigorating autumn of freedom and equality. Nineteen-sixty-three is not an end, but a beginning. Those who hope that the Negro needed to blow off steam and will now be content will have a rude awakening if the nation returns to business as usual. There will be neither rest nor tranquility in America until the Negro is granted his citizenship rights. The whirlwinds of revolt will continue to shake the foundations of our nation until the bright day of justice emerges.

But that is something that I must say to my people who stand on the warm threshold which leads into the palace of justice. In the process of gaining our rightful place we must not be guilty of wrongful deeds. Let us not seek to satisfy our thirst for freedom by drinking from the cup of bitterness and hatred.

We must forever conduct our struggle on the high plane of dignity and discipline. We must not allow our creative protest to degenerate into physical violence. Again and again we must rise to the majestic heights of meeting physical force with soul force. The marvelous new militancy which has engulfed the Negro community must not lead us to a distrust of all white people, for many of our white brothers, as evidenced by their presence here today, have come to realize that their destiny is tied up with our destiny. And they have come to realize that their freedom is inextricably bound to our freedom. We cannot walk alone.

And as we walk we must make the pledge that we shall always march ahead. We cannot turn back. There are those who ask the devotees of civil rights, "When will you be satisfied?" We can never be satisfied as long as the Negro is the victim of the unspeakable horrors of police brutality. We can never be satisfied as long as our bodies, heavy with the fatigue of travel, cannot gain lodging in the motels of the highways and the hotels of the cities. We cannot be satisfied as long as the Negro's basic mobility is from a smaller ghetto to a larger

(4) How effective is this metaphor of the "check" and "promissory note"? Would this metaphor work if members of your class were the intended listeners?

(5) Given the times and what you know of Martin Luther King's reputation during this time in history, how would you estimate King's credibility prior to the speech (his intrinsic credibility)? (6) Did King do anything in the speech to further establish his credibility (extrinsic credibility)? (7) How would you describe King's terminal credibility to his immediate audience after the speech?

(8) What is the thesis of this speech? Was this thesis appropriate given the general climate of the times, the specific occasion, the immediate audience, and King's purpose?

(9) What is the general purpose of this speech? The specific purpose? (10) What response did King want from his immediate audience? What response did King want from the black community? From the white community? From the country at large?

(11) What kinds of reasoning can you identify in this speech? Was the reasoning logical? Effective?

(12) What kinds of motivational appeals does King use? Are these generally effective? (13) What to you is the single most effective motivational appeal?

(14) What organizational pattern did King use in this speech? Was this pattern effective? (15) Was this speech organized on the basis of primacy or recency? (16) Was a climax or an anticlimax order used? Was this order effective? What specific evidence can you cite to support your conclusions?

(17) How effective are the specific examples King uses throughout the speech? (18) What other kinds of supporting materials does King use?

(19) How effective is the repetition of "I have a dream"?

This speech is regarded by many as a model of stylistic excellence. Examine the language used. (20) How effective is it? (21) What stylistic elements make it effective? Do some stylistic elements detract from its effectiveness? Explain.

(22) How would you characterize this speech on an oral-written style continuum? What specific phrases can you point to in support of your conclusion?

Each speaker has his or her own style. Another speaker's style—especially a speaker as unique as King—cannot easily be adapted. (23) What aspects of King's style would be inappropriate for you to adapt to your own speaking? (24) What aspects would be appropriate? On what basis do you make this distinction?

one. We can never be satisfied as long as our children are stripped of their selfhood and robbed of their dignity by signs stating "For Whites Only." We cannot be satisfied as long as a Negro in Mississippi cannot vote and a Negro in New York believes he has nothing for which to vote. No, no, we are not satisfied, and we will not be satisfied until justice rolls down like waters and righteousness like a mighty stream.

I am not unmindful that some of you have come here out of great trials and tribulations. Some of you have come fresh from narrow jail cells. Some of you have come from areas where your quest for freedom left you battered by the storms of persecution and staggered by the winds of police brutality. You have been the veterans of creative suffering. Continue to work with the faith that unearned suffering is redemptive.

Go back to Mississippi, go back to Alabama, go back to South Carolina, go back to Georgia, go back to Louisiana, go back to the slums and ghettos of our northern cities knowing that somehow this situation can and will be changed. Let us not wallow in the valley of despair.

I say to you today, my friends, so even though we face the difficulties of today and tomorrow, I still have a dream. It is a dream deeply rooted in the American dream.

I have a dream that one day this nation will rise up and live out the true meaning of its creed: "We hold these truths to be self-evident; that all men are created equal."

I have a dream that one day on the red hills of Georgia the sons of former slaves and the sons of former slaveowners will be able to sit down together at the table of brotherhood; I have a dream—

That one day even the state of Mississippi, a state sweltering with the heat of injustice, sweltering with the heat of oppression, will be transformed into an oasis of freedom and justice; I have a dream—

That my four little children will one day live in a nation where they will not be judged by the color of their skin but by the content of their character; I have a dream today.

I have a dream that one day down in Alabama, with its vicious racists, with its governor having his lips dripping with the words of interposition and nullification, one day right there in Alabama little black boys and black girls will be able to join hands with little white boys and white girls as sisters and brothers; I have a dream today.

I have a dream that one day every valley shall be exalted, every hill and mountain shall be made low, and rough places will be made plane and crooked places will be made straight, and the glory of the Lord shall be revealed, and all flesh shall see it together.

This is our hope. This is the faith that I go back to the South with. With this faith we will be able to hew out of the mountain of despair a stone of hope. With this faith we will be able to transform the jangling discords of our nation into a beautiful symphony of brotherhood. With this faith we will be able to work together, to pray together, to struggle together, to go to jail together, to stand up for freedom together, knowing that we will be free one day.

This will be the day. . . . This will be the day when all of God's children will be able to sing with new meaning "My country 'tis of thee, sweet land of liberty, of thee I sing. Land where my fathers died, land of the pilgrims' pride, from every mountainside, let freedom ring," and if America is to be a great nation—this must become true.

So let freedom ring—from the prodigious hilltops of New Hampshire, let freedom ring; from the mighty mountains of New York, let freedom ring—from the heightening Alleghenies of Pennsylvania!

Let freedom ring from the snowcapped Rockies of Colorado.

Let freedom ring from the curvaceous slopes of California!

But not only that; let freedom ring from Stone Mountain of Georgia!

Let freedom ring from Lookout Mountain of Tennessee!

Let freedom ring from every hill and mole hill of Mississippi. From every mountainside, let freedom ring, and when this happens . . .

When we allow freedom to ring, when we let it ring from every village and every hamlet, from every state and every city, we will be able to speed up that day when all of God's children, black men and white men, Jews and Gentiles, Protestants and Catholics, will be able to join hands and sing in the words of the old Negro spiritual, "Free at last! free at last! thank God almighty, we are free at last!"

(25) What type of conclusion did King use? Was this effective?

(26) What one feature of this entire speech do you find most effective? (27) What one feature do you find least effective?

(28) What do you remember most after reading this speech? (29) What public speaking principle might you derive on the basis of what you remember from this speech?

SOURCE: "I Have A Dream" by Martin Luther King, Jr. Reprinted by arrangement with the Heirs to the Estate of Martin Luther King, Jr., c/o Joan Daves Agency as agent for the proprietor. Copyright © 1963 by Martin Luther King, Jr., copyright renewed 1991 by Coretta Scott King.

Are You Too Busy to Think? Change Comes from the Questions We Ask—William J. Banach

My business is creating strategic advantage. I help people envision preferred futures and develop plans for getting there. My clients tend to be ahead of the curve. Here's why: They understand that thinking is the first step to being a step ahead.

But most people don't have time to think. They're too busy working!

Strange, isn't it?

How many times have you heard people say that they do their best thinking in the car. But when they pull into the park-

(1) How effectively does Banach involve his audience? (Remember that the audience consists of members of the Association of Wisconsin School Administrators.)

(2) How does Banach gain attention in his introduction? (3) Does Banach continue to use attention-gaining devices throughout his speech? (4) Does Banach establish a speaker-audience-topic relationship? If so, how? (5) Does Banach orient or preview his speech for his listeners? If so, how?

(6) Does Banach avoid the major pitfalls of introductions? Does he apologize or pretend? Make hollow promises? Preface his introduction?

(7) What is the thesis of this speech? How is it presented in the speech? For example, is it explicitly stated? Implied? (8) Is this thesis appropriate to the speaker's audience?

(9) What is the general purpose of the speech? The specific purpose? (10) Do you think the speaker accomplishes his purpose? On what do you base your conclusion?

(11) Does this example of the delay in textbooks and the inevitability of their being outdated convince you that textbooks are in fact outdated? (12) How might you verify Banach's claim?

(13) How effective was the Woodpecker theme? Would it be effective with your class as an audience?

ing lot, they turn off the car and shut down their thinking … so they can get to work.

Perhaps that's why there are too few new ideas. Perhaps that's why much of what we do looks like much of what we've done.

Here's your chance to rebel. Take time to think . . . right now. Shut the door. Get comfortable. Read the rest of this article. Then stare out the window. Indulge yourself in 20 minutes of thinking—30 if you're radical.

To get started, use Banach's Woodpecker Questions. These are questions for which we have an answer, but we're really not sure it's correct. (The classic is: "Do woodpeckers get headaches?" Scientists tell us the woodpecker's brain is wrapped in a huge mucous pad, so the bird can bang away all day and never get headaches. So, while the answer to the question is "no," we're not really sure.)

Woodpecker Question 1: Why do we use textbooks? We think we know the answer, but are we really sure? Information is doubling every $2\frac{1}{2}$ years—every 900 days! By the time today's kindergartner moves through the grades to graduation, the body of information will quadruple!

Now, add the data above to this: It takes about 10 years to get a textbook into print. From the time the author conceives ideas, develops thoughts, writes, edits, hooks up with a publisher, rewrites, and engages in myriad other steps, a decade passes. Next, a school district curriculum review committee spends two years evaluating the book before making a recommendation (which then passes through the administrative hierarchy before approval by the school board). Finally, the school district adopts a brand-new 12-year-old book . . . and students use it for five to seven years, sometimes more.

In this scenario, the student at the end of the line is using a 19-year-old book (10 + 2 + 7). This leads to a dead duck question: How can a student keep current by reading a 19-year-old book? (We have an answer to dead duck questions and we're sure it's right; e.g., "Do dead ducks quack?")

Woodpecker Question 2: Why do schools have to be places? Twenty percent of Americans work at home. The percentage is destined to increase.

Many of these home-based workers have computers, fax machines and sophisticated telephone equipment. Long distance they look and sound like "real" companies. And who else has access to the technology which makes home-based employment possible? The children of these workers.

So, why should students be transported to a place? They can get their lesson on video, from the best instructors in the world. Why should students spend time in an ill-equipped lab? They can do computer simulations. Why should they write out their lessons longhand? They can use word processors and fax their lessons to school.

During the 1990s we will repackage education. Learning will take place in the home, in the community, at school and in between. And by the dawning of the new century we will have dramatic new designs for the delivery of schooling.

"What about socialization?" asks Brontosaurus Skepticus. "Students won't learn how to interact with one another." The fact is there isn't much socializing at school. A lot of kids don't know a lot of kids. Think about it. In a high school there are typically five or six 55-minute periods with five minutes for passing from one class to the next. How do you socialize when you have to rush from one place to another and be quiet once you get there? (Woodpecker Question 2a!)

Woodpecker Question 3: Why don't we teach to the test? Obviously, it wouldn't be fair . . . or so we have learned.

But, if you think about it, education is one of the few arenas where participants often don't know what's expected of them . . . until it's too late.

In every sport, the objective is clear and the evaluation criteria are known before the game begins. Basketball players know they have to get the ball through the hoop more frequently than members of the other team. In baseball, the objective is to score more runs; in football, more points.

Other professions know the objectives in advance. For example, in medicine everyone works to heal the patient. In fact, the patient is part of the process. He/she knows in advance of any treatment which procedures will be performed, the expected outcomes, and his/her role in the process.

But in education the objectives aren't clear. Most school districts can't tell students and their parents what to expect from a twelve-year investment. (Sorry, Brontosaurus Skepticus, we haven't explained what we mean by "a quality education for every child" . . . nor have we defined "skills for the changing world of work" or "producing learners who will be fully functioning members of a multifaceted society.")

Perhaps we should start by spelling out what we want students to learn. Then we should tell them the objectives and expectations up front. We should also make clear their responsibility in the process. Maybe that's all that blocks effective teacher-student-parent partnerships. Maybe that's all that is keeping some students from saying, "Now I understand."

Woodpecker Question 4: Why can't groups come up with solutions? Pick an answer: (a) They don't have all the data. (b) There are usually too many people in the group. (c) Group members don't get along. (d) None of the above.

The correct answer is d, none of the above. Groups can't come up with solutions because solutions—real solutions!—are situational and personal.

Groups are good at identifying issues and obstacles, but they can't accommodate specific situations, local politics and delicate interrelationships. During group process, people tend

(14) How does Banach establish his credibility (competence, moral character, and charisma)? Which dimensions does Banach stress? (15) Are these attempts sufficient? Are they effective?

(16) Do any of these "Woodpecker Questions" lead you to question your own educational experiences? Why or why not?

(17) What are the major propositions of this speech? How effectively are they highlighted?

(18) How would you evaluate Banach's use of language? Is the language direct or indirect? High or low in abstraction? Objective or subjective? Formal or informal? Accurate or inaccurate? What specific examples can you give to support your conclusions about the language of his speech?

(19) Would you characterize the style of the speech as oral or written? What specific language elements can you use to support your conclusion?

(20) Is the language used generally clear? Vivid? Appropriate to the speaker, audience, and topic? Personal? Forceful? What specific elements can you point to in support of your conclusion?

(21) Which of the propositions do you think would be the most powerful for his audience of administrators? Which would be the most powerful for your class as an audience?

(22) How effectively does Banach demonstrate the inability of groups to solve problems? Are you ready to accept Banach's conclusion? If not, what additional data would you need?

(23) Considering that Banach is addressing school administrators, is this proposition about the defensiveness of educators well positioned? Would you have used it earlier or at about this point? Why?

(24) What organizational pattern is used? Was this effective?

(25) How would you describe the internal organization of the speech? For example, did the speaker use primacy or recency? Was this a wise decision, in your opinion? (26) Did the speaker use climax or anticlimax order? Was this a wise decision?

(27) What types of supporting material does the speaker use? Examples and illustrations? Definitions? Testimony? Statistics? Are these effectively used?

(28) What are the major forms of reasoning used? From specific instances? Analogy? Causes and effects? Sign? Is the reasoning sound? Does the reasoning pass the logical tests?

(29) What types of motivational appeals does the speaker use? Are these effective, given the speaker's audience?

to get sidetracked thinking about how they can survive the problem at home . . . or giving silent thanks that, in the end, it will be Bob or Mary who will have to handle the flak and deal with the fallout.

Getting everybody to agree that there is a problem is not a problem. In fact, every group can come to consensus on the dimensions of the problem and agree on a problem-solving model. But groups can't develop—let alone implement!—a common solution, and that's why groups always reach the point where "it's time to go home and do something."

Good administrators learn from group process, combine new information with what they know, bounce ideas off people "back home," and develop a solution.

This approach does not preclude citizen involvement or building decision-making teams. In fact, wise leaders involve people in things that affect their destiny. But realize that groups cannot take responsibility, and that's why there is often a gap between what they propose and what works. It is the job of the person in charge to accommodate the variables and develop localized solutions that have a chance. (This is why we have "ring leaders" and "team captains." Eventually, someone has to take responsibility.)

Woodpecker Question 5: Why are educators so defensive? Well, reading scores are down and violence is up; teachers aren't dedicated and administrators don't care. There are all kinds of reasons to be defensive and cover the flanks. But this is a dead duck question with lame duck answers. The reality is that educators have been assigned both blame and responsibility for society's problems. Most critics follow what's wrong with society (crime, drugs, violence, ill-prepared workers, etc.) by saying: "The schools have to improve!" (Notice that they don't say schools are a reflection of society and we are society so we must improve our schools.)

Nothing new here. America's educational system has taken responsibility in the past. Think about it. The industrial era required workers who were obedient, could handle routine work, didn't have to think too much and understood the importance of being on time. Look at the schools. They stressed discipline, drill and practice, not questioning your elders and being in your seat ". . . by the time the bell rings." Our schools produced the workforce industrial America demanded.

How well did the schools do? (Dead duck question!) American productivity reached new highs. Our quality of life surpassed anything forecasters imagined. U.S. graduate schools enrolled more foreign students than the graduate schools of all other nations combined. And our system of public education was envied throughout the world.

Now we are six decades into the Information Age. No one is sure of the future, and, hence, there is a lot of finger-pointing—people seeking to blame someone for the instability characterizing their lives. And guess what institution is front and center?

We demand more from our public schools than any other institution (with the possible exception of marriage). And they have produced what we have demanded.

But now the rules have changed. Knowledge is capital. There are new alliances in an international economy. Competition is being redefined, and so is work. We live in a period of turbulence, and during such times we tend to grab for the familiar and cling to the past.

But, our new age dictates a renaissance in education. Schools must accommodate the change in our society. They must become sensitive to marketplace forces, tailored to customer needs, and future focused. The changes ahead will redefine our concept of school. They also provide promise for an even better system of public education.

Get involved in the transformation. Start by asking questions. Think about the answers. Share the thoughts. Lead the revitalization wherever you are.

Need more?

Why do teachers have to be people? Okay, why do they have to be people trained as teachers?

Why do we set up evaluation systems that make schools look bad?

Why are our schools structured like the factories of the Industrial Age that ended 50 years ago?

Why do we spend so much time on squeaking wheels while ignoring the things that hum along?

Why is everything "bolted on" to the curriculum instead of integrated in?

Why do we lecture all the time?

Change comes from the questions we ask. Questions allow us to think, thinking allows us to make connections, connections produce understanding . . . and that's what leads to strategic advantage and preferred tomorrows.

Before you go back to work, think about it.

(30) How effective was the speaker's use of questions throughout the speech?

(31) What type of conclusion does Banach use? Does it effectively summarize and bring the speech to a definite close?

(32) Does Banach avoid the common faults of conclusions? Does he apologize? Introduce new material? Dilute his position in any way? Drag out the conclusion?

(33) What is your overall evaluation of this speech? That is, if this speech were given in your class, what grade would you give it? (34) What is the major strength of this speech as you see it? (35) What is the major weakness? How might this weakness have been corrected?

(36) How effective do you think the speech title is? What titles do you think would work better? Why? What would be an absolutely inappropriate title? Why?

SOURCE: William J. Banach is executive director of the Institute for Future Studies, Macomb Community College. This speech was delivered to the Association of Wisconsin School Administrators, Milwaukee, Wisconsin, October 25, 1990. The speech is reprinted from William J. Banach "Are You Too Busy to Think?" *Vital Speeches of the Day* 57, March 15, 1991. Reprinted by permission.

Folger, Joseph P., & Poole, Marshall Scott (1984). *Working Through Conflict: A Communication Perspective.* Glenview, IL: Scott, Foresman.

Freedman, J., & Fraser, S. (1966). Compliance Without Pressure: The Foot-in-the-Door Technique. *Journal of Personality and Social Psychology* 4:195–202.

Frey, Kurt J., & Eagly, Alice H. (1993). Vividness Can Undermine the Persuasiveness of Messages. *Journal of Personality and Social Psychology* 65 (July):32–44.

Frymier, Ann Bainbridge, & Gary M. Shulman (1995). "What's in It for Me?": Increasing Content Relevance to Enhance Students' Motivation. *Communication Education* 44 (January):40–50.

Gabor, Don (1989). *How to Talk to the People You Love.* New York: Simon & Schuster.

Garner, Alan (1981). *Conversationally Speaking.* New York: McGraw-Hill.

Gephardt, Richard A. (1995). The Democratic Challenge in the 104th Congress. *Vital Speeches of the Day* 61 (January 15):197–201.

Gibb, Jack (1961). Defensive Communication. *Journal of Communication* 11: 141–148.

Glaser, Connie Brown, & Smalley, Barbara Steinberg (1992). *More Power to You! How Women Can Communicate Their Way to Success.* New York: Warner.

Gordon, Thomas (1975). *P.E.T.: Parent Effectiveness Training.* New York: New American Library.

Goss, Blaine (1989). *The Psychology of Communication.* Prospect Heights, IL: Waveland Press.

Goss, Blaine, Thompson, M., & Olds, S. (1978). Behavioral Support for Systematic Desensitization for Communication Apprehension. *Human Communication Research* 4:158–163.

Gronbeck, Bruce E., McKerrow, Raymie E., Ehninger, Douglas, & Monroe, Alan H. (1994). *Principles and Types of Speech Communication,* 12th ed. New York: HarperCollins.

Gross, Ronald (1991). *Peak Learning.* Los Angeles: Jeremy P. Tarcher.

Guerra, Stella (1986). *Vital Speeches of the Day* 52 (September 15):727.

Hall, Edward T., & Hall, Mildred Reed (1987). *Hidden Differences: Doing Business with the Japanese.* New York: Doubleday, Anchor Books.

Hamlin, Sonya (1988). *How to Talk So People Listen.* New York: Harper & Row.

Haney, William (1973). *Communication and Organiza-tional Behavior: Text and Cases,* 3rd ed. Homewood IL: Irwin.

Hayakawa, S. I., & Hayakawa, Alan R. (1990). *Language in Thought and Action,* 5th ed. New York: Harcourt Brace Jovanovich.

Hecht, Michael, & Ribeau, Sidney (1984). Ethnic Communication: A Comparative Analysis of Satisfying Communication. *International Journal of Intercultural Relations* 8:135–151.

Heinrich, Robert et al. (1983). *Instructional Media: The New Technologies of Instruction.* New York: Wiley.

Heldmann, Mary Lynne (1988). *When Words Hurt: How to Keep Criticism from Undermining Your Self-Esteem.* New York: Ballantine.

Henley, Nancy M. (1977). *Body Politics: Power, Sex, and Nonverbal Communication.* Englewood Cliffs, NJ: Prentice Hall.

Hensley, Carl Wayne (1992). What You Share Is What You Get: Tips for Effective Communication. *Vital Speeches of the Day* 58 (December 1):115–117.

Hensley, Carl Wayne (1994). Divorce: The Sensible Approach. *Vital Speeches of the Day* 60 (March 1):317–319.

Hersey, Paul, & Blanchard, Ken (1988). *Management of Organizational Behavior: Utilizing Human Resources.* Englewood Cliffs, NJ: Prentice-Hall.

Hess, Ekhard H. (1975). *The Tell-Tale Eye.* New York: Van Nostrand Reinhold.

Hess, Jon A. (1993). Teaching Ethics in Introductory Public Speaking: Review and Proposal. In *Basic Communication Course Annual* V (September), ed. Lawrence W. Hugenberg (pp. 101–126). Boston: American Press.

Hewitt, John, & Stokes, Randall (1975). Disclaimers. *American Sociological Review* 40:1–11.

Hickey, Neil (1989). Decade of Change, Decade of Choice. *TV Guide* 37 (December 9):29–34.

Hickson, Mark L., & Stacks, Don W. (1989). *NVC: Nonverbal Communication: Studies and Applications,* 2nd ed. Dubuque, IA: Brown.

Hocker, Joyce L., & Wilmot, William W. (1991). *Interpersonal Conflict,* 3rd ed. Dubuque, IA: Brown.

Hoft, Nancy L. (1995). *International Technical Communication: How to Export Information About High Technology.* New York: Wiley.

Infante, Dominic A. (1988). *Arguing Constructively.* Prospect Heights, IL: Waveland Press.

Infante, Dominic A., Rancer, Andrew S., & Womack, Deanna F. (1993). *Building Communication Theory,* 2nd ed. Prospect Heights, IL: Waveland Press.

Jackson, William (1985). *Vital Speeches of the Day* 51 (September 15)

Jacob, John E. (1995). *Vital Speeches of the Day* 61 (July 1): 572–574.

Jacobs, Harvey (1985). *Vital Speeches of the Day* 51 (May 1).

Jaksa, James A., & Pritchard, Michael S. (1988). *Communication Ethics: Methods of Analysis.* Belmont, CA: Wadsworth.

James, David L. (1995). *The Executive Guide to Asia-Pacific Communications.* New York: Kodansha International.

Janis, Irving (1983). *Victims of Group Thinking: A Psychological Study of Foreign Policy Decisions and Fiascoes,* 2nd ed. Boston: Houghton Mifflin.

Jensen, J. V. (1985). Teaching Ethics in Speech Communication. *Communication Education* 34:324–330.

Jensen, J. Vernon (1985). Perspectives on Nonverbal Intercultural Communication. In *Intercultural Communication: A Reader,* 4th ed., ed. Larry Samovar & Richard E. Porter (pp. 256–272). Belmont, CA: Wadsworth.

Johnson, Geneva B. (1991). *Vital Speeches of the Day* 57 (April 15):393–398.

Johnson, Kenneth G., ed. (1991). *Thinking Creatically.* Concord, CA: International Society for General Semantics.

Kemp, Jerrold E., & Dayton, Deane K. (1985). *Planning and Producing Instructional Media,* 5th ed. New York: Harper & Row.

Keohane, Nannerl O. (1991). *Vital Speeches of the Day* 57 (July 15):605–608.

Kesselman-Turkel, Judi, & Peterson, Franklynn (1982). *Note-Taking Made Easy,* Chicago: Contemporary Books.

Kim, Hyun J. (1991). Influence of Language and Similarity on Initial Intercultural Attraction. In *Cross-Cultural Interpersonal Communication,* ed. Stella Ting-Toomey & Felipe Korzenny (pp. 213–229). Newbury Park, CA: Sage.

Kim, Young Yon, ed. (1986). *Interethnic Communication: Current Research.* Newbury Park, CA: Sage.

Kim, Young Yon (1991). Intercultural Communication Competence. In *Cross-Cultural Interpersonal Communication,* ed. Stella Ting-Toomey & Felipe Korzenny (pp. 259–275). Newbury Park, CA: Sage.

Kim, Young Yun, & Gudykunst, William B., eds. (1988). *Theories in Intercultural Communication*. Newbury Park, CA: Sage.

Kinsley, Carol W. (1994). What Is Community Service Learning? *Vital Speeches of the Day* 60 (November 1):40–43.

Kleinke, Chris L. (1978). *Self-Perception: The Psychology of Personal Awareness*. San Francisco: Freeman.

Kleinke, Chris L. (1986). *Meeting and Understanding People*. New York: Freeman.

Knapp, Mark, & Hall, Judith (1992). *Nonverbal Behavior in Human Interaction*, 3rd ed. New York: Holt, Rinehart & Winston.

Kohn, Alfie (1989). Do Religious People Help More? Not So You'd Notice. *Psychology Today* (December):66–68.

Korzybski, Alfred (1933). *Science and Sanity: An Introduction to Non-Aristotelian Systems and General Semantics*. Concord, CA: International Society for General Semantics.

Kramarae, Cheris (1981). *Women and Men Speaking*. Rowley, MA: Newbury House.

Lambdin, William (1981). *Doublespeak Dictionary*. Los Angeles: Pinnacle Books.

Lamkin, Martha (1986). *Vital Speeches of the Day* 52 (December 15):152.

Langer, Ellen J. (1978). Rethinking the Role of Thought in Social Interaction. In *New Directions in Attribution Research*, Vol. 2, ed. J. H. Harvey, W. J. Ickes, & R. F. Kidd (pp. 35–58). Hillsdale, NJ: Erlbaum.

Langer, Ellen J. (1989). *Mindfulness*. Reading, MA: Addison-Wesley.

Larson, Charles U. (1992). *Persuasion: Reception, and Responsibility*, 6th ed. Belmont, CA: Wadsworth.

Leathers, Dale G. (1992). *Successful Nonverbal Communication: Principles and Applications*, 2nd ed. New York: Macmillan.

Lee, Alfred McClung, & Lee, Elizabeth Briant (1995). The Iconography of Propaganda Analysis. *ETC.: A Review of General Semantics* 52 (Spring):13–17.

Leeds, Dorothy (1988). *Powerspeak*. Englewood Cliffs, NJ: Prentice Hall.

Levitt, Arthur (1995). Consumer Protection. *Vital Speeches of the Day* 61 (January 15):194–197.

Lidstad, Richard (1995). *Vital Speeches of the Day* 61 (July 1): 559–561.

Ling, Joseph T. (1993). Design for the Environment. *Vital Speeches of the Day* 59 (August 1):629–632.

Linkugel, Wil A., Allen, R. R., & Johannesen, Richard L., eds. (1978). *Contemporary American Speeches*, 4th ed. Dubuque, IA: Brown & Benchmark.

Littlejohn, Stephen W. (1992). *Theories of Human Communication*, 4th ed. Belmont, CA: Wadsworth.

Littlejohn, Stephen W., & Jabusch, David M. (1987). *Persuasive Transactions*. Glenview, IL: Scott, Foresman.

Loden, Marilyn (1986). *Vital Speeches of the Day* 52 (May 15):472–475.

Loftus, Elizabeth, & Palmer, J. C. (1974). Reconstruction of Automobile Destruction: An Example of the Interaction Between Language and Memory. *Journal of Verbal Learning and Verbal Behavior* 13:585–589.

Lucas, Stephen E. (1995). *The Art of Public Speaking*, 5th ed. New York: McGraw-Hill.

Lunsford, Charlotte (1988). *Vital Speeches of the Day* 54 (September 15):731.

Lurie, Alison (1983). *The Language of Clothes*. New York: Vintage.

Lustig, Myron W., & Koester, Jolene (1996). *Intercultural Competence: Interpersonal Communication Across Cultures*, 2nd ed. New York: HarperCollins

Mackay, Harvey B. (1991). *Vital Speeches of the Day* 57 (August 15):656–659.

MacLachlan, John (1979). What People Really Think of Fast Talkers. *Psychology Today* 13 (November):113–117.

Malandro, Loretta A., Barker, Larry, & Barker, Deborah Ann (1989). *Nonverbal Communication*, 2nd ed. New York: Random House.

Marien, Michael (1992). *Vital Speeches of the Day* 58 (March 15):340–344.

Markway, Barbara G., Carmin, Cheryl N., Pollard, C. Alex, & Flynn, Teresa. *Dying of Embarrassment: Help for Social Anxiety and Phobia*. Oakland, CA: New Harbinger Publications, 1992.

Marshall, Evan (1983). *Eye Language: Understanding the Eloquent Eye*. New York: New Trend.

Martel, Myles (1989). *The Persuasive Edge*. New York: Fawcett.

Marwell, G., & Schmitt, D. R. (1967). Dimensions of Compliance-Gaining Behavior: An Empirical Analysis. *Sociometry* 39:350–364.

Maslow, Abraham (1970). *Motivation and Personality*. New York: HarperCollins.

Matsuyama, Yukio (1992). *Vital Speeches of the Day* 58 (May 15):461–466.

McCarthy, Michael J. (1991). *Mastering the Information Age*. Los Angeles: Jeremy P. Tarcher.

McCroskey, James C. (1993). *An Introduction to Rhetorical Communication*, 6th ed. Englewood Cliffs, NJ: Prentice Hall.

McGill, Michael E. (1985). *The McGill Report on Male Intimacy*. New York: Harper & Row.

McLaughlin, Margaret L. (1984). *Conversation: How Talk Is Organized*. Newbury Park, CA: Sage.

McMahon, Ed (1986). *The Art of Public Speaking*. New York: Ballantine.

McNamara, Robert (1985). *Vital Speeches of the Day* 51 (July 1):549.

Miller, Gerald, & Parks, Malcolm (1982). Communication in Dissolving Relationships. In *Personal Relationships, Vol. 4: Dissolving Personal Relationships*, ed. Steve Duck (pp. 127–154). New York: Academic Press.

Miller, Sherod, Wackman, Daniel, Nunnally, Elam, & Saline, Carol (1982). *Straight Talk*. New York: New American Library.

Moghaddam, Fathali M., Taylor, Donald M., & Wright, Stephen C. (1993). *Social Psychology in Cross-Cultural Perspective*. New York: W. H. Freeman

Morris, Desmond, Collett, Peter, Marsh, Peter, & O'Shaughnessy, Marie (1979). *Gestures: Their Origins and Distribution*. New York: Stein & Day.

Murphy, Richard (1958). The Speech as Literary Genre. *Quarterly Journal of Speech* 44 (April): 117–127.

Naisbitt, John (1984). *Megatrends: Ten New Directions Transforming Our Lives*. New York: Warner.

Napier, Rodney W., & Gershenfeld, Matti K. (1989). *Groups: Theory and Experience*, 4th ed. Boston: Houghton Mifflin.

Nichols, Ralph (1961). Do We Know How to Listen? Practical Helps in a Modern Age. *Communication Education* 10:118–124.

Nichols, Ralph, & Stevens, Leonard (1957). *Are You Listening?* New York: McGraw-Hill.

Nickerson, Raymond S. (1987). Why Teach Thinking? In *Teaching Thinking Skills: Theory and Practice*, ed. Joan Boykoff Baron & Robert J. Sternberg (pp. 27–37). New York: Freeman.

Orr, James F., III (1993). Learning to Learn. *Vital Speeches of the Day* 59 (September 15):725–728.

Orski, C. Kenneth (1986). *Vital Speeches of the Day* 52 (February 1):274.

Osborn, Alex (1957). *Applied Imagination,* rev. ed. New York: Scribners.

Page, Richard A., & Balloun, Joseph L. (1978). The Effect of Voice Volume on the Perception of Personality. *Journal of Social Psychology* 105:65–72.

Payan, Janice (1990). *Vital Speeches of the Day* 56 (September 1):697–701.

Pearson, Judy C. (1985). *Gender and Communication.* Dubuque, IA: Brown.

Pease, Allen (1984). *Signals: How to Use Body Language for Power, Success, and Love.* New York: Bantam.

Pei, Mario (1956). *Language for Everybody.* New York: Pocket Books.

Penfield, Joyce, ed. (1987). *Women and Language in Transition.* Albany: State University of New York Press.

Penn, C. Ray (1990). *Vital Speeches of the Day* 56 (December 1): 116–117.

Peterson, Houston, ed. (1965). *A Treasury of the World's Great Speeches.* New York: Simon & Schuster.

Peterson, Russell W. (1985). *Vital Speeches of the Day* 51 (July 1):549.

Peterson, Susan (1995). Managing Your Communication. *Vital Speeches of the Day* 61 (January 1):188–190.

Pratkanis, Anthony, & Aronson, Elliot (1991). *Age of Propaganda: The Everyday Use and Abuse of Persuasion.* New York: Freeman.

Price, Hugh B. (1995). Public Discourse. *Vital Speeches of the Day* 61 (January 15):213–216.

Qubein, Nido R. (1986). *Get the Best from Yourself.* New York: Berkley.

Rankin, Paul (1929). Listening Ability. In *Proceedings of the Ohio State Educational Conference's Ninth Annual Session.*

Reed, Warren H. (1985). *Positive Listening: Learning to Hear What People Are Really Saying.* New York: Franklin Watts.

Reynolds, Christina L., & Schnoor, Larry G., eds. (1991). *1989 Championship Debates and Speeches.* Normal, IL: American Forensic Association.

Richardson, Margaret Milner (1995). Taxation with Representation. *Vital Speeches of the Day* 61 (January 15):201–203.

Richmond, Virginia P., & McCroskey, James C. (1992). *Communication: Apprehension, Avoidance, and Effectiveness,* 3rd ed. Scottsdale, AZ: Gorsuch Scarisbrick.

Richmond, Virginia, McCroskey, James, & Payne, Steven (1987). *Nonverbal Behavior in Interpersonal Relationships.* Englewood Cliffs, NJ: Prentice Hall.

Riggio, Ronald E. (1987). *The Charisma Quotient.* New York: Dodd, Mead.

Robinson, Janet, & McArthur, Leslie Zebrowitz (1982). Impact of Salient Vocal Qualities on Causal Attribution for a Speaker's Behavior. *Journal of Personality and Social Psychology* 43:236–247.

Rockefeller, David (1985). *Vital Speeches of the Day* 51 (March 15):328–331.

Rogers, Carl (1970). *Carl Rogers on Encounter Groups.* New York: Harrow Books.

Rolland, Ian M. (1993). Toward a *Working* Health Care System. *Vital Speeches of the Day* 59 (June 15):524–527.

Rosenthal, Peggy (1984). *Words and Values: Some Leading Words and Where They Lead Us.* New York: Oxford University Press.

Rosenthal, Robert, & Jacobson, L. (1968). *Pygmalion in the Classroom.* New York: Holt, Rinehart & Winston.

Rothwell, J. Dan (1982). *Telling It Like It Isn't: Language Misuse and Malpractice/What We Can Do About It.* Englewood Cliffs, NJ: Prentice Hall.

Ruben, Brent D. (1985). Human Communication and Cross-Cultural Effectiveness. In *Intercultural Communication: A Reader,* 4th ed. Larry A. Samovar & Richard E. Porter (pp. 338–346). Belmont, CA: Wadsworth.

Rubenstein, Eric (1992). *Vital Speeches of the Day* 58 (April 15):401–404.

Ruchlis, Hy (1990). *Clear Thinking: A Practical Introduction.* Buffalo, NY: Prometheus Books.

Ruggiero, Vincent Ryan (1987). *Vital Speeches of the Day* 53 (August 15).

Ruggiero, Vincent Ryan (1990). *The Art of Thinking: A Guideto Critical and Creative Thought,* 3rd ed. New York: HarperCollins.

Samovar, Larry A., & Porter, Richard E. (1991). *Communication Between Cultures.* Belmont, CA: Wadsworth.

Samovar, Larry A., & Porter, Richard E., eds. (1988). *Intercultural Communication: A Reader,* 5th ed. Belmont, CA: Wadsworth.

Samovar, Larry A., Porter, Richard E., & Jain, Nemi C. (1981). *Understanding Intercultural Communication.* Belmont, CA: Wadsworth.

Schaefer, Charles E. (1984). *How to Talk to Children About Really Important Things.* New York: Harper & Row.

Schnoor, Larry G. (1994), ed. *1991 and 1992 Championship Debates and Speeches.* River Falls, WI: American Forensic Association.

Seidler, Ann, & Bianchi, Doris (1988). *Voice and Diction Fitness: A Comprehensive Approach.* New York: Harper & Row.

Silber, John R. (1985). *Vital Speeches of the Day* 51 (September 15).

Singer, Marshall R. (1987). *Intercultural Communication: A Perceptual Approach.* Englewood Cliffs, NJ: Prentice Hall.

Smith, Raymond W. (1995). Advertising and the Interactive Age. *Vital Speeches of the Day* 61 (April 1):358–361.

Snyder, Richard (1984). *Vital Speeches of the Day* 50 (January 1).

Spitzberg, Brian H., & Cupach, William R. (1984). *Interpersonal Communication Competence.* Newbury Park, CA: Sage.

Spitzberg, Brian H., & Cupach, William R. (1989). *Handbook of Interpersonal Competence Research.* New York: Springer-Verlag.

Spitzberg, Brian H., & Hecht, Michael L. (1984). A Component Model of Relational Competence. *Human Communication Research* 10:575–599.

Sprague, Jo, & Stuart, Douglas (1988). *The Speaker's Handbook,* 2nd ed. San Diego: Harcourt Brace Jovanovich.

Stark, Peter B. (1985). *Vital Speeches of the Day* 51 (October 1).

Steil, Lyman K., Barker, Larry L., & Watson, Kittie W. (1983). *Effective Listening: Key to Your Success.* Reading, MA: Addison-Wesley.

Sternberg, Robert J. (1987). Questions and Answers About the Nature and Teaching of Thinking Skills. In *Teaching Thinking Skills: Theory and Practice,* ed. Joan Boykoff Baron & Robert J. Sternberg (pp. 251–259). New York: Freeman.

Swets, Paul W. (1983). *The Art of Talking So That People Will Listen.* Englewood Cliffs, NJ: Prentice Hall/Spectrum.

Teng-Hui, Lee (1995). *Vital Speeches of the Day* 61 (August 1): 611–613.

Thorne, Barrie, Kramarae, Cheris, & Henley, Nancy, eds. (1983). *Language, Gender, and Society.* Rowley, MA: Newbury House.

Toulmin, Stephen, Rieke, Richard, & Janik, Allen (1979). *An Introduction to Reasoning.* New York: Macmillan.

Trenholm, Sarah (1986). *Human Communication Theory.* Englewood Cliffs, NJ: Prentice Hall.

Truax, C. (1961). A Scale for the Measurement of Accurate Empathy. *Wisconsin Psychiatric Institute Discussion Paper No. 20.* Madison, WI: Wisconsin Psychiatric Institute.

Valenti, Jack (1982). *Speaking Up with Confidence: How to Prepare, Learn, and Deliver Effective Speeches.* New York: Morrow.

Vasile, Albert J., & Mintz, Harold K. (1996). *Speaking with Confidence: A Practical Guide.* New York: HarperCollins.

Verderber, Rudolph F. (1991). *The Challenge of Effective Speaking,* 8th ed. Belmont, CA: Wadsworth.

Wade, Carole, & Tavris, Carol (1990). *Learning to Think Critically: The Case of Close Relationships.* New York: HarperCollins.

Warnick, Barbara, & Inch, Edward S. (1989). *Critical Thinking and Communication: The Use of Reason in Argument.* New York: Macmillan.

Watson, Arden K., & Dodd, Carley H. (1984). Alleviating Communication Apprehension Through Rational Emotive Therapy: A Comparative Evaluation. *Communication Education* 33:257–266.

Weinstein, Fannie (1995). Professionally Speaking. *Profiles: The Magazine of Continental Airlines* 8 (April):50–55.

Wells, Theodora (1980). *Keeping Your Cool Under Fire: Communicating Non-Defensively.* New York: McGraw-Hill.

Wharton, Clifton R., Jr. (1994). The Myth of Superpower. *Vital Speeches of the Day* 60 (January 15):204–207.

Whitman, Richard F., & Timmis, John H. (1975). The Influence of Verbal Organizational Structure and Verbal Organizing Skills on Select Measures of Learning. *Human Communication Research* 1:293–301.

Williams, Andrea (1985). *Making Decisions.* New York: Zebra.

Wolf, Florence I., Marsnik, Nadine C., Tacey, William S., & Nichols, Ralph G. (1983). *Perceptive Listening.* New York: Holt, Rinehart & Winston.

Yoshida, Susumu (1995). *Vital Speeches of the Day* 61 (March 1):301–306.

Credits

Index

Abstraction, language and, 267–268
Abstracts
  computerized, 128
  journal, 127
Academic American Encyclopedia, 125
Accenting errors, 310–311
Accents, 62
Acceptance speech, 413–418
  cultural influence in, 424
  examples of, 414–416
  length of, 417
  pitfalls of, 416–418
  principles of, 413–414
Access, 127
Accountability, speaker ethics and, 14
Accuracy, language and, 270–273
Achievement, as motivational appeal, 385
Active listening, guidelines for, 68
Active verbs, 284
Actuate, speech to, 251–253
Adaptation, audience analysis and, 197–206
Adding sounds, errors of, 311
Advantages-disadvantages organization pattern, 223
Affiliation, as motivational appeal, 384
Agee, Warren K., 165
Agenda, group, 432
Agenda-setting, 73
Age of audience, in audience analysis, 24–25, 183–185
Alisky, Marvin, 149
Allen, Steve, 122
Alliteration, 285
Allness, as thinking error, 271
Almanacs, 127–128
Altercasting, 380
Alternative Press Index, 127
Altruism, as motivational appeal, 382
America: History and Life on Disc database, 130
American Men and Women of Science, 126
Amplifying materials, 147–162
  comparison and contrast, 159–160
  definitions, 159
  examples, 148–150
  narration, 148, 151–153
  quotations, 159
  repetition and restatement, 160
  simple statement or series of facts, 160

statistics, 156–158
testimony, 153–156
Analogy
  figurative, 366–367
  literal, 366
  reasoning from, 366–368
Anderson, Donna, 234
Anticlimax order, 224, 225
Antithesis, 285
Antithetical sentences, 292
Anton, Maria Lucia R., 451
Anxiety, intercultural situations and, 44. *See also* Speaker apprehension
Apologies, avoiding, 236, 396–397
Application questions, 7, 447–448
Applied Science and Technology Index, 127
Apprehension. *See* Speaker apprehension
Appropriateness
  of humor, 278
  wording and, 286–288
Approval, as motivational appeal, 384
Archambault, David, 239
Argument, 360–376. *See also* Persuasive speech; Reasoning
  corroborative support in, 362
  evidence and, 361–363
  Toulmin model to analyze, 374–376
  unbiased sources in, 362–363
Aristotle, 5
Articulation, 309–310
Articulation problems
  correction of, 310
  errors of addition, 310
  errors of omission, 309
  errors of substitution, 310
Art Index, 127
Aslett, Don, 308
Assertiveness, charisma and, 400
Assimilation as obstacle to listening, 67
Assimilationist perspective, 16
Attack, 73
  criticism as, 85
Attention of audience, gaining, 116, 164, 230–232
Attitudes
  of audience, 178–179
  persuasive speech and, 342, 348–351

473

expressiveness and, 302
extemporaneous speaking, 299–300
eye contact and, 302
feedback from audience, responding to, 302
impromptu speaking, 297
memorized speech, 298–299
monotonous patterns, 301
naturalness of, 300
notes, use of, 303–304
pauses, 311–312
predictable patterns, 301
pronunciation, 310–311
rehearsing, 31, 315–317
reinforcement of message and, 300
speaking from manuscript, 298
speech criticism and, 89
voice, 307–309
Delivery outline, 259–261
Democratic leader, 440
Demonstration, speech of, 333–336
audiovisual aids in, 334
developing, 334–335
temporal organization of, 333
Dempsey, Brenda, 148
Denotation, 268–269
Description, speech of, 326–329
audiovisual aids, 328
descriptive categories, use of variety of, 327–328
development of, 328–329
example topics, 326–327
organizational pattern for, 327
Desensitization, systematic, 48
DeVries, Mary A., 185, 284, 396
Dewey, John, 433
Dictionary of American Biography, 126
Dictionary of Canadian Biography, 126
Dictionary of National Biography, 126
Dictionary of Scientific Biography, 126
Dictionary of topics, 103–107
Difference, measures of, 156
Directness
language and, 267
styles of, 62
Directory of American Scholars, 126
Discovery questions, 7, 447
Display rules, 62–63, 205, 313
Disraeli, Benjamin, 271
Diversity, cultural, 16. *See also* Culture
Dole, Bob, 402
Door-in-the-face technique in persuasive speech, 347–348
Do's and Taboos Around the World (Axtell), 99
Dress, speaking occasion and, 300

Educational level of audience, 187–189
Education Index, 127
Effectiveness standard of criticism, 81
Ehrlich, Henry, 231

Either-or thinking, 270–271
E-mail, 135–138
Emerson, Ralph Waldo, 3
Emery, Edwin, 165
Empathy
audience analysis and, 181–182
listening with, 69
Emphatic language, charisma and, 400
Encarta, 125
Encyclopaedia Britannica, 124–125
Encyclopedia Americana, 125
Encyclopedia Judaica, 125
Encyclopedia of Bioethics, 125
Encyclopedia of Buddhism, 125
Encyclopedia of Islam, 125
Encyclopedia of Philosophy, 125
Encyclopedia of Religion, 125
Encyclopedias, 124–125
Engleberg, Isa, 335
Enthusiasm, charisma and, 400
ERIC (Education Resources Information Center) database, 130–131, 132
Ethical listening, 14–15
honest hearing, 15
honest responses, 15
Ethical merit standard of criticism, 81
Ethics of speaker, 12–14. *See also* Critical evaluation/critical thinking; Persuasive speech
audience-centered approach and, 14
clear and present danger and, 14
credibility and, 343
motivational appeals and, 387
plagiarism and, 13, 142
propaganda, unethical persuasion through, 70–73
rating scale for evaluation of, 13–14
truthfulness and, 13
understandability of material and, 14
Ethnocentrism, 63–65
Eulogy, 423
Evaluation, of spoken messages, 59–60
Evaluation questions, 7, 447
Evidence, argument, 361–363
Examples, 148–150. *See also* Illustrations; Narration
critical evaluation of, 148–149
using, 150
Exemplary narratives, 151
Expectations
of audience, 191
as obstacle to listening, 67
role, 431
Expertise, competence and, 394–397
Expert panel, 443
Experts, as information source, 123
Explanatory narratives, 151
Expressiveness, in delivery of speech, 302
Extemporaneous speaking, 204, 299–300
Extrinsic credibility, 392